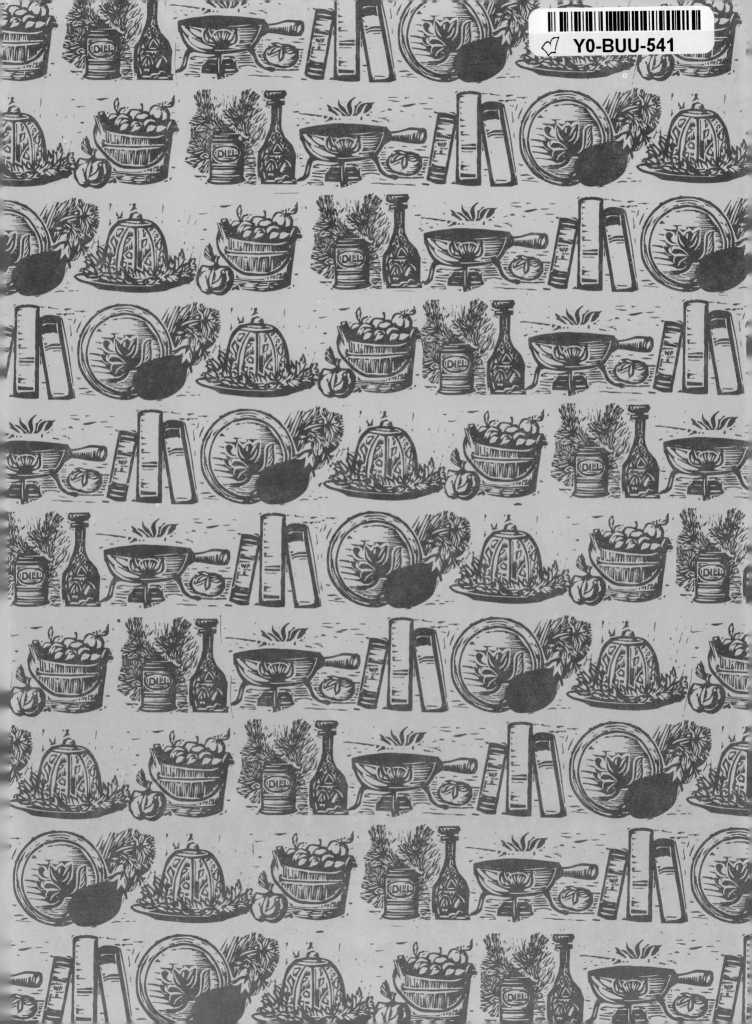

Y0-BUU-541

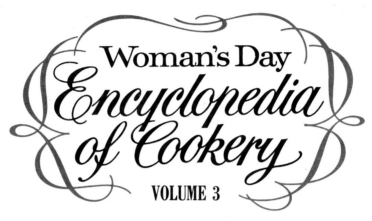

Woman's Day
Encyclopedia of Cookery

VOLUME 3

*in 12 volumes—over 2,000 pages—
with more than 1,500 illustrations in color,
1,000 entries and 8,500 recipes
1,200 menus, 50 specialty cook books
and a host of delightful features by distinguished food writers.*

Prepared and edited by the Editors of Woman's Day
Editor: EILEEN TIGHE
Managing Editor: EVELYN GRANT   *Food Editor:* GLENNA MCGINNIS
Art Consultant: HAROLD SITTERLE   *Photographic Editor:* BEN CALVO
Associates: OLIVIA RISBERG, CHARLOTTE SCRIPTURE,
CAROLYN STORM, JOHANNA BAFARO

SPECIAL PROJECT STAFF
Editor: NIKA STANDEN HAZELTON   *Art Director:* LEONARD A. ROMAGNA
Associates: L. GERALDINE MARSTELLER, HELEN FEINGOLD,
SUSAN J. KNOX, INEZ M. KRECH

FAWCETT PUBLICATIONS, INC.   NEW YORK

PRINTED AND BOUND BY
FAWCETT-HAYNES PRINTING CORPORATION
ROCKVILLE, MARYLAND

Table of Contents

VOLUME 3

CATFISH TO CRENSHAW

Definitions and 636 Recipes
How to buy, store, prepare, cook, and serve ·
Nutritive Food Values · Caloric Values

To help you plan more varied meals
with the recipes in this volume

Foreword

To the best of our knowledge, no work of this magnitude ever has been undertaken by any author, editor, or publisher in America. The editors of Woman's Day, with a special staff of experts, present to you this Encyclopedia of Cookery, a comprehensive and colorful library on all culinary matters. The twelve-volume encyclopedia contains in its 2,000 pages over 8,500 recipes from all over the world, 1,500 food illustrations in color, 1,200 menus, 50 special cook books and over 1,000 food definitions. In addition, there are full details about all foods, their nutritive and caloric values, how to buy, serve, prepare, and cook them. There is a history of food and cooking, articles on nutrition, diet, entertaining, menu planning, herbs and spices. Every topic of culinary interest is covered. Five years of intensive work have gone into its preparation, backed by twenty-five years of food and cookery experience in the publication of Woman's Day.

We think you will find this Encyclopedia of Cookery the most complete and authoritative work ever published on the subject. It is a library for everyone who cares about good food and the fine art of preparing it.

The Editors

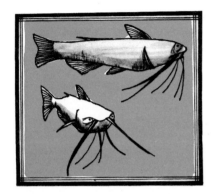

CATFISH—A fresh-water fish that derives its name from its barbels, or feelers, which resemble a cat's whiskers. The catfish lives in streams, primarily in the Mississippi Valley, where it is dear to the hearts of many small boys with only a bamboo pole and a bent-pin hook for fishing equipment. The most handsome member of the family, and the best eating, is the channel cat, which weighs from five to ten pounds. The smaller bullhead (up to a pound or so in weight) is the most common. The channel cat is usually baked; the bullhead is fried. There is also a salt-water catfish, sometimes called the hogfish, which is available cured.

Caloric Value

☐ 3½ ounces, raw, fresh-water = 103 calories

BAKED STUFFED CATFISH

    1 catfish (3½ to 4 pounds)
    1 cup soft bread crumbs
    ½ teaspoon salt
    ½ teaspoon pepper
    1 teaspoon each minced onion and
      parsley
    1 teaspoon pickle relish
    1 egg, beaten
    ¼ cup butter or margarine, melted
      Flour
    6 strips salt pork
    1½ cups fish stock or water

Wipe fish with damp paper towel. Mix next 7 ingredients, and stuff fish with the mixture. Use skewers to close the cavity or tie fish with string. Rub all over with melted butter. Roll in flour. Make S-shape slits in each side of fish and slip a pork strip into each. Bake in preheated moderate oven (350°F.) 40 to 60 minutes, basting frequently with the stock. Makes 6 servings.

FRIED CATFISH

    2 pounds catfish
    1 teaspoon salt
    ⅛ teaspoon pepper
    ½ cup sifted bread crumbs or cornmeal
    1 egg, well beaten, mixed with
      1 tablespoon water
    ¼ cup fat
      Lemon wedges

Skin catfish and fillet by removing backbone; cut into portions. Season with salt and pepper. Dip into crumbs, into beaten egg, then into crumbs again. Sauté in hot fat for about 12 minutes, until golden brown, turning once. Garnish with lemon and serve hot. Makes 4 servings.

CAULIFLOWER—*Brassica oleracea* is the Latin name of this member of the cabbage family, which Mark Twain once defined as "cabbage with a college education." The word is a combination of the Latin *caulis,* meaning "stalk," and *floris,* "flower."

Cauliflower has been grown for centuries in the coastal regions of the Mediterranean and in Asia Minor. The oldest records date to the 6th century B.C., and the Roman naturalist Pliny wrote about the vegetable in the 2nd century A.D. By the 12th century the Spaniards were eating as many as three varieties, introduced into Spain by the Arabs who once occupied it. In France and England it has been known since the 1600's, and it has been grown on our shores for over 200 years.

Availability—All year round. Peak crop September through November. Produced by a great many states but primarily in California and New York.

Purchasing Guide—Select a firm, compact head with white or creamy-white, clean flowerets and bright green leaves. The entire white edible portion is called the "curd." Spotted or bruised curd should be avoided unless it can be trimmed without causing waste. Size of head does not affect quality. If the leaves have grown through the curd, they affect the appearance only.

Storage—Keep in moisture-proof container or film bag in the refrigerator.

☐ Refrigerator shelf or vegetable compartment, raw: 3 to 5 days
☐ Refrigerator shelf, cooked and covered: 1 to 4 days
☐ Refrigerator frozen-food compartment, prepared for freezing: 1 month
☐ Freezer, prepared for freezing: 11 months

Nutritive Food Values—Cauliflower is a good source of vitamin C; a fair source of iron.

☐ 3½ ounces, raw = 27 calories
☐ 3½ ounces, cooked = 31 calories

Basic Preparation—Cut away the woody base and tough outer leaves. Tender green leaves may be left on or saved and used as salad greens. The head may be left whole or separated into flowerets. Wash in cold running water, holding head or flowerets upside down.

Have about 1 inch of water boiling in a saucepan. Add ½ teaspoon salt per cup of flowerets or head. A slice of lemon or a little lemon juice added to the water helps keep cauliflower white. Cook for 5 minutes, uncovered, then cover. Flowerets cook in 5 to 10 minutes; heads in 15 to 20 minutes. Do not overcook or cauliflower will discolor.

☐ **To Freeze**—Use firm white cauliflower with tough leaves and stalks removed. Cut into flowerets about 1 inch in diameter. Soak flowerets in salted water (¼ cup salt to 1 quart cold water) for 30 minutes. Rinse. Scald in boiling water for 4 minutes. Chill in ice water. Pack flowerets closely in package to prevent air spaces. Allow ½-inch headspace.

CAULIFLOWER SOUP

    1 medium cauliflower
    ¼ cup butter
    2 tablespoons grated onion
    2 tablespoons grated celery
    2 tablespoons all-purpose flour
    4 cups hot chicken bouillon
    2 cups hot milk or light cream
      Salt and white pepper
    1 egg yolk

Cauliflower in Cheese Puff

Hot Cauliflower with Shrimps

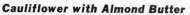

Cauliflower with Almond Butter

Cauliflower Soup

¼ cup heavy cream
2 tablespoons Madeira

Trim cauliflower. Cook in boiling water until tender. Drain; divide into flowerets. Reserve about one fourth of flowerets. Force remaining cauliflower through a strainer or food mill, or purée in blender. Melt butter and cook onion and celery in it for 2 minutes. Stir in flour. Do not brown. Gradually stir in hot bouillon. Add strained cauliflower. Stir in hot milk or cream. Season with salt and pepper to taste. Cook over medium heat, stirring constantly, until sauce coats spoon. Beat egg yolk with heavy cream. Remove soup from heat and gradually stir into egg yolk. Stir in Madeira. Add cauliflowerets. Serve very hot. Makes about 2 quarts.

HOT CAULIFLOWER WITH SHRIMPS

¼ cup butter
¼ cup all-purpose flour
1 cup milk
1 cup light or heavy cream
1 teaspoon salt
¼ teaspoon white pepper
½ cup heavy cream, whipped
1 large cauliflower
2 cups chopped cooked shelled shrimps
12 whole shrimps

Melt butter and stir in flour. Gradually add milk and cream, stirring constantly. Cook over low heat, stirring all the time, until sauce is thick and smooth. Stir in salt and pepper and fold in whipped cream. While making the sauce, cook trimmed cauliflower whole in boiling salted water until tender. Drain; place on hot plate and keep hot. Add chopped shrimps to sauce and heat thoroughly. Pour sauce over cauliflower and decorate with whole shrimps. Makes 4 servings.

CAULIFLOWER IN CHEESE PUFF

1 large cauliflower
1½ cups medium white sauce
¾ cup grated Cheddar cheese
4 eggs, separated
1 teaspoon sugar
Salt and pepper

Trim cauliflower and break into flowerets. Cook in boiling salted water until barely tender. Put in buttered shallow baking dish; reserve a few flowerets for garnish. Make white sauce; add cheese. Beat egg yolks, sugar, salt and pepper to taste, and add to white sauce. Beat egg whites until stiff and fold into sauce. Pour over cauliflowerets. Bake in preheated moderate oven (350°F.) for 20 minutes, or until sauce is firm. Garnish with remaining flowerets. Makes 4 to 6 servings.

CAULIFLOWER WITH ALMOND BUTTER

1 small cauliflower
¼ cup butter
¼ cup slivered blanched almonds

Cook cauliflower in boiling salted water until tender. Drain; keep hot. Heat butter and sauté almonds in it until golden

brown. Place cauliflower in hot serving dish. Top with almond butter. Makes 3 to 4 servings.

CAVIAR—*By James A. Beard*—Caviar is fish roe which has been sieved, lightly pressed, and treated with salt. It may come from any of the following fish, among others: beluga (which of course is a member of the sturgeon family), sterlet, sturgeon, salmon, carp, herring, whitefish, or cod. The greatest producers of caviar are in the region of the Caspian Sea, where both the Russians and the Iranians have created a major industry. True caviar is also found in the Gironde in France, at the mouth of the Columbia river in Oregon, and in Lake Michigan. Still other sources of caviar include Scandinavia and some German waters.

The finest caviar is the firm grayish egg with a minimum of salt. Occasionally there is a small amount of pinkish-gray caviar, which brings a premium price. There is also a small amount of what is known as "golden caviar," which is a variant on the gray.

The best caviar comes in large tins and is kept at a low temperature, around 30°F. Most other caviar, including the red variety, is vacuum-packed in jars or tins and stored at room temperature on shelves.

Pressed caviar is washed in an acidulated solution, then brined and drained, placed in bags and lightly pressed. It is preferred by some connoisseurs to the finely granulated beluga or sterlet caviar.

Dried caviar is sun-cured usually, and is cut in slices or granulated and mixed with seasonings before serving. The French provincial dish *Poutargues* is made with dried roe, mixed with onion, bread crumbs, and oil.

Service

Fine caviar should be served on a bed of crushed ice; special dishes are made for this purpose. It is best accompanied by toast, although some people prefer dark

bread. Lemon juice is all the seasoning it needs. The classic condiments for caviar, however, are finely chopped onion, chopped egg white, and chopped egg yolk. Some people like the addition of sour cream. If one buys top-grade caviar (which markets for something over $40 for fourteen ounces) he would do better to eschew embellishment. Next to being served plain probably the finest way to present caviar is with *blinis,* pancakes of buckwheat flour, with shredded potatoes or shredded carrots. These are served hot with cold caviar and sour cream and are widely popular as hors-d'oeuvre.

Canapés and open-face sandwiches of caviar are also popular. The Germans do a famous canapé with half caviar and half raw chopped beef dressed with onion and lemon juice.

Another service, found in Europe and occasionally on transatlantic liners, is a baked potato served with caviar and sour cream.

Caviar is used in Russian dressing for hors-d'oeuvre and salads, and in several white wine sauces for fish. Red caviar and sour cream are used as a garniture for omelets and for stuffed eggs. Caviar is also a much-prized complement with raw oysters on the half shell.

CAYENNE—The hot, pungent red pepper known as cayenne is prepared by grinding the dried ripe fruit of several species of the Capsicum plant, chiefly *Capsicum frutescens* and *C. annum.*

Cayenne is an ingredient of sausage seasonings and curry powders. When used with a light hand, it gives a zestful flavor to meat, fish, poultry, cheese, and egg dishes, and to sauces.

CELERIAC—This dark, turnip-rooted European variety of celery also goes by the names of celery root or celery knob. Only the root is eaten. Celeriac was developed from the same wild species as celery and was first described by Italian and Swiss botanists around 1600. A hundred years later it was common food in Europe, and is still much used in continental Europe. In the United States, it is used as a hot vegetable or a cold salad and as a flavoring for soups and stews. Celeriac is seldom eaten raw. It is excellent creamed, au gratin, or chilled and served as a salad or hors-d'oeuvre with a French or mayonnaise dressing.

Availability—Available from August through May with the peak month in October.

Purchasing Guide—Select firm, crisp roots; the quality and characteristics are similar to those of other root vegetables. The smaller roots are better; large ones tend to be hollow and woody.

Storage—Remove and discard leaves and root fibers. Plan to use it within a week.
☐ Refrigerator shelf or vegetable compartment, raw: 1 to 4 days
☐ Refrigerator shelf, cooked and covered: 4 to 5 days

Caloric Value
☐ 3½ ounces, raw = 40 calories

Basic Preparation—Wash well with vegetable brush. Cut off top of root; peel and cut celeriac into slices, julienne, or dice.

Have about 1 inch of water boiling in a saucepan. Add sliced, diced, or julienne celeriac and about ½ teaspoon salt per cup of celeriac. Cover; cook for 20 to 30 minutes. Drain, season, and serve with butter or a cream sauce.

Celeriac can also be cooked whole without peeling. Remove top and cook in enough boiling salted water to cover. Cook until just tender when pierced with a fork; do not overcook. Peel, slice, dice, or julienne.

CELERIAC AU GRATIN
1½ pounds celeriac (about 3 roots)
Salt and pepper
½ cup shredded process American cheese
1½ cups thin white sauce
¼ cup fine dry bread crumbs, mixed with 2 tablespoons melted butter

Cut off celeriac tops. Peel roots and dice. Cook in 1 inch of boiling salted water for about 20 minutes, or until tender. Drain and place in shallow casserole. Mix cheese with hot white sauce until melted. Pour over celery roots and season to taste. Top with buttered crumbs and bake in preheated moderate oven (375° F.) for 20 minutes, or until browned. Makes 4 servings.

CELERIAC SALAD
Remove celeriac tops. Peel roots and slice or dice. Cook in 1 inch of boiling salted water for about 20 minutes, or until tender. Do not overcook. Drain and

marinate immediately in a little French dressing. Chill, and serve on salad greens.

CELERY (Apium graveolens)—A popular stalk vegetable which is a cultivated version of a white-flowered herb that grew wild in both Europe and Asia. The leaves, stalk, and root of cultivated celery are all edible.

Celery was used as a medicinal herb first, but in the 16th century the Italians began using the celery stalks raw and boiling the root as a vegetable.

Celery was first grown commercially in this country in the early 19th century, and new strains with a greater delicacy of flavor were developed progressively. The two main varieties grown today are "Golden Heart," a blanched white variety grown under paper to prevent chlorophyll from forming and turning the celery green, and "Pascal," a slower-growing, tall green variety.

Splendid as a fresh, crunchy raw stalk, celery is also a delicious cooked vegetable. Fried, braised, or with a sauce, it makes an excellent accompaniment to roast meats and poultry.

Availability—Celery is available in markets the year round. It is sold in whole bunches with leaves, and in trimmed bunches. Florida, California, and Arizona produce the largest crops.

Purchasing Guide—Look for crisp, firm stalks with fresh leaves; the stalks should snap easily. Avoid bunches that have cracked, bruised, or loosened stalks. Stalks having air holes in the central portion, sometimes caused by frost, are undesirable.

Storage—Remove leaves and save for future use in soups and salads. Trim roots. Wash well, using a vegetable brush to remove sand; shake dry. Celery will keep best if stalks are not separated from root. Place leaves in film bag; wrap stalks in foil.

☐ Refrigerator shelf or vegetable compartment, raw: 3 to 8 days
☐ Refrigerator shelf, cooked and covered: 4 to 5 days

Caloric Value
☐ 3½ ounces, raw = 17 calories

Basic Preparation—Inner stalks are usually reserved to serve raw, outer ones cut up for cooking. Celery leaves can be dried for use in cooking.

To revive slightly wilted celery, place it in a bowl of ice water for a short time.
☐ **To Serve, Raw**—Break stalks apart and leave whole or cut into desired lengths for relish dish or "dunking." Celery curls, fine slices, or tiny strips are other ways to prepare celery.
☐ **To Boil**—Put about 1 inch of boiling water or bouillon in saucepan. Add ½ teaspoon salt and diced or thinly sliced celery. Cover; cook for 15 minutes. Drain. Season and serve with butter or a cream sauce.
☐ **To Braise**—Place celery cut into 3- to 4-inch lengths in a saucepan. Add ½ cup chicken bouillon, ½ teaspoon salt, and 2 tablespoons butter to every 1½ pounds celery. Cover tightly and simmer for 25 minutes, or until tender. Liquid left in saucepan may be reduced and thickened and served with the celery.

FRIED CELERY
Dip pieces of cooked celery into beaten egg, then coat with fine dry bread crumbs mixed with grated Parmesan cheese. Fry in deep fat at 360°F. on a frying thermometer until delicately browned, or brown in skillet in a small amount of vegetable oil or butter.

CELERY SAUTÉ
4 slices of bacon, cubed
¼ cup minced onions or shallots
3 cups celery, cut into 1-inch pieces
1 cup tomato sauce
½ cup beef gravy
6 slices of toast, cut into triangles

Fry bacon until crisp. Remove pieces and reserve. Sauté onions in the fat until golden brown. Add celery pieces, tomato sauce, and beef gravy. Cover and simmer until celery is tender, adding more tomato sauce if necessary. Serve over toast triangles, sprinkled with crisp pieces of bacon. Makes 4 to 6 servings.

BAKED CELERY WITH CHEESE AND HAM
3 cups celery, cut into julienne strips
3 cups chopped boiled or baked ham
2 cups grated sharp Cheddar cheese
½ cup butter or margarine
¼ cup all-purpose flour
1 cup chicken bouillon
1 cup light cream
Salt
¼ cup dry bread crumbs

Cover celery strips with salted water and cook until tender. Drain. In a well-greased 2-quart casserole, alternate layers of celery, ham, and grated cheese. Melt ¼ cup butter. Stir in flour. Gradually stir in chicken bouillon and cream. Cook over low heat, stirring constantly, until smooth and thick. Season to taste with salt. Pour sauce over filled casserole. Sprinkle top with dry bread crumbs. Drizzle ¼ cup melted butter over top. Bake in preheated moderate oven (350° F.) for 25 to 30 minutes, or until top is browned and mixture is bubbly. Makes 6 servings.

CELERY SALT—The product of a combination of ground celery seed and fine salt. It is gray-beige in color with a flavor like heavily salted celery. Available ground. Use as a seasoning in vegetable and clam juices, soups, salad dressings, croquettes, eggs, and with fish and potato dishes.

CELERY SEED (Apium graveolens)— Celery seed is a tiny, olive-brown seed obtained from the celery plant in its wild form. Wild celery, sometimes called smallage, is stronger in flavor and tougher in texture than celery cultivated for the table. We obtain most of our celery seed from India, with additional imports from France and the Netherlands. Commercial celery salt is made by combining celery seed with salt. The flavor of celery seed is almost identical with that of the vegetable celery. This seasoning is excellent in pickling, salad dressings, and in fish and vegetable dishes.

ODORI FINI (Herb Seasonings)
½ teaspoon celery seed
½ teaspoon curry powder
1 teaspoon ground ginger
¼ teaspoon cayenne
½ teaspoon grated lemon rind
2 heaping tablespoons fine bread crumbs

Blend all spices well with bread crumbs. Rub meat with olive oil and herb blend. Let meat stand in refrigerator for 8 to 24 hours before cooking. Cook or roast meat as usual. Makes about 3 tablespoons mixture, enough for a 4-pound roast or 8 chops. Excellent with pork.

CEREAL—An edible seed, also called grain, of the grass family. The most common cereal grasses are barley, corn, oats, rice, rye, and wheat. (Buckwheat, millet, and sorghum are not true cereals in the botanical sense, though they are used as cereals.) Cereal grains are used in the making of bread, flour, pastas, and breakfast foods, which are also called cereals. The word "cereal" goes back to Ceres, the Roman goddess of grain. Spring festivals beseeching her for fruitful harvests were called *cerealia*. As far back as 8,000 B.C. the Lake Dwellers of Switzerland cleared land for grain fields and used primitive plows to cultivate them, thus providing food for themselves and their animals.

Cereals are the most important food of man and the animals he has domesticated. Their history is the history of civilization. Before primitive man learned how to grow cereals, all of his time and energy had to go into hunting enough food to keep himself and his family alive. The growing of cereal crops gave him foods that could be stored and transported easily, and long intervals of leisure during which to develop the skills and arts which distinguish civilized man from the savage. To this day, cereal grains provide more food for less effort than any other crops. They contain a higher percentage of carbohydrates than other food plants, and a considerable amount of proteins as well as some fat and vitamins.

Cereal grasses will grow in practically any climate, from the tropics to the Arctic, and under many different soil and moisture conditions. In the north there is barley and rye, in the temperate zones wheat, and in warmer areas maize, or corn, and rice. An enormous amount of exciting scientific research in all parts of the world has increased the quality of cereals as well as their nutritive values.

Cereal Terminology—Each grain of cereal contains three elements: the bran, which refers to the thin outer protective layers of the seed; the endosperm, which is the largest part of the seed; and the germ, or embryo, which is that portion of the seed containing the elements of new growth. *Whole-grain* cereal contains the nutrients of all three elements. *Enriched* cereal has synthesized vitamins and minerals added above the level found in the whole-grain. *Restored* cereal is made from the parts of one or more grains to which nutrients have been added to bring their level back up to what they would be in whole-grain cereal.

Cereal Types—Cereals can be divided into three types: hot or cooked; quick-cooking; and ready-to-eat. Farina and oatmeal are examples of the hot and/or quick-cooking cereals. Quick cooking does not mean that they have been partially cooked, but rather that they are made in smaller, thinner particles which decrease the cooking time needed. The list of ready-to-eat cereals is vast with flakes, puffs, nuts, and shredded biscuits available, sweetened and unsweetened, and with various flavorings added.

Baby cereals are precooked, quickly mixed with water or milk, and easily digested. They may be made of a single grain or a combination of grains. The cereals are enriched with vitamins and minerals.

Purchasing Guide—Since the cereal product is not visible when purchased, select a brand in which you have confidence. Individually wrapped servings cost more than the large economy-size boxes. Cereals requiring long cooking are usually less expensive than the quick-cooking or ready-to-eat varieties. Select the cereal that is most convenient and economical for your use.

Storage—Store tightly covered in cool dry place. Ready-to-eat cereals are packaged with an inner wrapping. Open carefully to keep this lining intact. The lining should be kept tightly folded to preserve the freshness of the cereal. Whole-grain cereals, even though unopened, should be refrigerated because of their fat content.

☐ Kitchen shelf, dry or uncooked: 2 to 3 months

☐ Refrigerator shelf, cooked: 2 to 4 days

☐ Whole-grain cereals, dry or uncooked, refrigerator shelf: 5 to 6 months

Nutritive Food Values—Whole-grain and enriched cereals provide energy in the form of carbohydrates as well as the B-complex vitamins, minerals, and some protein. The combination of milk and cereal provides good sources of a wide variety of nutrients. Whole-grain cereals are high in vitamin E. All cereals are low in vitamins A, D, C, except for yellow corn which contains vitamin A.

Used as breakfast foods and breakfast products, the caloric value of 3½ ounces of the dry or ready-to-eat varieties ranges from 330 to 400 calories (an average serving is about 1 ounce); the cooked cereals range from a low of 42 calories for 3½ ounces of regular dry farina to a high of 75 calories for 3½ ounces of the rolled wheat products. (The specific caloric values for these grains raw, cooked, and as flour will be found under the entry for each grain.)

Basic Preparation—For best results, follow directions on the package.

☐ **To Cook Hot Cereal**—Measure ingredients accurately. Water must be boiling before cereal is added. Sprinkle cereal *slowly* into water to avoid lumping. Stir cereal while it thickens. Reduce heat and cook for the required time. Cereals may be reheated or kept warm in a double boiler.

A RULE OF THUMB

	CEREAL	WATER	SALT
Flaked	1 cup	2 cups	½ teaspoon
Whole and Cracked	1 cup	4 cups	1 teaspoon
Granular	1 cup	5 to 6 cups	1¼ to 1½ teaspoons

☐ **To Crisp Ready-to-Eat Cereal**—Place in a shallow pan and put in a hot oven for a few minutes.

Instead of granulated sugar with cereal, you can use a cinnamon-sugar mixture, brown sugar, corn syrup, honey, maple syrup, jams, and preserves.

VARIATIONS FOR HOT CEREAL

■ Use milk or chocolate milk instead of water for cooking cereal.

■ Add 1 teaspoon ground cinnamon to the salted boiling water just before cereal is stirred in.

■ **Fruit-Blended Oatmeal**—Stir 2 cups quick or old-fashioned rolled oats into 4 cups briskly boiling water to which 1 teaspoon salt has been added. Add 1 cup fresh, frozen, or canned peaches, drained; 1 cup fresh or frozen strawberries, drained; or 1 cup fresh or canned pineapple, drained. Cook quick oats for 1 minute, stirring occasionally. Cook old-fashioned oats for 5 minutes or longer. Cover pan, remove from heat, and let stand for a few minutes. Makes 4 to 6 servings.

■ Just before serving, stir in cut-up prunes, dates, apricots, raisins, currants, or nut meats.

■ Put a pat of butter in the center of a bowl of cereal. Or sprinkle cereal with a slice of crisp bacon, crumbled.

■ Drop a few semisweet chocolate pieces into a bowl of cereal.

■ Put one of the following into bowl before adding the cereal:
a marshmallow
a chocolate cream
a gumdrop
several jelly beans
a spoonful of preserves or marmalade
a maraschino cherry

SERVING VARIATIONS FOR READY-TO-EAT CEREAL

■ Top cereal with small chunks of plain fruit-flavored or fruited gelatin dessert.

■ Mix two kinds of ready-to-eat cereal in serving bowl.

■ Serve cereal with sliced bananas, berries, sliced nectarines, or any other favorite fruit.

■ Serve cereal in a cantaloupe half so children can eat the "bowl."

■ Instead of plain milk or cream, use:
chocolate milk
eggnog made from 1 egg and 1 cup milk
malted milk made by beating 2 tablespoons malted milk into 1 cup milk.

CERVELAT

CERVELAT—A smoked sausage made of finely ground beef chuck and pork, seasoned with salt, sugar, and red and black pepper. It is one of Europe's favorite sausages because of its tastiness and long-keeping qualities, and it comes in a number of varieties depending on locality.

CHAFING DISH—This handsome cooking utensil is used to cook at the table, and has its own source of heat, such as an alcohol lamp, candle, solid fuel burner, or an electric unit. The word developed from the Latin *calefacere,* "to make warm," through the Middle English *chaufen* which means the same thing.

Chafing-dish cookery dates back to the ancient Romans at least, as a chafing dish found in the ruins of Pompeii proves. Beautifully designed chafing dishes were the prized possessions of our colonial forebears. The greatest vogue for chafing-dish cookery was at the turn of the century, when hostesses gracefully cooked delicious dishes at the table for their admiring families and friends.

WELSH RABBIT

2 walnuts of butter (about 3 tablespoons)
3 pounds best fresh rat cheese, grated (this means Cheddar)
⅓ to ½ bottle ale
½ teaspoon salt
¼ teaspoon pepper
1 teaspoon paprika
4 teaspoons English powdered mustard
6 to 8 slices of buttered toast

Melt butter. Add cheese and stir constantly until melted to consistency of cold molasses. Add ale and seasonings. When mixture bubbles all over, drop in toast slices, one at a time. Turn toast over with fork and spoon and serve while piping hot. Makes 6 to 8 servings.

SCOTCH WOODCOCK

1 tube anchovy paste
5 slices of toast, buttered generously on both sides
4 egg yolks
1 cup light cream

Spread anchovy paste on one side of toast. Beat yolks with cream and pour into chafing dish. Stir until thick. Serve on toast.

CRABMEAT À LA DEWEY

1 small green pepper, minced
1 can (4 ounces) pimientos, cut into pieces
¼ teaspoon nutmeg
1 can (6½ ounces) crabmeat
Simple or Rich Cream Sauce
Saltines

Add all ingredients except saltines to Simple Cream Sauce. When bubbling hot, serve on saltines, or on toast or boiled rice, if desired. Makes 4 servings.

Simple or Rich Cream Sauce

For 2 cups sauce: melt 2 tablespoons butter or margarine in saucepan. Blend in 3 tablespoons flour, ½ teaspoon salt, and ⅛ teaspoon white pepper. Gradually stir in 2 cups milk and cook, stirring, until smooth and thickened.

■ **Rich Cream Sauce**—substitute 1 cup light cream for 1 cup of the milk.

CREAMED HAM, EGGS, AND MUSHROOMS IN A CHAFING DISH

2 tablespoons butter
1 cup sliced mushrooms
2 cans (10½ ounces each) cream of mushroom soup
¾ cup milk
1½ cups cooked cubed ham
6 hard-cooked eggs, quartered
Toast Cups

In the kitchen, heat butter and cook mushrooms in it for 3 minutes until golden brown. In chafing dish, combine cream of mushroom soup and milk. Blend thoroughly. Add ham and simmer, stirring frequently, for 5 minutes. Add mushrooms and hard-cooked eggs. Stir lightly, taking care not to break the eggs. Serve in Toast Cups or over thin slices of toast, or in patty shells. Makes 6 servings.

Toast Cups

Cut crust from 6 slices of day-old bread. Brush both sides well with melted butter. Press into muffin pans. Toast in preheated hot oven (400°F.) for about 10 minutes. Makes 6 cups.

CHAMPIGNON—*Champignon* is the French word for mushroom. It comes from *champ,* French for "field," implying that mushrooms grow in the fields.

CHANTILLY—This French word describes whipped cream that has been sweetened and flavored; it is also used for any dish, such as potatoes or sauce, to which whipped cream, sweet or unsweetened, has been added.

CHANTILLY POTATOES

Cook, drain, and mash enough potatoes to make 3 cups. Season with butter, salt, and pepper; shape into a mound on a

Creamed Ham, Eggs, and Mushrooms in a Chafing Dish

pie pan. Whip ½ cup heavy cream until stiff; season with salt, paprika, and a dash of cayenne. Fold in ½ cup grated Cheddar cheese. Spread on potato mound. Bake in preheated moderate oven (375° F.) for about 15 minutes. Makes 4 servings.

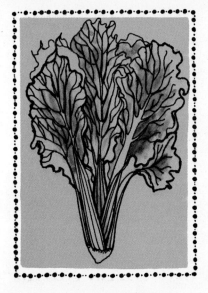

CHARD or SWISS CHARD

CHARD or SWISS CHARD—This vegetable is a variety of beet, of which the leaves and stalk, not the root, are eaten. When Aristotle wrote of beets in the 4th century B.C., he was referring to chard. Chard is a wholesome vegetable, and a favorite of home gardeners, since it is easy to grow and requires minimum care.

Availability—Chard is available only in the summer months.

Purchasing Guide—Look for tender, fresh green leaves and crisp stalks of white or reddish hue.

Storage—Like other greens, once it has been washed and trimmed, it should be stored in a moisture-proof bag in the refrigerator. Plan to use within 2 days.

Nutritive Food Values—Chard has all the attributes of the green leafy vegetables. It is an excellent source of vitamin A, a very good source of iron, and a good source of vitamin C.

☐ 3½ ounces, raw = 25 calories

Basic Preparation—Remove root ends; separate the leaves and stalks. Cut the stalks into 2-inch lengths; cut up the leaves if they are large. Wash thoroughly several times.

Cook in a small amount of boiling water until tender; 10 to 15 minutes for the stalks, 5 to 10 minutes for the leaves. Drain; season with salt and pepper, butter or margarine, and lemon juice, if desired. Or sauté stalks in melted butter in a skillet over low heat for a few minutes; stir; cover and cook until tender, about 15 to 20 minutes.

CHARD WITH CHEESE SAUCE

2 pounds chard
2 teaspoons salt
2 tablespoons butter
2 tablespoons all-purpose flour
½ cup milk
¼ pound process American cheese, diced

Wash chard, cut out heavy ribs, and cut into 1-inch pieces. Cook in ½ inch of boiling salted water, covered, for 5 minutes. Shred chard leaves, add to ribs, and cook for 5 minutes more. Drain well and press out excess liquid. Melt butter in saucepan; add flour. Stir to moisten flour. Gradually add milk, stirring constantly, and cook over medium heat until thickened. Add cheese and stir until cheese melts. Combine with chard in 1½-quart casserole and bake, uncovered, in preheated slow oven (325°F.) for about 45 minutes. Makes 4 servings.

CHARD AND GREEN ONIONS

4 slices of bacon
2 pounds chard
½ teaspoon salt
1 bunch green onions, cut into 1-inch lengths
1 hard-cooked egg, sieved

Fry bacon in skillet, remove, drain, and keep warm. Wash chard, cut away heavy ribs, and shred leaves. Put in skillet with bacon fat. Add salt and onions. Cover and cook slowly until tender. Put in serving dish; crumble bacon and sieved egg over top. Makes 6 servings.

CHARLOTTE RUSSE—This elegant lady of the dessert family consists of a molded shell of ladyfingers filled with a sumptuous Bavarian cream. The dessert appears on the table well chilled and fancifully decorated with glacé fruit, whipped cream, and candied flowers.

Carême, the indefatigable creator of luxurious desserts, is said to have created this beauty in honor of the Russian Emperor Alexander. This may be so, but the dessert existed in Paris under the name of Charlotte Parisienne long before Carême traveled to Russia. It was the favorite of high-ranking French and foreign ministers.

Sisters to this dessert are the "Charlottes des Fruits," and in particular the "Charlotte des Pommes," or apple charlotte. This kind of charlotte is always served hot, and consists of a shell of crisp bread filled with cooked fruit.

CHARLOTTE RUSSE

1 envelope unflavored gelatin
1 cup milk
4 eggs, separated
½ cup sugar
¼ teaspoon salt
¼ teaspoon vanilla extract
2 cups heavy cream, whipped
12 ladyfingers, split
⅓ cup glace fruit

Soften gelatin in milk in top of double boiler. Beat egg yolks and add to milk together with ¼ cup sugar and the salt. Cook over simmering (not boiling) water, stirring constantly, until mixture is thickened and smooth. Stir in vanilla. Cool. Stir occasionally to prevent crust from forming on top of custard. Beat egg whites until foamy. Beat in remaining sugar, 1 tablespoon at a time. Fold egg whites and 1 cup heavy cream, whipped, into custard. Line a greased 2-quart charlotte mold or springform with ladyfingers. Fill with custard. Chill for at least 4 hours. Run a knife around the charlotte carefully. Unmold by removing sides of springform carefully but leave bottom of pan in place. Decorate with glacé fruit and 1 cup heavy cream, whipped, forced through a pastry tube. Makes 8 servings.

CHARLOTTE DES POMMES
(Apple Charlotte)

6 to 8 slices of bread
   Melted butter or margarine
8 cups quartered peeled cored tart apples
½ cup sugar
½ teaspoon each of ground nutmeg and cinnamon
   Chopped almonds
   Cream or custard sauce

Brush bread slices generously with butter and cut bread into strips. Use some to line a 1½-quart casserole. Cook apples in a small amount of water until tender; drain and mash slightly. Mix in sugar and spices; use to fill lined casserole. Sprinkle with almonds. Top with remaining bread. Bake in preheated hot oven (400°F.) for about 25 minutes. Turn out on serving plate. Serve warm with cream. Makes 6 servings.

CHAUD-FROID—Literally translated, this French culinary term means "hot-cold." It refers to a sauce which begins hot and ends cold, and also to a method of coating food with this sauce.

The sauce is rich, well-seasoned, and stiffened with unflavored gelatin. Usually it is a white sauce but it can also be a brown sauce. *Chaud-froid* sauce is used to coat chicken, ham, cold meat, fish, and seafood. It should contain some stock made from the food it is to coat, such as chicken stock for a chicken *chaud-froid,* or fish stock for a seafood *chaud-froid. Chaud-froid* dishes are not only delicious but are also very elegant in appearance and most appropriate for buffets. Since *chaud-froid* is basically an aspic, foods can be decorated with sprays of flowers and leaves, or with edible decorations made from lemon rind, black olives, truffles, carrots, green peppers, fresh herbs, pimientos, eggs, and vegetables diced or cut into fancy shapes and patterns.

SUPRÊMES OF CHICKEN JEANETTE
6 chicken breasts, skinned, boned, and cut into halves to make 12 supremes
2 cups boiling chicken broth
7 tablespoons butter
3 tablespoons all-purpose flour
1 cup hot milk
   Salt and pepper
2 envelopes unflavored gelatin

Place chicken breasts in heavy saucepan. Cover with boiling chicken broth and add 3 tablespoons butter. (The butter will keep the chicken breasts juicy.) Simmer over low heat for 35 to 40 minutes, or until chicken breasts are tender. Drain; reserve 1¼ cups broth for sauce. Chill chicken breasts. Melt remaining butter and stir in flour. Cook, stirring constantly, until smooth. Do not let brown. Combine 1 cup of reserved hot chicken broth and the hot milk and stir into butter-flour mixture. Cook, stirring constantly, until sauce is smooth and thickened. Season with salt and pepper to taste. Soften gelatin in ¼ cup reserved chicken broth. Stir into hot sauce. Cook over medium heat, stirring constantly, until gelatin is thoroughly melted. Cool sauce, stirring occasionally, to prevent a skin from forming. Chill until it has the consistency of egg white, or is thick enough to coat a spoon, but not thicker.

Place chicken breasts on serving platter. Spoon a layer of sauce over chicken breasts. Chill to set. Repeat process until chicken breasts are thoroughly coated. If sauce thickens, warm over hot water to right consistency. After final coating, decorate chicken with cut olives, vegetables cut into fancy shapes, or fresh tarragon leaves. Place sprigs of watercress or parsley around chicken. Refrigerate until serving time. Makes 6 servings.

Note: For cooked seafood or fish, use this basic *chaud-froid* sauce, but replace the chicken broth with fish stock or clam juice.

CHAYOTE—The gourdlike fruit of a trailing vine of tropical America, which is eaten as a vegetable, chayote has a deeply ribbed, greenish-white rind and one soft seed. It was the principal food of the Aztecs and Mayas, and although it has long been grown in California and our southern states, it has only lately become a commercial crop.

Chayote is extremely bland and its main virtues are that it is low in starch and that it keeps its shape even when overcooked. It can be boiled—peeled or unpeeled—fried, baked, stuffed, or combined with other foods such as meats and vegetables. Since chayote has practically no flavor of its own, it should be well seasoned.

Chayote should be stored in the refrigerator.

Caloric Value

☐ 3½ ounces = 28 calories

BOILED CHAYOTE
Wash chayote and cut crosswise through seed into ¾-inch slices, or cut into cubes. Put in 1 inch of boiling salted water in saucepan, cover, and simmer for 10 to 15 minutes, or until tender. Drain, and serve with butter, hollandaise, tomato, or cream sauce.

Chayotes au Gratin
Prepare chayotes as in Boiled Chayote. Drain well and place in buttered baking dish. Cover with medium white sauce and sprinkle generously with grated Cheddar cheese and some buttered crumbs. Bake in preheated hot oven (400°F.) for about 15 minutes.

STUFFED CHAYOTES

3 chayotes of uniform size (about 2 pounds)
1 pound beef round steak, ground
1 onion, chopped
¼ cup uncooked rice
2 tablespoons soft butter or margarine
   Salt and pepper
   Olive oil
2⅓ cups (one 1-pound, 3-ounce can) tomatoes

Wash chayotes, cut into halves, and scoop out pulp and reserve. Mix remaining ingredients except last 2. Fill chayotes with mixture. Brown reserved pulp lightly in a little olive oil. Put chayotes in a greased shallow baking dish and pour pulp and tomatoes over top. Bake in preheated slow oven (325°F.) for about 1½ hours. Makes 6 servings.

CHEESE—A natural miracle and a universal food, cheese is made from milk which has been thickened and separated into two substances: a liquid called "whey" and a soft semisolid called "curd." Generally it is the curd which is pressed, treated, and ripened into a great variety of cheeses.

Cheese is one of the oldest foods known to humanity, and has appeared in one form or another wherever man has grazed animals and used their milk. It is a nearly perfect food with a great many of the essential food elements the body needs, such as proteins, fats, and vitamins, with the excellent taste and enormous variety to make it appealing to all. The amount of these nutritional elements varies with the different kinds of cheeses, but they are always there. Cheese is a most adequate meat substitute, and in countries where meat is prohibitively expensive, the people get most of their proteins from regular cheese eating. Pliny, the Roman chronicler, tells of the Persian philosopher Zoroaster, who, in the 6th century B.C., lived for twenty years on nothing but cheese. On the basis of half a pound a day, Zoroaster must have eaten his way through 3,650 pounds of cheese.

Cheese was made and eaten in Biblical times. The ancient Romans not only made cheese, they introduced cheese making to such distant parts of their empire as Great Britain. Throughout the Middle Ages, the great monasteries of Europe were famous cheese-making centers. And Italy, from early days, excelled in good cheese: the famous blue-veined Gorgonzola was made in the Po Valley as early as 879 A.D.

When the Pilgrims set sail on the Mayflower, they took round Dutch cheeses along with them. Until 1850 all the cheese in America was made on farms, and very often by the women. Most of it was cottage cheese, the simplest kind to make, but some farmers also made Cheddar, the way they had seen it made in their native England. The first American cheese factory was started in 1851 by Jessie Williams in Oneida County in the state of New York. Until the early 1900's most American cheese was made in New York where the surroundings were ideal: fine pastures, ample water, a good climate, and healthy cattle. By and by the industry traveled westward, especially to Wisconsin, which also had perfect cheese-making conditions. Today it is made in almost every state of the Union. Practically all American cheese is made from cow's milk, which must be pasteurized.

Availability—Both domestic and imported cheeses and cheese products are available in food stores the year round.

Purchasing Guide—Generally speaking, cheese products are divided into four groups:

Natural Cheese (nonprocessed)—Refers to a cheese made directly from milk curds or, in some cases, whey. There are probably only 18 distinct types of natural cheese, although cheese making has been so widespread that no entirely satisfactory grouping has ever been made, and more than 400 specific variations of these basic types are known. The characteristic flavor and texture of natural cheeses are dependent on several factors: the type and quality of milk used; whether it is whole, partly skimmed, skimmed, or whole milk enriched with cream; the method of curdling the milk: acid or rennet; the ripening process: type of bacteria or mold used; addition of salt or seasonings; temperature, humidity, and length of ripening.

Process Cheese (pasteurized process)—A product made from one or more natural cheeses. The selected cheeses are ground, heated, and stirred with an emulsifier and water to form a smooth, homogenous, fluid mixture. The mixture is packaged in loaf-shaped, foil-lined cardboard containers. The pasteurization prevents further ripening and improves the keeping quality. Process cheese is easy to slice and melts readily.

Process Cheese Food (pasteurized process)—Has a lower fat content and more moisture than process cheese. It is softer and spreads more easily. It is made the same way that process cheese is, except that it contains less cheese and has additional dairy products (milk, nonfat dry milk, cream, or whey solids) and water added to it. Fruits, vegetables, meats, spices, and flavorings may also be added. However, by law at least 51 per cent of the weight of the finished cheese food must be cheese.

Process Cheese Spread (pasteurized process)—Is made in the same way that process cheese food is except that an edible stabilizer is added. The moisture content is higher and the fat content is lower. It must be spreadable at room temperature (70°F.). Fruits, vegetables, or meats may be added.

Cheeses can also be classified as soft, semisoft, hard, and very hard. Choose cheese according to how you plan to use

it. Soft cheeses are very perishable; buy only as much as you are planning to use at one time. Hard cheeses keep very well and can be purchased several pounds at a time, in one piece. Cut when ready to use. Natural cheeses are sold, by weight, in wedges cut from wheels.

Process cheese and cheese spreads can be purchased in quantity because they have good keeping qualities.

Storage—Soft cheeses, such as cottage cheese, should be tightly covered and placed in the coldest part of the refrigerator.

Hard natural cheeses should be tightly wrapped in a double thickness of wax paper, aluminum foil, or plastic film and refrigerated. Cut edges may be buttered or coated with melted paraffin. Hard cheeses will keep for several weeks in the refrigerator if properly protected from mold contamination and drying out. If hard cheese begins to get too dry, wrap in a clean cloth dampened with vinegar or water. Keep cloth damp.

Strong cheeses should be wrapped as above and placed in a tightly covered container in the refrigerator. Should mold develop on natural cheeses, it is not harmful. Cut or scrape it off before using.

Process cheeses or cheese spreads should be kept in their original wrapper or container; or wrapped tightly in foil or plastic film and refrigerated. If un-

opened, they will keep well at room temperature, on the kitchen shelf.

☐ Soft, refrigerator shelf: 1 to 2 weeks
☐ Soft, refrigerator frozen-food compartment, prepared for freezing: 2 months
☐ Soft, freezer, prepared for freezing: 1 year
☐ Hard, refrigerator shelf: 3 to 9 months
☐ Hard, refrigerator frozen-food compartment, prepared for freezing: 1 year
☐ Hard, freezer, prepared for freezing: 1 to 2 years
☐ Cheese in jars, Spreads, kitchen shelf, unopened: 1 year
☐ Cheese in jars, Spreads, refrigerator shelf, opened and covered: 2 to 3 weeks

Do not freeze process cheeses, cottage, or cream cheese: they tend to become watery when thawed.

Nutritive Food Values—Cheese is a good source of protein, calcium, and riboflavin. It is impossible to list caloric values for the hundreds of known cheeses and the many cheese products, but 3½ ounces of most natural cheeses contain between 300 and 400 calories. The exception is cottage cheese: uncreamed, 3½ ounces contains 86 calories; creamed, 106 calories.

Basic Preparation—All natural cheeses, except cottage cheese, should be removed from the refrigerator at least one half to one hour before serving, for best flavor. Cottage cheese is served chilled.

☐ **To Cook**—Cheese is sliced, cubed, or grated for use in recipes. Soft cheeses should be shredded on a coarse grater. Hard cheeses are grated on a fine grater. Some cheeses are quite heavily salted; adjust recipes accordingly.

Cook cheese at low temperatures. Too much heat will toughen it and make it stringy. Heat can also cause separation of the fat from the protein. Process cheese melts at a lower temperature than natural cheese and makes a smoother sauce. For best results when cooking with cheese on top of the range, use a double boiler. Only when cheese is to be cooked for a very short time can high temperatures be used. Dried-out cheese is good for cooking; however, very dry grated cheese will not melt when heated unless moisture is added, so use it for such things as soup or spaghetti sauce.

☐ **To Freeze**—*Some natural* cheeses may be frozen in small pieces, 1 pound or less: Brick, Cheddar, Edam, Gouda, Muenster, Port Salut, Swiss, Provolone, and Mozzarella. Wrap tightly in moisture-proof container or wrapper; freeze quickly at 0°F. or lower. Frozen cheese will keep for several months.

Thaw it in the refrigerator and use as soon as possible after thawing.

1—Provoloncini, 2—Bel Paese, 3—Pot Cheese, 4—Irish Blarney, 5—Pineapple, 6—Mozzarella, 7—Provolone, 8—English Cheddar, 9—Switzerland Swiss, 10—Pepato, 11—Muenster, 12—Baby Gouda, 13—Sardo, 14—New York State Cheddar, 15—Sage, 16—Blue, 17—Romano, 18—Edam

The world's best-known cheeses

How many cheeses are there? Basically, there are only about eighteen distinctly different types, that is, cheeses made by different methods to produce different characteristics.
The hundreds we know by name are all variations of one or the other of these basic categories.
Some are named for the place where they are made,
others after a landmark of the community, and some to describe their distinctive flavor.
The cheeses listed on this chart are the world's best known.
They can all be found in food and cheese stores throughout the United States.

ASIAGO: Made from whole milk; imported is made from partly-skimmed milk. **Characteristics:** Dark surface, creamy inside; hard, granular texture; piquant flavor. **Uses:** Eating; Cooking.

BAKER'S CHEESE: Made from skim milk. **Characteristics:** White, resembles Cottage Cheese, however is softer and finer grained; slightly sour flavor. **Uses:** Eating; Cooking (its more common use).

BEL PAESE (a trade name): Made from whole milk. **Characteristics:** Gray-brown surface, light-yellow inside; soft texture; delicate flavor. **Use:** Eating.

BLUE: Made from whole milk. **Characteristics:** White interior with blue veins; semisoft, crumbly; piquant flavor that gets stronger with age; usually foil-wrapped. **Uses:** Eating; Cooking.

BRICK: Made from whole milk. **Characteristics:** Yellow-brown surface, creamy yellow inside; semisoft; mild but pungent flavor, midway between Cheddar and Limburger. **Use:** Eating.

BRIE: Made from whole milk, sometimes skimmed. **Characteristics:** Brown, edible crust, creamy yellow inside; soft; resembles Camembert; mild to pungent. **Use:** Eating.

CACIOCAVALLO: Made from whole milk. **Characteristics:** Light-brown, glossy surface, yellowish-white color; smooth, firm body; without eyes; slightly salty, smoky flavor; spindle-shape, cord bound. **Uses:** Eating; Grating when old and dry.

CAMEMBERT: Made from whole milk. **Characteristics:** Gray-white, edible crust; soft, creamy interior; full flavor. **Use:** Eating (Before serving store at room temperature until runny.)

CANTELLE (a trade name): Made from whole milk. **Characteristics:** Red waxed surface, yellow interior; mild flavor; similar to Trappist cheese. **Uses:** Eating; Cooking.

CHEDDAR: Made from whole milk. **Characteristics:** Yellow-brown surface, cream to deep-orange color; firm cheese; mild flavor when fresh; sharper the more cured and aged; English Cheddar is generally a little drier and milder than the American. **Uses:** Eating; Cooking.

CHESHIRE: Made from whole milk. **Characteristics:** Yellow surface, cream to deep-yellow color; firm, more crumbly than Cheddar; sharp flavor the more aged. **Uses:** Eating; Cooking.

COLBY: Made from whole milk. **Characteristics:** Deep yellow; softer body and more open texture than Cheddar (it contains more moisture and for this reason won't keep as well as Cheddar). **Uses:** Eating, Cooking.

COON: Made from whole milk. **Characteristics:** Cheddar-type cheese with dark surface; crumbly texture; sharp tangy flavor. **Uses:** Eating; Cooking.

COTTAGE CHEESE: Made from skim milk with cream and salt added. **Characteristics:** White; soft; pleasant sour taste. **Uses:** Eating; Cooking.

> **SKIM-MILK COTTAGE CHEESE:** A form of Cottage Cheese with no cream added.
> **POT CHEESE:** A form of Skim-milk Cottage Cheese with a larger, dry curd; neither cream nor salt added.

CREAM CHEESE: Made from cream and milk. **Characteristics:** White; smooth, soft texture; delicate, slightly acid taste. **Uses:** Eating; Cooking.

EDAM: Originally made of whole milk but now the fat content is reduced. **Characteristics:** Red waxed surface, yellowish inside; semisoft to hard; mild flavor. **Uses:** Eating; Cooking.

FARM: (Farmer's or Pressed): Made from whole or partly-skimmed milk. **Characteristics:** White, dry form of Cottage Cheese; pressed into parchment paper packages. **Use:** Cooking.

FETA: Made from ewe's milk; sometimes goat's milk. **Characteristics:** White; soft; salty cheese. **Uses:** Eating; Cooking.

FONTINA: Made from whole milk; imported may be made from ewe's milk. **Characteristics:** Slightly yellow with oiled surface; semisoft to hard; delicate, nutty flavor. **Uses:** Eating; Cooking; Grating when aged.

GAMMELOST: Made from skimmed, sour milk. **Characteristics:** Golden brown; semisoft to hard. **Use:** Eating.

GJETOST: Made from cow's and goat's milk whey or goat's milk whey, only. **Characteristics:** Golden brown; semisoft to hard; sweet uncheeselike flavor. **Use:** Eating.

GORGONZOLA: Made from whole milk. **Characteristics:** Clay-colored exterior, white with blue veins inside; semisoft, crumbly texture; piquant flavor. **Use:** Eating.

GOUDA: Made from whole or partly-skimmed milk. **Characteristics:** Usually red surface, yellow interior; semisoft to hard; similar to Edam but milk is skimmed; mellow flavor; Irish Blarney cheese is similar, but has holes like Swiss; domestic (Baby) Gouda is softer and often has a slightly sour flavor. **Use:** Eating.

GRUYÈRE: Made from whole milk. **Characteristics:** Light yellow, firm with small holes; tastes like Swiss only slightly sharper; U. S. Gruyère is a foil-wrapped, process cheese. **Uses:** Eating; Cooking.

HAND CHEESE: Made from sour milk and skim milk. **Characteristics:** Soft; pungent, sour-milk cheese; so named because originally it was molded into final shape by hand. **Use:** Eating.

JACK (Monterey): Made from whole, partly-skimmed, or skim milk. **Characteristics:** Mild, Cheddar-type cheese; whole-milk Jack is semisoft; Jack made from partly-skimmed or skim milk is called grating-type, dry Jack, or dry Monterey. **Uses:** Eating; Cooking; Grating.

LIEDERKRANZ (a trade name): Made from whole milk. **Characteristics:** Russet surface, creamy inside; soft; robust taste and aroma, like a mild Limburger. **Use:** Eating.

LIMBURGER: Made from whole milk. **Characteristics:** Grayish-brown surface, creamy white inside; semisoft; full, aromatic taste. **Use:** Eating.

LIPTAUER: Made from ewe's milk and some cow's milk. **Characteristics:** Pickled pot cheese; can be prepared at home. **Use:** Eating.

MOZZARELLA: Made from whole milk or partly-skimmed milk. **Characteristics:** White; semisoft, mild cheese. **Uses:** Eating; Cooking.

MUENSTER: Made from whole milk. **Characteristics:** Yellow-tan surface, white to light-yellow interior; semisoft; tastes like Brick only milder. **Uses:** Eating; Cooking.

MYSOST: Made from cow's milk whey. **Characteristics:** Light brown; sweetish taste. **Use:** Eating.

NEUFCHÂTEL, NEUCHÂTEL: Made from whole or skim milk or mixture of milk and cream. **Characteristics:** White; soft; mild cheese. Bondon, Malakoff, Petit Suisse, and Petit Carré are other French cheeses that differ from Neufchâtel mainly in fat content, size, and shape. The spelling "Neuchâtel" without the "f" is used for this cheese when it originates in Switzerland. **Use:** Eating.

PARMESAN: Made from partly-skimmed milk. **Characteristics:** Dark-green or black surface, whitish inside; hard, granular texture; flavor gets stronger with age; very old Parmesan is a delicacy. **Uses:** Eating when fresh; Grating when older.

PEPATO: Made from mixture of whole cow's and goat's milk. **Characteristics:** Light, grayish color; hard and dry; peppercorns added. **Use:** Grating.

PETIT SUISSE: Made from fresh, whole milk with cream. **Characteristics:** Soft, rich, unripened French cheese. **Use:** Eating.

PINEAPPLE: Made from whole milk. **Characteristics:** A Cheddar type, shaped like a pineapple and usually hard. **Uses:** Eating; Cooking.

PONT L'ÉVÊQUE: Made from whole or slightly skimmed milk. **Characteristics:** Yellow; soft; sharp-flavored. **Use:** Eating.

POONA: Made from whole milk. **Characteristics:** Pale; soft; aroma like mild Limburger. **Use:** Eating.

PORT SALUT: Made from whole or partly skimmed milk. **Characteristics:** Russet surface, creamy inside; elastic curd, semisoft; mild flavor like Gouda; aroma like Limburger (Made by Trappist monks). **Use:** Eating.

PRIMOST: Made from whey. **Characteristics:** Light brown; soft; mild flavor. **Use:** Eating.

PROVOLONE: Made from whole milk. **Characteristics:** Yellowish; hard; smoky flavor; link-shape or round and hangs from strings; Provoloncini is a smaller version of the same cheese. **Uses:** Eating; Cooking.

REGGIANO: Made from whole milk. **Characteristics:** Very hard; sharp, pungent flavor; granular; nearly the same as Parmesan. **Use:** Grating.

RICOTTA: Made from whey. **Characteristics:** White; soft; like Cottage Cheese. **Uses:** Eating; Cooking.

ROMADUR: Made from whole milk or partly-skimmed milk. **Characteristics:** Soft; whole-milk Romadur is similar to Liederkranz; aroma like Limburger only milder. **Use:** Eating.

ROMANO (Incanestrato): Made from partly-skimmed cow's, goat's or ewe's milk. **Characteristics:** Greenish-black surface, whitish inside; granular and hard texture; sharp flavor. **Use:** Grating.

ROQUEFORT: Made from ewe's milk (A French regulation limits use of the word Roquefort to cheese made in the Roquefort area from ewe's milk). **Characteristics:** White, blue-green veins; crumbly, semisoft to hard; sharp flavor. **Uses:** Eating; Cooking.

SAGE: Made from whole or partly-skimmed milk. **Characteristics:** Green, mottled appearance throughout; sage flavored (At one time, green sage leaves were added to the curd before it was hooped. Now sage extract is added for flavor). **Uses:** Cooking; Grating.

SAMSOE: Made from whole milk. **Characteristics.** Semihard; mild, sweet, nutty flavor. **Uses:** Eating; Cooking.

SAPSAGO: Made from slightly sour, skim milk. **Characteristics:** Light-green color; very hard; pungent, flavored with powdered clover leaves; small, conical shape. **Uses:** Eating; Grating.

SARDO: Made from whole cow's milk. **Characteristics:** Cream to gray color; firm and smooth. **Uses:** Eating; Cooking.

SBRINZ: Made from whole or partly-skimmed milk. **Characteristics:** Gray-green surface, white inside; hard, granular texture; medium-sharp flavor. **Use:** Grating.

STILTON: Made from whole milk. **Characteristics:** Cream-colored with blue-green veins; wrinkled surface; crumbly; sharp flavor. **Use:** Eating.

SWISS (Emmentaler): Made from whole milk. **Characteristics:** Light-yellow interior with holes that develop in the curd as the cheese ripens; elastic body; mild, nutty flavor. **Uses:** Eating; Cooking; Grating.

TILSITER (Ragnit): Made from whole or skim milk. **Characteristics:** Slightly yellow; medium firm, similar to Brick cheese; medium-sharp taste, similar to mild Limburger. **Uses:** Mostly eating; Sometimes cooking.

TRAPPIST: Made from whole cow's milk; ewe's or goat's milk may be added. **Characteristics:** Pale yellow; semisoft; mild flavor; similar to Port Salut. **Use:** Eating.

VACHERIN: Made from whole milk. **Characteristics:** Firm, hard rind and very soft interior; aromatic. **Use:** Eating.

WENSLEYDALE: Made from whole cow's milk. **Characteristics:** White; soft; delicately flavored; when aged, it is a medium-hard, blue-veined cheese, similar to Stilton; cylindrical in shape with a strong flavor. **Uses:** Eating; Cooking.

cheese cook book

A delicious collection
of recipes for appetizers,
soups, main dishes,
salads, breads,
sandwiches,
sauces, and desserts
featuring the cheeses
americans love best

APPETIZERS

CHEESE MUSHROOM CANAPÉ

Wash small mushrooms. Remove stems and save for soup or sauce. Make holes in caps slightly larger. Fill with ½ teaspoon of any cheese spread, or cottage cheese mixed with chives, well seasoned, for a low-calorie canapé.

BRANDIED CHEDDAR CHEESE

1 pound sharp American Cheddar cheese, shredded
2 tablespoons butter
1 teaspoon sugar
  Dash of cayenne
½ cup brandy

Have cheese and butter at room temperature. Add sugar, cayenne, and ¼ cup brandy; mix or beat with electric mixer until quite smooth. Gradually add remaining ¼ cup brandy, mixing until creamy. Store in covered crock in refrigerator. Keeps indefinitely. Makes about 2 cups.

Individual Pizzas

Split English muffins; rub each half with garlic; brush with oil. Top with tomato sauce, slice of Mozzarella cheese, anchovy, dash of oregano. Heat in preheated moderate oven (375°F.) for 8 minutes. Cut into small pieces for appetizers.

CHEDDAR-CHEESE STICKS

2 cups sifted all-purpose flour
¾ teaspoon salt
⅛ teaspoon paprika
¾ cup butter
6 ounces sharp American Cheddar cheese, shredded (1½ cups)
⅓ cup water (about)

Sift dry ingredients. Cut in ½ cup butter. Add cheese and mix well; then add enough water to hold ingredients together. Roll out on floured board to rectangle 14 x 8 inches. Dot with 2 tablespoons butter; fold corners into center. Roll out again, dot with 2 tablespoons more butter; fold again. Wrap in wax paper and chill for about 30 minutes. Roll out ¼ inch thick. With pastry wheel, cut into scalloped strips ½ x 4 inches. Put on ungreased cookie sheets. Bake in preheated hot oven (400°F.) for 8 to 10 minutes. Makes about 4½ dozen.

MALAXE

½ cup mashed Roquefort or blue cheese
½ cup butter
2 tablespoons Calvados, Armagnac, applejack, or brandy

Malaxe means mixture, and this one comes from Normandy. Mix cheese with butter until smooth. Add liquor. Mix until smooth and creamy. Spread on dry toast or on dark breads such as rye or pumpernickel. Makes 1 cup.

COTTAGE-STUFFED CELERY

Mix 1 cup dry cottage cheese with 1 to 2 tablespoons light cream, ½ teaspoon salt, and ⅓ cup chopped olives or finely chopped nuts. Fill crisp celery stalks with mixture; sprinkle with paprika, and chill. Serve in bite-size pieces.

SOUPS

CHEESE SOUP WITH CROUTONS

1 medium onion, sliced
1 cup chopped celery
¼ cup butter
¼ cup all-purpose flour
½ teaspoon powdered mustard
1 teaspoon Worcestershire
½ teaspoon each of garlic salt and monosodium glutamate
2 bouillon cubes
2 cups water
1 medium carrot, diced
4 cups milk
6 ounces sharp American Cheddar cheese, shredded (1½ cups)
  Salt and pepper
  Croutons

Cook onion and celery in butter in large saucepan for about 5 minutes. Blend in flour and seasonings. Add next 3 ingredients. Bring to boil; cover and simmer for 15 minutes. Add milk and heat almost to boiling. Add cheese; stir until cheese is melted. Season to taste. Serve at once with croutons. Makes 1½ quarts.

LEEK SOUP WITH CHEESE

5 leeks, sliced
¼ cup uncooked rice
3 cups chicken bouillon
  Salt and pepper
1 cup (¼ pound) grated Swiss cheese
1 cup white wine

Put leeks and rice in saucepan. Add water just to cover. Simmer for 20 minutes, or until rice is tender. Add chicken bouillon. Let come to a boil. Season to taste. Melt cheese with wine in top part of double boiler. Mix well. Put a good spoonful of cheese sauce in each serving of soup. Makes 4 or 5 servings.

Note: Crisp French bread is good with this soup.

CHEDDAR-TUNA CHOWDER

2 cups boiling water
  Salt
1 large potato, peeled and cut in ½-inch dice
½ cup each carrot and celery, diced
1 small onion, chopped
¼ cup butter or margarine
¼ cup all-purpose flour
2 cups milk
¾ pound sharp Cheddar cheese, shredded
1 can (6½ ounces) tuna, drained and flaked
1 can (8 ounces) cream-style corn
  Pinch of dried rosemary
  Few drops of hot pepper sauce
  Chopped chives

Put water in saucepan and season with salt. Add next 4 ingredients, bring to

boil, cover and simmer for 10 minutes; do not drain. In small kettle, melt butter and blend in flour. Gradually stir in milk and cook, stirring, until smooth and thickened. Add cheese and stir until melted. Add vegetables and liquid, tuna, corn, rosemary, and hot pepper sauce. Add salt to taste and serve with a garnish of chives. Makes about 2 quarts, or 6 servings.

MAIN DISHES

CHEESE PIE WITH BACON

  Pastry for 1-crust 9-inch pie, unbaked
1½ cups (6 ounces) grated Swiss cheese
8 slices crisp bacon, crumbled
3 eggs
1 cup heavy cream
½ cup milk
½ teaspoon salt
¼ teaspoon pepper
  Dash of cayenne
½ teaspoon powdered mustard

Roll pastry to ⅛-inch thickness and line 9-inch pie pan; flute edges. Sprinkle cheese and bacon into pan. Beat remaining ingredients together and pour into lined pan. Bake in preheated moderate oven (375°F.) for 45 minutes. Cut into wedges. Makes 6 servings.

FISH GRILL

1 pound fillet of flounder
  Salt and pepper to taste
1 tablespoon grated onion
2 tomatoes, peeled and diced
  Butter
½ cup grated Swiss cheese

Wash fish. Drain and place in buttered shallow baking dish. Sprinkle with salt, pepper, and grated onion. Place diced tomatoes on top of fish. Dot with butter. Place under medium broiler heat. Cook until fish will flake slightly, about 20 minutes. Sprinkle with cheese. Return to broiler and cook until cheese is melted. Makes 4 servings.

CHEESE-BAKED HAM AND VEGETABLES

6 hard-cooked eggs, sliced
1 can (4 ounces) mushrooms, drained
1½ cups diced cooked ham
1 package (10 ounces) frozen asparagus, cooked
3 cups Cheese Sauce (see page 359)
  Dash of hot pepper sauce
  Dash of Worcestershire
  Pinch of salt
  Pepper to taste
2 tablespoons white wine
  Bread crumbs

Place sliced eggs, mushrooms, ham, and asparagus in layers in a shallow baking dish. Make Cheese Sauce. Add seasonings and wine and pour sauce over asparagus. Sprinkle top with a thin layer of bread crumbs. Bake in preheated moderate oven (350°F.) for 25 minutes. Makes 6 servings.

Note: Use cooked chicken or any leftover meat in place of ham.

Onions Ménagère ▼   **Cheese-Apple-Noodle Pudding** ▲

Stuffed Pancakes with Cheese Sauce

HAM AND NOODLES

2 cups cooked medium noodles
   (about 1 cup dry)
2 tablespoons butter
2 tablespoons all-purpose flour
½ teaspoon salt
   Dash of pepper
2 cups milk
1 cup diced cooked ham
1 cup (¼ pound) diced Swiss, Cheddar,
   or Parmesan or 1 cup cottage cheese

Cook noodles according to directions on package until just tender. Drain. Melt butter. Remove from heat. Blend in flour and seasonings. Gradually add milk, mixing until well blended. Cook over low heat, stirring constantly, until thick and smooth. Remove from heat. Add ham and cheese. Add noodles. Pour into greased 2-quart casserole and bake in preheated moderate oven (350°F.) for 20 to 25 minutes, or until top is bubbly and slightly brown. Makes 4 to 6 servings.

VEAL PARMIGIANA

1 pound very thin veal steak
1 onion, minced
2 garlic cloves, minced
6 tablespoons olive oil
2⅓ cups (one 1-pound, 3-ounce can)
   tomatoes
1¼ teaspoons salt
¼ teaspoon pepper
1 can (8 ounces) tomato sauce
   Dash of oregano
¼ cup fine dry bread crumbs
   Grated Parmesan cheese
1 egg, beaten
½ pound Mozzarella cheese, sliced

Cut veal into serving pieces. Cook onion and garlic in 3 tablespoons olive oil for 5 minutes. Add tomatoes broken with fork; add salt and pepper. Simmer, uncovered, for 10 minutes. Add tomato sauce and oregano. Simmer for 20 minutes longer. Combine crumbs and ¼ cup grated cheese. Dip veal into egg, then into crumbs; brown in 3 tablespoons oil in skillet. Transfer veal to shallow baking dish. Pour about two thirds of sauce over veal, top with Mozzarella, then with remaining tomato mixture. Sprinkle with rest of grated cheese. Bake in preheated moderate oven (375°F.) for 30 minutes. Makes 4 servings.

VEAL CHOPS LUCULLUS

4 veal chops cut 1 inch thick
   Salt and pepper
4 thin slices of ham
4 thin slices of Swiss cheese
   Butter or shortening
   Hot water

Make pocket in each veal chop. Sprinkle with seasonings. Insert ham and cheese in pocket. Secure with toothpicks. Brown on both sides in hot fat. Remove excess fat. Add hot water. Cover. Simmer until chops are tender. If desired, thicken gravy. Makes 4 servings.

CHEESE, CHICKEN, AND CAULIFLOWER CASSEROLE

1 onion, sliced thin
½ green pepper, coarsely chopped
⅓ cup diced celery
3 tablespoons butter
3 tablespoons all-purpose flour
2 cups milk
2 carrots, sliced thin
1 tablespoon chopped parsley
1½ cups cooked chicken
   Salt and pepper to taste
   Dash of paprika
1 small cauliflower, separated into
   flowerets and cooked
½ pound Swiss cheese, sliced

Sauté onion, pepper, and celery in butter until tender. Stir in flour, then gradually add milk and cook over low heat until smooth and slightly thickened. Add carrots, parsley, chicken, and seasonings and simmer for 15 minutes. Stir this mixture occasionally. Add cauliflower. Place in a shallow casserole. Top with cheese slices. Bake in preheated moderate oven (350° F.) until cheese is melted, about 15 minutes. Makes 6 servings.

CREAMY MACARONI AND CHEESE

1½ cups (6 ounces) elbow macaroni
2 tablespoons margarine
4½ tablespoons all-purpose flour
¼ teaspoon powdered mustard
¾ teaspoon salt
¼ teaspoon pepper
3 cups milk
¾ teaspoon Worcestershire
½ small onion, grated
8 ounces sharp cheese, shredded
3 tablespoons fine dry bread crumbs
1½ tablespoons melted margarine

Cook macaroni in boiling salted water according to package directions. Drain and put in greased 2-quart casserole. Melt margarine; blend in flour, mustard, salt, and pepper. Remove from heat and add milk gradually. Cook until thickened, stirring constantly. Add Worcestershire, onion, and cheese; stir until cheese begins to melt. Pour over macaroni. Sprinkle with crumbs mixed with melted margarine. Bake in preheated moderate oven (375°F.) for 30 minutes. Makes 4 to 6 servings.

CREAMY EGGS AND CHEESE

2 tablespoons butter or margarine
¾ cup diced sharp process cheese
2 tablespoons water
8 eggs, beaten
   Salt and pepper to taste

Melt butter in large skillet. Add cheese and water; cook slowly, stirring, until cheese melts. Add eggs, salt, and pepper. Cook slowly until eggs are set, scraping mixture frequently during cooking. Makes 4 servings.

CHEESE OMELET

2 tablespoons margarine
8 eggs
1 teaspoon salt
¼ teaspoon pepper
1 tablespoon water
1 cup shredded process American
   cheese

Melt margarine in 10-inch skillet. Beat eggs, salt, pepper, and water until blended. Pour into skillet. Cook over low heat; as mixture begins to set, lift with spatula to let uncooked portion go to bottom of pan. When almost set, sprinkle with cheese and increase heat to brown bottom. Loosen edges of omelet and fold in half. Serve from skillet or put on hot serving platter. Makes 4 servings.

GOLDEN BUCK

2 tablespoons butter
½ pound process American cheese, cubed
⅓ cup milk
   Salt and pepper
   Powdered mustard
4 slices of hot toast
4 poached eggs

Melt butter in top part of double boiler over hot water. Add cheese and stir until melted. Stir in milk; when thick, season well. Serve on toast, topped with a poached egg. Makes 4 servings.

SPIEDINO ALLA ROMANA

Remove crust from a loaf of French bread. Cut loaf into slices about ⅓ inch thick. Cut cheese into slices the same size and thickness as bread. (Use Mozzarella or very new Monterey Jack.) Place alternate slices of bread and cheese on a skewer until there are 3 slices of cheese with a bread slice on the outside at each end; this is one helping. Preheat baking dish and place skewers in it. Bake in preheated very hot oven (450°F.) just long enough for cheese to melt and bread to brown. If bread hasn't browned, place under broiler for a few minutes. Now prepare this essential sauce: Melt 1 cup butter. Chop 6 anchovy fillets and simmer in butter for 5 minutes. When bread and cheese skewers are done, pour sauce over each helping. Serve as hot as you can.

INDIVIDUAL CHEESE STRATAS

8 slices of rye or white bread
2 medium onions, minced
8 slices (½ pound) process American
   cheese
1 teaspoon salt
   Dash each of cayenne and paprika
   Chopped parsley
2 eggs, beaten
2 cups hot milk

Arrange alternate layers of bread, onion, and cheese in 4 individual 1½-cup baking dishes, having cheese on top. Combine remaining ingredients and pour over top. Set dishes in shallow pan of water and bake in preheated moderate oven (375°F.) for about 25 minutes, or until custard is just set and bread is puffy. May be baked in one large shallow 2-quart baking dish, if desired. Makes 4 servings.

CHEESE-BEEF PATTIES

Mix 1½ pounds ground beef, 1½ teaspoons salt, and ⅛ teaspoon pepper. Shape into 8 thin patties. Cut 4 ounces smoked cheese into 8 slices. Put 2 slices between each 2 patties, sandwich fashion, and press together. Panfry or broil slowly until browned and of desired doneness. Makes 4 servings.

STUFFED PANCAKES WITH CHEESE SAUCE
½ pound sausage meat, cooked and drained
1 package (10 ounces) frozen chopped spinach, cooked
1 cup finely chopped cooked chicken
¼ cup grated Romano cheese
⅛ teaspoon ground thyme
⅛ teaspoon pepper
Butter
1 cup milk
2 eggs, beaten
½ cup sifted all-purpose flour
1 teaspoon baking powder
½ teaspoon salt
Cheese Sauce

Combine first 6 ingredients to make stuffing. Heat 2 tablespoons butter and the milk until butter is melted. Cool slightly. Add next 4 ingredients and mix until smooth. Pour batter, 2 tablespoons at a time, into buttered 6-inch skillet. Tip pan to make round. Fry until browned on both sides. Cool; spread each with stuffing. Roll up and put in broilerproof shallow baking dish. Cover with Cheese Sauce. Broil for 5 minutes. Makes 6 servings.

Cheese Sauce

Melt 3 tablespoons butter; blend in 3 tablespoons all-purpose flour. Add 1½ cups light cream; cook, stirring, until thickened. Stir in ½ cup grated Parmesan cheese. Season to taste. Makes about 1½ cups.

SWISS-CHEESE PIE
Pastry for 1-crust 9-inch pie, unbaked
2 cups (½ pound) Switzerland Swiss cheese, grated
1 tablespoon all-purpose flour
3 eggs, well beaten
1 cup milk or light cream
Salt and pepper to taste

Line a deep pie plate with pastry. Chill. Dredge cheese with flour. Place cheese evenly on pastry. Mix eggs with milk and seasonings. Pour mixture over cheese. Bake for 15 minutes in preheated hot oven (425°F.), then reduce heat to slow (325°F.), and bake for 30 minutes longer, or until knife inserted in center of pie comes out clean. Serve hot or warmed over, never cold. Makes 4 servings.

■ **Variation 1**—Instead of making a large cheese pie, you may use the above ingredients for small, individual tartlets. Proceed as above but bake in preheated hot oven (400°F.) for 20 to 25 minutes only. Serve hot or warmed over, never cold.

■ **Variation 2**—To the ingredients above you can add: 4 strips of crisp bacon, crumbled; or 1 large onion, chopped and sautéed; or ½ cup finely minced boiled or smoked ham; or ½ cup finely minced cooked chicken. Add bacon or onion or

ham or chicken and place in pastry-lined pie pan with floured cheese.

SWISS FONDUE
FOR THIS DISH YOU WILL NEED:
1 earthenware casserole holding about 4 cups, or a chafing dish, or a similarly shaped cooking utensil with a handle.

1 alcohol stove, the flame of which is easily adjustable; or any electric plate with an asbestos pad, that will hold the cooking utensils securely.

THESE ARE THE INGREDIENTS FOR 2 SERVINGS:
2 cups (½ pound) Switzerland Swiss cheese, shredded
1½ tablespoons all-purpose flour
1 garlic clove
1 cup Neuchatel wine (or any light dry wine of the Rhine, Reisling, or Chablis types)
Salt and pepper
Nutmeg (optional)

3 tablespoons kirsch or 2 tablespoons light rum, brandy, applejack, or other nonsweet brandy (optional, but very desirable)

1 loaf French or other crusty bread, or at least 4 hard rolls cut into bite-size pieces, each of which must have at least one side of crust

Dredge cheese with flour. Rub cooking utensil with garlic. Pour in wine and set over very slow heat. When wine is heated to the point that air bubbles rise to the surface (it must not boil), stir with a fork and add cheese by handfuls, each handful to be completely absorbed and dissolved before another one is added. Keep stirring until mixture starts bubbling lightly. At this point add a little salt and pepper and a dash of nutmeg (optional). Finally add and thoroughly stir in kirsch, if desired. Remove bubbling fondue from heat and set immediately on preheated table heating equipment.

Spear a piece of bread with a fork, going through soft part first and securing the points in the crust. The idea is not to lose your bread when you dip it into fondue (first loser pays for the works is often the rule). Dunk bread with a stirring motion until your neighbor takes over to give you a chance to enjoy your morsel. While each one takes his leisurely turn, his stirring will help maintain the proper consistency of the fondue and will assure that each piece is thoroughly coated with melted cheese.

Care should be taken that fondue keeps bubbling lightly. This is done by regulating heat or by turning it off or on. If fondue becomes a little too thick at any time, this can be rectified by stirring in a little preheated—never, never cold—wine. Toward the end, some of the melted cheese will form a brown crust at the bottom of the utensil. When that happens, keep heat low in order to prevent

cracking of the utensil. The crust can easily be lifted out with a fork and is considered to be a special delicacy.

BAKED CHEESE FONDUE
2 cups milk, scalded
2 cups soft stale bread crumbs
1½ cups shredded sharp American Cheddar cheese
1 teaspoon salt
Dash of cayenne
4 eggs, separated

Pour hot milk over the bread crumbs. Stir in cheese, salt, and cayenne. Beat egg whites until stiff. Beat egg yolks and stir into milk mixture. Fold in stiffly beaten whites. Pour into greased 2-quart casserole. Bake in preheated moderate oven (350°F.) for 35 to 40 minutes. Makes 4 to 6 servings.

TOP-HAT CHEESE SOUFFLÉ
1½ cups milk
¼ cup butter or margarine
¼ cup all-purpose flour
Salt
Cayenne
½ pound (2 cups) Cheddar cheese, finely grated
4 eggs, separated

Bring milk to a boil; remove from heat. In another saucepan, melt butter over low heat. Stir in flour and blend until smooth. Add all the milk at once. Stir mixture until smooth. Cook, stirring constantly, for 2 to 3 minutes. Season with salt and cayenne to taste. Remove from heat; cool for 3 minutes. Add cheese and stir until melted. Beat in egg yolks, one at a time. Cool mixture. Beat egg whites until they stand in stiff peaks. Fold carefully and quickly into mixture. Turn into a 2-quart baking dish. For top-hat effect, run the tip of a teaspoon in a track around soufflé mixture about 1¼ inches from edge. Bake in a preheated moderate oven (375°F.) for 30 to 45 minutes, depending on whether a runny or firmer soufflé is wanted. Serve immediately. Makes 4 to 6 servings.

Note: The baking dish may be greased or ungreased. A greased baking dish will cause the soufflé to rise more easily.

● ● ● ● ● ● ●

VEGETABLES AND PASTA

● ● ● ● ● ● ●

COTTAGE GREEN-NOODLE CASSEROLE
¼ pound green noodles
1 cup cottage cheese
½ cup dairy sour cream
1 onion, minced
1 small garlic clove, minced
1 teaspoon steak sauce
1 teaspoon seasoned salt
Dash of pepper
½ cup soft bread crumbs
½ cup shredded American Cheddar cheese

Cook noodles in salted boiling water until tender. Drain and mix with remaining ingredients except last 2. Put in shal-

Creamy Macaroni and Cheese

low 1-quart baking dish. Sprinkle with combined crumbs and cheese. Bake in preheated moderate oven (350°F.) for 30 minutes. Makes 4 servings.

Note: This casserole is a wonderful accompaniment for cold meats on a buffet table.

SPAGHETTI PARMIGIANA

8 ounces spaghetti
1 garlic clove, minced
¼ cup margarine or olive oil
1½ cups grated Parmesan cheese

Cook spaghetti following directions on package, adding garlic to water. Drain. Add remaining ingredients and toss lightly until well blended. Makes 4 servings.

CHEESE SPINACH PIE

1 package (10 ounces) frozen chopped spinach
1 cup cottage cheese
2 eggs, beaten
1 teaspoon caraway seeds
1 teaspoon seasoned salt
¼ teaspoon seasoned pepper
Dash of nutmeg
2 tablespoons grated Parmesan cheese
Paprika
1 tablespoon butter

Cook spinach and drain. Add next 6 ingredients. Place in a small shallow casserole or 8-inch pie pan. Sprinkle with Parmesan and paprika and dot with butter. Bake in preheated moderate oven (350°F.) for about 20 minutes. Makes 4 servings.

ONIONS MÉNAGÈRE

1 pound onions
Easy Cheese Sauce (about 2 cups) (Below)
½ cup grated cheese
Butter

Parboil onions. Arrange in buttered shallow baking dish. Pour Easy Cheese Sauce over onions. Sprinkle with grated cheese. Dot with butter. Broil until heated through and golden. Makes 4 servings.

■ **Variation**—Beets may be used in the same way.

CHEESE AND RICE BALLS

2 cups cooked rice
½ cup grated Parmesan cheese
1 egg, well beaten
1 tablespoon melted butter
2 teaspoons prepared mustard (optional)
1 teaspoon salt
Dash of pepper
½-inch cubes of your favorite cheese
Bread crumbs
Fat for deep frying

Mix rice and grated cheese. Add egg, butter, and seasonings. Blend well. Cover each cube of cheese with rice mixture. Form into balls. Be sure that there are no open places in the balls, so that cheese won't seep out and separate from rice. Dip into bread crumbs. Fry in deep hot fat (365°F.) for 5 to 8 minutes, or until slightly brown on all sides. Makes 12 to 16 balls, depending on size.

Note: These balls are a fine way to use leftover rice. In Italy, they're called *suppli* and are also eaten as snacks, with wine.

CHEESE-CORN FRITTERS

2 cups cooked cream-style corn
2 eggs, beaten
1 cup shredded Cheddar cheese
¾ cup sifted all-purpose flour
1 teaspoon each of baking powder and salt
¼ teaspoon pepper

Mix all ingredients and drop by tablespoons into hot deep fat (375°F. on a frying thermometer). Fry until golden brown and done, turning once. Drain. Makes 6 servings.

● ● ● ●

SALADS

OREGON CHEESE SALAD

Mix 1 cup each of packaged grated American cheese and chopped filberts or walnuts, ½ cup dairy sour cream, and dash of salt. Arrange 8 fresh or canned pear halves on salad greens. Sprinkle with fresh orange juice and spread with cheese mixture. Serve as is, or stud with halved seeded grapes. Makes 4 servings.

COTTAGE PEAR SALAD

6 to 10 pear halves (one 1-pound can)
Water
1 package (3 ounces) lime-flavored gelatin
2 tablespoons fresh lemon juice
1 canned pimiento
½ cup crushed pineapple
1 cup cottage cheese
2 tablespoons chopped green pepper
Salad greens

Drain pears and add enough water to syrup to make 1¾ cups; heat liquid. Pour hot liquid over gelatin and stir until dissolved. Add lemon juice, and cool. Pour a thin layer of gelatin into a deep round dish or layer-cake pan. Chill until almost set. Put a small strip of pimiento in tip of each pear half and arrange cut side down in pan. Fold chopped pimiento, pineapple, cheese, and green pepper into remaining gelatin. Pour over pears and chill until firm. Unmold on salad greens. Makes 6 to 8 servings.

● ● ● ● ● ● ● ●

SAUCES AND DRESSINGS

EASY CHEESE SAUCE

3 tablespoons butter
3 tablespoons all-purpose flour
¾ teaspoon salt
½ teaspoon Worcestershire (optional)
⅛ teaspoon pepper
1½ cups milk
1 cup grated sharp Cheddar or Swiss cheese or 1 jar cheese with smoky flavor

Melt butter. Remove from heat. Blend in flour and seasonings. Gradually add milk,

stirring until well mixed. Cook over low heat, stirring constantly, until thick and smooth. Cook for 5 minutes longer. Add cheese. Stir until well blended. Makes about 2 cups.

QUICK CHEESE SAUCE

2 cups (½ pound) processed American cheese, chopped or grated
½ cup milk

Melt cheese in top part of double boiler over hot water. Add milk and stir until well blended. Makes about 2 cups.

MORNAY SAUCE

2 tablespoons butter
2 tablespoons all-purpose flour
½ teaspoon salt
⅛ teaspoon white pepper
1 cup milk
1 egg yolk
½ cup (⅛ pound) grated Swiss or other cheese

Melt butter. Remove from heat. Blend in flour, salt, and pepper. Gradually add milk, stirring until smooth and well blended. Cook over low heat, stirring constantly, until thick. Beat in egg yolk and cheese. Cook for 3 minutes longer. Makes about 1¼ cups.

BLUE-CHEESE DRESSING

⅔ cup crumbled blue cheese
Dash of garlic salt
2 tablespoons cider vinegar
¼ cup salad oil

Put cheese and garlic salt in small bowl and beat in vinegar. Gradually add oil, beating constantly with rotary beater. Makes 1 cup.

● ● ● ●

BREADS

CHEESE SPOON BREAD

¾ cup cornmeal
1 teaspoon salt
Dash of pepper
1 tablespoon sugar
1 cup water
2 tablespoons shortening
2 cups milk
½ pound process American cheese
3 eggs, beaten

Mix first 6 ingredients in saucepan and add 1 cup milk. Cook over moderate heat, stirring constantly, until thickened and boiling. Remove from heat. Reserve one third of cheese to slice for top. Cut remaining cheese into cubes; add to cooked mixture; stir until cheese melts. Add remaining milk and eggs; mix well. Pour into greased 1½-quart shallow baking dish and top with reserved cheese slices. Bake in preheated slow oven (325°F.) for about 50 minutes, until almost set. Serve at once from baking dish. Makes 4 servings.

COTTAGE PANCAKES

Beat 6 eggs until light. Mash 1½ cups cottage cheese, or beat in electric mixer

or with rotary beater, until almost smooth. Add to eggs with ½ teaspoon salt and ½ cup all-purpose flour; mix well. Drop by tablespoons onto lightly greased griddle and bake until browned. Serve hot, with syrup. Makes about 2 dozen 3-inch cakes.

AMERICAN-CHEESE FRITTERS

1 egg, beaten
½ cup milk
1 teaspoon Worcestershire
1 tablespoon instant minced onion
 or 1 small onion, minced
 Dash of hot pepper sauce
2 cups packaged biscuit mix
1½ cups diced process American cheese
 Fat for frying
 Tart jelly

Mix first 5 ingredients and add to biscuit mix. Mix well and stir in cheese. Drop by tablespoons into hot deep fat (365° F. on a frying thermometer) and fry until golden brown. Drain on absorbent paper. Serve with jelly. Makes about 20.

SANDWICHES

FRENCH-TOASTED CHEESE SANDWICHES

8 slices of bread
8 slices of process American cheese
2 eggs
¾ cup milk
¼ teaspoon salt
 Butter or margarine

For each sandwich, put 2 slices of bread together with 2 slices of cheese. Beat eggs and add milk and salt. Dip sandwiches into egg mixture and fry slowly on both sides until bread is delicately browned and cheese is melted. Makes 4 servings.

CROQUE MONSIEUR

8 slices of stale bread
 Butter, softened
8 thin slices of Swiss cheese
4 slices of boiled ham
½ cup grated Swiss cheese
1 cup Medium White Sauce
 Paprika

Spread bread with butter. Then make into 4 sandwiches, using 2 slices of cheese and 1 slice of ham for each sandwich. Cut into halves and tie lightly with string. Sauté in melted butter until browned on both sides. Add grated cheese to White Sauce. Heat until cheese is melted. Remove strings from sandwiches. Place 2 half sandwiches on each plate; cover with Sauce. Sprinkle with paprika. Makes 4 servings.

Medium White Sauce

Melt 2 tablespoons butter. Stir in 2 tablespoons flour. Gradually stir in 1 cup milk. Season to taste.

DESSERTS

COTTAGE-CHEESE DESSERT

½ pound cottage cheese
¼ cup sugar

¼ teaspoon each of almond and
 lemon extract
½ cup almonds, blanched and chopped
¼ teaspoon ground cardamom

Beat cheese with electric mixer until as smooth as possible. Add remaining ingredients; mix thoroughly. Let stand at room temperature for 1 to 2 hours, or for a few hours in refrigerator. Makes 4 servings.

CHEESE À LA CRÈME

1 package (3 ounces) cream cheese
1 pound cream-style cottage cheese
1 cup heavy cream
 Mint leaves
 Fruit

Beat cream cheese and cottage cheese until smooth and creamy. Gradually beat in cream, beating until thick. Stand strainer (or colander) in bowl deeper than strainer. Line strainer with several thicknesses of cheesecloth. Pour in mixture; tie cloth. Let drain overnight in refrigerator. Untie; turn out on plate; remove cheesecloth. Decorate top with mint leaves. Surround with sugared whole berries, melon, or other fruit. Makes 6 to 8 servings.

CREAM-CHEESE MOUSSE

1 envelope unflavored gelatin
1½ cups sugar
1 cup pineapple juice
1 cup fresh orange juice
 Juice of 1 lemon
12 ounces soft cream cheese
1½ teaspoons almond extract
¼ teaspoon salt
½ cup toasted, slivered blanched
 almonds
1 cup heavy cream, whipped

Set refrigerator control for coldest setting. Combine gelatin with sugar in saucepan. Add pineapple juice and cook over low heat, stirring, until gelatin and sugar are dissolved. Cool. Add orange and lemon juice. Blend cheese with next 3 ingredients. Stir in first mixture; fold in cream; pour into freezing trays and freeze until firm. Makes 8 servings.

COTTAGE PRUNE SOUFFLÉ

½ cup butter
½ cup sugar
4 eggs, separated
½ cup finely chopped uncooked soft
 prunes
1 cup cottage cheese, sieved
1 cup dairy sour cream
1 tablespoon fresh lemon juice

Cream butter and sugar until light and fluffy. Beat in egg yolks. Add prunes, cheese, sour cream, and lemon juice. Beat egg whites until stiff but not dry. Fold into first mixture. Pour into buttered 2-quart casserole and set in a pan of hot water. Bake in preheated moderate oven (350°F.) for 1 hour, or until set. Makes 6 servings.

CHEESE-APPLE-NOODLE PUDDING

1½ cups wide noodles, cooked
2 cups (one 1-pound can) sliced apples,
 undrained

1 cup cottage cheese
½ cup dairy sour cream
1 cup raisins
¼ cup granulated sugar
½ teaspoon ground cinnamon
½ cup firmly packed dark brown sugar
¼ cup fine dry bread crumbs
2 tablespoons soft butter or margarine
 Heavy cream

Mix first 7 ingredients and pour into buttered 2-quart casserole. Mix brown sugar, bread crumbs, and butter until crumbly. Sprinkle crumbs over noodles. Bake in preheated moderate oven (375° F.) for about 20 minutes. Serve warm with cream. Makes 6 to 8 servings.

PINEAPPLE-CHEESE PIE

1½ cups creamed cottage cheese, sieved
1 tablespoon all-purpose flour
⅛ teaspoon salt
1 cup heavy cream
⅔ cup granulated sugar
 Grated rind of 1 lemon
 Juice of 1 lemon
3 eggs, separated
 Pastry for 1-crust 9-inch pie,
 unbaked
½ cup pineapple preserves
 Confectioners' sugar

Combine cheese, flour, and salt. Stir in cream, granulated sugar, rinds, and juice. Beat egg whites until stiff. Beat yolks until thick. Add yolks to cheese mixture and fold in whites. Line 9-inch pie pan with pastry. Spread pastry with preserves. Pour in cheese mixture. Bake in preheated very hot oven (450°F.) for 10 minutes. Reduce heat to moderate (350° F.); bake for 45 minutes longer, or until firm. Cool; sprinkle with confectioners' sugar. Makes 8 servings.

CREAM-CHEESE TOPPING FOR GINGERBREAD

Cream a 3-ounce package of cream cheese with 3 tablespoons milk, 1 tablespoon sugar, and grated rind of ½ lemon. Makes about ⅓ cup.
Note: Spoon over gingerbread; sprinkle with nuts.

DESSERT CHEESE TRAY

A variety of cheeses makes the finest ending for the best of meals. Arrange cheese on a wooden tray or a large platter. Tastes differ, so try to offer a wide choice: some mild cheese, some sharp, some smooth, some soft. Consider: Gorgonzola, Roquefort, Edam or Gouda, American Cheddar, brick, Stilton, Swiss, Camembert, cottage, cream, Trappist, Gjetost, pineapple, Liederkranz, and Bel Paese. Remember to serve them at room temperature. Add crisp crackers of several sizes and kinds and, if you like, your favorite jelly or preserve. Since fruit and cheese are good companions, have a bowl of fresh fruit near.

Cheeses on the dessert board pictured at right are: Gouda, Camembert, Gruyère, and American Cheddar.

Cheddar-Tuna Chowder

Top-Hat Cheese Soufflé

Cheese Pie with Bacon

Everybody Loves Cheesecake

by James A. Beard

If you're as fond of cheesecake as I am, you might like to join me in honoring its inventor. It seems to me that anyone who could think up such a fantastically wonderful concoction deserves a statue in his memory. The only difficulty in memorializing cheesecake's originator is that no one has the faintest idea who he, or she, was. It might have been an ancient Greek, for they made cheesecakes of a simple kind.

Cheesecake isn't at all new. It's a rediscovery. When I was twenty years younger, cheesecake wasn't so widely known as it is today, and the art of making it was pretty much of a specialty in restaurants serving German, Austrian, or French cuisine. Nowadays, it has grown so popular that it rivals apple pie as an American favorite.

About two centuries ago it was a standard item in most family cook books. In those days farmers made their own cheese, and the farm housewife used the fresh curd to make delectable pastries flavored with spices or lemon or candied peels and raisins. These confections were variously known as "chess pyes," court cheesecakes, or lemon cheesecakes. Throughout Europe, wherever dairy products abounded, people feasted on cheesecakes.

The earliest published recipe I have found appears in a famous 18th-century

DeLuxe Cheesecake

Violet-Topped Cheesecake

Strawberry-Pineapple Refrigerator Cake

Blueberry-Decorated Cheesecake

Dream Cheesecake

cook book, *The Art of Cookery Made Plain and Easy*, by Mrs. Glasse. This recipe begins: "Take a pint of cream, warm it, and put to it five quarts of milk warm from the cow, then put runnet to it and just give it a stir; and when it is come, put the curd in a linen bag; let it drain well away from the whey but do not squeeze it much. Then put it to your mortar and pound as fine as butter."

Today's housewife need only go to the nearest food store and buy pot cheese, dry curd cheese, farmer's cheese, cream cheese, or cottage cheese and have the makings of a fine cheesecake.

The cheesecake recipes that I have collected here from across the country and in Europe are fascinating in their variety. Some are firm and rich; others are light, almost like a soufflé in texture; others are creamy. (A point to remember: a degree of shrinkage takes place in baking most cheesecakes.)

The recipe for the Bohemian Restaurant Cheesecake takes patience but the result is authentically old-fashioned. I include recipes for the much admired cheesecakes from the Pump Room in Chicago, from the Secret Harbor Restaurant in Los Angeles, from Grison's in San Francisco, and Lindy's restaurant in New York. In this variety, there is cheesecake to suit everybody's preference.

DREAM CHEESECAKE

¼ cup butter or margarine, melted
1 cup fine graham-cracker crumbs (about 16 large crackers)
1 teaspoon cream of tartar
6 eggs, separated
  Sugar
19 ounces cream cheese
3 tablespoons flour
½ teaspoon salt
1 pint dairy sour cream
1 teaspoon vanilla extract

Have all ingredients at room temperature. Butter generously a 9-inch springform pan. Mix butter and crumbs well; reserve ¼ cup and press remainder firmly on bottom of pan. Add cream of tartar to egg whites and beat until foamy. Gradually add 3 tablespoons sugar and beat until stiff; set aside. Beat cheese until soft. Mix 1½ cups sugar, the flour and salt. Gradually beat into cheese. Add egg yolks, one at a time, beating thoroughly after each. Add sour cream and vanilla; mix well. Fold in egg whites thoroughly and pour mixture into prepared pan. Sprinkle with reserved ¼ cup crumbs. Bake in preheated slow oven (325°F.) for 1¼ hours, or until firm. Turn off heat, open oven door and leave cake in oven for 10 minutes. Remove from oven and let stand on cake rack away from drafts until cool. Chill. (Cake will shrink some as it cools.)

MAD HATTER CHEESECAKE

1½ cups fine graham-cracker crumbs
½ cup fine chopped pecans or walnuts
¾ teaspoon ground cinnamon
½ cup melted butter
1 pound cream cheese
3 eggs, well beaten
1 cup sugar
¼ teaspoon salt
  Inside scrapings from 1 vanilla bean
½ teaspoon almond extract
  Grated rind of 1 lemon
3 cups sour cream

Have cheese and eggs at room temperature. Mix well first four ingredients and put aside ¼ cup of the mixture. Pat remainder firmly onto bottom of 9-inch springform pan. Cream cheese until light and fluffy. Add eggs, sugar, salt, and flavorings; beat until smooth and well blended. Fold in sour cream. Pour into prepared pan and sprinkle top with reserved crumbs. Bake in preheated moderate oven (350°F.) for 45 minutes, or until firm. Turn off heat and let cake stand in oven for about 30 minutes. Cool.

BLUEBERRY-DECORATED CHEESECAKE

  Crumb Crust
2 packages (7½ ounces each) farmer cheese or 1 pound creamed cottage cheese
  Sugar
2 tablespoons flour
¼ teaspoon salt
4 eggs, separated
2 tablespoons butter or margarine, melted
1 teaspoon vanilla extract
2 tablespoons grated lemon rind
1 cup dairy sour cream
2 teaspoons unflavored gelatin
  Water
2 cups fresh blueberries
  Dash each of mace and cinnamon

Have filling ingredients at room temperature. Make Crumb Crust and press firmly on bottom and sides of buttered 9-inch springform pan. Force cheese through food mill or sieve. Gradually beat in 1 cup sugar; then add flour and salt. Add egg yolks, one at a time, beating thoroughly after each. Beat in butter, vanilla, lemon rind, and sour cream. Fold in stiffly beaten egg whites. Pour into pan and bake in preheated very slow oven (275°F.) for 1½ hours, or until firm. Remove from oven and cool on rack away from drafts.

To make glaze, sprinkle gelatin on ¼ cup cold water. Wash and drain berries. Put 1 cup in saucepan with 2 tablespoons water. Bring to a full rolling boil. Press through food mill or sieve. Return pulp to saucepan with 3 tablespoons sugar and the spices. Heat; add gelatin and stir until dissolved. Chill until slightly thickened; spread on top of cake and decorate with remaining 1 cup berries. Chill until glaze is firm.

Crumb Crust

1⅓ cups fine graham-cracker, vanilla-wafer, or zwieback crumbs

⅓ cup butter or margarine, melted
⅓ cup sugar

Mix all ingredients thoroughly. (Add a little cinnamon, if desired.) An electric blender is convenient for making fine crumbs. Or, put crackers in a plastic bag and crush fine with a rolling pin. (Packaged graham-cracker crumbs are available in most food stores.)

BOHEMIAN RESTAURANT CHEESECAKE

2 tablespoons butter (about)
  Fine graham-cracker crumbs
1 pound farmer's cheese
  Sugar (about ¾ cup)
½ teaspoon salt
½ cup sifted all-purpose flour
  Grated rind of 1 lemon
1 large egg
1 tablespoon fresh lemon juice
⅔ cup skim milk
1 tablespoon vanilla extract
3 tablespoons powdered glucose or dextrose
3 tablespoons water
6 egg whites
⅛ teaspoon cream of tartar

Have all ingredients at room temperature. Butter 9-inch springform pan; dust lightly with graham-cracker crumbs. Force cheese through a food mill or a fine strainer. Add butter, 2 tablespoons sugar, salt, flour, grated lemon rind, egg, and lemon juice. Cream well. Gradually beat in milk. Add vanilla. Put ⅔ cup sugar in saucepan; add glucose and water. Cook to 240°F. on a candy thermometer. Beat egg whites and cream of tartar until almost stiff. Gradually beat in syrup; then beat until mixture stands in stiff peaks. Fold carefully into cheese mixture. Pour into prepared pan. Bake in preheated hot oven (400°F.) for 8 minutes. Decrease to slow (325°F.) and bake for 35 to 45 minutes longer. Turn off heat and let cake stand in oven for about 1 hour. Cool, and remove rim of pan.

PUMP ROOM CHEESECAKE

  Butter
  Fine graham-cracker crumbs
1 pound fine cottage cheese
7 tablespoons cornstarch
6 egg yolks
⅛ teaspoon salt
1 teaspoon vanilla extract
⅔ cup boiling milk
1¾ cups sugar
⅔ cup water
4 egg whites
  Confectioners' sugar

Have cheese and eggs at room temperature. Butter 9-inch springform pan; dust lightly with graham-cracker crumbs. Force cheese through a food mill or a fine strainer. Add cornstarch, egg yolks, salt, and vanilla. Cream well. Gradually beat in milk. Mix sugar and water in saucepan and cook to 234°F. on a candy thermometer. Beat egg whites until almost stiff. Gradually beat in syrup. Then beat until mixture stands in stiff peaks. Fold carefully into cheese mixture. Pour into prepared pan. Bake in preheated hot oven (400°F.) for 15 minutes. Decrease heat to slow (300°F.) and bake for 30 minutes longer, or until firm. Turn off heat and let cake stand in oven for about 1 hour. Cool, and remove rim of pan. Sprinkle top lightly with confectioners' sugar.

THE GEVASCI'S RICOTTA TART

2 cups plus 1 tablespoon sifted all-purpose flour
1 teaspoon baking powder
¼ teaspoon salt
¾ cup soft butter
2 tablespoons brandy
1½ pounds ricotta (Italian pot cheese)
2 tablespoons chopped almonds
3 tablespoons toasted pine nuts
2 tablespoons chopped angelica or citron
4 eggs
1 cup sugar
1½ teaspoons vanilla extract
Confectioners' sugar

Have butter, cheese, and eggs at room temperature. Mix 2 cups flour, baking powder, and salt. With hands work in butter. Gradually add brandy, mixing lightly just until dough holds together. Chill. Then roll about two thirds of dough ⅛ inch thick and use to line 10-inch pie pan. Mix 1 tablespoon flour, cheese, nuts, and angelica. Beat eggs until light and lemon-colored. Gradually beat in sugar; add vanilla. Stir into cheese mixture. Pour into lined pie pan. Roll remaining pastry to ⅛-inch thickness and cut into strips. Arrange lattice-fashion on pie. Bake in preheated moderate oven (375°F.) for 40 minutes, or until firm. Cool. Just before serving, sift confectioners' sugar lightly on top.

GRISON'S STEAK HOUSE CHEESECAKE

1¼ cups fine zwieback crumbs
½ teaspoon ground cinnamon
1¼ cups sugar
Melted butter (about ⅔ cup)
1½ pounds fine cottage cheese, sieved
6 eggs, separated
½ teaspoon salt
1 teaspoon grated lemon rind
1 teaspoon fresh lemon juice
⅓ cup heavy cream

Have cheese and eggs at room temperature. Mix well crumbs, cinnamon, ¼ cup sugar, and 6 tablespoons melted butter. Sprinkle sides of buttered 9-inch springform pan lightly with crumbs. Then press most of remaining crumbs firmly onto bottom of pan, reserving a few for the top. Stir ½ cup sugar, cheese, egg yolks, salt, rind, and juice for 10 minutes. Blend in cream. Beat egg whites until almost stiff. Gradually beat in ½ cup sugar; then beat until mixture stands in stiff peaks. Fold carefully into cheese mixture. Lightly stir in ¼ cup melted butter. Pour into prepared pan and sprinkle with reserved crumbs. Bake in preheated moderate oven (350°F.) for 1 hour and 10 minutes, or until firm.

Turn off heat and let cake stand in oven for about 30 minutes. Cool; remove rim of pan.

ELENA ZELAYETA'S POSTRE DE MAMON

1½ cups water
1¼ cups sugar
2 tablespoons butter
4 eggs, separated
¼ cup brandy
8 slices poundcake
½ pound Monterey Jack cheese or Mozzarella, sliced
Ground cinnamon

Have all ingredients at room temperature. Boil sugar and water for 3 minutes; add butter; stir until melted. Beat egg whites stiff; then beat yolks well. Add sugar syrup to yolks, stirring constantly. Add brandy. Fold in egg whites. Put 4 slices of poundcake in shallow 2-quart baking dish. Cover cake with half of cheese. Bathe with half of syrup mixture. Top with remaining cake and cheese. Spoon remaining syrup over top. Bake in preheated slow oven (325°F.) for 30 minutes, or until set. Sprinkle with cinnamon and serve warm. Makes 8 servings.

TROPICAL CHEESE TARTS

Pastry (2 cups flour recipe), unbaked
4 eggs
½ cup sugar
⅛ teaspoon salt
1 cup milk
1 teaspoon vanilla extract
1 cup fine cottage cheese
1 cup flaked coconut

Have all ingredients at room temperature. Line 3- or 4-inch tart pans with pastry. Beat eggs in top part of double boiler. Add sugar, salt, milk. Put over boiling water and cook until thickened, stirring constantly. Remove from heat and add vanilla. Fold in cheese and coconut. Pour into prepared pans. Bake in preheated hot oven (425°F.) for 15 to 18 minutes. Makes 12 small or 7 large tarts.

LINDY'S STRAWBERRY-GLAZED CHEESECAKE

Cookie Crust
1¼ pounds cream cheese
¾ cup sugar
1½ tablespoons all-purpose flour
¾ teaspoon each of grated lemon and orange rind
¼ teaspoon vanilla extract
3 eggs
1 egg yolk
2 tablespoons heavy cream
Strawberry Glaze

Have cheese and eggs at room temperature. Make Cookie Crust. Cream cheese until softened. Beat in next five ingredients. Add eggs and egg yolk, one at a time, beating well after each addition. Stir in cream. Pour into baked crust. Bake in preheated very slow oven (250°F.) for 1 hour, or until firm. Cool. Top with Strawberry Glaze.

Cookie Crust

Mix 1 cup sifted all-purpose flour, ¼

cup sugar, 1 teaspoon grated lemon rind, and scrapings from the inside of a small piece of vanilla bean. Add 1 egg yolk and ½ cup soft butter. Using your hands, mix until blended. Pat or spread onto bottom and sides of 10-inch pie pan. Bake in preheated hot oven (400°F.) for 10 minutes, or until lightly browned.

Strawberry Glaze

Wash and hull 1 quart fresh strawberries. Crush enough of the small uneven-size berries to make 1 cup. Put through strainer. Keep remainder whole. Put crushed berries, ¾ cup sugar, ¼ cup cold water, dash of salt, and 1½ tablespoons cornstarch in saucepan. Boil for 2 minutes, stirring constantly. Stir in 1 teaspoon butter and enough red food coloring to tint desired shade. Cool slightly. Arrange whole berries on top of cooled cheesecake, and spoon glaze on berries and cake. Chill.

JIM BEARD'S REFRIGERATOR CHEESECAKE

1 box (6 ounces) zwieback
½ cup butter
¾ cup sugar
Dash of nutmeg, cinnamon, or ginger
2 envelopes unflavored gelatin
1 cup cold water
3 eggs, separated
1 pound cream cheese
1 teaspoon fresh lemon juice
Grated rind of 1 lemon
1 teaspoon vanilla extract
1 cup heavy cream
Candied cherries
Angelica

Have butter, eggs, and cheese at room temperature. Crush zwieback fine in plastic bag with rolling pin, or in electric blender. Mix well with butter, ¼ cup sugar, and spice. Press firmly onto bottom of a 9-inch springform pan. Bake in preheated hot oven (400°F.) for 10 minutes. Cool. In top part of double boiler soften gelatin in cold water for 5 minutes. Beat in egg yolks and ½ cup sugar. Put over boiling water and cook, stirring constantly, until slightly thickened. Cream cheese until softened. Gradually beat in hot mixture. Add flavorings; cool. Beat egg whites until stiff but not dry. Whip cream until stiff. Fold whites and cream into cheese mixture. Pour into prepared pan; chill until firm. Remove rim. Decorate top with candied cherries and bits of angelica.

PINEAPPLE CHEESECAKE

1½ cups fine vanilla-wafer crumbs
¼ cup melted butter
1 tablespoon fresh lemon juice
¾ cup plus 1 tablespoon sugar
¾ cup pineapple preserves
1 pound cream cheese
3 eggs, separated
2 tablespoons all-purpose flour
½ teaspoon salt
⅔ cup undiluted evaporated milk
1 teaspoon vanilla extract
⅔ cup heavy cream

Have cheese, eggs, and milk at room temperature. Mix crumbs, butter, lemon juice, and 1 tablespoon sugar with hands. Blend well. Press half of mixture onto bottom of 9-inch springform pan. Bake in preheated slow oven (325°F.) for 5 minutes. Cool. Put rim around bottom and butter rim. Press remaining crumb mixture about halfway up rim. Spread preserves on bottom crust. Cream cheese well. Beat in egg yolks. Gradually beat in ½ cup sugar, the flour and salt. Blend in milk and vanilla. Beat egg whites until almost stiff. Gradually beat in ¼ cup sugar. Fold carefully into first mixture. Pour into prepared pan. Bake in slow oven (325°F.) for 50 minutes, or until set. Cool, then chill. Remove rim of pan. Whip cream until stiff, put in pastry tube, and decorate edge of cake.

CHARCOAL ROOM CHEESECAKE

Johnny Johnston's Charcoal Room, New York City

    ¾ cup fine graham-cracker crumbs
    2 tablespoons butter
    1 cup plus 5 tablespoons sugar
    1½ pounds cream cheese
    3 eggs
    2 teaspoons vanilla extract
    2 cups sour cream
    ½ cup toasted slivered blanched
       almonds

Have butter, cheese, and eggs at room temperature. Mix crumbs, butter, and 2 tablespoons sugar with hands. Blend well. Press on bottom of 9-inch springform pan. Cream cheese well. Slowly beat in 1 cup sugar. Then add eggs, one at a time, beating well after each addition. Add 1 teaspoon vanilla. Pour into prepared pan. Bake in preheated moderate oven (350°F.) for 20 minutes, or until set. Remove from oven, and increase heat to extremely hot (500°F.). Mix sour cream, 3 tablespoons sugar, and 1 teaspoon vanilla. Spread on cake. Return to oven and bake for 5 minutes. Cool, then chill. Remove rim of pan and sprinkle top of cake with almonds.

JAY'S FAMOUS CHEESE PIE

Jay de Laval was a restless soul who swam the Pacific by day and cooked by candlelight at night. I first met him in Jay's small restaurant, little more than a shack really, down where Santa Monica Canyon meets the sea in Southern California. His selected customers would pay any price for anything cooked by Jay and wait outside his tiny door for long periods of time, for Jay's Restaurant was too small to serve more than 12 people.

At the height of his success, Jay sailed one day for the faraway Virgin Islands, learned to wear an earring in one ear, in true native style, drifted to the west coast of Mexico, and the ever increasingly popular Acapulco. And that's the

last I heard of him. But he gave me a recipe for which I shall always be grateful. Many have imitated it, few have achieved it, Jay originated it.

    1⅓ cups fine graham-cracker crumbs
    ¼ cup melted butter
    3 packages (3 ounces each) cream
       cheese
    ½ cup plus 5 tablespoons sugar
    2 eggs, beaten
    1 teaspoon vanilla extract
    2 cups sour cream
    ⅛ teaspoon ground cinnamon

Have cheese and eggs at room temperature. Mix crumbs and butter well with hands. Press onto bottom and sides of 9-inch pie pan. Bake in preheated moderate oven (350°F.) for 5 minutes. Cream cheese well. Gradually beat in ½ cup sugar. Add eggs and ½ teaspoon vanilla; beat well. Pour into prepared pan. Bake in slow oven (325°F.) for 20 minutes, or until firm. Mix sour cream, ½ teaspoon vanilla, 5 tablespoons sugar, and the cinnamon. Spread on pie. Return to oven and bake for 5 minutes. Cool, then chill.

SECRET HARBOR CHEESECAKE

Secret Harbor Restaurant, Los Angeles

    1¼ cups fine graham-cracker crumbs
    ⅓ cup firmly packed brown sugar
    ¼ cup butter
    1 pound cream cheese
    1¼ cups granulated sugar
    5 eggs
    2 teaspoons vanilla extract
    1 teaspoon almond extract
    1½ cups sour cream
       Shaved sweet or semisweet
       chocolate

Have butter, cheese, and eggs at room temperature. Mix crumbs, brown sugar, and butter with hands. Blend well. Press on bottom of 9-inch springform pan. Bake in preheated moderate oven (350°F.) for about 10 minutes. Cream cheese well. Gradually beat in ¾ cup granulated sugar. Then add eggs, one at a time, beating well after each addition. Add 1 teaspoon vanilla and ½ teaspoon almond extract. Pour into prepared pan. Bake in moderate oven (350°F.) for 35 minutes, or until set. Remove from oven and increase heat to extremely hot (500°F.). Mix sour cream, ½ cup granulated sugar, 1 teaspoon vanilla, and ½ teaspoon almond extract. Spread on cake. Return to oven and bake for 5 minutes. Cool, then chill. Remove rim of pan, and sprinkle shaved chocolate around edge of cake.

CANNOLI

    4 cups sifted all-purpose flour
    1 egg
    3 egg yolks
    2 tablespoons cooking oil
       Grated rind of ½ lemon
    ¼ teaspoon ground cinnamon
    1 tablespoon pulverized or instant
       coffee
    1¾ cups sugar

    Sauterne (about 1 cup)
       Fat for deep frying
    2 pounds ricotta
    1 teaspoon vanilla extract
    ¼ cup finely chopped citron
    ½ cup semisweet chocolate pieces

Put flour in bowl; add egg, 1 egg yolk, oil, lemon rind, cinnamon, coffee, and ¼ cup sugar. Mixing with hands, add just enough sauterne to hold ingredients together to form a dough. Put on floured board and knead until smooth and elastic. Chill for several hours. Cut off pieces of dough about the size of a walnut, and roll very thin on a well-floured board. Cut rounds using a 5-inch cutter or saucer. Wrap each around a *cannoli* mold or piece of wood the thickness of a broomstick and about 5 inches long. Secure with 2 beaten egg yolks. Drop (mold and all) into hot deep fat (375° F. on a frying thermometer) and fry until well browned. Remove and drain on absorbent paper. Cool slightly, then push molds out one end. Just before serving, mix 1½ cups sugar, ricotta, and remaining ingredients. Fill *cannoli* and serve. Makes about 3 dozen.

DALE'S CHEESECAKE

    1½ cups fine graham-cracker crumbs
    ⅓ cup brown sugar
    ⅓ cup melted butter
    ½ teaspoon ground cinnamon
    12 ounces cream cheese
    2 eggs
    ½ cup granulated sugar
    ½ teaspoon vanilla extract
    1 cup sour cream

Have cheese and eggs at room temperature. Mix well first four ingredients. Reserve 3 tablespoons, and press remainder firmly with spoon into buttered 9-inch pie pan. Cream cheese until soft. Add eggs, one at a time, beating well after each addition. Add sugar and vanilla and beat until blended. Pour into pie shell. Bake in preheated moderate oven (350°F.) for 35 minutes, or until firm. Spread top with sour cream, and sprinkle with reserved crumbs. Cool, then chill.

DE LUXE CHEESECAKE

Cookie-Dough Crust

    5 packages (8 ounces each)
       cream cheese
    1¾ cups sugar
    3 tablespoons all-purpose flour
    ¼ teaspoon salt
       Grated rind 1 lemon
       Grated rind ½ orange
    5 eggs
    2 egg yolks
    ¼ cup heavy cream
       Whipped cream or whipped topping

Make Cookie-Dough Crust. Beat cheese until soft. Mix sugar, flour, and salt; gradually blend into cheese, keeping mixture smooth. Add grated rinds. Add eggs and egg yolks, one at a time, beating thoroughly after each. Blend in cream. Pour into pan. Bake in preheated very hot oven (475°F.) for 15 minutes. Reduce heat to very slow (225°F.) and bake 1 hour longer. Turn off heat and leave cake in oven for 15 minutes. Remove from oven and let stand on cake rack away from drafts until cold. Chill. When ready to serve, remove sides of pan. Put cake on serving plate and decorate top with whipped cream. (Cake will shrink some as it cools.)

Cookie-Dough Crust

1 cup sifted all-purpose flour
¼ cup sugar
 Grated rind 1 lemon
1 egg yolk
½ cup soft butter or margarine

Mix flour and sugar. Add remaining ingredients and mix well. Chill. Roll one third of dough to cover bottom of 9-inch springform or loose-bottomed pan. Bake in preheated hot oven (400°F.) for about 8 minutes. Butter sides of pan; put bottom with crust inside it. Cool. Roll remaining dough in two strips, 2½ inches wide and 14 inches long; press onto sides of pan. (If strips break, just patch and press smooth with fingers.)

STRAWBERRY-PINEAPPLE REFRIGERATOR CAKE

1 cup fine corn-flake crumbs
¼ cup soft butter or margarine
1¼ cups sugar
½ teaspoon ground cinnamon
3 envelopes unflavored gelatin
3 eggs, separated
¾ teaspoon salt
1½ cups milk
1½ pounds (3 cups) creamed cottage cheese
 Grated rind and juice 1½ lemons
1½ cups heavy cream
 Sweetened halved strawberries and pineapple tidbits

Have cheese and eggs at room temperature. Mix well crumbs, butter, ¼ cup sugar, and cinnamon. Press firmly on bottom of 9-inch springform or loose-bottomed pan; chill. In top part of double boiler combine 1 cup sugar and gelatin. Add egg yolks, salt, and milk; beat with rotary beater until blended. Cook over simmering water, stirring, until slightly thickened. Cool. Force cheese through food mill or sieve. Beat into first mixture with lemon rind and juice. Whip cream until stiff and fold with stiffly beaten egg whites into mixture. Pour into prepared pan and chill until firm. Remove sides of pan and put cake on serving plate. Decorate with strawberry halves and pineapple.

VIOLET-TOPPED CHEESECAKE

1 pound cream cheese
3 eggs
 Sugar
¼ teaspoon salt
½ teaspoon almond extract
½ pint dairy sour cream
½ teaspoon vanilla extract
 Candied violets
 Angelica or green candied cherries

Have cheese, eggs, and sour cream at room temperature. Beat cheese until fluffy. Add eggs, ⅔ cup sugar, ⅛ teaspoon salt, and almond extract. Beat until thick and lemon-colored. Pour into buttered 9-inch pie pan. Bake in preheated moderate oven (350°F.) for 25 minutes. Cool on rack for 20 minutes. Mix well sour cream, 1½ tablespoons sugar, ⅛ teaspoon salt, and vanilla. Spread on cake. Bake in preheated moderate oven (350°F.) for 10 minutes. Cool; then chill thoroughly. Decorate with violets and leaves made of angelica.

CHEF—In French, the word means "chief," but in both French and English it has become a culinary term for a superior male cook, head of his kitchen. To be a chef means that a man has embraced a definite profession, studying, serving an apprenticeship, and working his way through specialized cooking positions until he becomes the head cook. Today, chefs go to school for a number of years, and the chefs' schools in Switzerland are renowned for the superior training they give to people from all over the world. Chefs of the leading restaurants and hotels in the English-speaking world have usually served their apprenticeship in Central Europe or in France.

Chefs are absolute masters of their kitchens, directing the many people who serve under them, including vegetable cooks, fry cooks, roast cooks (*rôtisseurs*), bakers, salad chefs, cold-meat chefs, and pastry chefs (*pâtissiers*). To this day, the world of chefdom is heavily influenced by French tradition.

The true chef is an artist of the kitchen and, like many artists, often a splendid, tempestuous creature. He must have not only a keen sense of taste, but also of touch and sight as well. All this must be combined with the ability to learn from past authorities and the creativity to originate new dishes. It is no wonder that in the best of times he is a rare phenomenon and worth his weight in gold.

In the roster of great chefs, Escoffier comes first to mind, for he was not only a genius in his own kitchen, but inspired and trained chefs the world over. He was fond of quoting the renowned Brillat-Savarin, who spoke for all great gastronomes when he said, "Beasts feed, man eats, but only the man of intelligence and true perceptiveness really dines."

There has been in the past as much rivalry between chefs as there is competition among hotels and wealthy patrons for their services. Carême, French master of the *cuisine classique,* claimed that neither Cambacérès nor Brillat-Savarin knew how to eat, but merely filled their stomachs. The latter deeply shocked him by actually falling asleep in his presence after a meal.

There were other great chefs, Beauvilliers, Ude, Francatelli, Urbain-Dubois, Montagne, but it is the story of the suicide of Vatel, the Swiss chef to the Prince de Condé, that conveys most poignantly the seriousness in which such masters held their profession. The episode is recounted in the letters of the famed Mme. de Sévigné, written in Paris in 1671. In those days the chef had responsibility for the ordering of the food, as well as its cooking, and the setting and decor of the tables. The Swiss chef, who was in charge of a dinner given in honor of the King, was in great despair. He had failed to provide enough meat to serve all the tables due to the arrival of more than the expected number of guests. The next morning he arose at four o'clock to hear that only two loads of fish had come in. Thinking he would again be lacking enough food to serve the King and his guests, he dashed to his apartments and stabbed himself. Too late the remainder of the fish arrived and the King expressed his deep regret, declaring that from then on he would permit only two tables to be set on the occasion of his visits.

As for trying to explain why great, creative cooks have practically always been men and not women, prudence dictates an unbreakable silence.

CHERRY—The small, smooth, long-stemmed, round-stoned fruit of a tree that has a birchlike bark and charming pink or white flowers. This delectable fruit originated in Asia Minor and was

Cherry Cake

named for the Turkish town Cerasus, now called Giresun, which is on the Black Sea.

The earliest known mention of cherries was made in 300 B.C. when Theophrastus, the Greek "Father of Botany," described both the tree and the fruit. Pliny credited Lucullus, Roman lover of food and luxury, with bringing the cherry to Rome after his victory over Mithridates, King of Pontus. Birds, too, played their part in spreading the fruit throughout Europe.

Early settlers of this country brought the cherry with them. In 1629 the Red Kentish cherry was already being cultivated in Massachusetts. Many a colonial home boasted of one or more cherry trees in the back yard. Certainly George Washington's family home did, and the cherry tree there became immortalized when Parson Weems wrote the *Life of George Washington: With Curious Anecdotes. Equally Honorable to Himself and Exemplary to His Young Countrymen.*

On our west coast, the sweet-cherry industry began in 1847 when pioneer horticulturist Henderson Luelling took cherries with him in a covered-wagonload of fruit to be planted in Oregon.

Cherries, one of Europe's favorite fruits, have always inspired painters and poets. Robert Herrick, the 17th-century English poet, took the words of the cherry vendor wending his way through old London and turned them into lyric praise of the fruit and a certain lady.

Cherry ripe, ripe, ripe, I cry,
Full and fair ones; come and buy;
If so be, you ask me where
They do grow, I answer, there,
Where my Julia's lips do smile;
There's the land, or cherry-isle.

And let us not forget the beauty of the flowering ornamental cherry trees, such as those grown by the Japanese. In 1912, as a token of good will from one capital to another, Yukio Ozaki, governor of Tokyo, presented 3,000 of these ornamental trees to the city of Washington. Now planted along the Tidal Basin, they have been a springtime joy to millions of visitors who come from afar to see them in bloom.

Cherries are divided into two groups: sweet and sour. Sweet cherries are the larger of the two, heart-shape, and firm yet tender. They are cultivated primarily west of the Rockies, although some are also grown in New York and in the Great Lakes' region. Sour cherries are rounder, softer-textured fruit, cultivated in the Atlantic States and west to the Mississippi. New York, Wisconsin, and Michigan lead in the production of sour cherries.

Americans consume more than 140,-000 tons of cherries each year; more than half of the sweet cherries and ninety per cent of the sour cherries are canned or frozen. Cherry pie, cherry ice cream, cherry jam, cherries jubilee, cherries in salads and fruit cups and meat casseroles, or just a brown paper bag filled with cherries for eating out-of-hand: cherries any way at all are very special.

CHERRY VARIETIES

☐ **Sweet Cherries**—Red, white or golden, and dark red, they are used both fresh and cooked.

Bing—Extra large, heart-shape, with flesh that ranges from deep dark mahogany to almost black. Firm, meaty, and with luscious flavor; skin smooth and glossy.

Chapman (also called Early Chapman) —Very large, roundish, purplish-blach flesh. Tender, sweet, and flavorful. Fruit matures early. This variety is said to have been produced from a seedling of the Black Tartarian.

Lambert—Large to extra large, roundish, mahogany to very dark red-fleshed cherry. Firm, meaty.

Republican (also called Black Republican or Lewelling)—Small to medium-size, heart-shape, purplish-black flesh with dark-colored juice. Mild, crisp, and sweet.

Royal Ann (also called Napoleon)—Large, heart-shape, light golden flesh color with pink or light red blush. Firm, meaty, juicy, with fine flavor. Skin is thin. Flesh bruises easily. The only light-fleshed variety that is important commercially. Mainly a canning variety.

Tartarian (also called Black Tartarian) —Large, heart-shape, purplish to black flesh. Tender, sweet, with excellent flavor. Skin is thin. Most popular of early mid-season varieties.

☐ **Sour (or Tart) Cherries**—Red to nearly black, they are hardier than sweet cherries and for the most part are used cooked.

Early Richmond—Roundish, full; clear medium red. Tender flesh, rather tough skin, excellent for cooking purposes. It is the first sour cherry on the market in late spring and is often confused with the Montmorency.

English Morello—Roundish; very deep red becoming almost black. Flesh dark red, tender and melting, tart and juicy. Good for all cooking purposes.

Montmorency—Roundish, slightly compressed; full clear medium red, very juicy. Best for pies, tarts, jellies, and all cooking. The most popular sour cherry in the United States.

☐ **Maraschino Cherries**—These are made from sweet cherries, usually Royal Ann, which are bleached, then pitted and steeped in a syrup made of sugar, water, a touch of oil of bitter almond, and food coloring. The history of this delicacy goes back some three hundred years to Italy, where a white sweet cherry was soaked in a cordial called "maraschino," which was made from another cherry, the marasca. The name was derived from the Latin *amarus,* meaning "bitter." Later the French created another version: cherries soaked in a sugar syrup. They named their version a maraschino cherry. Once imported to this country maraschino cherries became very popular, and in time homegrown cherries and syrup were developed to produce an all-American product.

Maraschino cherries are used in candies, cookies, cakes, sauces, as well as in fruit cups and fruit salad, and alcoholic beverages.

Availability—Look for sweet cherries in markets from May through August, depending on locality. For sour cherries, the main season starts in June and ends in August.

Cherries in cans or jars are chiefly light and dark sweet cherries, with or without pits; and red sour, or tart, cherries, always pitted. Other canned or processed cherry products include: pie fillings, sauce, some juice blended with other fruit juices, preserves, and candied, glacéed, and maraschino cherries.

Sweet and sour frozen cherries are also available, as are frozen cherry pies.

Purchasing Guide—Select bright, fresh-appearing, plump, ripe cherries with good color for their variety. Sweet cherries should be firm; sour cherries, medium firm. Avoid immature cherries, indicated by smaller size, hard texture, and poor color; they are likely to have less juice. Overripe cherries, also bad buys, are usually soft, dull, and shriveled or leaky. Cuts and bruises on cherries forecast mold and decay formation where injured. Cherries with stems keep better; but if used promptly, stemmed cherries are a better buy because of greater yield.

☐ 1 quart with stems = 1½ pounds = 3 cups, stemmed and pitted, or 2 cups juice

☐ 1 quart, stemmed = 2 pounds = 4 cups, pitted, or 2 cups juice

Select canned sweet or sour cherries according to preference and use planned. Select top quality grades for use when the cherries will show, as in cocktails, compotes, salads, desserts, and garnishes. When they will be used chopped or mixed with other foods, as in sherbets, cobblers, and sauces, other grades are thriftier. The can label will state:

Variety—Light or dark sweet cherries or red sour cherries.

Preparation—Pitted or unpitted (the latter is not always designated).

Packing liquid—Light, heavy, or extra-heavy syrup, sugar, or artificial noncaloric sweeteners, water, or cherry juice. Dietetic-pack cherries are generally considered as artificially sweetened. Spices, flavorings, and vinegar may be added but these must be stated on label.

For maraschino cherries, you can choose either the red variety flavored with almond and packed with or without stems, or the green-colored, flavored with mint and packed only without stems. Cherries packed without stems will cost less than those with stems. Candied or glacéed maraschino cherries are also available in both red and green, generally for holiday cooking at Christmas and Easter.

Storage—Sort and discard any spoiled cherries. Store in refrigerator, unwashed.

Packaged candied cherries keep well in screw-top jars in the refrigerator.

- Fresh, refrigerator shelf: 3 days to 2 weeks
- Fresh, refrigerator frozen-food compartment, prepared for freezing: 2 months
- Fresh, freezer, prepared for freezing: 1 year
- Canned, light cherries, kitchen shelf: 3 years
- Canned, dark cherries, kitchen shelf: 1 year
- Canned, refrigerator shelf, opened and covered: 4 to 5 days
- Frozen packaged cherries and pies, refrigerator frozen-food compartment: 2 months
- Frozen packaged cherries and pies, freezer: 1 year
- Maraschino, refrigerator shelf, tightly covered: 2 months

Nutritive Food Values—Fresh cherries, both sweet and sour, contain small amounts of vitamins and minerals. Canned and frozen cherries are similar in food value except that those processed with sugar contain more calories.

- Fresh, sweet, 3½ ounces = 70 calories
- Fresh, sour, 3½ ounces, raw = 58 calories
- Canned in light syrup, sweet, 3½ ounces = 65 calories
- Canned in light syrup, sour, 3½ ounces = 74 calories
- Maraschino, 3½ ounces = 116 calories

Basic Preparation—Wash before eating or cooking. Sort again for spoilage. Drain well. An easy way to pit is to use one end of a paper clip. This forms a hook and pits can be pried out. The tip of a vegetable parer may also be used. Do not squeeze out the pit, since this causes much of the juice to be lost and the cherry collapses.

- **To Freeze Red Sour Cherries**—Wash and pit. Pack in freezer container and cover with either a sugar or syrup pack:
  Sugar Pack: 1 cup sugar for every 4 cups cherries.
  Syrup Pack: 4 cups water for every 6 cups sugar. Cook until syrup is clear. Cool. Put cherries into freezer container and cover with syrup. Allow ½-inch headspace.
- **To Freeze Sweet Cherries**—Wash and pit. Pack in freezer container and cover with syrup pack (see above). Add ½ teaspoon ascorbic acid to every quart of syrup. Allow ½-inch headspace. Cover.

SWEET CHERRIES

PORK CHOPS WITH CHERRIES

4 pork chops
Fat
Salt and pepper to taste
1 can (1 lb. 1 ounce) pitted light sweet cherries
¼ cup slivered almonds
6 whole cloves
1 tablespoon cider vinegar

Brown pork chops in a little fat. Season with salt and pepper. Combine cherries and syrup from can with almonds, cloves, vinegar, and a little red food coloring, if desired. Pour over chops and simmer, covered, for 30 minutes. Makes 4 servings.

CLAFOUTIS
(French Cherry Pudding)

1 cup milk
2 tablespoons brandy
6 tablespoons granulated sugar
3 eggs
2 teaspoons vanilla extract
⅔ cup sifted all-purpose flour
2 tablespoons melted butter
3 cups pitted black sweet cherries, or canned drained Bing cherries, or frozen sweet cherries
Confectioners' sugar

Place all ingredients except 2 tablespoons granulated sugar, the cherries, and the confectioners' sugar in a blender and blend at high speed for 1 minute. Place one fourth of batter in a buttered 2-quart casserole; place on an asbestos mat over low heat for a minute or two to set the batter on the bottom of the dish. Cover with the cherries and sprinkle with remaining granulated sugar. If canned or frozen cherries are used, omit sugar. Pour over remaining batter; bake in preheated hot oven (400°F.) for 45 minutes to 1 hour, or until puffed and golden brown. Sprinkle with confectioners' sugar and serve warm. Makes 4 to 6 servings.

CHERRIES JUBILEE

½ cup sugar
Dash of salt
1 tablespoon cornstarch
1 cup water
1 pound pitted dark sweet cherries
2 to 4 tablespoons brandy
1 pint vanilla ice cream

Combine sugar, salt, cornstarch, and water. Add cherries; cook until thickened, stirring constantly. Pour brandy over top, ignite, and spoon immediately over ice cream. Makes 4 servings.

CHERRY BOUNCE

3 pounds black sweet cherries
1 pound loaf sugar
1 tablespoon whole allspice
1 cinnamon stick
1 tablespoon whole cloves
1 quart whisky

Wash cherries and remove stems. Put cherries in a wide-mouthed 2-quart jar in layers with loaf sugar and spices. Pour whisky over all. Let stand at room temperature, covered, for at least 2 months. The longer it stands, the better it tastes. Makes 2 quarts.

SOUR CHERRIES

CHERRY CAKE

1 package active dry yeast, or 1 cake compressed yeast
¼ cup water*
¾ cup milk, scalded and cooled to lukewarm
½ cup butter or margarine, melted
Granulated sugar
1 teaspoon salt
1 egg, slightly beaten
3 to 3½ cups all-purpose flour
1 cup red-cherry preserves
Confectioners' sugar
Red sour pitted cherries, packed in syrup

*Use very warm water (105°F. to 115° F.) for dry yeast; use lukewarm (80°F. to 90°F.) for compressed. Sprinkle dry yeast or crumble cake into water. Let stand for a few minutes; then stir until dissolved. Mix with milk, butter, ⅓ cup granulated sugar, salt, and egg. Add 2½ cups of the flour, and beat until smooth. Stir in enough more flour to make a soft dough. Turn out on lightly floured board, and knead until smooth and elastic, about 5 minutes. Put in buttered bowl, cover and let rise in warm place until doubled, about 1½ hours. When light, punch down. Turn out on lightly floured board, and knead lightly. Divide dough into 4 equal pieces. Shape each piece into a roll about 8 inches long. Cut each in 8 pieces. Roll each piece into a ball, and dip in granulated sugar. Put a layer of balls in greased 9-inch tube pan so that balls barely touch. Put small dots of cherry preserves between balls. Proceed until all ingredients are used. Cover, and let rise until doubled, about 1 hour. Bake in preheated moderate oven (375°F.) for 30 to 35 minutes. Turn out, and cool on rack. When cold, put on serving plate, and sift confectioners' sugar over top. Just before serving, decorate with well-drained pitted red cherries.

Cherry Tarts

Deep-Dish Cherry Pie with Shortcake Crust

Cherries Jubilee

Pork Chops with Cherries

CHERRY DUMPLINGS

1 can (1 pound) pitted red sour cherries
1 cup sugar
1 cup sifted cake flour
1 teaspoon baking powder
¼ teaspoon salt
Grated rind of 1 orange
⅓ cup milk
2 teaspoons butter, melted

Put undrained cherries and ¾ cup sugar in large deep skillet and bring to boil. Mix and sift ¼ cup sugar, the flour, baking powder, and salt into bowl. Add remaining ingredients and mix lightly. Drop from tablespoon into boiling mixture, making 4 to 6 dumplings. Cover and cook gently for 20 minutes. Serve warm. Makes 4 to 6 servings.

CHERRY BATTER PUDDING

2 tablespoons butter or margarine
2 cups sugar
2 eggs
2 cups sifted all-purpose flour
2 teaspoons baking powder
½ teaspoon salt
1 cup milk
1 can (1 pound) pitted red sour cherries
1 cup water

Mix butter and ½ cup sugar. Beat in eggs well, one at a time. Add mixed and sifted dry ingredients alternately with milk. Mix well and pour into greased 9-inch pan. Drain cherries; combine juice and water and bring to boil. Sprinkle cherries over batter; cover with 1½ cups sugar; pour boiling liquid over top. Bake in preheated moderate oven (375°F.) for 45 minutes. Serve warm. Makes 6 servings.

DEEP-DISH CHERRY PIE WITH SHORTCAKE CRUST

1 can (1 pound) pitted red sour cherries
¾ cup plus 2 tablespoons sugar
2 tablespoons all-purpose flour
Dash of salt
1 tablespoon fresh lemon juice
1 tablespoon butter
1 cup prepared biscuit mix
¼ cup milk

Drain cherries and reserve juice. Combine ¾ cup sugar with flour and salt. Gradually stir in cherry juice. Cook over low heat until thickened, stirring constantly. Cool slightly. Stir in lemon juice, butter, and cherries; pour into 1-quart casserole. Combine biscuit mix and 2 tablespoons sugar; add milk and beat well. Spoon batter over cherries. Bake in preheated hot oven (400°F.) for 20 to 25 minutes, or until brown. Makes 4 servings.

FRESH SOUR-CHERRY PIE

1⅓ cups sugar
3 tablespoons all-purpose flour
1 tablespoon cornstarch
⅛ teaspoon salt
1½ pounds (4 cups) pitted fresh red sour cherries
¼ teaspoon almond extract
Pastry for 2-crust 9-inch pie, unbaked
1½ tablespoons butter

Combine sugar, flour, cornstarch, and salt. Mix with cherries, adding extract. Roll out pastry. Use half to line a deep 9-inch pie pan; trim. Pour in cherry mixture and dot with butter. Cut remaining pastry into ⅝-inch strips. Arrange pastry strips, lattice fashion, over all. Seal edges with water. If a glazed topping is desired, carefully brush lattice with evaporated milk or egg white. Bake in preheated hot oven (425°F.) for 10 minutes; reduce heat to moderate (350°F.) and continue baking about 30 minutes longer, or until crust is well done. **Note:** 4 to 5 tablespoons flour, 3 tablespoons quick-cooking tapioca, or 2½ to 3 tablespoons cornstarch may be used as the thickening agent, instead of the mixture of flour and cornstarch.

Canned Sour-Cherry Pie

Follow recipe above, using 3 cups drained (two 1-pound cans) water-packed red sour cherries and 1 cup sugar.

Frozen Sour-Cherry Pie

Follow recipe above, using 2 packages (1 pound each) frozen red sour cherries, thawed, and ½ cup sugar.

CHERRY BAVARIAN

1 envelope unflavored gelatin
⅔ cup sugar
⅛ teaspoon salt
1 can (1 pound) water-packed pitted red sour cherries
2 eggs, separated
¼ teaspoon almond extract
¼ teaspoon red food coloring
1 cup heavy cream, whipped

Mix gelatin with ⅓ cup sugar and the salt. Drain cherries; reserve juice. Beat juice with egg yolks and stir mixture into gelatin. Cook over low heat, stirring constantly, until gelatin dissolves. Add almond extract and food coloring. Fold in cherries. Chill until thickened. Beat egg whites until stiff but not dry. Gradually beat in remaining sugar, 1 tablespoon at a time. Fold egg whites and whipped cream into cherry mixture. Pour into 6 individual molds. Chill until firm; unmold by dipping into warm water for a few seconds. Garnish with whipped cream. Makes 6 servings.

CHERRY PARFAIT

1 box (3 ounces) cherry gelatin
¾ cup sugar
1 cup hot water
Dash of salt
2 cups milk
2 tablespoons fresh lemon juice
¼ teaspoon almond extract
1 can (1 pound) water-packed pitted red sour cherries
½ cup heavy cream

Dissolve gelatin and sugar in hot water. Add salt, milk, lemon juice, almond extract, and juice drained from canned cherries. Freeze until mushy. Beat until light and fluffy. Beat in heavy cream. Fold in cherries. Pile in parfait glasses. Freeze until firm. Makes 8 servings.

CHERRY TARTS

1 can (1 pound) water-packed pitted red sour cherries
4 teaspoons cornstarch
½ cup sugar
Few drops of red coloring
Four 4½-inch baked tart shells
Dairy sour cream

Drain cherries and measure juice. Add enough water to make ¾ cup. Mix juice with cornstarch and sugar. Cook over low heat, stirring constantly, until smooth and thick. Add cherries and a few drops of red coloring. Cool. Pour mixture into 4 tart shells. Garnish with sour cream. Makes 4 servings.

CHERRY ROLY-POLY

1 cup prepared biscuit mix
2 teaspoons butter
¼ cup light cream
Melted butter
1 cup drained canned pitted red sour cherries
2 tablespoons diced candied lemon peel
Cherry Sauce, I

Blend together biscuit mix and butter; add cream and stir well. Turn out on a lightly floured board; knead for 30 seconds. Roll out into a rectangle ¼-inch thick. Brush with melted butter. Top with cherries and lemon peel. Roll up as for jelly roll. Place on buttered baking sheet; brush with melted butter. Bake in preheated hot oven (425°F.) for 20 minutes. Slice and serve hot with Cherry Sauce, I. Makes 6 servings.

Cherry Sauce, I

¾ cup cherry juice
½ cup sugar
⅛ teaspoon salt
1½ teaspoons potato flour or cornstarch
¼ cup drained canned pitted red sour cherries
1 tablespoon butter
1 tablespoon fresh lemon juice

Stir cherry juice into a mixture of sugar, salt, and potato flour. Cook over low heat for 5 minutes, stirring constantly. Add cherries, butter, and lemon juice. Serve hot. Makes 1 cup sauce.

CHERRY UPSIDE-DOWN CAKE

¾ cup butter or margarine
½ cup firmly packed light brown sugar
1 can (1 pound) water-packed pitted red sour cherries
2 teaspoons grated lemon rind
½ cup granulated sugar
1 egg
1½ cups sifted all-purpose flour
2 teaspoons baking powder
½ teaspoon salt
½ cup milk
Cherry Sauce, II

Melt ¼ cup butter in 9-inch square baking pan. Sprinkle with brown sugar. Drain cherries; reserve juice for sauce. Spoon cherries evenly over brown sugar. Sprinkle with grated lemon rind. Cream ½ cup butter. Gradually add granulated sugar, beating until light and fluffy. Beat in egg. Sift flour with baking powder and salt. Add dry ingredients alternately with milk, beginning and ending with dry ingredients. Spread mixture on cherries. Bake in preheated moderate oven (375° F.) for 30 minutes. Cut cake into squares and serve with Cherry Sauce, II. Makes about 6 large servings.

Cherry Sauce, II

Blend 2 tablespoons sugar and 2 teaspoons cornstarch. Add reserved cherry juice (about ¾ cup); cook until thickened. Makes about ¾ cup sauce.

MARASCHINO CHERRIES

CHERRY-PISTACHIO PARFAIT

Flavor whipped cream with a little maraschino-cherry juice and chopped cherries. Fill parfait or other tall glass (fruit-juice glass can be used) alternately with cherry-whipped cream mixture and pistachio ice cream. Top with a whole maraschino cherry or chopped pistachio nuts. Serve at once or store in freezer.

MARASCHINO-CHERRY CAKE

- ½ cup shortening
- 1¼ cups sugar
- ½ teaspoon almond extract
- 16 maraschino cherries, cut fine
- 2 cups plus 6 tablespoons sifted cake flour
- 3 teaspoons baking powder
- ¾ teaspoon salt
- ¼ cup cherry juice
- ½ cup milk
- 4 egg whites
  Marshmallow Frosting

Cream shortening well; add sugar gradually, beating until light and fluffy. Add almond extract. Mix cherries with 2 tablespoons flour. Sift remaining flour with baking powder and salt. Beginning and ending with dry ingredients, add to cream mixture alternately with combined cherry juice and milk, beating until smooth. Beat egg whites until stiff but not dry and fold into flour mixture. Pour into two pans (8 x 8 x 2 inches) lined on the bottom with wax paper, then greased. Bake in preheated moderate oven (350°F.) for about 35 minutes. Cool for 5 minutes. Turn out on racks, peel off paper, and cool. Spread Marshmallow Frosting between layers and on top and sides. Garnish with more cut maraschino cherries, if desired.

Marshmallow Frosting

- 1½ cups sugar
- ⅓ cup water
- ¼ teaspoon salt
- 2 egg whites
- 1½ teaspoons light corn syrup
- 1 teaspoon vanilla extract
- 1 cup miniature marshmallows or 16 large marshmallows, cut up
  Red food coloring

Combine first 5 ingredients in top part of double boiler. Beat with rotary beater until mixed. Place over rapidly boiling water; beat constantly for 7 minutes, or until frosting forms peaks. Remove from heat, add vanilla and marshmallows, and beat until smooth and of spreading consistency. Add a few drops of food coloring, if desired.

CHERRY-PINEAPPLE JAM

- 3½ cups sugar
- 2½ cups (one 1-pound, 4½ ounce can) crushed pineapple
- ½ cup halved maraschino cherries
- ¾ cup water
- 1 box powdered fruit pectin

Measure sugar and set aside. In large saucepan mix pineapple, cherries, and water. Add pectin and mix well. Bring to a hard boil. At once stir in sugar. Stirring constantly, bring to a full rolling boil and boil hard for 1 minute. Remove from heat and skim off foam. Then stir and skim by turns for 5 minutes to prevent floating fruit. Ladle quickly into hot sterilized glasses and seal with hot paraffin. Put on lids. Makes 7 medium glasses.

CHERRY LIQUEUR—A number of well-known European liqueurs and brandies are made from special strains of cherries cultivated for the purpose. The best known ones are Kirsch, a strong, colorless spirit made in France, Switzerland, and Germany; Cherry Heering, a rich, red cordial made in Denmark; and cherry brandy made in Holland and England.

CHERVIL (Anthriscus cerefolium)—This delicate herb, used to flavor soups, salads, and stews, is a favorite in American herb gardens. Chervil is an annual, and grows to a height of two feet. In appearance, it resembles a delicate parsley with lacy leaves. The flowers are tiny and white.

Chervil is one of the most famous of *fines herbes,* or "fine herbs," on which French cooking relies so much. It is an essential ingredient in the classic *Béarnaise* Sauce and is used as an ingredient or a garnish with omelets, in mixed salads, and in stews. It is good also in potato dishes, such as potato soup or salad.

Greeks and Romans enjoyed this herb as a vegetable, eating the leaves and boiling the roots. The Roman writer Pliny, offering one more addition to the long list of hiccup remedies, suggested some chervil seed in vinegar. Chervil was grown in the 9th century in the gardens of the Benedictine monastery in St. Gall, Switzerland. The Saxons in England kept this attractive herb as a potherb and in Holland and Denmark it has always been a special favorite. The first mention of chervil in American cooking occurs at the beginning of the 19th century.

Chervil may be used fresh or dried. It is more flavorful when fresh. The adventuresome may cook the root as any other root vegetable.

CHESTNUT—The edible nut of a tree of the same name. In the old childhood riddle, "First I am frosted, Then I am beaten, Then I am roasted, Then I am eaten," chestnut was the answer. It was customary to beat the chestnut tree with poles after the first frost in order to obtain the shiny, dark brown chestnuts in their prickly coating. For urban Americans there was the chestnut vendor, who may still be seen in eastern cities patiently turning his roasting chestnuts over a charcoal fire. There is nothing better on a crisp autumn day than a bag full of warm, smoky, sweet chestnuts.

The ancient Greeks imported their trees from Asia Minor. Theophrastus wrote that Mount Olympus, the home of the gods, abounded in chestnut trees. Romans imported chestnuts from Kastanum in Asia Minor and *Castanea* is still the botanical name for chestnut. There are several varieties of European chestnuts, referred to as the French, the Italian, and the Spanish chestnut.

The chestnut tree was once one of America's great trees. It flourished in New England and southward through the

Appalachian Mountains to Alabama. Thoreau had a chestnut tree growing behind his house and in the winter he used the nuts as a substitute for bread. Early Americans not only ate the chestnuts but also used the wood for fence posts and ships' masts. Today, tragically enough, few of these magnificent trees remain. The villain was a parasitic fungus borne from Asia and deadly to the chestnut. First identified in 1904 in New York, this fungus proved dramatically effective in stripping the country of its great chestnut trees. Ironically enough, the Japanese and Chinese chestnut trees, which may have carried the blight originally, are being used in experiments to produce a tree that will resist the disease.

The Japanese chestnut is smaller than the American tree. It is blight resistant but its nuts are less sweet. The Chinese chestnut is a more attractive tree with sweeter nuts.

Today we think of the chestnut as a holiday food or an autumn treat, but the chestnut has served many peoples as a vital staple. In southern Europe it has been extensively cultivated as a standard food for centuries and used much as we use wheat or corn. Peasants of Italy, France, Greece, and Spain went to work with a pocketful of chestnuts to sustain them as they worked. In time of crop failure or food shortage, there remained the abundant chestnut, high in food value and capable of being ground into flour for bread, biscuits, or fritters, or made into a thick soup.

Chestnuts are peeled (both the hard brown outer shell and the thin bitter brown inner peel), and are eaten in a variety of ways. They may be boiled or roasted, and served with a glass of wine. With turkey, goose, wild duck, or pheasant, they serve as a glorious stuffing, and with all of these meats, as well as with pork and sausages, they go well as a vegetable in mashed or whole braised form. Braised chestnuts also combine deliciously with red cabbage, Brussels sprouts, mushrooms, onions, and carrots. Imported canned chestnuts, sweetened or unsweetened, are of excellent quality and are a great convenience.

Availability—Fresh chestnuts are available from about mid-September to March and are sold primarily in bulk, in the shell. Most of them are imported from Spain or Italy.

☐ 1 pound = about 35 to 40 raw chestnuts in the shell = about 2½ cups, shelled and peeled.

Also available in specialty food stores are canned cooked chestnuts, both sweetened and unsweetened, whole or as a purée; preserved chestnuts, whole or in pieces in heavy sugar syrup; and glazed chestnuts, called *Marrons Glacées*.

Dried chestnuts can be found in food stores in Italian and Spanish neighborhoods. During the winter, they are also sold ground as a flour.

Purchasing Guide—Select nuts which look plump and unshriveled, with shells free from blemishes and cracks.

Storage—Keep fresh chestnuts in a cool, dry place. Shelled nuts should be stored in a covered container. Refrigerate open cans or jars of chestnuts.

☐ Fresh, kitchen shelf, unshelled: 4 to 5 days
☐ Fresh, refrigerator shelf, cooked and covered: 3 to 4 days
☐ Canned and preserved, kitchen shelf: 1 year
☐ Canned and preserved, refrigerator shelf, opened and covered: 1 week
☐ Dried, kitchen shelf: 2 months
☐ Dried, refrigerator shelf, cooked and covered: 1 week

Nutritive Food Values—Chestnuts provide some protein, iron, and B vitamins, but their main contribution is calories.
☐ Fresh, 3½ ounces = 194 calories
☐ Dried, 3½ ounces = 377 calories

Basic Preparation

☐ **To Cook, Shell, and Blanch**—Slash the flat side of each chestnut with a sharp knife. Place chestnuts in pan of cold water. Bring to a boil; boil for 1 minute and remove from heat. With a slotted spoon remove 3 or 4 chestnuts at a time from water. Peel off outer shells and brown inner skins, taking care to keep chestnuts whole. Keep unpeeled chestnuts warm in water until peeling time or the inner skin won't come off.

☐ **To Roast**—Slash the flat side of shell with a sharp knife. Place on cookie sheet in hot oven (400°F.) for 15 to 20 minutes, tossing occasionally. Serve piping hot.

☐ **To Purée**—Cook, shell, and blanch nuts. Cook in boiling water, stock, or milk to cover (depending on future use) for 35 minutes, or until tender. Drain. Strain through a sieve or a food mill, or whirl in a blender.

☐ **To Reconstitute Dried Chestnuts**—Soak overnight in enough water to cover. Simmer the next day in about 5 inches of water until chestnuts are puffed up and tender. Use as you would fresh-cooked chestnuts, cup for cup.

WHOLE BRAISED CHESTNUTS
2 to 3 cups peeled chestnuts (about 1 pound whole raw or 35 chestnuts)
1 cup chicken consomme (about)
1 tablespoon cornstarch
2 tablespoons red or white wine, sherry, or water
Salt and pepper
¼ cup butter

Place chestnuts in heavy saucepan or casserole. Cover with consommé to the depth of ½ inch. Mix cornstarch and wine to a smooth paste. Pour over chestnuts. Add salt and pepper to taste and dot with butter. Simmer, covered, over lowest possible heat for 50 minutes, or until chestnuts are tender. Serve as separate dish or mix with braised red cabbage or Brussels sprouts. Makes 4 to 6 servings.

CHESTNUT PURÉE
5 cups peeled chestnuts (about 2 pounds whole raw or about 70 chestnuts)
1 celery stalk
1 bouquet garni (2 parsley sprigs, ½ bay leaf, and ⅛ teaspoon thyme tied in cheesecloth)
1½ cups chicken consomme (about)
3 tablespoons butter, softened
Salt and pepper

Place peeled chestnuts in heavy saucepan. Add celery, *bouquet garni,* and enough consommé to cover chestnuts to the depth of 1½ inches. Simmer, uncovered, over lowest possible heat for 50 minutes, or until chestnuts are tender. Do not let them become mushy. Drain and remove *bouquet garni.* Purée chestnuts through a food mill or a sieve, or whirl in a blender. Return to saucepan and heat through. Beat in butter and salt and pepper to taste. Serve very hot. Makes 4 to 6 servings.

CHESTNUT STUFFING FOR TURKEY
1 cup butter or margarine
1 cup minced onion
1 teaspoon each of ground thyme and sage
1½ teaspoons salt
¾ teaspoon pepper
⅓ cup chopped parsley
¾ cup chopped celery and leaves
2 quarts soft stale-bread crumbs or cubes
1 pound chestnuts, cooked, shelled and chopped

Melt butter in skillet and add all ingredients except last two. Cook for 5 minutes. Add crumbs and chestnuts. Use as stuffing for turkey. Makes about 10 cups.

SAUSAGE AND CHESTNUT STUFFING FOR CHICKEN
1 small onion, chopped
¼ cup butter or margarine
½ pound pork sausage meat
2 pounds chestnuts
2 teaspoons salt
¼ teaspoon pepper
¼ teaspoon ground thyme
2 tablespoons chopped parsley
1 cup soft stale-bread cubes

Cook onion in butter for 3 minutes. Add sausage meat and cook for 5 minutes longer. Cook and shell chestnuts and mash them coarsely. Add onion mixture and remaining ingredients; mix well. Use as stuffing for chicken. Makes about 6 cups.

MONTE BIANCO DI CASTAGNE (Mont Blanc of Chestnuts)
3 cups milk
⅛ teaspoon salt

¾ cup sugar
1½ pounds chestnuts
2 cups heavy cream, whipped and
　vanilla flavored

Scald milk with salt and sugar. Score chestnuts across flat side with sharp knife. Cover with cold water and bring to a boil. Boil for 15 minutes. Drain, shell, and peel off brown skin. As each chestnut is readied, drop it into the milk. Cook in top part of double boiler until chestnuts are very tender. (This takes 30 to 45 minutes, depending on chestnuts.) Drain, reserving milk for custard or other dessert. Over large serving dish, preferably silver, force chestnuts through a coarse sieve, a potato ricer, or a food mill into the shape of a mound. The chestnuts must be very light and fluffy. Smooth whipped cream over chestnut mound. Do not press down. Chill. To be perfect, it should be made a short time before eating. Makes 8 to 10 servings.

ITALIAN CHESTNUT-CHOCOLATE DESSERT

4 ounces sweet cooking chocolate
½ cup sweet butter
1 teaspoon vanilla extract
1½ cups canned chestnut creme
　Whipped cream
　Chocolate curls

Melt chocolate in top part of double boiler over hot water. Cream butter until fluffy. Stir in vanilla and chestnut crème. Beat in melted chocolate and beat until absolutely smooth. Line bottom of 8-inch layer-cake pan or pie pan, or 8-inch square pan with wax paper. Press mixture into pan. Chill. Unmold and remove wax paper. Decorate with whipped cream and chocolate curls. Makes 12 servings.

CHICKEN—This domesticated bird, whose meat and eggs are such an important and popular source of food, originated in the jungles of southeastern Asia. There, in the dense bamboo forests and thickets, strutted and crowed a wild jungle fowl not unlike our Bantam rooster. How did this small bird come to circle the globe and, through its domesticated progeny, provide so much delight for the hungry gourmet?

He got an early start, possibly as early as 1400 B.C., and men were responsible, for no doubt the wild jungle fowl proved a tasty morsel for the hungry hunter. This same hunter, when he turned explorer, carried the bird with him, eastward from island to island across the Pacific, and westward, following the mountain valleys and rivers, across Asia to Europe.

As a newcomer in Europe, the small jungle fowl must have been a somewhat rare bird and was looked upon as sacred. Long before Chicken Little proclaimed that the sky was falling in, her ancestors, as objects of divination, were foretelling doom and good fortune. Publius Claudius, commander of the Roman fleet during the first Punic War in the 3rd century B.C., desired to bring about good fortune and offered food to his sacred birds. It is said that they would not eat and he hurled them into the sea. He suffered a humiliating defeat in the battle of Drepanum. Later, however, the Romans discovered a more satisfactory use for their sacred fowl: as an excellent addition to the banquet table.

By the 16th century the small bird had won its place in Europe, for the French king, Henry of Navarre, could envision no greater goal than a chicken cooking in every Frenchman's pot. In the 18th century French farmers were force-feeding their birds with paste containing aniseed and other fragrant spices in order to produce a more flavorful chicken.

In 1607 early settlers brought chickens to the American Colonies, and in Jamestown small home flocks were raised, mainly for their feathers which were used to stuff feather beds. Later, in America, chicken was served at a Mount Vernon reception for General Lafayette. As the American cuisine developed, chicken became a preferred dinner dish, prepared differently in various parts of the country, but no matter what the specialties the young broiler-fryer birds were the most desired of all the flock.

Availability—Available all year round. Peak season is May to October.

A wide and ever-growing variety of chicken and chicken products are available canned and frozen. There are also some freeze-dried chicken products available.

Purchasing Guide—All market types of chicken may be purchased whole. Broiler-fryer parts are sold as breasts, legs, backs, necks, and wings. Most market chickens are sold ready-to-cook: eviscerated, free from pinfeathers, and thoroughly cleaned. The neck and giblets (liver, gizzard, heart) are usually packaged separately and placed in the body cavity of the whole bird, or included with the packaged, cut-up chicken. The market types of ready-to-cook chicken are:

☐ Broiler or Fryer—Weighs ¾ to 3½ pounds.

☐ Capon—Weighs 4 to 8 pounds; used for roasting.

☐ Roaster—Weighs 2½ to 5 pounds.

☐ Rock Cornish (game) Hen—Weighs up to 2 pounds; used for roasting, broiling, and baking.

☐ Stewing Chicken, Hen or Fowl—Weighs 2½ to 5 pounds or over; has less tender meat; used for stewing and braising.

Choose chickens that have short legs, a plump body, and unbruised skin. A good fat covering is an indication of tender meat.

Storage—Loosen any tight transparent film packaging and place chicken immediately in the coldest part of the refrigerator.

☐ Refrigerator shelf, raw: 2 days

☐ Refrigerator shelf, cooked and covered: 1 to 2 days

☐ Refrigerator frozen-food compartment, raw, prepared for freezing: 1 week

☐ Freezer, raw, prepared for freezing: 6 to 7 months; giblets: 2 to 3 months

☐ Freezer, cooked, without gravy, prepared for freezing: 1 month

☐ Freezer, cooked, in sandwiches, prepared for freezing: 1 month

☐ Freezer, fried, prepared for freezing: 3 months

☐ Freezer, cooked, with gravy, or as a main dish, prepared for freezing: 6 months

Do not refreeze once thawed. Use within two days of thawing.

Nutritive Food Values—Chicken is an excellent source of high-quality protein, very good to excellent for niacin, and a fair source of iron. Broiler-fryers are lower in fat and calories than most other meats. The light meat of chicken has a lower fat content and is higher in niacin than the dark meat; however, it is lower in iron.

☐ Light meat without skin, 3½ ounces, raw = 117 calories

☐ Light meat without skin, 3½ ounces, cooked, roasted = 166 calories

☐ Dark meat without skin, 3½ ounces, raw = 130 calories

☐ Dark meat without skin, 3½ ounces, cooked, roasted = 176 calories

Basic Preparation—Rinse chicken in cold water. Drain and pat dry. If chicken is frozen, thaw in refrigerator; allow 12 to 24 hours for broiler-fryers and longer for larger birds. Or place wrapped chicken in a pan under cold running water; allow ½ to 1 hour for broiler-fryers and longer for larger birds.

Most people prefer chicken cooked

well done. Fully cooked young chicken sometimes appears underdone due to the red color around the bone. This is caused by internal pigment moving from the inside to the outside of the bone and does not affect eating quality. Since dark meat requires longer cooking than white meat, allow 8 to 9 minutes extra time when cooking dark meat pieces.

☐ **To Roast**—Don't stuff bird until ready to roast; if stuffing and bird are prepared in advance, refrigerate them separately. Stuff chicken lightly just before roasting. Tuck wing tip into back to hold neck skin. Truss the legs and rub the bird with softened butter. Place on rack, breast side down, in shallow roasting pan in a slow oven (325°F.). Turn chicken breast side up for the last 15 minutes of cooking for added color and a crisp skin; increase the temperature to hot (425° F.) for 15 minutes before removing from oven. When drumstick moves up and down easily, chicken is ready.

☐ **To Broil**—Preheat broiler, setting oven temperature at moderate (350°F.). Season broiler chicken and brush with melted butter or margarine. Place chicken halves or quarters, skin side down, on lightly greased broiler rack. Place broiler pan as far away from heat as possible. Broil for 20 minutes on each side. Brush chicken with butter after turning. Length of time under broiler depends on size of chicken and type of broiling equipment. After 40 minutes, prick chicken with skewer or cake tester. If juice is red, chicken needs additional cooking.

☐ **To Sauté**—Coat bottom of skillet with mixture of butter and salad oil or vegetable shortening. A 10-inch skillet will require 2 tablespoons butter and 1 of oil or shortening. Dry chicken thoroughly or it will not brown. Place chicken pieces, skin side down, in butter and oil. Brown on one side, turn and brown on the other side. Remove pieces as they are browned. Add more butter if necessary. Season chicken and place dark meat pieces in skillet. Cover and cook for 8 to 9 minutes. Add white meat pieces; cover and cook for 15 minutes, or until tender. Turn and baste chicken several times during cooking.

☐ **To Fry**—Dredge cut-up broiler-fryer with seasoned flour. Heat ½ inch of oil or vegetable shortening in skillet. Place larger pieces of chicken, skin side down, in skillet over moderate heat. Brown, then add smaller pieces and giblets. Turn pieces and brown other side. Reduce heat and fry, uncovered, for 15 to 25 minutes on each side.

☐ **To Braise**—Season cut-up broiler-fryer. Place, skin side down, in a skillet with about ¼ cup oil. Brown over high heat, reduce heat, and add ½ cup consommé. Cover; cook 30 minutes, or until tender.

☐ **To Stew**—Place chicken in large kettle with seasonings and water to cover. Cover and simmer for 1 to 3 hours, or until tender. Time depends on the size and age of chicken. If not to be used immediately, cool chicken and broth for a short time; then refrigerate.

☐ **To Barbecue**—Place broiler-fryer halves or quarters, skin side up, on barbecue grate 6 inches from heat. Brush with barbecue sauce. Grill slowly, turning frequently and basting with sauce. Allow 45 minutes to 1 hour, depending on size of bird. Chicken can be barbecued this way using an indoor broiler.

☐ **To Bone, Whole Chicken**—Wash and pat dray. Remove the wings. With a sharp, small pointed knife, cut the bird down the center back to the tail. Remove the tail section. Using the point of the knife against the bones of the bird, cut away the skin and flesh from the back and ribs. When the legs are reached, cut the joint at the hip to remove the leg, bone and all. Do the same with the wings, leaving the wing bone for later removal. Continue cutting the meat away from the bones until the breastbone is reached. Carefully cut the skin away from the top of the breastbone. Now, with the sharp knife, cut and scrape away the meat from the leg and wing bones. In doing this the wing and leg will be turned inside out when the bone is removed. Turn legs and wings right side out. Now the bird is ready for stuffing or rolling.

☐ **To Bone, Chicken Breasts**—Turn skin side down. With the fingers push against the ribs of the breast until the joints holding the breastbone break. Push the flesh away from the breastbone until it is just attached at the top. Pull out the breastbone and the piece of cartilage attached to it. With a sharp knife which has a sharp point, carefully cut the meat away from the rib bones. Continue cutting carefully until the wishbone is reached. Remove the wishbone and the remaining rib section. Fold skin over meat and stuff or cook as is.

☐ **To Freeze, Whole Chicken, Uncooked** —Wash and pat dry. Do not stuff chicken before freezing. Truss chicken to make body as compact as possible. Wrap chicken tightly in moisture- vaporproof material. Seal.

☐ **To Freeze, Chicken Parts, Uncooked** —Proceed as above. Wrap individual pieces or as many pieces as you need for one meal in one package. Make sure pieces fit together tightly to avoid air spaces which promote spoilage.

TIMETABLE FOR ROASTING
STUFFED, CHILLED CHICKEN AND UNSTUFFED CHICKEN

For greatest accuracy, insert meat thermometer in thigh of chicken, not touching a bone. When chicken is wrapped in foil, push thermometer through foil.

KIND OF CHICKEN	APPROXIMATE READY-TO-COOK WEIGHT (POUNDS)	AMOUNT OF STUFFING (QUARTS)	INTERNAL TEMPERATURE WHEN DONE	APPROXIMATE TOTAL COOKING TIME AT 325°F. (HOURS)
Broiler or Fryer	1½ to 2½	¼ to ½	190°F.-200°F.	1¼ to 2*
Rock Cornish (Game) Hen (defrosted)	1 to 1¼	¼ to ⅓ Cup	200°F.	1
Roaster (also Rock Cornish Roaster)	2½ to 4½	½ to 1¼	190°F.-200°F.	2-3½**
Capon	4 to 8	1¼-1¾	200°F.	3-5

*Or roast unstuffed at 400°F. for ¾ to 1½ hours.
**Or roast unstuffed at 400°F. for 1½ to 2¾ hours.

CHICKEN
COOK BOOK—Roasted or stewed,
baked, barbecued or fried,
creamed, sauced or seasoned,
chicken is an all-time international favorite

Breast of Chicken, Tropicale

ROAST CHICKEN WITH SAUSAGE-NUT STUFFING

1 roasting chicken (3½ to 4 pounds)
1 lemon
    Sausage-Nut Stuffing
1 tablespoon chicken or sausage fat
    Celery leaves and rosemary
1 tablespoon minced onion
½ cup light cream
2 tablespoons brown sugar

Wash and dry chicken. Rub skin with cut lemon. Stuff body and neck cavities of chicken lightly with Sausage-Nut Stuffing, and truss. Rub with fat; then sprinkle with celery leaves, rosemary, and onion. Wrap loosely in foil and put on rack in open shallow pan. Roast in preheated slow oven (325°F.) for 1½ hours. Open foil and pull it away from chicken. Brush with mixture of cream and brown sugar. Continue roasting and basting for 1 hour, or until chicken is tender and well browned. Makes 6 servings.

Sausage-Nut Stuffing

¼ cup sausage meat
¼ cup butter or margarine
2 tablespoons minced onion
½ teaspoon paprika
¾ teaspoon salt
¼ cup chopped celery
¼ cup chopped parsley
3½ cups soft stale-bread crumbs
⅓ cup chopped pecans or other nuts
    Milk

Cook sausage until golden brown, breaking up with fork. Add butter and onion. Cook for 2 or 3 minutes. Remove from heat and add next 6 ingredients. Add enough milk to moisten and mix well.

ROAST CHICKEN WITH BANANAS

1 roasting chicken (3½ to 4 pounds)
    Salt and pepper
1 large onion
    Butter or chicken fat
    Gravy coloring
4 bananas
¼ cup butter
¼ teaspoon ground ginger

Sprinkle the inside of a 3½- to 4-pound roasting chicken with salt and pepper. Place 1 large onion, halved, inside the bird. Tie legs together. Rub outside of chicken with softened butter. Sprinkle outside with salt and pepper. Place, uncovered, in preheated moderate oven (350°F.). Every 15 minutes (for a total of 45 minutes to 1 hour, depending on size of chicken), baste with chicken drippings. Examine the color of chicken carefully 15 minutes before bird is done; if it isn't a rich brown, turn oven to extremely hot (500°F.) for remaining time. Remove chicken to hot platter and keep warm while making gravy. This is best done by turning off oven heat and putting chicken back in oven with oven door left open.

Tip roaster over a mixing bowl and pour off some of fat but not all. (A caution here: do not throw away this fat. It has a number of splendid uses: frying potatoes, creaming another roasting or broiling chicken.) Place roasting pan on top of stove over medium heat. Add a little boiling water, approximately ¼ to ½ cup, and with a large metal spoon scrape and stir chicken drippings sticking to bottom of pan until well blended with water. Add a few drops of gravy coloring. The gravy must be dark in color, rich in texture. If necessary, a little more water may be added, but be careful not to add too much.

Cut 4 bananas into halves crosswise. Melt ¼ cup butter in a skillet. Sprinkle bananas with ginger and fry gently in butter until soft, turning several times. Place around chicken. Makes 4 servings.

ROAST CHICKEN, INDIA STYLE

1 roasting chicken (3½ to 4 pounds)
½ cup raw rice
1 can (10½ ounces) condensed mushroom soup
½ teaspoon curry powder
6 ripe olives, chopped
2 tablespoons chopped onion
2 tablespoons butter or margarine, melted

Wash and dry chicken. Cook and drain rice. Mix rice, ½ cup soup, ¼ teaspoon curry powder, olives, and onion. Stuff chicken with the mixture and truss. Put in baking pan and brush with butter. Cover lightly with foil and roast in preheated slow oven (325°F.) for 2½ to 3 hours, removing foil about 45 minutes before end of roasting time to allow for browning. Serve chicken and stuffing with sauce made from remaining soup, heated, and ¼ teaspoon curry powder. Makes 5 to 6 servings.

BARBECUED BROILED CHICKEN

1 broiling chicken (about 2½ pounds)
½ cup butter or margarine
1 teaspoon salt
2 tablespoons vinegar
1 teaspoon sugar
1 tablespoon Worcestershire
1 teaspoon onion salt
¼ teaspoon pepper
½ cup water

Wash chicken and dry on absorbent paper. Arrange, skin side down, on rack. Combine remaining ingredients and heat until butter is melted. Brush chicken with some of mixture and put in preheated broiler about 4 inches from heat. Broil for 50 to 60 minutes under medium heat, turning 3 or 4 times and brushing with barbecue mixture. Makes 4 servings.

CHICKEN MARENGO

3 tablespoons olive oil
1 tablespoon butter
1 frying chicken (about 3 pounds), cut up
1 tablespoon all-purpose flour
1 teaspoon salt
½ teaspoon pepper
1 garlic clove, crushed
½ cup dry white wine
⅓ cup canned tomatoes or 1 tablespoon tomato paste dissolved in 3 tablespoons water
3 medium tomatoes, peeled, seeded, and chopped
½ teaspoon crumbled dried thyme
½ pound mushrooms, sliced
2 tablespoons chopped parsley
4 cooked lobster tails or 8 cooked shelled deveined jumbo shrimps (optional)
2 slices of bread, trimmed of crust and fried in butter (optional)
4 eggs, fried in hot olive oil (optional)

Heat oil and butter in large heavy skillet. Sauté chicken in it until browned on all sides. Remove chicken to casserole and keep hot. Blend flour into skillet pan juices. Cook, stirring constantly, for 2 to 3 minutes. Season with salt and pepper. Add garlic, wine, and canned tomatoes. Bring to a boil. Add fresh tomatoes, thyme, mushrooms, and parsley. Cook over medium heat, stirring frequently, for about 5 minutes. Pour sauce over chicken pieces in casserole. Cook, covered, over low heat, or in preheated moderate oven (350°F.), for 30 minutes, or until chicken is tender. If to be served in the manner of an elegant French restaurant, arrange chicken and sauce on large heated serving platter. Surround with lobster or shrimps, and with fried bread slices cut on the diagonal to form triangles. Top each bread piece with a fried egg. Makes 4 servings.

CHINESE WALNUT CHICKEN

4 whole chicken breasts
1 tablespoon cornstarch
    Salt
½ teaspoon pepper

½ teaspoon sugar
2 tablespoons soy sauce
5 tablespoons cooking oil
½ cup coarsely chopped walnuts
1 cup smoked ham, diced in ½-inch squares (about 4 slices packaged variety)
½ cup hot chicken broth

Bone breasts, discarding skin; or have butcher do it. Press with hands to make of uniform thickness. Cut in 1½-inch squares. Mix cornstarch, ½ teaspoon salt, the pepper, sugar, 1 tablespoon soy sauce, and 2 tablespoons oil. Add chicken and stir to coat evenly. Sauté walnuts until golden in 1 tablespoon oil. Sprinkle with ½ teaspoon salt. Heat remaining oil, add chicken mixture and stir-fry for 2 minutes. Add ham and walnuts and stir-fry for about 5 minutes. Stir in remaining soy sauce and broth, scraping up brown bits from bottom of pan. Cook for 1 minute longer. Makes 6 to 8 servings.

CHICKEN À L'ORANGE

1 frying chicken (about 3 pounds), cut up
Salt and pepper
¼ cup all-purpose flour
¼ cup shortening or cooking oil
1 cup fresh orange juice
½ cup chili sauce
¼ cup chopped green pepper
1 teaspoon prepared mustard
½ to 1 teaspoon garlic salt
2 tablespoons soy sauce
1 tablespoon molasses
3 medium oranges, peeled and sliced into half-cartwheels

Wash and dry chicken pieces and season with salt and pepper. Dredge with flour. Heat shortening in skillet, add chicken, and brown lightly on all sides. Remove chicken to 3-quart casserole. Drain fat from pan. To skillet add remaining ingredients except orange slices and simmer for 2 or 3 minutes. Pour sauce over chicken in casserole. Cover and bake in preheated moderate oven (350°F.) for 50 to 60 minutes, or until chicken is tender. Just before serving, add oranges. Makes 4 servings.

OLD HOMESTEAD CHICKEN PIE

1 stewing hen (about 4 pounds), cut up
5 cups water
1 onion
2 celery stalks
2 parsley sprigs
Salt
2 cups (one 1-pound can) onions
1 package (10 ounces) frozen carrots and peas, cooked
6 tablespoons flour
Pepper
Pastry (2 cups flour recipe), unbaked
1 egg, slightly beaten

Wash chicken. Simmer chicken, covered, in water with onion, celery, parsley, and 1 teaspoon salt for 3 hours, or until tender. Remove chicken; cool broth. Re-

move meat from bones and cut into large pieces. Put in 2-quart baking dish with onions and carrots and peas. Remove fat from cooled broth. Melt ¼ cup of the fat (add butter if there is not enough) and stir in flour. Add 3 cups of the broth and cook until thickened. Season to taste. Pour over chicken and vegetables and keep hot. Cover with pastry. Make slits in crust to let steam escape; brush with egg. Bake in preheated hot oven (425°F.) for 30 minutes. Makes 6 servings.

BAKED CHICKEN AND PRUNES

3 tablespoons cooking oil
6 medium onions, cut into ¼-inch slices
2 tablespoons all-purpose flour
2 frying chickens (about 3½ pounds each), cut up
Salt and pepper
1½ pounds dried prunes
2 cans (8 ounces each) tomato sauce

Put oil in bottom of large deep casserole. Add onions and sprinkle with flour. Add half of chicken pieces and sprinkle them with salt and pepper. Add half of prunes. Repeat layers of chicken, seasonings, and prunes. Pour tomato sauce over all. Cover and bake in preheated moderate oven (350°F.) for 2 hours. Makes 8 servings.

COUNTRY CAPTAIN

2 frying chickens (about 3 pounds each), cut up
½ cup butter or margarine
2 medium green peppers, chopped
1 garlic clove, minced
2 small onions, chopped
2⅓ cups (one 1-pound, 3-ounce can) tomatoes
½ cup seedless raisins
½ cup blanched almonds
1 teaspoon curry powder
1 teaspoon crumbled dried thyme
Salt and pepper
2 cups partially cooked rice

Fry chicken in hot butter until brown. Remove chicken to a casserole. Pour off butter. To skillet add green peppers, garlic, onions, tomatoes, ¼ cup each of raisins and almonds, and the seasonings.

Simmer for 5 to 10 minutes. Put rice in casserole with chicken and cover with tomato mixture. Sprinkle with remaining raisins and nuts. Cover casserole and bake in preheated hot oven (400°F.) for 30 minutes, or until chicken is tender and rice is done. Makes 6 to 8 servings.

CHICKEN BAKED IN CREAM

1 frying chicken (about 3 pounds), cut up
Flour
Salt and pepper
2 cups light cream
Hot milk

Wash chicken and dry on absorbent paper. Roll in flour seasoned with salt and pepper and place in shallow baking pan. Almost cover chicken with cream. Bake, uncovered, in preheated slow oven (325°F.) for about 2 hours. Turn chicken pieces after first hour. If gravy is too thick, add a little more light cream. At serving time, place chicken pieces on a heated serving dish and keep warm. Stir enough hot milk into gravy to give it the right consistency and pour over chicken pieces. Makes 4 servings.

CHICKEN IN A POT

2 frying chickens, about 2½ pounds each, cut in quarters
½ cup olive oil
1 large onion, minced
1 garlic clove, minced
1 teaspoon salt
¾ teaspoon pepper
1 medium tomato, chopped, or ½ cup drained canned tomatoes
½ cup dry white wine

In Dutch oven or heavy kettle, brown chicken in olive oil until golden brown. Sprinkle with onion, garlic, the salt and pepper. Cover and simmer for 30 minutes. Add tomato and wine and simmer for 30 minutes longer, or until chicken is tender. Makes 8 servings.

CHICKEN ROSEMARY

1 broiling chicken (about 2½ pounds), cut into small pieces
Salt and pepper
1 garlic clove, minced
½ cup cooking oil
½ teaspoon dried rosemary
Fine dry bread crumbs

Wash and dry chicken pieces and put in shallow baking dish. Sprinkle with salt and pepper. Add remaining ingredients except crumbs. Then sprinkle with crumbs. Marinate for several hours, turning now and then and adding more crumbs. Put on rack on broiler pan about 6 inches from heat and brown for 25 minutes on one side and 15 minutes on the other, until golden brown. Makes 4 servings.

BROILED DEVILED CHICKEN

1 broiling chicken (about 2½ pounds)

Olive oil
1 tablespoon crushed red pepper flakes
   (or less for a milder dish)
   Salt
   About ¼ cup dry white wine or
1 tablespoon lemon juice and
3 tablespoons water combined

Split chicken and crush flat, bones and all, with a meat mallet or a rolling pin. Brush both sides lavishly with olive oil. Sprinkle with red pepper and salt. Broil about 4 inches from source of heat for 15 minutes on each side, basting with a little olive oil. Transfer chicken to a hot dish and keep hot. Put broiler pan with drippings over heat and stir in wine. Bring to a boil and pour over chicken. Makes 4 servings.

CHICKEN À LA PROVIDENCE
(Shown on Cover)
2 whole chicken breasts
4 chicken thighs
   Salt
1 bay leaf
   Parsley
   Water
   Flour
   Butter or margarine
2 medium onions, sliced
4 carrots, peeled, cut in ¼-inch slices
   and cooked
2 teaspoons fresh lemon juice
2 egg yolks, slightly beaten
   White pepper
8 slices bacon, cut in 1-inch pieces and
   fried until crisp
   Chopped parsley

Put chicken, 1 teaspoon salt, the bay leaf, 1 sprig parsley, and enough water to cover chicken in large saucepan. Bring to boil, cover and simmer for 45 minutes, or until chicken is tender. Remove chicken and boil the liquid until reduced to 2 cups. Remove skin and bones from chicken, keeping pieces of meat as large as possible. Dredge meat lightly with flour and brown in 2 tablespoons butter. Remove chicken and brown onion lightly in remaining drippings in skillet. Put layers of chicken, carrot, and onion in 2-quart casserole. Cover and put in preheated moderate oven (350°F.) to heat while making sauce. In saucepan, melt 2 tablespoons butter and blend in 2 tablespoons flour. Gradually add 2 cups broth and cook, stirring, until smooth and slightly thickened. Add lemon juice. Pour mixture over egg yolks, beating constantly. Season to taste with salt and pepper. Pour over contents of casserole, sprinkle with bacon and garnish with chopped parsley. Makes 4 servings.

SOUTHERN-FRIED CHICKEN WITH CREAM GRAVY
1 frying chicken (about 3½ pounds),
   cut up
½ cup plus 2 tablespoons
   all-purpose flour
1½ teaspoons salt
¾ teaspoon pepper

¼ cup butter or margarine
¼ cup shortening
2 cups milk

Wash chicken and dry on absorbent paper. Roll in ½ cup flour seasoned with salt and pepper. Melt butter and shortening in skillet. Add chicken and brown quickly on all sides. Reduce heat, cover, and continue cooking for 25 minutes, or until tender, turning occasionally. Remove cover during last 10 minutes of cooking. Drain on absorbent paper and arrange on hot platter. To make gravy, drain off all but 2 tablespoons fat. Add 2 tablespoons flour and the milk and cook until thickened, stirring constantly. Season to taste. Makes 4 servings.

CRISPY OVEN-FRIED CHICKEN
Cut chicken into serving pieces. Wash and pat dry. Sprinkle pieces with salt and pepper. Dip pieces into melted butter or margarine. Roll pieces in corn-flake crumbs. Place pieces in well-greased shallow baking pan and drizzle melted butter over pieces. Bake in preheated slow oven (325°F.) for 1 hour, or until chicken is tender.

LOW-CALORIE FRIED CHICKEN
Cut chicken into serving pieces. Wash and pat dry. Sprinkle pieces with salt and pepper. Dip pieces into milk and roll in corn-flake crumbs, coating each piece well. Place pieces in well-greased shallow baking pan and bake in preheated slow oven (325°F.) for 1 hour, or until chicken is tender.

BREAST OF CHICKEN, TROPICALE
2 large whole chicken breasts,
   cut into halves
   Salt and pepper
   Butter (about ⅔ cup)
8 ounces medium noodles
1 pound mushrooms, chopped
2 tablespoons minced onion
   Few parsley sprigs, chopped
½ cup fine dry bread crumbs
4 slices of canned pineapple
3 tablespoons all-purpose flour
2½ cups milk
½ cup pineapple juice
2 egg yolks, beaten
½ cup heavy cream, whipped
¼ cup grated Parmesan cheese

Wash and dry chicken breasts. Season with salt and pepper and sauté in ¼ cup butter until lightly browned. Cover and cook for 25 minutes, or until tender, turning occasionally. Cook and drain noodles. Season with salt, pepper, and butter and put in flat broilerproof dish. Arrange chicken on top and keep warm. Cook mushrooms and onion in butter remaining in chicken skillet. Add parsley and crumbs and mix well; season. Put a pineapple slice on each chicken breast and top with a mound of mushroom mixture. Melt 3 tablespoons butter and blend in flour. Add milk and pineapple juice and cook until slightly thickened. Add small amount of mixture to egg yolks. Put back in saucepan and cook, stirring, for a few minutes longer. Fold in whipped cream and season to taste. Pour over chicken and sprinkle with cheese. Put under broiler until browned. Makes 4 servings.

SUPRÊMES DE VOLAILLE
(Boneless Chicken Breasts)
A *suprême de volaille* is a skinless, boneless raw breast of chicken that has been removed from one side of the bird. Each chicken has two of them. They are one of the glories of French cooking, and are cooked in countless, delicious ways.

French kitchen terminology also speaks of *côtelette de volaille,* a *suprême* with the upper part of the wing left attached.

Good French cooking never cooks a *suprême* in liquid, but broils, sautés, or cooks it in butter in a covered saucepan. The trick of cooking *suprêmes* perfectly is not to overcook them, because even a minute's overcooking will make them tough and dry. A *suprême,* depending on size, cooks in 6 to 8 minutes. To test for doneness, the top of it should be pressed lightly with a finger. If it is still soft and gives to the touch, it is not yet done; to be done, the flesh should spring back with a little resilience. A perfectly cooked *suprême* is white, with a very faint pink blush. It is juicy, with clear yellow juices.

Suprêmes de Volaille à Blanc
Bone breasts from 2 frying chickens as directed in Basic Preparation, page 378. After sautéing for 6 to 8 minutes in ¼ cup butter, remove chicken to a hot platter and keep warm. To drippings in skillet, add ¼ cup each chicken stock or bouillon and dry white wine. Cook down until syrupy. Stir in 1 cup heavy cream and cook until slightly thickened. Season with salt, pepper, and lemon juice. Pour over breasts and sprinkle with chopped parsley. Makes 4 servings.

Chicken Breasts with Mushrooms
Follow recipe above, sautéing 1 minced

green onion and ¼ pound mushrooms, sliced, in the drippings for 5 minutes before stirring in the stock and wine.

DEEP-FRIED CHICKEN

2 frying chickens (about 2½ pounds each)
½ cup all-purpose flour
1½ teaspoons salt
¾ teaspoon pepper
Fat for deep frying

Wash chicken and drain on absorbent paper. Roll in seasoned flour. Heat deep fat to 370°F. on a frying thermometer, or until a 1-inch bread cube browns in 1 minute. Fry 3 or 4 pieces at a time in hot fat for 12 to 15 minutes, or until golden brown and tender. Drain on absorbent paper. Keep hot in warm oven until all pieces are fried. Makes 4 servings.

■ **Variation**—Add 1 teaspoon ground ginger to the seasoned flour.

BATTER-DIPPED FRIED CHICKEN

1 frying chicken (about 3½ pounds)
1 cup water
1½ teaspoons salt
1 cup sifted all-purpose flour
1 teaspoon baking powder
1 teaspoon poultry seasoning
¼ teaspoon pepper
Milk
1 egg, beaten
Fat for deep frying

Wash chicken, dry on absorbent paper, and put in saucepan. Add water and 1 teaspoon salt. Cover, bring to boil, and simmer for 30 minutes. Drain, reserving broth. Cool chicken. To make batter, sift remaining ½ teaspoon salt, the flour, baking powder, poultry seasoning, and pepper. Add enough milk to broth to make ¾ cup; add egg and stir into flour mixture. Heat deep fat to 375°F. on a frying thermometer or until a 1-inch bread cube browns in 1 minute. Dip chicken into batter with tongs and fry 3 or 4 pieces at a time in hot fat until golden brown. Drain on absorbent paper and keep hot in warm oven until all pieces are fried. Makes 4 servings.

CHICKEN ON THE WING

2 pounds chicken wings
2 tablespoons butter or margarine
1 teaspoon salt
1 teaspoon paprika or curry powder
1 cup chicken bouillon (dissolve bouillon cube in hot water)
Fat for deep frying
½ cup ketchup
¼ cup prepared mustard
Batter
1 egg
⅔ cup milk (about)
1⅓ cups sifted all-purpose flour
½ teaspoon salt
1½ teaspoons baking powder

Wash chicken and dry on absorbent paper. Put wings in casserole or baking dish; dot with butter; season with salt

Danish Chicken

and paprika and pour in bouillon. Bake, covered, in preheated moderate oven (350°F.) until tender, about 45 minutes. Meanwhile, prepare batter. Beat egg; pour drippings from chicken into measuring cup and add milk to make ⅔ cup. Add to egg. Sift flour, salt, and baking powder into egg and milk and beat until smooth. Heat deep fat to 365°F. on a frying thermometer, or until a 1-inch bread cube browns in 1 minute. Dip chicken into batter with tongs; fry 3 or 4 pieces at a time in hot fat for 3 to 5 minutes per side, or until golden brown. Drain on absorbent paper and keep hot in warm oven until all pieces are fried. Blend ketchup and mustard; serve with chicken. Makes 4 servings.

DANISH CHICKEN

1 roasting chicken (about 4 pounds)
  Salt and pepper
1 large bunch of parsley
3 to 4 tablespoons butter or margarine
¼ cup water
1 cup heavy cream
1 tablespoon all-purpose flour

Wash chicken inside and out. Pat dry with paper towels. Season inside with salt and a liberal amount of pepper. Wash parsley, break off stems, and stuff whole bunch inside chicken. Melt butter in a Dutch oven and slowly brown chicken on all sides. Add water, cover, and simmer until drumstick doesn't show pink when pulled away from bird, about 45 minutes. For the last 15 minutes remove cover and add cream, keeping heat very low to prevent curdling. Remove cooked chicken to platter. Thicken drippings with flour blended with a little cold water. Season to taste with salt and pepper. Spoon cooked parsley from chicken and serve with chicken. Serve the gravy separately in a bowl. Makes 4 servings.

CHICKEN GUMBO

1 frying chicken (about 3½ pounds),
  cut up
2 cups water
2 medium onions, sliced
  Tops from 2 celery stalks
2 bay leaves
1 teaspoon monosodium glutamate
2 teaspoons salt
2 tablespoons butter or margarine
1 medium green pepper, chopped
4 cups (two 1-pound cans) tomatoes
3 parsley sprigs, chopped
½ teaspoon hot pepper sauce
⅓ cup uncooked rice
½ pound fresh okra, sliced
1 teaspoon filé powder

Wash chicken pieces and put in kettle. Add water, 1 onion, celery, bay leaves, monosodium glutamate, and 1 teaspoon salt. Bring to boil, cover, and simmer for 40 minutes. Remove from heat; strain broth and return to kettle. Remove meat

from bones in large pieces. Cut into bite-size pieces; return to broth. Melt butter, add remaining onion and green pepper, and cook for about 5 minutes. Add to chicken with 1 teaspoon salt, tomatoes, parsley, and hot pepper sauce. Simmer for 20 minutes. Add rice and okra; simmer for 20 minutes longer. Remove from heat, and stir in filé powder. Makes 4 generous servings.

CHINESE SMOKED CHICKEN

Rub 1 whole frying chicken (about 3 pounds) inside and out with soy sauce and let stand for 30 minutes. Cover with boiling salted water and simmer for 40 minutes. Drain and pat dry. Line a kettle slightly larger than the chicken with foil. Put ⅓ cup packed brown sugar on foil. Put chicken in kettle on a trivet above the sugar. Draw foil over top of chicken and seal by folding over. Put kettle over low heat and smoke chicken for 20 minutes. Remove from foil; cut into small pieces. Makes 4 servings.

CHICKEN STEW, BRUNSWICK STYLE

1 frying chicken (about 3½ pounds),
  cut up
1½ teaspoons salt
¼ teaspoon pepper
2 tablespoons shortening
1 large onion, chopped
2½ cups water
2 cups (one 1-pound can tomatoes)
⅓ cup sherry
1 tablespoon Worcestershire
1 package (10 ounces) frozen
  Lima beans
1 cup canned, fresh, or frozen
  sliced okra
1 package (10 ounces) frozen cut corn
½ cup fine dry bread crumbs

Wash chicken and dry on absorbent paper. Season with salt and pepper. Heat shortening in Dutch oven or large kettle; add onion and chicken. Cook until lightly browned. Add water, tomatoes, sherry, and Worcestershire. Cover and simmer for 40 minutes. Add beans and okra and simmer for 10 minutes. Add corn and

crumbs and simmer for 10 minutes longer. Season to taste. Makes 6 servings.

POULET VALLÉE D'AUGE

2 pounds chicken breasts or thighs
½ cup butter or margarine
2 tablespoons brandy
2 tablespoons chopped chives or
  green onion tops
2 tablespoons chopped parsley
¼ teaspoon crumbled dried thyme
1 teaspoon salt
  Pepper to taste
½ cup sauterne
½ cup heavy cream

Wash chicken and drain on absorbent paper. Brown slowly in butter. Lower heat and continue cooking, uncovered, for 15 minutes, turning occasionally. Pour in brandy and ignite; shake pan until flame dies. Add chives, parsley, thyme, salt, pepper, and sauterne. Cover and cook until chicken is tender, about 45 minutes. Arrange on platter. To make sauce, add cream slowly to drippings, stirring rapidly so mixture blends smoothly. Pour over chicken or serve separately. Makes 4 servings.

Note: 1 teaspoon grated orange rind and 1 tablespoon fresh orange juice can be added just before removing sauce from heat.

COQ AU VIN

1 frying chicken (about 3 pounds),
  cut up
¼ cup butter
8 small boiling onions, peeled
8 small carrots, scraped
1 garlic clove, minced
2 tablespoons all-purpose flour
2 cups dry red wine
1 small bay leaf
1 tablespoon minced parsley
¼ teaspoon each of ground savory
  and thyme
1 can (4 ounces) button mushrooms
1½ teaspoons salt
¼ teaspoon pepper

Cut chicken into quarters, or smaller pieces if you prefer. Remove spinal cord and neck to improve appearance of the breast. Melt butter in a skillet and brown chicken pieces over medium heat. Remove chicken pieces to a plate and set aside. Put onions and carrots in the skillet. Brown very lightly. Add garlic. Stir in flour, then gradually stir in wine. When wine is well blended, add bay leaf, parsley, savory, and thyme. Pour in liquid from can of mushrooms; add salt and pepper. Return chicken to pan and add mushrooms. Cover and simmer slowly for 20 to 30 minutes, or until chicken and vegetables are tender. Serve with mashed potatoes. Makes 3 or 4 servings.

Note: The better the wine, the better the dish!

CHICKEN STEAMED IN LEMON BUTTER

½ cup butter
  Juice of 1 lemon
1 teaspoon salt
1 garlic clove
  Dash of pepper
½ teaspoon paprika
1 frying chicken (about 3 pounds),
  cut up

Put all ingredients except chicken in skillet and heat. Arrange chicken pieces on rack in skillet. Cover and steam over low heat for 45 minutes, or until tender, turning several times. Makes 4 servings.

POULE AU RIZ

1 whole stewing chicken, about 5 pounds
4 to 6 cups water
1 carrot, cut in chunks
2 celery stalks and tops, cut in pieces
1 bay leaf
2 large parsley sprigs
1 large onion, sliced
2 garlic cloves
½ teaspoon dried thyme
  Salt
10 whole black peppercorns
  Paprika
1 cup uncooked rice
4 tablespoons butter or margarine
⅓ cup all-purpose flour
1 cup light cream or milk
1 egg yolk, beaten
½ teaspoon white pepper
½ teaspoon Worcestershire
¼ teaspoon nutmeg

Put chicken in kettle with enough water to come at least halfway over chicken. Add next 7 ingredients, 1 teaspoon salt and peppercorns. Sprinkle with paprika. Bring to boil, cover and simmer for 3 hours, or until chicken is tender. About 45 minutes before chicken is cooked, remove 2 cups chicken broth and strain. Cook rice in this until it is tender and most of the liquid is absorbed, about 30 minutes. Rice should be rather moist. When chicken is tender, remove to a warm platter and keep warm. Strain 2 cups broth. Melt 3 tablespoons butter

Chicken Loaves: Hot with Curry Sauce, Cold and Jellied

Chinese Walnut Chicken

Chicken in a Pot

Poule au Riz

Far Eastern Kebabs

and blend in flour. Add 2 cups broth and cook, stirring, until smooth and thickened. Stir in cream. Add small amount of mixture to egg yolk. Stir into remaining sauce. Add seasonings and simmer for about 10 minutes longer. Do not boil. Add remaining butter. Serve chicken on bed of rice on platter, or with rice at each end in mounds. Spoon some of the sauce over the chicken and serve the remainder in a sauce-boat. Makes 6 to 8 servings.

CHICKEN MONTMORENCY

2 cups, about (one 1-pound, 1-ounce can), black cherries
1 frying chicken (about 3 pounds), cut up
  Salt, pepper, and paprika
3 tablespoons butter
1 tablespoon all-purpose flour
1 teaspoon sugar
⅛ teaspoon each of ground allspice and cinnamon
1 chicken bouillon cube
¼ teaspoon red food coloring

Drain cherries, reserving liquid. Wash and dry chicken pieces and sprinkle with salt, pepper, and paprika. Brown chicken on all sides in hot butter. Remove from skillet. To skillet add ¼ teaspoon salt, the flour, sugar, and spices; blend with drippings. Gradually stir in cherry liquid. Add chicken and remaining ingredients, except cherries. Cover, bring to a boil, and simmer for 40 minutes, or until chicken is tender. Add drained cherries for last 5 minutes of cooking time. Put chicken on serving platter and cover with sauce. Makes 4 servings.

CHICKEN FRICASSEE

1 hen, cut in pieces
  Boiling water
2 teaspoons salt
¼ teaspoon white pepper
2 celery stalks, including leaves
1 medium onion, sliced
1 sprig parsley
1 bay leaf
½ cup milk
½ cup flour
2 egg yolks, beaten (optional)

Wash chicken pieces and put in kettle. Cover with boiling water. (Pieces can first be browned in a little fat, if desired.) Bring to boil, cover, and simmer 1 hour. Add next 6 ingredients and simmer 2 hours longer, or until tender. Remove meat. Leave as is or remove bones and skin. Keep warm. Skim excess fat from liquid and measure liquid. There should be 4 cups. If not enough, add water to make 4 cups. Blend milk and flour. Gradually add a little of the hot liquid. Stir into remaining hot liquid and cook, stirring, until thickened. Beat in egg yolks, if using them, and strain over

chicken. Serve with hot cooked rice or noodles; with biscuits, dumplings, corn bread, or riced potato. Makes 6 servings.

CHICKEN LOAVES

Steam two 3-pound chickens in 2 cups water with 1 teaspoon salt, 1 teaspoon instant minced onion, and 2 parsley sprigs for 45 minutes, or until done. Remove from broth, cool; remove meat from bones. Strain broth and reserve. Cut breast meat in large pieces; put in loaf pan (7 x 3 x 2 inches) and cover with broth to fill pan. Chill.

Cut up remaining chicken. Melt 2 tablespoons margarine in 2 cups hot milk. Mix with chicken, 2 cups soft, stale bread crumbs, ¼ teaspoon pepper, 1 teaspoon each of salt and monosodium glutamate, ¼ cup chopped celery, 2 tablespoons minced green pepper, 1 diced pimiento, and 4 beaten eggs. Put in well-greased loaf pan (9 x 5 x 3 inches). Bake in preheated moderate oven (350°F.) for 1 hour. Each loaf makes 4 servings.

Note: Serve hot loaf with curry sauce and cooked asparagus spears. For sauce, add 1 tablespoon curry powder to 1 can (10¾ ounces) chicken gravy, and heat.

Serve jellied loaf cold with a tart Waldorf salad.

FAR EASTERN KEBABS

4 whole chicken breasts, skinned and boned
½ teaspoon ground ginger
¼ teaspoon dried chili peppers
⅛ teaspoon powdered mustard
⅛ teaspoon ground cardamom or finely crushed cardamom seed
⅛ teaspoon turmeric
1 teaspoon curry powder
1 tablespoon yogurt or buttermilk
2 teaspoons fresh lemon juice
1 teaspoon salt
  Small onions, cut in ¼-inch slices
  Lemon quarters, sprinkled with paprika
  Parsley

Flatten skinned and boned chicken with hands and cut in 2-inch pieces. Mix re-

maining ingredients, except last 3, to a thick paste. Add chicken pieces and stir to coat well. Let stand for 1 hour at room temperature. Thread on skewers, alternating several pieces with a slice of onion. Repeat until 4 skewers are filled. Set across shallow pan and broil slowly for 15 minutes, or until done, turning once during cooking. Serve at once garnished with lemon quarters and parsley. Makes 4 servings.

COOKED CHICKEN

COOL CURRIED CHICKEN SOUP

1 medium onion, sliced
2 apples, cored, peeled, and sliced
1 tablespoon butter
1 teaspoon all-purpose flour
1 teaspoon curry powder, or more to taste
  Salt, pepper, cayenne
2 cups chicken bouillon
½ cup dry white wine
½ cup diced cooked white chicken
1 cup light cream

Cook onion and apples in melted butter until soft. Mix flour with curry; add to first mixture and cook slowly, stirring often, for about 5 minutes. Season with salt, pepper, and a dash of cayenne. Add bouillon and wine and cook slowly for 10 minutes, stirring constantly. Rub entire mixture through a fine sieve, cool, and chill in refrigerator. At serving time add diced chicken and well-chilled cream. Serve very cold. Makes 3 to 4 servings.

CHICKEN HASHED IN CREAM

2 cups diced cooked chicken
1 cup light cream
3 tablespoons butter or margarine
3 tablespoons all-purpose flour
1 teaspoon salt
⅛ teaspoon white pepper
1½ cups milk
3 egg yolks
1 teaspoon instant minced onion
2 tablespoons grated Parmesan cheese

Simmer chicken in cream until cream is reduced to about half. Melt butter and blend in flour and seasonings. Gradually add milk and cook, stirring, until thickened. Add about ½ cup of this sauce to chicken mixture and stir in 1 egg yolk and the onion. Beat a little of the sauce into remaining egg yolks. Put back in saucepan with remaining sauce and cook for a few minutes longer. Stir in 1 tablespoon of the cheese. Pour chicken mixture into shallow broilerproof dish, cover with sauce and top with remaining cheese. Brown under broiler. Makes 4 servings.

CHICKEN PILAF

2 cups cooked chicken in strips
½ cup butter
⅓ cup coarsely chopped walnuts
1 tablespoon instant minced onion
1 teaspoon salt
½ teaspoon pepper
¼ teaspoon ground coriander
2 cups uncooked rice
4 cups boiling chicken bouillon
2 medium tomatoes, peeled, seeded, and chopped

Cook chicken in butter over low heat for 3 minutes. Add walnuts and cook for 2 minutes longer. Add onion, salt, pepper, and coriander. Add rice and cook for 5 minutes, stirring. Pour in boiling bouillon. Add tomatoes, bring to boil, cover, and simmer for 20 minutes, or until rice is tender and liquid completely absorbed. Remove from heat and let stand for 5 minutes before serving. Makes 4 to 6 servings.

CHICKEN-HAM MOUSSE

¾ cup each of milk and chicken bouillon
1 envelope unflavored gelatin
2 egg yolks
1 cup ground cooked ham
¾ teaspoon paprika
1 pimiento, chopped
¾ cup heavy cream
Onion salt
Salt and pepper
1 cup ground cooked chicken
1 tablespoon prepared horseradish
Few parsley sprigs, chopped

Put milk and bouillon in top part of double boiler; sprinkle gelatin on liquids to soften. Beat in egg yolks. Put over boiling water and cook, stirring constantly, until mixture is slightly thickened and coats a metal spoon. Put half (about ¾ cup) of mixture in each of two bowls and cool. To one bowl add ham, paprika, and pimiento. Whip cream until stiff and fold half into ham mixture. Add onion salt and salt and pepper to taste. Pour into 3½-cup loaf pan and chill until firm. Store remaining cream in refrigerator. To second bowl add chicken, horseradish, and parsley. When ham layer is firm, fold remaining cream into chicken mixture. Add salt and pepper to taste. Pour over ham layer and chill until firm. To serve, unmold and cut into slices. Makes 4 servings.

BAKED CHICKEN HASH

2 cups chopped cooked chicken
1 medium onion, chopped
1 raw potato, chopped
2 pimientos, diced
2 carrots, shredded
½ teaspoon salt
2 tablespoons chopped parsley
½ teaspoon poultry seasoning
2½ cups chicken gravy

Combine all ingredients and mix well.

Put in 1½-quart casserole. Cover and bake in preheated moderate oven (350° F.) for 45 minutes. Uncover and bake for about 15 minutes longer. Serve with additional gravy. Makes 4 servings.

CHICKEN SALAD

2 cups diced cooked chicken
1 cup diced celery
½ teaspoon salt
Dash of pepper
½ cup mayonnaise or salad dressing
Lettuce or other salad greens
Wedges of hard-cooked egg, olives, sliced cucumber, tomato wedges, radishes, pickles, sliced cooked beets, or asparagus spears (all optional)

Mix first 5 ingredients and serve on salad greens, adding garnishes as desired. Makes 4 servings.

Note: For variety, salad can be served in tomato shells, cream-puff shells, or soft rolls.

CHICKEN GIBLETS

CHICKEN-LIVER APPETIZERS

1 pound chicken livers
½ cup soy sauce
½ cup water
¼ cup sherry
1 tablespoon sugar
1 green onion
2 slices fresh gingerroot
¼ teaspoon peppercorns
1 clove star anise

Blanch chicken livers with boiling water. Rinse and drain. Mix soy sauce, water, sherry, and sugar and bring to a boil. Cut green onion into ½-inch slices and add with chicken livers, gingerroot, peppercorns, and anise to first mixture. Simmer for 10 minutes. Cool in liquid. Cut livers into pieces and serve on toothpicks as an appetizer.

Note: A few drops of anise extract, available at some markets and drugstores, can be substituted for star anise.

CHICKEN LIVERS AND BARLEY

½ cup butter, margarine, or bacon fat
1 onion, minced
½ pound mushrooms, sliced
1 cup medium pearl barley
2 cups chicken bouillon
1 pound chicken livers
Salt and pepper

Heat ¼ cup butter in heavy saucepan. Add onion and cook for 2 or 3 minutes. Add mushrooms and cook for 5 minutes. Add barley and brown lightly. Stir in bouillon. Cover, and simmer for 25 minutes, or until barley is tender and liquid absorbed. Sauté chicken livers in remaining butter. Season to taste. Stir into barley. Makes 4 to 6 servings.

CHICKEN LIVERS WITH FRIED NOODLES

½ pound fine egg noodles
Cooking oil
Salt
1 pound chicken livers
2 tablespoons diced celery
2 tablespoons sliced green onion
Pinch of pepper
1 cup chicken bouillon
2 tablespoons cornstarch
¼ cup water
2 teaspoons soy sauce

Cook noodles in boiling salted water until tender. Drain, rinse with cold water, and chill. Heat 2 tablespoons oil in heavy skillet, add noodles and ½ teaspoon salt, and cook noodles, stirring, for 6 minutes. Remove to a heated platter and keep warm. Add more oil to skillet, if necessary, to make 2 tablespoons. Sauté chicken livers, celery, and onion, stirring, for 5 minutes. Season with pepper. Add bouillon, cover pan, and simmer for 5 minutes. Mix together cornstarch, water, and soy sauce. Add slowly, stirring, and cook until thickened. Serve on noodles. Makes 4 to 6 servings.

CHICKEN LIVERS AND RICE, ORIENTAL STYLE

1 cup uncooked rice
1 can (10½ ounces) condensed beef bouillon
1¼ cups water
1 pound chicken livers, chopped
2 tablespoons minced onion
2 tablespoons chopped green pepper
3 tablespoons butter
2 tablespoons soy sauce
¼ teaspoon ground ginger

In saucepan combine first 3 ingredients. Bring to boil, cover, and simmer for 15 minutes, or until rice is tender and liquid absorbed. In skillet, brown chicken livers, onion, and pepper in butter. Stir in soy sauce and ginger. Spoon rice onto serving dish. Put chicken livers in center. Makes 4 servings.

SWEET-AND-PUNGENT CHICKEN LIVERS

1 pound chicken livers
2 tablespoons cooking oil

Salt and pepper
3 green peppers
1 can (9 ounces) sliced pineapple
1 cup chicken bouillon
½ cup vinegar
½ cup sugar
3 tablespoons cornstarch
1 tablespoon soy sauce
Hot steamed rice

Cut each chicken liver into 2 or 3 pieces. Sauté in oil until lightly browned, and season. Set aside on a hot platter. Remove seeds from green peppers and cut peppers into 1-inch pieces. Cut pineapple slices into 6 pieces each. Simmer peppers and pineapple in bouillon for 3 minutes. Mix vinegar, sugar, cornstarch, and soy sauce. Add to green peppers and pineapple and cook, stirring, until thickened. Pour over chicken livers and serve with steamed rice. Makes 6 servings.

CHICKEN GIZZARDS IN SAUCE PIETRO

¼ pound salt pork, chopped fine
1 tablespoon olive oil
1 small onion, minced
2 garlic cloves, minced
1 pound chicken gizzards, chopped
2 parsley sprigs, minced
¼ to ½ teaspoon crushed dried
  red pepper
¼ teaspoon ground cloves
½ teaspoon crumbled dried marjoram
½ teaspoon salt
1 cup dry red wine
2 cups (one 1-pound can)
  Italian-style tomatoes
2 cans (6 ounces each) tomato paste
4 cups water
8 ounces thin spaghetti or
  fine egg noodles
  Grated Romano or Parmesan cheese

Put salt pork in kettle with next 3 ingredients and cook until pork is golden brown. Add gizzards, herbs, and salt and cook for a few minutes. Add wine and simmer for about 25 minutes. Add tomatoes, paste, and water and simmer until fairly thick. Cook and drain spaghetti. Sprinkle platter with cheese; add some spaghetti and more cheese and sauce. Repeat until all is used, ending with sauce and cheese. Makes 6 servings.

CHICKEN STUFFINGS

BREAD STUFFING

1 small onion, minced
½ cup butter or margarine
4 cups day-old bread crumbs or cubes
½ teaspoon salt
½ teaspoon poultry seasoning or
  ¼ teaspoon each of ground sage
    and thyme
¼ teaspoon celery seed
2 parsley sprigs, chopped

Cook onion in butter for 5 minutes. Add remaining ingredients and mix lightly. Makes 3 cups.

Rice Stuffing

Make Bread Stuffing, substituting 3 cups cooked rice (¾ cup raw) for bread crumbs.

Corn-Bread Stuffing

Make Bread Stuffing, substituting 2 cups crumbled unsweetened corn bread for half of bread crumbs.

Giblet Stuffing

Make Bread Stuffing, adding chopped cooked chicken giblets.

Potato Stuffing

Make Bread Stuffing, substituting 3 cups cold riced potato for 3 cups bread crumbs. Add 1 egg and 2 tablespoons milk.

Nut Stuffing

Make Bread Stuffing, adding ½ cup chopped nuts.

CHICK-PEA (*Cicer arietinum*)—The chick-pea, also known as garbanzo bean, Spanish bean, or *ceci* pea, is native to and extensively grown in southern Europe. The plant is a branching, bushy annual which is well adapted to arid and semiarid regions. The sparse foliage is poisonous, eliminating any use of the plants as forage. Large green pods produce one or two edible seeds, or peas, that wrinkle as they dry and are picturesquely described as looking like rams' heads. Peas vary in size and color (white, red, and black) in the different varieties. They are most important as a food in many parts of Asia, Africa, and Central America, and are much used in Italian, Spanish, and Mexican cooking.

In ancient times chick-peas were cultivated by Jews, Greeks, and Egyptians. The Romans used both the black and white varieties. Herbalists of the 16th, 17th, and 18th centuries delighted in the many colors these peas came in. Today the white chick-pea is the most common. The red variety is grown in eastern countries and the black variety is now considered more curious than useful.

Chick-peas have a nutty flavor, which lends itself to cooking in many ways, and are one of the most nutritious of the legumes. They can be served as a vegetable, added to soups and stews, used in sauces and salads, or marinated and served as an appetizer.

Availability—Dried chick-peas are available in 1-pound packages and in bulk. Canned chick-peas, cooked and ready to use, are also available.

Storage

☐ Dry, kitchen shelf: 1 year
☐ Canned, kitchen shelf: 1 year
☐ Refrigerator shelf, cooked or canned, opened and covered: 1 week

Nutritive Food Values—Good source of protein, iron, and thiamine.

☐ 3½ ounces, dry = 360 calories

Basic Preparation—Rinse dry chick-peas in cold water. Place in saucepan with water to cover. Bring to a boil. Remove from heat and soak for 1 hour. Add 1 teaspoon salt for each cup of chick-peas. Bring to a boil again, then simmer, covered, for about 2 hours, or until tender, adding more water if necessary. Drain well and cool.

SPANISH CHICK-PEA SOUP

1¾ cups chick-peas, washed
  and drained
4 cups water
1 garlic clove, minced
2 onions, chopped
1 green pepper, chopped
1 tablespoon cooking oil
4 cups ham broth
1 large potato, diced
⅓ cup diced ham
½ pound chorizos (Spanish sausages)
  or frankfurters
  Salt and cayenne

Soak peas overnight in water; do not drain. Cook garlic, onions, and green pepper in oil in heavy kettle for about 5 minutes; do not brown. Add soaked undrained chick-peas and ham broth; simmer for about 1½ hours, until chick-peas are just tender. Add potato, ham, and sliced *chorizos;* cook for about 30 minutes, until potato is tender. Season to taste with salt and cayenne. Makes about 2 quarts or 8 to 10 servings.

ITALIAN CHICK-PEA SALAD

Drain a can of chick-peas. Marinate for 1 hour in well-seasoned French dressing. Before serving, pour off excess dressing and sprinkle thickly with chopped parsley.
Note: Serve this salad instead of potatoes with fish or meat.

MEXICAN CHICK-PEA SALAD

2 cups cooked or canned chick-peas,
  drained
1 canned green chili, chopped
½ medium green pepper, chopped
1 pimiento, chopped
1 cup diced celery
2 tablespoons capers
¼ cup chopped green onions and tops
¼ cup olive oil
2 tablespoons vinegar
  Salt and pepper
  Salad greens

Mix first 7 ingredients. Add oil and vinegar and toss lightly. Season to taste with salt and pepper and serve on greens. Makes 4 servings.

CHICORY (Succory)—This salad green is a member of the endive family, with finely cut, feathery leaves that have dark green edges and almost white centers. It originated in Europe but was naturalized in America and has been a farm crop here since the turn of the century. Its slightly bitter flavor is a welcome addition to salads. In France it is also eaten braised.

Some varieties of chicory are cultivated for their roots, which are roasted, then ground, and added to certain coffees as stretchers. This is a French and Creole practice, followed in this country chiefly in Louisiana. This coffee is marketed as New Orleans coffee.

Availability—Fresh chicory is available throughout the year.

Roasted chicory is available in packages and in bulk. It can be added to coffee in any quantity desired.

Purchasing Guide—Choose crisp, fresh greens that are tender and bright in color. Fresh chicory is usually sold by weight.

Storage—Place unwashed greens in a tightly covered container in the refrigerator and wash as needed. Plan to use within two days.

Store roasted chicory in a tightly covered jar or canister, as it tends to absorb moisture.

Nutritive Food Values—An excellent source of vitamin A.

☐ 3½ ounces, raw = 20 calories

Basic Preparation—Trim and wash greens thoroughly, discarding wilted or discolored leaves. Dry well and chill before serving.

PANNED CHICORY

Cook 2 quarts (about 2 pounds before chopping) finely chopped chicory in 2 tablespoons bacon fat, butter, or margarine in a large heavy saucepan for 3 to 5 minutes, stirring constantly. Season to taste. Makes 4 servings.

CHIFFON—The word is used to describe both a cake and a pie, each of which, not surprisingly, is light-textured and fluffy. Each is also a comparative newcomer to cookery. A professional baker invented chiffon pie in the early 1920's. It was so fluffy with beaten egg whites that his mother said it reminded her of a pile of chiffon. It was so named. This pie is always served chilled.

The cake was invented by another professional baker in the 1940's, and the novelty of it was that it used a liquid shortening, cooking oil, instead of the usual solid shortenings.

CHOCOLATE CHIFFON PIE

    2 ounces (2 squares) unsweetened
        chocolate
    ½ cup sugar
    ¼ teaspoon salt
    1 cup milk
    1 envelope unflavored gelatin
    ¼ cup cold water
    3 eggs, separated
    ½ teaspoon vanilla extract
        9-inch pie shell, baked

Combine chocolate, sugar, salt, and milk in top part of double boiler; heat. When chocolate is melted, beat with rotary beater until blended. Add gelatin soaked in water; stir until dissolved. Add gradually to beaten egg yolks, stirring constantly. Return to heat; cook for 2 minutes. Add vanilla; mix well; chill. When slightly thickened, beat with rotary beater until foamy. Fold into stiffly beaten egg whites. Pour into cooled pie shell; chill. Makes 6 to 8 servings.

CHIFFON CAKE

    1 cup egg whites (about 7 or 8)
    ½ teaspoon cream of tartar
    2¼ cups sifted cake flour
    1½ cups sugar
    3 teaspoons baking powder
    1 teaspoon salt
    ½ cup cooking oil
    5 egg yolks
    ¼ cup cold water
    ½ cup milk
    2 teaspoons vanilla extract
    2 teaspoons grated lemon rind

In a large mixing bowl beat egg whites until foamy; add cream of tartar and beat until whites are stiff but not dry. In a second bowl sift together next 4 ingredients. Make a well, add oil, egg yolks, water, milk, vanilla, and lemon rind. Beat until smooth. Pour egg-yolk mixture over egg whites gradually, gently folding in until blended. Pour into ungreased 10-inch tube pan. Bake in preheated slow oven (325°F.) for 55 minutes, then at moderate (350°F.) for 20 minutes. Invert pan on cake rack; let stand until cold. Remove from pan and frost as desired. Makes 10 to 12 servings.

CHIFFONADE—Literally translated, this French term means "made of rags." In French culinary usage, it stands for vegetables cut into fine strips or ribbons,

and, more specifically, for lettuce and sorrel cut into shreds and cooked in butter or cream. Most chiffonades are used as garnish for soups.

In America, chiffonade is a salad dressing in which shredded vegetables and hard-cooked eggs are added to a standard French dressing.

CHIFFONADE DRESSING

    ⅔ cup French dressing
    1 hard-cooked egg, chopped
    2 tablespoons strips of cooked beet
    2 tablespoons strips of green pepper
    2 tablespoons chopped parsley
    2 teaspoons chopped chives or
        green onions
    1 teaspoon chopped onion

Combine all ingredients and mix thoroughly. Store in covered jar. Shake jar before using. Makes about 1⅓ cups dressing.

CHILDREN'S FOOD—For the food of very young children, consult your doctor, or special literature recommended by him. The food of older children is generally quite a different matter, and the article that follows may prove helpful.

The Cook Strikes Back
by Mary W. Littell

There are many hazards involved in being a mother, but falling into the pit of catering to children's eating preferences can be the deadliest one of them all. The worst part is that everything creeps up on you so gradually that before you know it, you have a Situation.

In the beginning of your life with children you can personally stuff your youngster with what's good for him. He eats it or else. Then when he is able to wield his own spoon, you can withhold his dessert if he refuses his carrots. But what can one do when he is old enough to sneak goodies after school? With appetite gone, he can sit at the dinner table and let his nonfavorite foods congeal on his plate.

This poses a problem. He says he isn't hungry and sometimes, I suppose, he isn't. But if he isn't hungry because he is full of candy bars, your former good eater will become a picker. A picker is a child who looks over the menu and eats only what he likes. There are two varieties of pickers: the natural-born type and the ones who acquire the habit. The natural-born picker is a hopeless case, I think, but there is still hope for those who only acquire the habit.

If you have but one child perhaps you can keep up with his whims. You know he doesn't like turnips, bacon, or stewed tomatoes, to take a for instance. So you try to serve other items just as good for him that he does like, such as Lima beans, ham, or tomato slices. This is easy. But if you have more than one child, trying to keep up with each one's likes and dislikes can make a mumbling wreck out of a healthy mother in no time at all.

With our three children, this subtle elimination of first one food and then another, by first one child and then another, began in such an insidious way that before I knew it I was knee-deep in their likes and dislikes.

If I put dinner on the table in bowls and platters, then I had to hover like Mother Hen while each child helped himself. If I didn't, he was likely to give himself nothing but potatoes or nothing but meat. If I served at the table, each spoonful I dished out was argued over. "That's too much." "You didn't give me enough." "Don't give me any of that stuff." To prevent the dinner hour from becoming a field of battle where my will power was put to the test each night, I decided to fix everyone's plate in the kitchen and present the accomplished fact to my merry dinner companions.

Since our children are old enough to express themselves, and well, I tried to remember as I served each plate: John doesn't like chicken, so he gets a small piece; Susan doesn't like mashed potatoes, so a small serving for her; Stephen doesn't like green beans, just a few beans on his plate.

On the other hand, I tried to keep in mind, John loves mashed potatoes, he gets a large portion; Stephen loves ham, two slices for him; and Susan adores Lima beans, so I give her a big spoonful.

We rocked along like this for quite a while because I have a very good memory. But the idea became contagious. The likes and dislikes became so many and varied and violent that once, when I put a large mound of mashed potatoes on Susan's plate and she protested, I found myself saying, "Oh, I'm sorry. I forgot you are the one who doesn't like them." You see how sinister this Motherhood can become? Apologizing to a five-year-old for giving her good food to eat!

Then one night I hit upon a solution and, believe me, if you can stand a period of utter chaos (I recommend waiting until your husband is out of town), it will work. I was about to put a pork chop on someone's plate when all of a sudden my mind went blank. It was quite the biggest and juiciest of the lot and very tasty-looking. For the moment

I couldn't remember who it was that liked pork chops. Was it John, Stephen, or Susan? And, just as suddenly, I didn't care. I'd spent a considerable part of my day buying the food, preparing it, cooking it, and now serving it. I just didn't give a popsicle who wanted what any more.

With a gleam in my eye, I dished up the plates to suit myself. The resulting din was deafening.

"You gave me too many potatoes. I hate mashed potatoes."

"I'm the one who likes corn. You didn't give me hardly any."

"How come I got such a little piece of meat? I love pork chops."

I think you get the idea. Whatever they had said they didn't like, they got, in quantity. Whatever they liked, they got only a scant helping of on their plates. Mothers can be pretty tricky too, you know, if pushed far enough. And I was at the brink.

I sat and let the roars go over my head while calmly eating my own dinner. When each of the small explosions had died down enough so that I could be heard, I pointed out that there had been a change in the kitchen. The cook was on strike. And since help is hard to get these days, they were stuck with their balky chef.

From now on, I announced, I was through trying to remember each one's little peccadilloes. There was more of everything for those who felt cheated, and those who felt they had got too much of some one food had jolly well better eat it. I had given up trying to remember their individual tastes.

They stared at me as if they had fallen among the enemy instead of their ever-loving mother. They were incredulous for days. The grumbling I bore in stoic silence. Since all our children were forcibly enrolled, years ago, in the Clean Plate Club (I'm President), they still feel honor-bound to eat what is on their plates, and they had some tough nights. They still do.

Some of the nose-holding and more ungentlemanly and unladylike noises denoting distaste had to be dealt with swiftly and firmly. Sometimes my husband and I ended up eating alone. And I wouldn't say it was happy times around the old ranch for a while.

But once they accepted their new life and their formidable new cook, the air cleared and we got back to normal as the worst complaints dropped off.

I still sit fascinated and watch as one child eats the food he dislikes first, and in large mouthfuls. That done, he enjoys his dinner. The other boy saves his least-liked food until last and watches me with hawklike eyes, never giving up hope that maybe this time I won't notice

that he hasn't yet eaten it. And the youngest child says in a loud voice, "Well, here goes," so that we will all watch her struggle with her pet dislike and then give her the equivalent of a good-conduct medal.

But we are making headway. Last week one puzzled youngster said, "Lima beans aren't so bad, are they?" as he ate a normal-size portion. The oldest youngster, when pressed, said he thought if he lived long enough he *might* get so he liked broccoli. And best of all was the youngest who ate all her portion of lamb under the impression that it was roast beef, which she loves. She never knew until she had finished that she had gobbled up the meat she always claimed she "hated."

I feel emancipated too, as I no longer try to remember who likes what or why. With gay abandon, I serve up the plates to look attractive and well balanced as to both variety and amount.

I cherish the hope that when our three children grow up and get invited out to dinner parties, they won't run across foods they have never tasted before and will therefore shun. And I hope they will have come to the conclusion that it isn't considered quite chic to put one pea or one string bean on their plates or a piece of meat so small you have to look twice to see it.

I know that there are some foods that some of them will never clap their hands over (frankly, I can't stand parsnips). But if they have learned enough so that every time certain foods appear on their horizons they can eat a small portion without gagging, washing it down with water, or going "Ugh!" this cook feels that it will have been worth the trouble.

CHILI (Capsicum frutescens)—A tropical American plant from whose small elongated pods, or peppers, we get cayenne (red) pepper and hot pepper sauce.

Chili powder is a blend of dried ground chili pepper pods, which may or may not contain other powdered herbs and spices. Our chili powder comes from a group of small, very hot Mexican chilies, ground and mixed with a larger, sweeter variety of Mexican chilies. The exact flavor and aroma depends upon the manufacturer of the particular blend. Most blends contain some ground cumin-seed and oregano. In addition garlic, cloves, or allspice may be used. Americans prefer a milder blend to the one used in Mexican and Spanish cuisines.

Chili powder is available in jars and shaker-top cans. It is a delightful seasoning in eggs, meat marinades, Spanish rice, sauces, and soups, with shellfish and sweet vegetables or, combined with butter and salt, on corn-on-the-cob.

CHILI POPCORN

Pop ½ cup shelled popcorn in a popcorn popper or covered 10-inch skillet. Turn popped corn into a large bowl. Melt 2 tablespoons butter or margarine and mix with 1½ teaspoons chili powder. Pour over hot popped corn. Mix well, but lightly. Makes 4 cups.

CHILI CHEESE FINGERS

Blend ½ cup grated sharp Cheddar cheese with ¼ cup butter or margarine and 1 teaspoon chili powder. Trim crusts from 8 slices of bread and toast only on one side. Spread untoasted side with chili-cheese mixture. Cut each into 4 fingers. Arrange on cookie sheet. Place under broiler to brown. Makes 32 fingers.

CHILI CON CARNE—A dish that is as old as the Aztec civilization in Mexico where it originated. "Chili with meat" is the literal translation of the Spanish words. The chili is minced red chili peppers or powder; the meat is beef; and another important ingredient is generally beans. Popular today in our Southwest, where Mexican influence in cookery is strong, it is also a favorite dish throughout the country because it is available canned, with or without beans.

CHILI CON CARNE
(Mild)

    ¾ pound chopped beef
    1 garlic clove, minced
    3 small onions, sliced
    2⅓ cups (one 1-pound, 3-ounce can)
         tomatoes
    1 teaspoon salt
    2 teaspoons chili powder
    4 cups (two 1-pound cans)
         red kidney beans

Combine first 3 ingredients in a large skillet and fry slowly for about 10 minutes. Add remaining ingredients and simmer for 10 minutes longer. Serve with crackers and shredded lettuce. Serves 4.

CHILI CON CARNE
(Hot)

    1 pound red, pink, or pinto beans,
         washed and drained
    6 cups water
    ⅓ cup chopped beef suet
    2 onions, chopped
    1 garlic clove, minced
    2 pounds lean beef, coarsely ground
    3 teaspoons salt
    ¼ teaspoon pepper
    1 to 3 teaspoons chili powder
    ¼ teaspoon crushed red pepper
    1 teaspoon paprika
    4 cups tomato juice

Cover beans with the water, bring to boil, and boil for 2 minutes. Let stand for 1 hour. Cover and simmer until tender, about 2 hours. Render beef fat in skillet, add onions and garlic, and cook until golden. Add meat; cook until meat separates and browns, stirring with fork. Add with remaining ingredients to beans. Simmer, uncovered, for about 1½ hours, stirring occasionally. Makes 8 servings.

Chili con Carne (Hot)

CHILI SAUCE

CHILI CON CARNE
(Heavy)

1 cup dried pinto or red beans,
  washed and drained
4 cups water
3 pounds lean beef
¼ cup olive oil
1 bay leaf
2 tablespoons chili powder
1 tablespoon salt
4 garlic cloves, minced
1 teaspoon each ground cuminseed
  and oregano
3 tablespoons paprika
3 tablespoons cornmeal
1 tablespoon all-purpose flour

Cover beans with the water, bring to boil, and boil for 2 minutes. Cover pan and let stand for 1 hour; then cook until tender. Drain and reserve liquid. Cut meat into ½-inch cubes and sear in hot oil. Add enough water to bean liquid to make 6 cups. Add to meat, cover pan, bring to boil, and simmer for 1 hour. Add bay leaf and next 6 ingredients. Simmer for 30 minutes. Blend cornmeal, flour, and cold water to make a paste. Stir into mixture; simmer for 5 minutes. Add beans and heat. Makes 6 servings.

CHILI SAUCE—This highly spiced sauce is made of tomatoes, onions, and chili peppers or powder. It is a Mexican staple and it adds flavor to bland food. It can be made at home or bought in bottles.

HOMEMADE CHILI SAUCE

2 tablespoons cooking oil
2 tablespoons all-purpose flour
1½ teaspoons chili powder
1 cup (8-ounce can) Spanish-type
  tomato sauce
2 tablespoons instant minced onion
¼ teaspoon instant minced garlic
1 teaspoon vinegar
1¼ cups (10½ ounce can) beef bouillon
½ teaspoon salt
¼ teaspoon pepper

Combine oil and flour in a 1-quart saucepan. Cook over low heat, stirring constantly, until flour is browned. Stir in remaining ingredients and blend until smooth. Simmer, stirring constantly, for 5 minutes, or until sauce is thickened. Makes 2 cups.

CHILL—To remove the heat from food or beverages by placing in a cold, but not freezing, temperature: in the refrigerator, on ice, or, as in the case of wine, in an ice and water pack. Chilling does not mean icing or freezing. Overchilling deprives most foods of flavor, especially seafood, salads, and fruits.

Yang Jo Kuo (Chafing Dish Lamb)

The Art of Chinese Cookery
by Mimi Ouei

Lin Yutang declares that if there is anything the Chinese are serious about, it is food. Eating is truly one of the joys of life. It was not unusual for a great poet, scholar, artist, or dramatist to write on cookery, for it also was a most respected art. Lin Yutang proves himself equally at home writing an article on Chinese cooking as he does writing on the aesthetics of Chinese calligraphy.

For centuries the fascinations of philosophical thinking have occupied the Chinese scholar, and philosophy has also had its influence upon the daily life of

Ch'ao Lung Hsia (Lobster Cantonese)

T'ang Ts'u Niu Ju Wan (Sweet-and-Sour Beef Balls)

La Chiso Ch'ao Chi
(Chicken Sautéed with Peppers)

Hung Shao Chu-Tzu (Red-Cooked Pork Shoulder)

the Chinese. This life, in order to be properly lived, must be enjoyed in a civilized manner. Confucius, a lover of good food, taught that good taste in food was to be cultivated as a part of artistic living. The Chinese scholar became a gourmet as well. Many table customs and practices of etiquette date back thousands of years to Confucius. Cooking became appreciated as an art in which the chef, not unlike a great French chef, became free to create. The philosophical teachings of Taoism, following the teachings of Lao-tse, also had their impact

upon Chinese cooking. The nourishment of the body for a happier and longer life was considered most important, which in turn gave impetus to the development of hygienic food. The great Chinese philosophers set about improving the situation described in an old Chinese proverb that bemoaned, "All man's diseases enter his mouth and all his mistakes fly out of it."

It is difficult to appreciate fully Chinese cooking without understanding the carefully sought-after relationships between the various ingredients and condi-

ments. It is the art of mixture that is the central principle around which the culinary arts of China were built. Chinese philosophy and art depend upon harmony; it is the unifying principle unto which all others are bound. Thus, it is the *harmonious* mixture in dishes and not a confusion of conflicting elements that is desired. The subtle combinations that are created more fully please the taste experience. "There is no man who does not eat and drink," decried Confucius, "but there are few who appreciate taste." This appreciation is derived from experiencing the various relationships, such as sweet and sour, smooth and crunchy, hot and cold, salty and bland. Great importance was given to aroma and visual appeal.

The preparation of Chinese food takes great care and in most cases a longer time than does the actual cooking. The technique of cutting is of prime importance. Many dissimilar ingredients blend into surprising harmony when cut to uniform size and shape. There is no main course, for there is interest in variety. The greater the occasion, the larger the number of dishes. A large banquet may consist of as many as twenty dishes, but a mouthful of some, or perhaps four or five of others, is all that is expected of the polite guest.

Pork is the primary meat of the Chinese. It is eaten almost daily in well-to-do households. For centuries the agrarian output of China depended upon the strong back of the water buffalo (the Chinese "cow") to plow the fields. It is understandable that they did not eat their dependable worker. Buddhism brought other reasons for leaving the sacred cow alone. Duck and chicken are also important in Chinese cookery; in fact, the Chinese pride themselves on the superior flavor of their chickens.

Buddhism not only held the cow as sacrosanct but respected all living things. This gave impetus to the highly skilled vegetable cookery in China. Soup is another dish in which the Chinese take great delight. Sometimes a light soup is served between courses to contrast with a previously served salty or dry dish.

Rice in China is not only the staple food, but the symbol of life and fertility. Hence at Chinese weddings, as well as our own, the custom of throwing rice is a wish that the couple be blessed with long life and many children. The poor in China are likely to subsist on a large quantity of rice, fewer vegetables, and even less meat.

SCHOOLS OF CHINESE COOKING

In general, there were five distinct types of cuisine developed through the centuries, namely, Canton, Fukien, Shantung, Szechwan, and Honan.

The Canton School—The Canton school of cooking is the best known outside of China, for the Cantonese were the travelers and the emigrants. Canton became rich after her doors were opened to foreign trade. With wealth came leisure and the desire for good food, and with its indulgence, a cuisine characterized by sautéing, roasting, and grilling was developed. Fried rice and fried noodles are also the specialties of this school.

The Fukien School—We from Fukien think that we have the best cuisine in China. There are not many examples of this type of cooking in the United States because the Fukienese, who were the sailors of China, settled in Thailand, Malaya, and other parts of Southeast Asia. This cuisine is characterized by all-around cooking, although many complain that too many soupy dishes are included.

The Shantung School—Shantung, besides having produced philosophers, has also produced good cooking. As Peking is so near, many people from Shantung migrated to the big city and took their cooking with them. So, although the dishes may have been perfected in Peking, they are native to Shantung. The foods in the northern part of the country are lighter than those of the south. Much of it is cooked in wine sauce and very little sautéing is done.

The Szechwan School—Till Chungking became a temporary capital, Szechwan, in the far west, had been left to her own devices. In summer it is terribly hot, and like all people who live in hot climates, the Szechwanese had developed a hot, very highly seasoned cuisine. This is the main characteristic of this school of cooking.

The Honan School—The capital of Honan was once the capital of China, and with the wealthier people flocking to the court, good cooking was in demand. Honan is the home of the sweet-and-sour dishes.

METHODS OF CHINESE COOKING

There are five main methods of preparing food in the Chinese manner. They are sautéing, red cooking (a kind of braising or stewing with soy sauce, a method known as *hung shao*, deep frying, steaming, and roasting which includes barbecuing, or grilling.

Sautéing—Of the five, the most characteristic method is sautéing. It is the most difficult, but it is worthwhile to master the secret of this method, for it is most versatile. Tenderness is all important. With meat, use lean fillet. Be sure that the meat is cut across the grain into the size desired. It is easier to cut the meat finely when it is frozen slightly. If the meat is not as thin as you would like it, pound it with a cleaver. If chicken is your choice, use the breast without the skin. Soak the slices in cold water with a little salt.

It is essential that everything be prepared before you start cooking because ingredients are put in seconds apart, and you do not have time to slice and cut, say, your gingerroot or bamboo shoots when you need them. Sliced vegetables, meat, and other ingredients should be set out on separate plates and within easy reach.

The straight-cutting method is most suitable for tender vegetables, for example, green onions. For harder vegetables, the diagonal method of slicing is better. A larger area cut across the grain will be exposed to the heat and to the absorption of the seasonings and juices.

Cutting is most important because it determines the appearance of the dish and the length of time it should be cooked. There are various forms of cutting meat: cut into fairly large pieces, cut into cubes of about 1½ inches, which are suitable for stewing and braising, or sliced, shredded, diced, or minced, for sautéing. A Chinese cook prefers to mince his meat with a cleaver rather than with a grinder.

Food, when cut into small sizes, cooks quickly and is easy to season. These two principles account for the distinctive taste of Chinese food. All Chinese food is cooked thoroughly yet remains wholesome. Very little water is added in the cooking, since the method of quick-frying brings out the natural juices of the food. This liquid makes enough sauce for the dish and is very tasty. Nothing is more abhorrent to a gourmet than to find a dish slopped over with a sauce composed of water and a thickening agent.

The liquid, which includes soy sauce, wine, and other juices accumulated during cooking, may be thickened with cornstarch just before serving, but this is not necessary and often not desirable. Take the pan off the heat just as the vegetable is turning a darker green and the meat still undercooked, as the food will continue to cook in the hot pan when off the heat. High heat is essential in sautéing.

Red cooking—Red cooking is a type of stewing with soy sauce known as *hung shao*. *Hung* means red and the cooking method is so called because soy sauce gives the juice a reddish color. Very often it is necessary to brown the meat first. Pork shoulder, stew beef, chicken, and duck are well suited to the *hung shao* method.

Deep frying—Deep frying is another common way of cooking in China. Cut the meat into medium-size pieces, marinate it in sherry, soy sauce, and other seasonings for about half an hour, and then fry it in deep fat. Pieces of meat may be dipped into a mixture of egg and flour and then deep fried and served with pepper and salt.

Steaming—Steaming is a favorite method of cooking à la chinoise. There are two kinds, wet steaming and dry. Western cooks usually employ the method of dry steaming in a double boiler in which the steam never actually touches the food. Chinese cooks wet-steam their food and that is why they have tiers of perforated partitions in the steamers.

Roasting—The mode of cooking used least in China is roasting, barbecuing, or grilling. This is due to the fact that fuel is expensive and hard to get. The typical Chinese oven for roasting is open and cooking is usually done on a spit. This is a very familiar sight to Americans today, with their outdoor barbecues and rotisseries.

Now, a few general hints: Everything, of course, has to be cleaned. Dried ingredients should be soaked in cold water until they soften, then cleaned and resoaked in hot water until very soft. When soft, remove from the liquid and drain and cut as directed.

Cooking time is given in the recipes, but the degree of heat is the controlling factor, so it is most important to keep your eye on the food. With practice, the experienced cook will be able to judge when a dish is ready. As a general rule, it is better to undercook than overcook, that is, everything except pork.

It is difficult to say just how many people a given recipe will serve. In Chinese meals, if there are more people, more dishes are prepared instead of making a dish larger. Most of the recipes given here will produce enough for four people when four dishes and a soup are served. However, the number of servings has been indicated for each recipe if you wish to use it American-style for a main dish.

Peanut oil or other cooking oil can be used interchangeably in all recipes.

CH'AO LUNG HSIA
(Lobster Cantonese)
Canton School

- 2 1-pound lobsters
- ½ pound lean pork
- 4 scallions, minced fine
- 1½ teaspoons salt
- 1 teaspoon pepper
- ¼ cup cooking oil
- 1 celery stalk, finely sliced
- 1 cup chicken bouillon
- 2 eggs

Thickening

- 2½ tablespoons all-purpose flour mixed with 2 teaspoons soy sauce
- ¼ cup lobster liquid (add water to make up the amount, if not enough)

Split lobster lengthwise and pick off broken shells. Cut off legs and claws with poultry shears. Discard very small legs and wash large legs and claws. Cut them at the joints with shears, and crack them well enough with a nutcracker so that meat can be extracted easily. Cut lobster in the shells into 1½-inch sections. Put all in a large bowl and save the lobster liquid. Mince pork and add the scallions, ½ teaspoon salt, and pep-

per. Heat a deep frying pan with the oil and remaining salt; when it is very hot, sauté pork and celery for 1 minute. Add lobster and claws and sauté for ½ minute; then slowly add bouillon and bring to a boil. Cover pan, reduce heat, and cook for 10 minutes, turning the lobster once. Add thickening to pan and simmer for 4 minutes. Beat eggs well and pour over lobster. After 1 minute, turn off heat. Pour mixture into a large hot bowl and serve immediately. Makes 2 servings.

SSU CHI TOU NIU JU
(Beef with Green Beans)
Canton School

- ½ pound top round of beef, thinly sliced
- ½ pound green beans
- 1½ cups boiling water
- 2 tablespoons cooking oil

Marinade

- 2 tablespoons soy sauce
- 1 teaspoon sugar
- 1 tablespoon cornstarch
- ½ teaspoon salt
- 1 tablespoon sherry

Coat sliced beef with marinating mixture and let it stand for 10 minutes. Trim beans and cut into 2-inch lengths. Pour boiling water over them; remove beans immediately and drain, but reserve ¼ cup of this water for later use. Heat oil in skillet; when it is hot, add meat and sauté for 20 seconds. Add beans and stir for another 20 to 30 seconds; then add reserved bean water to mixture. Cover, turn down heat, and simmer for 1 minute. Serve on a shallow dish immediately. Makes 2 servings.

HUNG SHAO NIU NAN
(Red-Cooked Shin of Beef)
Fukien School

- 2 tablespoons cooking oil
- 2 pounds shin of beef
- ⅛ teaspoon pepper
- 2 slices of fresh gingerroot
- 1 garlic clove
- 1 scallion, halved
- 1 teaspoon salt
- 2 teaspoons sugar
- ¼ cup soy sauce
- 1 teaspoon sesame-seed oil
- 1 tablespoon sherry
- Enough water to cover meat

Heat oil in a frying pan; when it is hot, add the meat and brown on both sides. Add pepper, gingerroot, garlic, and scallion. Transfer meat mixture to a saucepan, add salt and sugar, and pour soy sauce, sesame-seed oil, and sherry over it. Add enough boiling water to cover meat. Bring liquid to a boil, cover, and turn down heat. Simmer slowly for

2½ hours. Remove meat and cut into slices ¼ inch thick; arrange on a shallow dish. Pour gravy over it and serve at once. Makes 4 servings.

T'ANG TS'U NIU JU WAN
(Sweet-and-Sour Beef Balls)
Honan School

- 1 egg
- 2 tablespoons all-purpose flour
- ½ teaspoon salt
- ⅛ teaspoon pepper
- 1 pound beef, finely minced
- ½ cup cooking oil
- 1½ teaspoons salt
- ⅓ cup chicken bouillon
- 1 slice of canned pineapple, cut into 8 chunks
- 1 pound spinach

Sauce

- 2 teaspoons cornstarch
- 2 teaspoons soy sauce
- ½ cup vinegar
- ½ cup sugar
- ½ cup chicken bouillon

Make a batter of first 4 ingredients. Shape meat into balls the size of a walnut and dip them into batter. Heat oil in a frying pan and 1½ teaspoons salt; when very hot, place balls in the pan and fry until browned on all sides. Remove to a shallow serving bowl and keep hot. Drain oil from pan except for 1 tablespoon; add bouillon and pineapple. Heat thoroughly for about 3 minutes over low heat. Blend ingredients for sauce and add to the pan. Stir constantly until thickened. Cook spinach and drain; put in a dish. Arrange meatballs on spinach and pour the sauce over them. Makes 4 servings.

TUNG SUN CH'AO JO
(Pork with Bamboo Shoots)
Canton School

- ¼ cup cooking oil
- 2 cups sliced bamboo shoots
- ½ pound pork, thinly sliced
- ¼ cup water

Marinade

- 2 tablespoons soy sauce
- ½ teaspoon salt
- 2 tablespoons sherry
- 1 tablespoon cornstarch

Heat 2 tablespoons oil in a frying pan; when it is hot, add bamboo shoots and sauté for 2 minutes. Remove from pan. Mix ingredients for marinade and coat sliced pork with this mixture. Reheat pan with remaining oil and sauté pork for about 5 minutes. Add bamboo shoots and the water and bring to a boil. Simmer for 1 minute, stirring all the time. Serve very hot in a shallow dish. Makes 4 servings.

HUNG SHAO CHU-TZU
(Red-Cooked Pork Shoulder)
Fukien School

One 6-pound pork shoulder
2 cups water
¼ cup sherry
1 cup soy sauce
4 slices of preserved gingerroot
4 scallions
1 tablespoon sugar
Hot cooked rice

Wash pork well and pull off any hairs there may be on the skin. Place the meat, skin side up, in a heavy saucepan with the water. Turn heat high; when water boils, pour the sherry over pork, then the soy sauce. Place gingerroot and scallions in the liquid. Cover pork, lower heat, and simmer for 1 hour. Turn the meat and simmer for another hour. Turn the meat again, add sugar, and cook for 30 minutes longer. The meat should now be tender enough to give way with chopsticks. Serve on a bed of rice in a deep bowl with the gravy poured over it. Makes 6 servings.

T'ANG TS'U CHU JO
(Sweet-and-Sour Pork)
Honan School

Oil for deep frying

Batter
1 egg
½ cup all-purpose flour
½ teaspoon salt
¼ cup water

1 pound pork shoulder, cut into ¾-inch cubes

Sauce
1 cup pineapple cubes
1 green pepper, cut into squares
½ cup vinegar
¼ cup firmly packed brown sugar
¾ cup water
1 tablespoon molasses

Thickening
2 tablespoons cornstarch
¼ cup water

Heat oil in a deep frying pan. Mix the batter. Dip pork cubes into batter and drop into the boiling oil. When cubes brown, remove them and drain on absorbent paper. Mix ingredients for the sauce in a pan and bring slowly to a boil, stirring constantly. Pour thickening into the sauce; when sauce becomes thick and smooth, add meat and mix well. When very hot, serve at once. Makes 4 servings.

YANG JO KUO
(Chafing-Dish Lamb)
Shantung School

Condiment Sauce
½ cup soy sauce
½ cup vinegar
½ cup sherry
½ cup hot pepper sauce
½ cup sesame paste or peanut butter
1 cup chopped scallions

2 pounds lamb tenderloin or boneless leg of lamb
¼ pound salted cabbage
1½ pounds celery cabbage
½ pound egg noodles
¼ pound pea starch vermicelli
6 cups chicken bouillon

Combine ingredients for Condiment Sauce. Cut lamb into very thin slices and arrange on a plate. Cut salted cabbage into small pieces; shred celery cabbage into 1½-inch pieces. Boil noodles for about 10 minutes and drain them very dry. Boil vermicelli for about 30 minutes and let it soak in the hot water until it is needed. Arrange all these ingredients attractively on separate dishes and place around the chafing dish on the table. Heat bouillon and pour half into chafing dish and half into a bowl on the table for replenishing. Add vegetables and some slices of meat to chafing dish and cook for five minutes. The noodles and vermicelli are added to chafing dish halfway through the meal. Individual rice bowls should be served to each diner with enough condiment sauce to coat easily each slice of meat. A bowl of noodles or vermicelli will nicely finish the meal. Makes 6 to 8 servings.

Note: Salted cabbage, egg noodles, and pea starch vermicelli are Chinese specialty items. Sesame paste can also be bought in stores catering to people of near-eastern origin.

YANG JO KAO (Jellied Lamb)
Fukien School

4 pounds shoulder of lamb
2 tablespoons sherry
½ cup soy sauce
1 teaspoon sugar
½ teaspoon salt
3 green onions
2 cups boiling water

Cut off and discard all fat from the meat, but be sure to keep all the bones, for this is where the gelatin will come from. Place meat and bones in a saucepan over high heat. Add sherry, soy sauce, sugar, and salt, and bring to a boil. Cut green onions into 1½-inch pieces and add to saucepan. Add water slowly; when it comes to a boil, turn heat low and simmer for 3 hours. Re-

move from heat and cool. Remove all the bones and discard. Transfer meat and liquid to a loaf pan (9 x 5 x 3 inches). When liquid is cold, skim the oil which floats on top and discard. Place pan in refrigerator overnight. Cut into ½-inch slices and serve cold. Makes 8 servings.

Note: Should the liquid not gel because of inadequate gelatinous stuff in the bones, melt 1 envelope unflavored gelatin in 2 cups hot liquid, mix well, and pour over meat. Put in the coldest part of refrigerator; it should gel in 2 or 3 hours.

CHA CHI (Deep-Fried Chicken)
Fukien School

1 broiling chicken (2 pounds)
Oil for deep frying
1 slice of fresh gingerroot
1 green onion, cut into 1-inch pieces

Marinade
1 tablespoon each of sherry and cornstarch
5 teaspoons soy sauce

Place chicken in a saucepan and add enough water to cover. Bring to a boil, turn down heat, and simmer for about 1 hour. Remove chicken from broth, bone it, cutting the meat into shreds about 2 inches long, and allow it to cool. Coat chicken with the marinade and allow it to stand for a few minutes. Heat a deep frying pan and add enough oil for deep frying. Add gingerroot and green onion. Fry the pieces of chicken in hot oil for about 1 minute, or until they become brown and crisp. Serve immediately. Makes 2 servings.

LA CHISO CH'AO CHI
(Chicken Sautéed with Peppers)
Szechwan School

1 teaspoon salt
1 teaspoon cornstarch
2 teaspoons sherry
¾ pound boned raw chicken, diced
½ cup cooking oil
1 tablespoon vegetable paste (Hoisin)
2 dried mushrooms, soaked and diced
2 small green peppers, diced
1 red chili, diced
1 bamboo shoot, diced

Mix first 3 ingredients. Add chicken and stir to coat well. Sauté chicken in ¼ cup oil for 2 minutes. Remove chicken. Add remaining oil to skillet. Add vegetable paste and sauté for 1 minute. Add mushrooms, pepper, chili, and bamboo shoot and sauté for 1 minute. Add chicken and heat, stirring. Serve at once. Makes 3 or 4 servings.

Note: This is a very spicy dish which must be eaten sparingly.

HSIEN CHI (Salted Chicken)
Canton School

1 broiling chicken (2½ pounds)
2 pounds salt

Wash chicken and dry it well with a cloth. Hang it in a draft to dry thoroughly. Put salt in a heavy pot big enough to hold the chicken, and heat the salt over medium heat. When salt is very hot, remove pot from heat and remove half of the salt. Make a hole in the center, but do not expose the bottom of the pan. Place the chicken, neck downward, in the salt and pack remaining salt around the chicken. Cover pan and cook over very low heat for about 1 hour. Remove chicken from salt, chop it Chinese style, and serve immediately as a side dish. This may also be served cold.

HSING JEN CHI TING
(Diced Chicken with Almonds)
Canton School

3 tablespoons cooking oil
1 teaspoon salt
2 cups diced raw chicken
2 tablespoons soy sauce
1 cup cooked peas
1 cup diced celery
½ cup canned mushrooms
1 cup boiling water
1 tablespoon cornstarch
¼ cup cold water
½ cup toasted almonds

Heat oil and salt in a deep frying pan; when very hot, add chicken and sauté for 3 minutes. Season with soy sauce and stir well. Add peas, celery, mushrooms, and boiling water very slowly; stir well. Cover pan and cook for about 4 minutes. Add cornstarch mixed with cold water, and lower heat. When the gravy thickens and becomes clear, remove from heat and transfer to a shallow plate. Sprinkle with toasted almonds. Serve very hot. Makes 4 servings.

WU HSIANG YA (Spiced Duck)
Fukien School

1 duck (5 pounds)
¾ cup sherry
¾ cup soy sauce
2 teaspoons powdered spices (use a combination of any five)

Clean duck well and remove all hairs Cut off tail and oil sacs and discard. Place in a large pan and pour sherry and soy sauce over it. Bring to a boil over high heat and brown each side of duck for 2 minutes. Coat duck well on each side with powdered spices; add enough water to half cover duck. Bring to a boil, cover, lower heat, and simmer for 1½ hours, turning every 20 minutes. Chop up duck Chinese style, or carve in the western way. Serve either hot or cold. Makes 4 servings.

Additional Chinese Recipes to Help You Plan a Complete Meal

CHI TAN T'ANG
(Chinese Egg-Drop Soup)

2 tablespoons cornstarch
6 cups chicken bouillon
2 tablespoons soy sauce
3 tablespoons vinegar
¼ teaspoon pepper
½ teaspoon monosodium glutamate
1 scallion, minced
3 eggs, beaten

In large saucepan mix cornstarch with small amount of cold bouillon. Add remaining bouillon and other ingredients except eggs. Bring to boil and simmer until clear, stirring occasionally. Gradually stir in eggs, season to taste, and serve at once. Makes about 1½ quarts.

CHU JOU PI CHI T'ANG
(Pork and Watercress Soup)

½ pound lean pork
4 cups water
4 cups concentrated chicken bouillon
1 small onion, thinly sliced
1 celery stalk, thinly sliced
1 teaspoon salt
¼ teaspoon pepper
1 cup firmly packed watercress, sliced

Cut pork into shreds, add to water, and simmer for 10 minutes. Add bouillon, onion, celery, salt, and pepper and simmer for 10 minutes more. Wash watercress and slice into 1-inch pieces. Add to soup and bring to a boil. Makes 1½ quarts, or 4 servings.

CHI TAN CHUAN
(Chinese Egg Rolls)

3 eggs
1 cup all-purpose flour
2 tablespoons cornstarch
2 cups water
½ teaspoon salt
1 cup chopped cooked shrimps, crabmeat, or lobster
½ cup finely diced celery
¼ cup each of minced cooked ham, water chestnuts, and bamboo shoots
1 tablespoon soy sauce
2 tablespoons minced green onion
Fat for frying

Beat 2 eggs slightly. Beat in flour, cornstarch, water, and salt. Heat a greased 7- or 8-inch skillet. Add 1 tablespoon batter and tip and tilt pan so that batter runs evenly over bottom of pan. Fry on one side only. Mix 1 egg and remaining ingredients except fat. Shape into finger-size rolls. Lay on cooked sides of pancakes and roll up, tucking in edges to seal in filling. A little uncooked batter can be used for sealing. Chill. Just before serving, brown in 2 inches of hot fat. Makes about 30.

RICE

To cook rice Chinese style, wash thoroughly and drain 1 cup long-grain rice. Put in a saucepan with water to cover rice 1 inch. Bring water to boil and boil over high heat, stirring occasionally, for 5 minutes, or until most of water boils off. Cover pan tightly and cook rice over low heat for 20 minutes more, or until just tender and dry.

CH'AO FAN
(Fried Rice)

No collection of Chinese recipes is complete without mention of Fried Rice, although it is difficult to give exact ingredients and quantities because Fried Rice is a versatile dish and an excellent way to use leftovers. Cooked meat and vegetables are combined with cooked rice, beaten eggs (sometimes the eggs are cooked first in a thin sheet and shredded), and seasonings, and stir-fried until thoroughly heated. For 4 cups cooked rice you will need 2 eggs, 1 cup each of shredded or diced meat and vegetables, and ¼ cup diced green onion. Pork, ham, chicken, beef, crabmeat, shrimps, or lobster can be used. Two or more vegetables can be combined to make the cup needed—mushrooms, water chestnuts, bamboo shoots, bean sprouts, or peas. Season with 2 tablespoons soy sauce and ½ teaspoon sugar. Makes 4 servings.
Note: For best results, start with well-chilled cooked rice.

CHA YUN T'UN
(Crisp Won Ton)

½ pound lean pork (chicken or shrimps can be substituted)
8 water chestnuts
2 green onions
2 teaspoons soy sauce
3 slices fresh gingerroot
1 teaspoon salt
Dash of pepper
½ teaspoon monosodium glutamate
Cha Yun T'un (Won Ton noodles)

Put pork, water chestnuts, and green onions in a chopping bowl and finely chop. Or force through food chopper, using fine blade. Mix with rest of ingredients except Won Ton noodles. Place a Won Ton noodle in front of you with one point facing you. Put 1 teaspoon filling on lower half of a Won Ton noodle and fold top half over, making a triangle. Moisten edges and press together, being sure you do not leave a

Chiang Lo Po
(Sweet-and-Sour Radishes)

Ch'ao Fan (Fried Rice)

Wu Dep Har (Butterfly Shrimps)

Niu Ju Chin Jow
(Beef with Green Peppers)

Cha Yun T'un
(Crisp Won Ton)

pocket of air inside. Now cross the right and left points by bringing them together on the fold opposite the point toward you. Moisten and press together. Fry in hot deep oil (375°F. on a frying thermometer) until brown. Serve as an appetizer. Or cook in chicken bouillon for soup garnish. Makes 36.

Won Ton Noodles

1½ cups sifted flour
1 teaspoon salt
1 egg
3 tablespoons water (about)
Cornstarch

Sift flour and salt into a bowl. Beat egg with a fork, add water, and add to flour. Work into a dough, adding more water if necessary. Turn out on a floured board and knead until smooth. Cover with a damp paper towel; let rest for 30 minutes. Rub a board with cornstarch; roll out dough very thin. Cut into 2½-inch squares.

CH'AO TAN
(Eggs, Cantonese Style)

6 eggs
½ teaspoon salt
½ teaspoon soy sauce
1 cup thinly sliced celery
1 cup chopped canned bean sprouts
½ cup chopped scallions
2 tablespoons cooking oil

Beat eggs with salt and soy sauce. Add vegetables. Heat oil in skillet; pour in egg mixture and cook slowly until almost set. Cut into quarters and turn; cook for about 3 minutes. Makes 4 servings.

WU DEP HAR
(Butterfly Shrimps)

1 pound raw jumbo shrimps
3 tablespoons all-purpose flour
1½ tablespoons cornstarch
1 tablespoon white cornmeal
¾ teaspoon baking powder
¾ teaspoon salt
½ cup milk
Cooking oil
Barbecue Sauce

Peel shrimps, leaving tails on. Make a deep slit along the back to "butterfly" shrimps, removing black vein as you do so. Mix flour, cornstarch, cornmeal, baking powder, and salt. Beat in milk, making a thin batter. Dip each shrimp into batter and fry in hot deep oil (375°F. on a frying thermometer) until golden brown, 2 or 3 minutes. Serve with Barbecue Sauce. Makes 4 servings.

Barbecue Sauce

Heat ¼ cup soy sauce, 2 tablespoons each of honey and sherry, ½ teaspoon salt, ⅛ teaspoon pepper, and 1 minced garlic clove.

CH'AO HSIA TAN
(Shrimp Omelet)

½ pound raw shrimps
1 teaspoon cornstarch
1 teaspoon soy sauce
1 teaspoon sherry
3 slices of fresh gingerroot, minced

3 tablespoons cooking oil
6 eggs
1 teaspoon salt
Dash of pepper
¼ teaspoon monosodium glutamate

Shell shrimps and remove black vein. Mix cornstarch, soy sauce, sherry, and gingerroot. Add to shrimps and mix well. Heat 2 tablespoons oil in skillet and sauté shrimps, turning once, until shrimps turn pink. Lightly beat eggs with a fork and add salt, pepper, and monosodium glutamate. Pour over shrimps and cook until lightly browned on bottom. Loosen omelet and invert on plate. Heat remaining oil and carefully slide omelet back into pan. Lightly brown on the underside. Makes 4 servings.

HSIEH FU YUNG
(Crab Fu Yung)

1 cup crabmeat
1 cup bean sprouts
½ cup shredded onion
½ cup finely sliced celery
3 tablespoons cooking oil
6 eggs
1 tablespoon soy sauce
1 tablespoon cornstarch
1 teaspoon salt
Dash of pepper
Sauce

Put crabmeat and bean sprouts in large bowl. If using canned sprouts, rinse and drain first. To cut onion into shreds, cut into halves from top to bottom. Put, cut side down, on cutting board and finely slice with the grain of the onion, or from top to bottom. Sauté onion and celery in oil until limp, about 5 minutes, and add to crabmeat. Beat eggs, add soy sauce, cornstarch, salt, and pepper. Pour over crabmeat and vegetables and mix thoroughly. Put 1 tablespoon mixture on greased griddle or skillet and brown. Turn and brown other side. Keep hot until all are cooked. Pour Sauce over top. Makes 4 servings.

Sauce

Cook until thick ½ cup water, 2 teaspoons sherry, 1 tablespoon soy sauce, and 2 teaspoons cornstarch.

Shrimp Fu Yung

Substitute 1 cup rinsed canned shrimps for the crabmeat in the recipe above.

NIU JU CHIN JOW
(Beef with Green Peppers)

1 pound lean beef, shredded
4 tablespoons soy sauce
2 teaspoons cornstarch
⅛ teaspoon pepper
6 medium green peppers, shredded
6 tablespoons cooking oil
1 teaspoon salt
¼ teaspoon monosodium glutamate

Mix beef with 2 tablespoons soy sauce, cornstarch, and pepper. Seed peppers and cut in julienne strips. Fry in 3 tablespoons oil. Remove, add remaining oil and fry beef until redness disappears. Add peppers, salt, monosodium glutamate,

and remaining soy sauce. Makes 4 to 6 servings.

VEGETABLES

For crispness when using canned bean sprouts, water chestnuts, or bamboo shoots, rinse well in cold water before adding to pan, and heat just to serving temperature. Snow peas, a Chinese delicacy, are available fresh or frozen at some markets.

LIANG PAN HUANG KUA
(Pickled Cucumbers)

2 medium cucumbers
2 teaspoons salt
½ cup vinegar
⅓ cup sugar
2 teaspoons minced fresh gingerroot
2 teaspoons sesame seeds

Wash cucumbers and pare lengthwise in ¼- to ½-inch strips, leaving every other strip of green skin on. Cut into halves lengthwise, remove seeds, and slice thinly. Put in bowl and add salt. Mix well and let stand for 1 hour. Put in cloth and squeeze out excess moisture. Mix remaining ingredients and bring to boil. Pour over cucumbers and chill. Makes 4 servings.

CHIANG LO PO
(Sweet-and-Sour Radishes)

1 bunch young radishes with fresh leaves
1 teaspoon salt
2 teaspoons soy sauce
2 tablespoons vinegar
2 tablespoons sugar
1 teaspoon sesame oil

Wash and trim radishes. With the flat side of a heavy Chinese knife or cleaver, gently crush the radishes, being careful not to break them into pieces. Wash leaves and cut into ½-inch pieces. Mix salt, radishes, and leaves and let stand for 10 minutes. Drain. Mix remaining ingredients and pour over radishes. Serve cold as a relish. Makes 4 servings.

PA PAO FAN
(Eight Treasures Pudding)

1½ cups glutinous rice (a special kind of opaque short-grain rice, obtainable in Chinese markets)
6 cups boiling water
½ cup sugar
6 candied red cherries
3 tablespoons diced candied citron
3 tablespoons diced candied orange peel
3 tablespoons diced preserved ginger
¼ cup white raisins
¼ cup dark raisins
12 dates, pitted
6 tablespoons whole blanched almonds
Sauce

Add rice to boiling water and simmer until water is almost absorbed. Lower heat, add sugar, and stir well. Continue to cook for several minutes until rice looks firm and water is absorbed. Grease an 8- or 9-inch round bowl. Put cherries in the center and arrange the other fruits and the nuts in circles around them, across the bottom and up sides of bowl.

Use in the order given. Add rice, being careful not to disturb the fruits. Cover the bowl with foil or wax paper and steam for 30 minutes. To serve, invert onto serving plate and serve with warm Sauce. Makes 6 servings.

Sauce

Mix 1 cup sugar and 2 tablespoons cornstarch; add 1 cup water and cook, stirring constantly, until thickened. Add ½ teaspoon almond flavoring.

HSING JEN PING
(Almond Cookies)

1 cup lard
1 cup sugar
1 egg
1 teaspoon almond extract
3 cups sifted all-purpose flour
1 teaspoon baking soda
1 teaspoon salt
  Red food coloring

Cream lard with sugar until light. Add egg and mix well. Add almond extract. Add sifted dry ingredients and mix well. Shape into 1-inch balls and put on ungreased cookie sheets. Flatten slightly by pressing center of cookies with thumb. Dip the end of a chopstick into coloring and touch top of each cookie. (Half an almond can be used instead of coloring.) Bake in preheated moderate oven (375° F.) for 10 minutes. Makes 4½ dozen.

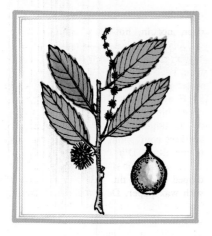

CHINQUAPIN—A tree and its edible fruit which, like chestnuts, belongs to the genus *Castanea*. Chinquapins grow in the southern United States and bear small, single-fruited burrs. Although not of the same quality as chestnuts, chinquapins are eaten in the same way.

CHITTERLINGS—The intestines of young pigs that have been emptied, turned inside out, and scraped clean while still warm. They are then soaked for twenty-four hours in cold salted water to cover, and washed at least six times before being cut up into two-inch lengths. It is advisable to scrape off the greater part of the fat, leaving only a little for flavor.

Chitterlings are very popular in the American South, and are a surprisingly tasty dish, eaten either boiled or deep fried.

BOILED CHITTERLINGS

2 pounds chitterlings, cut up
2 onions, minced
2 bay leaves
2 sprigs fresh thyme or pinch of
    ground thyme
½ teaspoon cayenne
2 garlic cloves, minced
2 teaspoons salt
¼ teaspoon pepper
4 cups water

Wash chitterlings 3 times and put in kettle with remaining ingredients. Bring to boil. Simmer, covered, for 2 hours, or until tender. Makes 6 servings.

DEEP-FRIED CHITTERLINGS

2 pounds boiled chitterlings
1 egg, slightly beaten
1 tablespoon water
  Fine cracker crumbs
  Fat for deep frying

Prepare chitterlings as in Boiled Chitterlings. Cut into pieces the size of oysters. Dip each piece into combined egg and water, then roll in crumbs. Fry in hot deep fat (370°F. on a frying thermometer) until golden brown. Makes 4 to 6 servings.

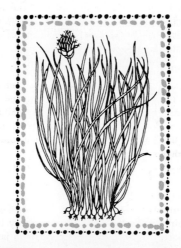

CHIVE **(Allium schoenoprasum)**—A member of the onion family, it grows in clumps of slender, green, tubular leaves. A hardy perennial, it is also a very decorative garden plant. Never growing over ten inches, chives make an attractive garden border or edging. They grow in average soil with plenty of sun. Their tiny lavender flowers will add a spot of color to your garden. Chives may be kept in a pot in a sunny kitchen window, as well as outdoors.

A great favorite since ancient times, the mild, onionlike fragrance of chives pleased peoples of Asia and northern Europe centuries before the Christian era. Since then the plant has held its position as one of the most popular culinary herbs cultivated in European herb gardens. Our American garden variety is a descendant of the original wild plant found in North America and Eurasia.

Potted chives are the harbingers of spring and they are sold at many food stores early in the season. Don't cut off the tops for they will brown where cut, but snip a few of the leaves at a time. Also, don't cut one plant more than four times during a season. When you divide your plants, which should be done every two or three years, save the tiny bulbs. They are delicious pickled and taste like small pickled onions.

Chives may be used to flavor any food in which a mild onion flavor is desired. Fresh chopped leaves are excellent in soups, eggs, vegetables, appetizers, cheeses, cream and other sauces, and in salad dressings. They should be cut and added to foods just before serving.

Chopped freeze-dried chives and chopped frozen chives are now available in food stores. When added to foods they regain their fresh appearance, texture, and flavor. Use about ½ teaspoon for each serving and use them as you would fresh chives.

CHIVE-SCRAMBLED EGGS

4 eggs
¼ cup milk or light cream
  Salt and pepper to taste
2 tablespoons butter or margarine
2 tablespoons minced chives

Beat eggs lightly with milk. Season. Melt butter in hot skillet; add egg mixture, lower heat, and add chives. Stir gently until done. Serve surrounded with toast tips and quarters of fresh tomatoes for breakfast or luncheon. Makes 2 servings.

CHOCOLATE—Chocolate and its brother, cocoa, are made from the beans of the cacao tree, a perennial evergreen tree of the cola family, botanically called *Theobroma*, or "food of the gods." The cacao tree is native to the hot humid forests of the Amazon basin, and it flourishes only in tropical climates. Chocolate is a mixture of roasted cocoa, cocoa butter (also obtained from the cacao bean), and very fine sugar.

It is truly a product of the New World. The word comes from the Mexican Indian *choco*, "foam," and *atl*, "water." It is said that Columbus brought some home to Spain with him, but the first Europeans to see it used were the Spaniards who invaded Mexico under Cortez in 1519. There they found chocolate in common use, flavored with spices, but unsweetened. It was the royal drink of the Aztecs: the Emperor Montezuma drank his chocolate from golden ceremonial goblets. Cocoa beans were also used as money.

Cortez introduced chocolate as a hot drink to Spain, where sugar and vanilla flavoring were added to it. By 1580 it was in common use and extremely popular. The Spaniards tried to hold on to their monopoly of the cocoa bean and the chocolate drink, and managed to do so for a hundred years. But in the middle of the 1600's, when the Spanish princess Maria Theresa married Louis XIV, the French started using chocolate. At about the same time cocoa began to be cultivated in the British West Indies and advertised in London. Chocolate shops sprang up throughout Europe, and the fashionables of the day sipped and gossiped in them.

The wives of the New England colonists knew chocolate and loved it. At first it was imported, but as early as 1765 a plant for making chocolate was started in Dorchester, Massachusetts. Chocolate as a drink became very popular; the earlier pioneers had thought tea and coffee on the thin side, but chocolate, full bodied and stimulating, was very nourishing. A tavern sign near Salem, Massachusetts, said:

Francis Symonds Makes and Sells
The best of Chocolate, also Shells.
I'll toll you if you have need
And feed you well and bid you speed.

Chocolate was also used in baking and the chocolate cake has become the darling of Americans of all ages.

The two greatest developments in the history of chocolate came in the 19th century. The first one was when a Swiss, Daniel Peter, thought of combining milk and chocolate for eating, and thus created the first milk chocolate. The second was due to another Swiss, who invented the process called "conching" by which chocolate is kneaded into a smooth and velvety texture. This replaced the coarsely grained chocolate that was current previously. The Swiss conche their chocolate as long as seventy-two hours (which is very long) and this accounts for the melting smoothness of Swiss chocolate.

Chocolate, apart from its palatability, has a considerable stimulating effect on the heart and the general musculature of the body. It is more than a delicacy; it is good solid food and nourishment and considered as such by many nations. Chocolate is a standard part of army rations in times of stress. Mountaineers carry chocolate with them as a matter of course. French children eat it instead of butter or jam with their bread. And the comfort derived from a chocolate bar when one is tired or depressed is not to be underestimated. It is little wonder that chocolate is America's favorite flavor. Housewives, confronted with a choice of desserts, should remember "when in doubt, make it chocolate."

THE TYPES OF CHOCOLATE AND THEIR USE

Unsweetened (or bitter) chocolate

Available in squares, it is the natural rich chocolate ground from cocoa beans. It is unsweetened and has a deep-bodied flavor that makes it ideal for baking and cooking.

Semisweet (or candy-making) chocolate

Available in squares, it is processed with a low viscosity to make it more fluid. It also has a satin gloss. Both these facts make it especially good for dipping. Is excellent for candy making and also is used for frostings, sauces, and baking.

Chocolate pieces

Available in bits, morsels, and pieces, this is a semisweet chocolate. They retain their shape to some extent in baking. Chocolate pieces are especially adapted to cookie baking. They are often eaten "as is" too.

Sweet cooking chocolate

Available in bars, this chocolate can be used both as a confection and in cooking. Since it is smooth in texture and sweet, it is excellent for chocolate drinks, refrigerator cakes, etc.

Milk chocolate

Available in bars; has dried milk added to the chocolate formula with a blend of other ingredients. It is lighter and milder than chocolate without milk added, and is used primarily as an eating chocolate.

Other chocolate products

There are also a great variety of chocolate products available. These include a semiliquid unsweetened chocolate, developed especially for baking, which requires no melting; chocolate milk by the quart; chocolate syrup, canned or in jars, some fortified with vitamins and minerals; chocolate sundae sauce; chocolate sprinkles; chocolate kisses; and endless other chocolate candies and bars, cakes, cupcakes, and cookies.

Storage—Chocolate should be stored in a cool, dry place, at a temperature of about 60°F. If chocolate becomes warm, the fat in it rises to the surface, forming a grayish film. This is not harmful, and the chocolate is perfectly usable. But if the wrapper gets oily, the chocolate has deteriorated.

☐ Kitchen shelf, wrapped: 1 year

☐ Refrigerator shelf, wrapped: 1 year

Nutritive Food Values—Chocolate contains an appreciable amount of fat and carbohydrates. It is a good source of quick energy.

☐ Unsweetened, 3½ ounces = 505 calories
☐ Semisweet, 3½ ounces = 507 calories
☐ Sweet, 3½ ounces = 528 calories
☐ Milk chocolate, 3½ ounces = 520 calories

HINTS FOR SUCCESSFUL CHOCOLATE COOKERY

■ Always use the chocolate called for in the recipe. Since different chocolates give different results, the chocolate specifically mentioned was carefully chosen for its particular effect or flavor.

■ Chocolate burns so easily it is best to melt it over hot water.

■ To make thin chocolate shavings for topping on pies or ice cream, use a vegetable parer. Have chocolate at room temperature. Refrigerate after cutting.

■ When grating chocolate, be sure that the grater is dry. Handle chocolate as little and as quickly as possible.

■ To dip chocolate for homemade confections, follow this simple rule: Grate 1 pound of semisweet chocolate squares as finely as possible. Place in top part of double boiler. Melt *extremely* slowly over, not in, hot water. Stir until the chocolate reaches the temperature of 130°F. on a candy thermometer. Remove from heat and cool to about 88°F. Heat water in bottom part of double boiler to 90°F. and remove from heat. Replace top of double boiler (with chocolate still in it) on bottom part of double boiler.

■ Have confections to be dipped at room temperature. Dip one piece at a time, using a candy or steel kitchen fork. Place dipped pieces on cake racks covered with wax paper. Decorate before coating is completely hardened. Allow confections to harden for at least 5 minutes after they have been decorated before removing them from paper. Do not work in warm or humid room. Choose a crisp day for dipping. Keep room temperature at about 60° to 70°F. Avoid drafts. Work quickly. Remember that practice makes perfect.

■ When making a beverage, there is less tendency to "settle out" if the chocolate is cooked with a small amount of water before adding the milk.

■ Because milk and chocolate scorch easily, it is best to cook chocolate beverages in a double boiler over low heat after the milk is added.

■ After cooking the beverage, beat it with a rotary beater before serving. The foam prevents the formation of scum.

Chocolate Cook Book

Delectable ways to use
this most luscious and irresistible of
all cooking ingredients in cakes
pies, cupcakes, cookies, desserts, frostings,
confections, drinks, sauces and syrups

CAKES AND PIES

SWEET-CHOCOLATE CAKE

    4 ounces (1 package) sweet cooking
       chocolate
    ½ cup boiling water
    1 cup butter or other shortening
    2 cups sugar
    4 eggs, separated
    1 teaspoon vanilla extract
 2½ cups sifted cake flour
    1 teaspoon baking soda
    ½ teaspoon salt
    1 cup buttermilk
       Coconut-Pecan Filling
       Chocolate Cream-Cheese Frosting

Melt chocolate in water; cool. Cream butter and sugar; add egg yolks, one at a time, beating thoroughly after each addition. Add vanilla and chocolate; mix well. Add sifted dry ingredients alternately with buttermilk; beat until smooth. Fold in stiffly beaten egg whites. Pour into three 8- or 9-inch layer-cake pans lined on bottom with greased wax paper. Bake in preheated moderate oven (350° F.) for about 35 minutes. Cool. Fill with Coconut-Pecan Filling and frost with Chocolate Cream-Cheese Frosting.

Coconut-Pecan Filling

In saucepan mix 1 cup undiluted evaporated milk, 1 cup sugar, 3 egg yolks, ½ cup butter or margarine, and 1 teaspoon vanilla extract. Cook, stirring, over medium heat for 12 minutes, or until mixture thickens. Add 1 cup flaked coconut and 1 cup chopped pecans. Beat until thick.

Chocolate Cream-Cheese Frosting

Cream 2 tablespoons butter and 4 ounces cream cheese; add 1½ ounces (1½ squares) unsweetened chocolate, melted, dash of salt, 1½ cups sifted confectioners' sugar, ¼ cup heavy cream, and ½ teaspoon vanilla extract. Mix well.

Orange Cream-Cheese Frosting

Use recipe for Chocolate Cream-Cheese Frosting but omit chocolate and vanilla; reduce cream to ⅛ cup. Cream 1½ tablespoons powdered orange juice with butter and cheese.

MILK-CHOCOLATE CAKE

 2¼ cups sugar
    3 tablespoons water
    2 squares (2 ounces) unsweetened
       chocolate, melted, or 2 envelopes
       no-melt unsweetened chocolate
    ¾ cup soft butter or margarine
    1 teaspoon vanilla extract
    4 eggs, separated
 2¼ cups sifted cake flour
    1 teaspoon cream of tartar
    ½ teaspoon baking soda
    ½ teaspoon salt

    1 cup milk
       Vanilla Cream Filling
     * Chocolate Cream-Cheese Frosting

Add ¼ cup sugar and the water to chocolate. Cream butter well. Add remaining 2 cups sugar gradually, beating until light and fluffy. Add vanilla, then egg yolks, one at a time, beating well after each addition. Add chocolate mixture and blend. Add sifted dry ingredients alternately with milk, beating until smooth. Fold in egg whites, beaten until stiff but not dry. Pour into three round 9-inch or four 8-inch layer pans, lined on the bottom with wax paper. Bake 9-inch layers in preheated moderate oven (350°F.) for about 50 minutes, and 8-inch layers about 40 minutes. Let stand for 5 minutes; then turn out on racks to cool. Remove paper. Put the layers together with Vanilla Cream Filling and spread top and sides of cake with Chocolate Cream-Cheese Frosting.

For Chocolate Cream-Cheese Frosting, double quantities given for recipe at left.

Vanilla Cream Filling

    ½ cup sugar
    3 tablespoons all-purpose flour
    ⅛ teaspoon salt
 1½ cups milk
    2 eggs, beaten
    ½ teaspoon vanilla extract

In top part of double boiler, mix ¼ cup sugar, the flour, and salt. Add ½ cup milk; stir until smooth. Pour in remaining 1 cup milk and cook over boiling water for 10 minutes, or until smooth and thickened, stirring constantly. Mix remaining ¼ cup sugar and the eggs. Add hot mixture slowly, stirring constantly. Put back in double boiler and cook for 5 minutes, or until very thick, stirring constantly. Cool, and add vanilla. Makes enough to fill four 8-inch or three 9-inch layers.

MIDNIGHT LACE CAKE

    2 ounces (2 squares) unsweetened
       chocolate
    1 cup milk
    ½ cup soft butter or margarine
 1½ cups sugar
    1 teaspoon vanilla extract
    2 eggs, separated
 1¾ cups sifted all-purpose flour
    2 teaspoons baking powder
    ½ teaspoon each of baking soda and
       salt
       Soft Chocolate Frosting

Cook chocolate with ½ cup milk until smooth and thickened, stirring. Cream butter and sugar. Add vanilla and egg yolks; beat well. Add sifted dry ingredients alternately with ½ cup milk; beat until smooth. Blend in cooled chocolate

mixture. Beat egg whites until stiff but not dry. Fold into batter. Pour into two 9-inch layer-cake pans lined on bottom with greased wax paper. Bake in preheated moderate oven (350°F.) for 30 minutes. Cool; frost with Soft Chocolate Frosting.

Soft Chocolate Frosting

In top part of double boiler over boiling water melt 2 ounces (2 squares) unsweetened chocolate in ¾ cup milk; beat to blend. Stir in 1½ tablespoons cornstarch blended with ¼ cup milk, 1 cup sugar, and dash of salt. Cook, stirring often, for 15 minutes, or until thick. Remove from water; add 1 tablespoon butter and 1 teaspoon vanilla extract; cool.

WISCONSIN CHOCOLATE CAKE

    ¾ cup cocoa (Dutch-process preferred)
 1¾ cups sugar
    4 eggs
    ½ cup milk
    ½ cup butter or margarine
    2 cups sifted all-purpose flour
    1 teaspoon baking powder
    1 teaspoon baking soda
    ½ teaspoon salt
    1 cup dairy sour cream
    1 teaspoon vanilla extract
       Glossy Chocolate Frosting
       Candied violets
       Candied green leaves

Cook until thick cocoa, ¾ cup of the sugar, 1 egg yolk, and milk. Stir constantly to prevent sticking. Cool. Cream butter until soft. Gradually add remaining 1 cup of sugar, beating until well blended. Add 1 whole egg and 2 egg yolks. Mix well. Stir in sifted dry ingredients alternately with sour cream. Add vanilla and cocoa mixture. Fold in egg whites which have been beaten until stiff but not dry. Pour into three 8-inch layer pans, lined on the bottom with wax paper. Bake in preheated moderate oven (350°F.) for 30 to 35 minutes. Turn out on racks and peel off paper. Cool, and thinly frost top and sides of cake with Glossy Chocolate Frosting. Decorate with violets and leaves.

Glossy Chocolate Frosting

Melt 6 ounces (6 squares) unsweetened chocolate. Add 1½ cups sifted confectioners' sugar, and 5 tablespoons hot water; beat well and add 1½ cups more sugar. Gradually beat in 6 egg yolks. When smooth and blended, beat in ½ cup soft butter or margarine. Makes enough frosting for tops and sides of three 9-inch layers.

CHOCOLATE FONDANT CAKE

    1 cup butter or margarine
    1 cup granulated sugar

1 cup firmly packed light brown sugar
4 eggs
3 ounces (3 squares) unsweetened chocolate, melted
1 cup freshly cooked and mashed potatoes
1 teaspoon almond extract
2 cups sifted cake flour
1 teaspoon each of baking soda, cream of tartar, and salt
½ teaspoon each of ground cloves and allspice
½ cup dairy sour cream
1 cup chopped California walnuts
1 cup chopped pitted dates
Fluffy White Frosting
Red food coloring
Chocolate sprinkles

Cream butter and sugars until light and fluffy. Add eggs, one at a time, beating well after each addition. Add chocolate, potatoes, and almond extract. Sift flour with soda, cream of tartar, salt, cloves, and allspice. Add to butter mixture alternately with cream. Fold in nuts and dates. Pour into 9-inch springform pan lined on bottom with greased wax paper, or into 3 lined 9-inch layer-cake pans. Bake in preheated moderate oven (350° F.) for about 1½ hours for springform pan, or about 30 minutes for layer-cake pans. Spread Fluffy White Frosting, tinted pink with red coloring, between layers and on top and sides of cooled cake. Sprinkle with chocolate sprinkles.

Fluffy White Frosting
2 egg whites
1½ cups sugar
⅛ teaspoon salt
⅓ cup water
2 teaspoons light corn syrup
1 teaspoon vanilla extract

In top part of double boiler combine egg whites, sugar, salt, water, and syrup. Put over boiling water and beat with rotary beater or electric mixer for 7 minutes, or until mixture will stand in stiff peaks. Add vanilla.

DIVA CAKE
1 cup soft butter or margarine
1½ cups sugar
1 teaspoon vanilla extract
2 ounces (2 squares) unsweetened chocolate, melted and cooled
5 egg yolks, well beaten
1½ cups sifted cake flour
1 teaspoon baking powder
¼ teaspoon baking soda
½ teaspoon salt
½ cup dairy sour cream or buttermilk
2 tablespoons strong coffee
2 egg whites, beaten stiff
Brown-Sugar Frosting

Cream butter, sugar, and vanilla. Blend in cooled chocolate. Add egg yolks; mix well. Add sifted dry ingredients and sour cream; beat until smooth. Add coffee. Fold in egg whites. Pour into two 9-inch layer-cake pans lined on bottom with greased wax paper. Bake in preheated moderate oven (350°F.) for about 30 minutes. Cool, and frost with Brown-Sugar Frosting.

Brown-Sugar Frosting
1 cup granulated sugar
½ cup firmly packed brown sugar
3 tablespoons dark corn syrup
¼ cup water
2 egg whites
¼ teaspoon each of salt and cream of tartar
1 teaspoon vanilla extract

Put all ingredients except vanilla in top part of double boiler; mix well. Put over boiling water and beat until mixture will hold a peak, about 4 minutes. Remove from water; add vanilla.

A MAN'S RUM CHOCOLATE CAKE
1 ounce (1 square) unsweetened chocolate
½ cup water
½ cup butter or margarine
1½ cups firmly packed light brown sugar
3 eggs
1¾ cups sifted cake flour
1½ teaspoons baking powder
¼ teaspoon salt
½ teaspoon baking soda
¼ cup dark rum
Rum Chocolate Frosting

Melt chocolate in water over very low heat, stirring constantly. Cool. Cream butter until fluffy. Gradually beat in sugar. Beat in eggs, one at a time, beating well after each addition. Sift flour with baking powder, salt, and soda. Add flour and chocolate alternately to egg mixture, beating until smooth. Stir in rum. Line three 8-inch layer-cake pans or two 9-inch pans with greased wax paper. Distribute batter equally among pans. Bake 8-inch layers in preheated moderate oven (350°F.) for 15 to 20 minutes, 9-inch layers for 20 to 25 minutes, or until cakes test clean. Cool for 5 minutes. Turn out on racks and peel off paper. When cool, fill and frost with Rum Chocolate Frosting.
Note: This is best made with an electric mixer.

Rum Chocolate Frosting
Melt 3 ounces (3 squares) unsweetened chocolate with ½ cup dark rum over low heat. Stir in 1 teaspoon vanilla extract. Add 4 cups sifted confectioners' sugar, 1 cup at a time, beating well after each addition. Beat in ¼ cup soft butter. Add a little more rum if necessary to make frosting of spreading consistency.

Milk-Chocolate Cake

HONEY CHOCOLATE CAKE
¼ cup soft butter or margarine
¾ cup sugar
½ teaspoon vanilla extract
2 eggs, separated
4 ounces (4 squares) unsweetened chocolate, melted and cooled
½ cup honey
2 cups sifted cake flour
1 teaspoon baking powder
½ teaspoon each of salt and baking soda
½ cup buttermilk
½ cup milk, scalded and cooled
Confectioners' Sugar Frosting

Cream butter, ½ cup sugar, and vanilla. Add egg yolks; beat well. Add cooled chocolate; blend. Gradually beat in honey. Add sifted dry ingredients and buttermilk; beat until smooth. Beat egg whites until stiff but not dry. Gradually add ¼ cup sugar, beating until very stiff and glossy. Fold into batter; stir in scalded milk. Pour into two 9-inch layer-cake pans lined on bottom with greased wax paper. Bake in preheated moderate oven (350°F.) for about 30 minutes. Cool, and frost with Confectioners' Sugar Frosting. Can be frozen.

Confectioners' Sugar Frosting
Cream ¼ cup soft butter or margarine and ¼ teaspoon salt. Gradually beat in 3 cups sifted confectioners' sugar alternately with 4 to 6 tablespoons scalded light cream. Add 1 teaspoon vanilla extract and beat until creamy and of good spreading consistency. Makes about 1¾ cups, or enough to spread top and sides of two 9-inch layers.

MOCHA CAKE
4 ounces (4 squares) unsweetened chocolate
⅔ cup hot water
1 cup soft butter or margarine
2¼ cups sugar
1½ teaspoons vanilla extract
4 eggs
3 cups sifted all-purpose flour
3 teaspoons baking powder
¾ teaspoon salt
2 teaspoons instant coffee
¾ cup milk
Cinnamon Mocha Frosting

Melt chocolate and stir in hot water; cool. Cream butter, sugar, and vanilla. Add eggs, one at a time, beating thoroughly after each addition. Add chocolate mixture; blend. Add sifted dry ingredients alternately with milk; beat until smooth. Pour into three 9-inch layer-cake pans lined on bottom with greased wax paper. Bake in preheated moderate oven (375°F.) for about 30 minutes. Cool; frost with Cinnamon Mocha Frosting.

Cinnamon Mocha Frosting
Cream until fluffy ½ cup soft butter or margarine, ¼ cup cocoa, 4 teaspoons instant coffee, and ½ teaspoon ground cinnamon. Add 4 cups confectioners' sugar alternately with ¼ cup undiluted evaporated milk (or enough to make frosting of spreading consistency). Add 1 teaspoon vanilla extract.

CHOCOLATE ANGEL FOOD
¾ cup sifted cake flour
¼ cup cocoa
1 cup egg whites
1 teaspoon cream of tartar
¼ teaspoon salt
1¼ cups sifted sugar
1 teaspoon vanilla extract
Chocolate Glaze

Sift flour and cocoa several times. Beat egg whites until frothy. Add cream of tartar and salt; beat until stiff but not dry. Gradually beat in sugar. Add flavoring. Then fold in sifted dry ingredients in fourths. Pour into ungreased 9-inch tube pan and bake in preheated moderate oven (325°F.) for about 1 hour. Invert pan on rack. Let stand until cold. Top with Chocolate Glaze.

Chocolate Glaze
Melt together 2 tablespoons butter and 2 ounces (2 squares) unsweetened chocolate. Beat in 2 tablespoons boiling water, 1 cup sifted confectioners' sugar, dash of salt, and ¼ teaspoon vanilla extract.

CHOCOLATE SPONGECAKE
1 cup sifted cake flour
⅓ cup cocoa
½ teaspoon baking powder
1½ cups sifted sugar
6 eggs, separated
½ teaspoon each of salt and cream of tartar
¼ cup water
1 teaspoon vanilla extract
Chocolate Glaze (see recipe above)

Sift flour, cocoa, baking powder, and 1 cup sugar. Beat egg whites with salt and cream of tartar until stiff but not dry. Gradually add ½ cup sugar and beat until very stiff. Combine egg yolks, water, and vanilla; add to dry ingredients and beat just to blend. Carefully fold yolk mixture into egg whites. Bake in ungreased 10-inch tube pan in preheated moderate oven (375°F.) for about 35 minutes. Cool in pan. Remove and top with Chocolate Glaze.

CHOCOLATE NUTCAKE
⅓ cup soft butter or other shortening
¾ cup sugar
1 egg
2 ounces (2 squares) unsweetened chocolate, melted and cooled
1⅓ cups sifted cake flour

¾ teaspoon baking soda
½ teaspoon salt
¾ cup buttermilk
1 teaspoon vanilla extract
1 cup coarsely chopped pecans or walnuts
Easy Chocolate Frosting
8 to 10 pecan or walnut halves

Cream butter and sugar. Add egg and beat until light. Blend in cooled chocolate. Sift dry ingredients; add alternately with buttermilk. Add vanilla and nuts. Pour into greased 8-inch tube pan 3 inches deep. Bake in preheated moderate oven (350°F.) for about 1 hour. Cool, frost with Easy Chocolate Frosting, and arrange nut halves around edge.

Easy Chocolate Frosting
Beat 1 cup confectioners' sugar, 2 ounces (2 squares) melted unsweetened chocolate, 1 egg, ½ teaspoon vanilla extract, and ⅛ teaspoon salt. Add heavy cream or undiluted evaporated milk to give spreading consistency.

GRANDMA'S CHOCOLATE CAKE
1 cup soft butter or margarine
2 cups sugar
3 eggs, separated
3 ounces (3 squares) unsweetened chocolate, melted and cooled
1¼ teaspoons active dry yeast
Water
2¾ cups sifted all-purpose flour
½ teaspoon salt
1 teaspoon baking soda
1½ teaspoons vanilla extract
Rich Mocha Frosting

Cream butter; gradually add sugar, beating until light and fluffy. Add egg yolks and beat until light. Blend in cooled chocolate. Dissolve dry yeast in ¼ cup warm water (105°F. to 115°F.). Add to chocolate mixture with sifted flour and salt. Beat whites until stiff; fold into mixture. Cover and let stand in warm place for about 4 hours. Dissolve soda in 3 tablespoons hot water and add with vanilla to batter; beat well. Pour into three 9-inch layer-cake pans lined on bottom with greased wax paper. Bake in preheated moderate oven (350°F.) for 35 minutes. Cool, and frost with Rich Mocha Frosting.

Rich Mocha Frosting
Cream ¼ cup soft butter or margarine. Add 3 egg yolks and beat well. Add 4½ cups confectioners' sugar, ¾ cup cocoa, ¼ teaspoon salt, and 1 teaspoon vanilla extract. Gradually beat in enough strong coffee to give frosting spreading consistency.

CHOCOLATE CREAM ROLL
5 eggs, separated
3 tablespoons cocoa

1 cup sifted confectioners' sugar
Dash of salt
1½ teaspoons vanilla extract
Confectioners' sugar
1 cup heavy cream
2 tablespoons granulated sugar
Thin Chocolate Glaze
Maraschino cherries with stems

Beat egg whites until stiff but not dry; set aside. Beat egg yolks until thick and lemon-colored. Sift next 3 ingredients and gradually beat into yolks. Fold in whites. Add 1 teaspoon vanilla. Pour into pan (13 x 9 x 2 inches) lined on bottom with greased wax paper. Bake in preheated hot oven (400°F.) for about 15 minutes. Turn out on wax paper lightly covered with confectioners' sugar. Cool; carefully peel off paper. Whip cream with granulated sugar until stiff. Add ½ teaspoon vanilla and spread on cake. Roll up and chill. Spread top and sides with Thin Chocolate Glaze and chill until firm. Decorate with cherries. Cut into slices. Makes 6 servings.

Thin Chocolate Glaze

Melt 1 package (4 ounces) sweet cooking chocolate and 1 tablespoon butter in 3 tablespoons water over low heat. Combine 1 cup confectioners' sugar and dash of salt in a medium-size bowl. Gradually add chocolate mixture, blending well. Stir in ½ teaspoon vanilla extract. Makes ¾ cup glaze, or enough to spread top of 8-inch layer cake or top and sides of one cake roll.

CHOCOLATE CHIFFON PIE

Crust
1½ cups graham-cracker or zwieback crumbs
⅓ cup unblanched almonds
6 tablespoons sugar
¼ cup light cream
½ cup melted butter or margarine
½ teaspoon ground cinnamon

Filling
1 envelope unflavored gelatin
¼ cup cold water
2 tablespoons hot water
4 eggs, separated
1 cup commercial chocolate sauce
⅛ teaspoon salt
1 teaspoon vanilla extract
½ cup sugar
Whipped cream
Shaved semisweet chocolate

Blend crumbs at low speed until very fine. Add almonds and blend fine at low speed. Remove from blender and mix thoroughly with remaining crust ingredients. Pat firmly into lightly buttered 10-inch pie pan. Prick bottom several times with fork tines. Bake in preheated moderate oven (375°F.) for 12 to 15 minutes. Cool. To make Filling, soften

gelatin in cold water. Add hot water and stir until dissolved. Put egg yolks in blender, add gelatin, cover and blend at low speed until thoroughly mixed. Add chocolate sauce, salt, and vanilla; blend at high speed for 4 or 5 seconds, or until thoroughly blended. Chill until consistency of raw egg white. With rotary beater, beat egg whites until foamy. Gradually add sugar and beat until very stiff. Fold into chocolate mixture. Pour into shell and chill. Decorate with whipped cream and shaved chocolate.

CHOCOLATE ANGEL PIE

4 eggs, separated
¼ teaspoon salt
½ teaspoon cream of tartar
1½ cups sugar
3 ounces (3 squares) unsweetened chocolate
1 cup heavy cream, whipped

Beat egg whites and ⅛ teaspoon salt until foamy; add cream of tartar. Continue beating, adding 1 cup sugar gradually, until very stiff. Spread 1-inch layer on bottom of greased 9-inch pie pan. Pile remaining egg white evenly around sides of pan. Bake in preheated very slow oven (250°F.) for 1 hour; cool. Melt chocolate in top part of double boiler over boiling water. Beat egg yolks, remaining sugar and salt, and 2 tablespoons water thoroughly; stir into chocolate. Cook over boiling water, stirring constantly, until very thick. Remove from heat and cool. Fold in whipped cream and pour into the cooled meringue shell. Chill overnight. Makes 6 to 8 servings.

BLACK-BOTTOM PIE

1 envelope unflavored gelatin
1¾ cups milk
4 eggs, separated
1 cup granulated sugar
½ teaspoon salt
4 teaspoons cornstarch
2 ounces (2 squares) unsweetened chocolate
1 teaspoon vanilla extract
Gingersnap-Crumb Crust
3 tablespoons rum
1 cup heavy cream, whipped
2 tablespoons confectioners' sugar

Soften gelatin in ¼ cup milk for 5 minutes. Scald remaining 1½ cups milk in top part of double boiler over boiling water. Beat egg yolks. Blend in ½ cup sugar, salt, and cornstarch. Add milk slowly, stirring constantly. Return to double boiler and cook over simmering water, stirring constantly, for 4 minutes, or until custard coats spoon. Remove from heat. Reserve ½ cup of custard. Add gelatin to remainder and stir until

dissolved. Chill. Melt 1½ ounces chocolate. Stir in reserved ½ cup custard and vanilla. Beat with rotary beater until blended. Cool. Pour into Gingersnap-Crumb Crust. Chill until firm. When remaining custard begins to set, add rum. Beat egg whites until stiff but not dry. Gradually beat in remaining granulated sugar. Fold in custard. Pour over chocolate mixture in pie. Chill until firm. Combine cream and confectioners' sugar. Put on pie with pastry tube or spread on top. Shave remaining chocolate over cream. Chill before serving. Makes 6 to 8 servings.

Gingersnap-Crumb Crust

Blend thoroughly 1¼ cups fine gingersnap crumbs and ¼ cup butter; press onto bottom and sides of deep 9-inch pie pan, using back of spoon. Bake in preheated moderate oven (350°F.) for about 10 minutes. Chill.

CUPCAKES AND COOKIES

SURPRISE CHOCOLATE CUPCAKES

½ cup butter
1½ cups sugar
2 cups sifted all-purpose flour
1 teaspoon baking soda
½ teaspoon salt
1 cup milk
3 eggs, beaten
2 ounces (2 squares) unsweetened chocolate
1 teaspoon vanilla extract
1 teaspoon lemon flavoring
The Surprise

Cream butter and sugar together. Sift flour with baking soda and salt; add to butter and sugar mixture alternately with ½ cup milk. Add beaten eggs. Melt chocolate with remaining ½ cup milk over low heat. Cool. Add to batter and stir in flavorings. Pour into greased 2½-inch muffin pans, filling cups about two thirds full. Bake in preheated moderate oven (350°F.) for 25 minutes, or until cakes test clean. Makes about 24.

The Surprise

Cut tops off cupcakes and reserve. Scoop out interior carefully so that cake shells don't break. Fill with sugared fresh raspberries or well-drained thawed, frozen raspberries. Top with sugared whipped cream. Place cake tops on whipped cream at an angle and decorate each with a raspberry or a candied cherry.

FUDGE-CAKE SQUARES

½ cup butter or margarine
2 tablespoons cocoa
2 eggs

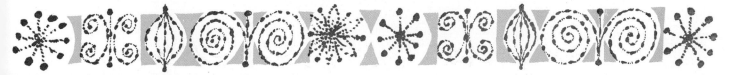

1 cup sugar
¾ cup sifted all-purpose flour
¼ teaspoon salt
1 teaspoon vanilla extract
1 cup chopped nuts
Fudge Frosting

Melt butter and blend in cocoa. Beat eggs; gradually beat in sugar. Stir in first mixture. Add sifted flour and salt; mix well. Add vanilla and nuts. Pour into greased 8-inch square pan and bake in preheated moderate oven (350°F.) for 30 to 40 minutes. Spread with Fudge Frosting to cover completely. Cool, and cut into 2-inch squares. Makes 16.

Fudge Frosting

2 cups sugar
2 tablespoons light corn syrup
⅔ cup milk
3 squares (3 ounces) unsweetened chocolate
¼ cup butter or margarine
1 teaspoon vanilla extract

Put the sugar, corn syrup, milk, and chocolate in large saucepan. Cook over medium heat, stirring until sugar is dissolved. Continue cooking until mixture forms a very soft ball when a small amount is dropped in very cold water (232°F. on a candy thermometer). Stir occasionally to prevent scorching. Remove from heat, add butter without stirring, and cool until bottom of pan feels lukewarm (about 1 hour). Then add vanilla and beat until frosting is creamy and barely holds its shape. Spread quickly on cake before frosting hardens. Makes about 2 cups, or enough to spread top and sides of 8-inch or 9-inch square cake.

CHOCOLATE MINT COOKIES

½ cup margarine
½ cup sugar
1 egg
½ teaspoon vanilla extract
2 ounces (2 squares) unsweetened chocolate, melted
1 tablespoon milk
2 cups sifted all-purpose flour
1 teaspoon baking powder
½ teaspoon salt
Mint Filling
Confectioners' Sugar Frosting
(see page 410)
Colored sugar

Cream margarine and sugar. Beat in egg, vanilla, and chocolate. Add milk and mix. Sift in flour with baking powder and salt. Shape dough in 2 rolls, 2 inches in diameter. Wrap in wax paper and chill overnight. Cut into thin slices and bake on ungreased cookie sheet in preheated moderate oven (350°F.) for 10 minutes, or until done. Cool. Spread Mint Filling on half of cookies. Top with remaining cookies. Frost with green-tinted Confec-

tioners' Sugar Frosting to which a few drops of peppermint extract have been added. Sprinkle a small round of colored sugar on each. Makes about 5 dozen double cookies.

Mint Filling

Cream ¼ cup butter. Add 2 cups sifted confectioners' sugar, a little at a time. Add a dash of salt, 1 tablespoon hot milk, and ¼ teaspoon peppermint extract. Mix well.

SPICY CHOCOLATE STICKS

4 eggs
2 cups firmly packed brown sugar
1 teaspoon ground cinnamon
¼ teaspoon each of ground allspice and cloves
4 ounces (1 package) sweet cooking chocolate, grated fine
1 teaspoon grated lemon rind
3 cups sifted all-purpose flour
1 teaspoon baking powder
1 cup chopped blanched almonds
¼ cup finely chopped candied orange or lemon peel

Beat eggs and sugar until light. Stir in spices, chocolate, and lemon rind. Sift flour and baking powder over almonds and candied peel and coat fruit thoroughly. Stir into egg mixture. If dough is too soft to roll out, add a little more flour, 1 tablespoon at a time. Roll out dough on lightly floured board to ¼-inch thickness. Cut into sticks 1 x 3 inches. Bake on greased cookie sheet in preheated moderate oven (350°F.) for 10 to 12 minutes. Makes about 4½ dozen.

FROSTINGS

BUTTER FROSTING

Cream ½ cup soft butter. Gradually add 1 pound sifted confectioners' sugar. Add dash of salt, 1 teaspoon vanilla extract, 3 ounces (3 squares) melted unsweetened chocolate, and about 3 tablespoons heavy cream. Beat until smooth and of spreading consistency. Makes enough to spread between and over top and sides of three 9-inch layers.

CHOCO-PEANUT FROSTING

Cream 2 tablespoons butter, ¼ cup smooth peanut butter, and ½ teaspoon salt. Blend in 2 ounces (2 squares) melted unsweetened chocolate. Add alternately 3 cups sifted confectioners' sugar and ⅓ cup milk, beating until smooth and well blended. Add 1 teaspoon vanilla extract.

CHOCO-SOUR CREAM FROSTING

Melt 12 ounces (1 large package) semi-

sweet chocolate pieces over hot water. Beat in 1 cup dairy sour cream and ⅛ teaspoon salt.

CREAMY CHOCOLATE FROSTING

Melt 4 ounces (4 squares) unsweetened chocolate in top part of double boiler over hot water. Beat 4 egg yolks with ⅔ cup sugar; add ½ cup heavy cream and ⅛ teaspoon salt. Pour slowly over chocolate, stirring constantly. Cook over hot water for 5 minutes, or until thickened, stirring. Cream 1¼ cups unsalted butter; add chocolate mixture, 1 tablespoon at a time, beating until blended. Chill until thick.

SEMISWEET FROSTING

Melt 3 packages (6 ounces each) semisweet chocolate pieces. Add 3 cups sifted confectioners' sugar, ⅓ cup soft butter, 1½ teaspoons vanilla extract, and about ⅓ cup hot milk, or enough to give spreading consistency. Beat until smooth. Makes enough for top and sides of three 9-inch layers.

BITTERSWEET CHOCOLATE FROSTING

Melt together ¼ cup butter or margarine and 4 squares unsweetened chocolate. Beat in ¼ cup boiling water, 2 cups sifted confectioners' sugar, ⅛ teaspoon salt and ½ teaspoon vanilla extract. Use as frosting for top and sides of 9-inch white layer cake. Decorate cake with preserved whole chestnuts.

WHIPPED-CREAM TOPPING

Whip 1 cup heavy cream with 2 tablespoons cocoa and 2 teaspoons sugar until almost stiff. Serve on plain cake. Makes about 2 cups.

DESSERTS

CHOCOLATE SOUFFLÉ

2 ounces (2 squares) unsweetened chocolate
2 cups milk
½ cup sugar
⅓ cup all-purpose flour
½ teaspoon salt
2 tablespoons butter or margarine
1 teaspoon vanilla extract
4 egg yolks, beaten until thick and lemon-colored
4 egg whites, stiffly beaten
Flavored, sweetened whipped cream

Melt chocolate in milk in top part of double boiler over boiling water. Beat with rotary beater until well blended. Mix sugar, flour, and salt; add small amount of chocolate mixture, stirring until smooth. Return to double boiler and cook until thickened, stirring constantly.

Chocolate Meringues

Surprise Chocolate Cupcakes

Spicy Chocolate Sticks

Chocolate Chiffon Pie

Chocolate Fondant Cake

Wisconsin Chocolate Cake

Bittersweet Chocolate Frosting for a white layer cake

Continue cooking for 5 minutes, stirring occasionally. Add butter and vanilla; cool slightly. Add egg yolks; mix well. Fold into egg whites. Pour into buttered 1½-quart casserole. Put in pan of hot water and bake in preheated moderate oven (350°F.) for 1¼ hours, or until firm. Serve at once with whipped cream. Makes 8 servings.

UNBAKED WARSAW CHOCOLATE TORTE
    1 cup sweet butter
 1½ cups superfine granulated sugar
    8 ounces (1 package) semisweet chocolate squares, grated fine (not melted)
    1 tablespoon grated orange rind
    3 cups finely ground California walnuts or filberts
  ½ teaspoon vanilla extract
 4 to 5 tablespoons heavy cream
    Thin Chocolate Glaze
      (see recipe on page 411
      Candied orange and citron peel and cherries

Cream butter until very light. Add 1 cup of the sugar gradually, beating well after each addition. The sugar must be perfectly absorbed in the butter so that no trace of graininess remains. Beat in chocolate and orange rind. Spread 1 cup of the ground nuts on the bottom of an 8-inch layer-cake pan with a removable bottom. Top with chocolate mixture. Smooth top with wet spatula or knife. Chill until mixture sets. Combine remaining ½ cup sugar and 2 cups nuts with vanilla and enough cream to make a mixture that spreads. Spread on chocolate and smooth. Ice thinly with Thin Chocolate Glaze. Decorate with flowers and designs made with strips of orange and citron peel and cherries. Chill. Serve without removing from pan bottom. Makes 10 to 12 servings.

Note: It is best to make this very rich, smooth dessert with an electric beater.

FRENCH CHOCOLATE MOUSSE
    8 ounces (two 4-ounce packages) sweet cooking chocolate
  ¼ cup water or strong coffee
    5 eggs, separated
    1 teaspoon vanilla extract or
    1 tablespoon rum, brandy, or kirsch
    Whipped sweet or dairy sour cream

Melt chocolate in water in top part of double boiler over hot water, stirring constantly. Cool. Beat in egg yolks, one at a time, beating well after each addition. Stir in flavoring. Beat egg whites until stiff but not dry. Fold carefully into chocolate mixture until just blended. Pile lightly in small individual white soufflé dishes (also called *pots de crème* dishes) or sherbet glasses. Chill for at least 8 hours or overnight. Fills 6 to 8 dishes, depending on size. Serve with a dab of whipped cream. (Sour cream is excellent).

LOW-CALORIE CHOCOLATE MOUSSE
    1 teaspoon unflavored gelatin
    1 ounce (1 square) unsweetened chocolate
  ¼ teaspoon salt
    1 tablespoon liquid sweetener (cyclamate type)
    1 teaspoon vanilla extract
    1 teaspoon grated orange rind
  ⅛ teaspoon cream of tartar
  ⅔ cup nonfat dry-milk solids

Soften gelatin in 2 tablespoons water. Melt chocolate with ¼ cup water in top part of double boiler over hot water. Stir until smooth; remove from heat. Stir in gelatin until dissolved. Add salt, liquid sweetener, vanilla, and orange rind. Chill until mixture begins to thicken, stirring occasionally. Pour ⅔ cup ice water into small mixing bowl; add cream of tartar and nonfat dry milk. With electric beater, beat for 5 minutes at high speed, until stiff peaks form. Add chocolate mixture, beating at low speed. Pour into 1-quart serving dish, refrigerator tray, or individual dishes. Freeze until firm. Makes 4 to 6 servings.

FUDGE BATTER PUDDING
    2 tablespoons melted butter or margarine
    1 cup sugar
    1 teaspoon vanilla extract
    1 cup sifted all-purpose flour
    8 tablespoons cocoa
    1 teaspoon baking powder
  ¾ teaspoon salt
  ½ cup milk
  ½ cup chopped nuts (optional)
 1⅔ cups boiling water

Mix butter, ½ cup sugar, and vanilla together. Sift flour, 3 tablespoons cocoa, baking powder, and ½ teaspoon salt together and add alternately with milk to first mixture; mix well and stir in nuts. (Nuts can be omitted, if preferred.) Mix together ½ cup sugar, 5 tablespoons cocoa, ¼ teaspoon salt, and boiling water. Turn into baking dish (10 x 6 x 2 inches); drop batter by tablespoonfuls on top. Bake in preheated moderate oven (350°F.) for 40 to 45 minutes. Serve warm or cold. Spoon out a portion of the cake and cover with sauce. Whipped cream, heavy cream, or top milk goes well with this pudding if it is served cold, because the chocolate sauce becomes quite thick. Makes 6 servings.

Note: When baked, the chocolate sauce is on the bottom, the cake on top.

Black-and-White Fudge Batter Pudding
Mix ½ large box or 1 small box white-cake mix as directed on label and substitute for chocolate batter in recipe above. Use same sauce.

QUEEN BONA'S DESSERT
    8 ladyfingers, split
  ⅓ cup sherry, rum, or brandy
  ⅓ cup toasted blanched almonds
  ¼ cup butter
  ½ cup sugar
    2 ounces (2 squares) unsweetened chocolate
  ¼ cup milk
    1 egg yolk
    1 teaspoon vanilla extract
    Walnut halves
    Candied cherries

Place ladyfingers on large platter. Sprinkle with sherry. Ladyfingers must be only slightly soaked, or they will fall apart. Grind almonds fine in blender or chop as fine as possible. Cream butter and sugar together until thoroughly blended. Melt chocolate in top part of double boiler over hot water. Beat together milk, egg yolk, and vanilla. Add mixture to chocolate in double boiler. Cook over simmering water until smooth, stirring constantly. Blend in butter-sugar mixture. Remove from heat. Beat with rotary beater until smooth. Cool. With a broad spatula, place half of ladyfinger halves on serving dish. Take care not to break. Carefully pour a thin layer of chocolate cream over ladyfingers. Cover with remaining ladyfingers. Cover with remaining chocolate cream. Decorate with nuts and cherries. Chill thoroughly. Makes 4 to 6 servings.

PEARS HÉLÈNE
    4 pears, peeled and cored*
    2 cups water
 1⅓ cups sugar
    1 teaspoon vanilla extract
 1 to 1½ pints vanilla ice cream
    Chopped walnuts, pecans, filberts, or chopped toasted blanched almonds (optional)
    Fudge Sauce

Cut pears into halves lengthwise. Boil water and sugar together for 5 minutes. Stir in vanilla. Add pears and simmer over low heat for 5 to 10 minutes, depending on quality and ripeness of fruit. Cool pears in syrup; drain. At serving time, place ice cream in glass serving dish. Arrange pears on it and sprinkle with nuts, if desired. Pass Fudge Sauce separately. Makes 4 servings.

*Drained canned pears can be used.

Fudge Sauce
Melt 4 ounces (4 squares) unsweetened chocolate and ¼ cup butter in top part of double boiler over hot water, stirring occasionally. Add ⅓ cup heavy cream

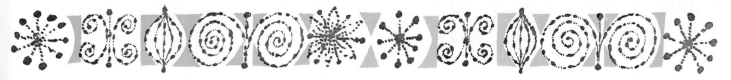

and 1 cup confectioners' sugar. Beat in 1 teaspoon vanilla extract. Stir until mixture is smooth. Serve over pears. Makes 1⅓ cups.

CHOCOLATE RASPBERRY CREAM

2 cups heavy cream
½ teaspoon vanilla extract
4 ounces (1 package) sweet cooking chocolate, grated fine
3 cups fresh raspberries or 2 packages (10 ounces each) thoroughly drained thawed frozen raspberries
¼ cup sugar (omit if frozen berries are used)

Whip cream with vanilla. Add chocolate and blend thoroughly. Reserve a few raspberries for garnish. Sprinkle sugar on remaining berries and fold into cream. Spoon into individual serving dishes or large glass serving bowl. Chill thoroughly. Before serving, decorate with reserved berries. Makes 6 to 8 servings.

CHESTNUT-CHOCOLATE VANILLA TARTS

1 square (1 ounce) unsweetened chocolate
3 tablespoons butter
1 teaspoon vanilla extract
¾ cup canned sweetened chestnut cream
½ package (about ⅓ cup) instant vanilla pudding
Heavy cream
6 baked, shallow tart shells, about 4½ inches in diameter
Whipped cream

Melt chocolate in top part of double boiler over hot water. Combine thoroughly with butter. Cool. Stir in vanilla. Blend with sweetened chestnut cream until very smooth. Chill. Beat vanilla pudding and 1 cup less 1 tablespoon heavy cream until thoroughly blended and fluffy, scraping the bottom of the bowl frequently. Chill. Fill one half of each tart with Chestnut-Chocolate Filling and the other with Vanilla Filling. Garnish with piped swirls of whipped cream. Makes 6 servings.

Note: You can buy chestnut cream at gourmet food or specialty stores.

CONFECTIONS

CHOCOLATE MERINGUES

2 egg whites
⅛ teaspoon salt
½ cup sugar
1 teaspoon vanilla extract
1 package (6 ounces) or 1 cup semisweet chocolate pieces

Beat egg whites with salt until stiff, but not dry. Add sugar 1 tablespoon at a time, beating for 2 minutes after each addition. Mixture should be very stiff and satiny. Stir in vanilla and fold in chocolate. Drop by teaspoonfuls onto ungreased cookie sheet. Bake in preheated slow oven (300°F.) for about 25 min-

utes. Makes about 3½ dozen.

Note: To make large meringues, drop mixture by tablespoonfuls onto cookie sheet and bake at 300°F. for 30 to 35 minutes. Put cooled meringues together with ice cream, allowing 2 for each serving.

GREEK CHOCOLATE BALLS

½ pound walnut meats
8 ounces sweet cooking chocolate
9 pieces of zwieback
½ teaspoon ground cinnamon
Confectioners' sugar
2 tablespoons rosewater

Put nuts, chocolate, and zwieback through food chopper, using fine blade. Add cinnamon, 1½ tablespoons sugar, and the rosewater. Form into 36 small balls. Roll in confectioners' sugar. Makes 3 dozen.

Note: No cooking is required to make these.

VIENNESE CHOCOLATE CONFECTION

2 cups ground blanched almonds
1 cup grated sweet cooking chocolate (about 1½ packages, 4 ounces each)
1 egg
½ cup sugar
½ cup finely diced citron
⅓ cup almonds, blanched and slivered
Superfine granulated sugar, white or colored

Combine ground almonds and chocolate. Beat egg and sugar until fluffy. Add to almond-chocolate mixture together with citron and slivered almonds. Heat mixture in top part of double boiler over hot water until warm, stirring constantly until well blended. Cool. Lightly spread a baking board or a sheet of wax paper with sugar. Put mixture on it and, between sugared hands, shape into a sausage about 11 inches long. Roll in fine sugar. Dry in cool place overnight. To serve, cut into thin slices. Makes about 1½ pounds.

CHOCOLATE CRINKLE CUPS

Melt 6 ounces (6 squares) semisweet chocolate in top part of double boiler over hot water. Place 6 to 8 paper cups (3 to 4 inches in diameter) in muffin pan. With a spoon, line inside of cups with melted chocolate, coating all folds evenly. Put muffin pan in refrigerator until ready to use. Then, with cool hands, quickly peel paper off cups. Fill with ice cream, whipped cream, or sherbet. Decorate filled cups with chocolate curls. Makes 6 to 8 servings.

DRINKS

BRAZILIAN CHOCOLATE

2 ounces (2 squares) unsweetened chocolate

1 cup water
¼ cup sugar
3 cups milk
1 tablespoon grated orange rind
¼ teaspoon almond extract
5 cinnamon sticks

Melt chocolate in water in top part of double boiler over hot water. Stir in sugar; bring to a boil over direct heat. Boil for 5 minutes, stirring constantly. Stir in milk, orange rind, and almond extract. Heat thoroughly. Before serving, beat with rotary beater until frothy. Serve with a cinnamon stick in each cup. Makes 5 cups.

GUATEMALAN CHOCOLATE

2 ounces (2 squares) unsweetened chocolate
2 tablespoons water
½ cup sugar
1 tablespoon cornstarch
2 cups freshly brewed strong black coffee
1½ teaspoons ground cinnamon
½ teaspoon vanilla extract
⅛ teaspoon salt
3 cups hot milk

Grate chocolate into top part of double boiler over boiling water. Add water and mix chocolate and water into a smooth paste. Add sugar mixed with cornstarch. Gradually stir in coffee. Beat until smooth. Cook for about 5 minutes, stirring occasionally. Stir in cinnamon, vanilla, salt, and milk. Blend thoroughly. Cook mixture for about 20 minutes, stirring occasionally. Before serving, beat with rotary beater until frothy. Makes about 6 cups, or 6 to 8 servings.

Note: This chocolate is also very good iced. It then has the consistency of a milk shake. It can be served as a dessert drink, with a topping of sweetened whipped cream.

SPANISH EGG CHOCOLATE

2 ounces (2 squares) unsweetened chocolate
2 cups milk
½ cup sugar
1 teaspoon vanilla extract
⅛ teaspoon ground cloves
1 egg

In top part of double boiler over hot water melt together chocolate and milk. Beat with rotary beater until blended. Stir in sugar, vanilla, and cloves. Beat egg until frothy in pitcher in which chocolate will be served. Pour chocolate over egg and beat again to a froth. Serve at once. Makes about 3½ cups or 4 servings.

SAUCES AND SYRUPS

LOW-CALORIE CHOCOLATE SAUCE

1½ ounces (1½ squares) unsweetened chocolate

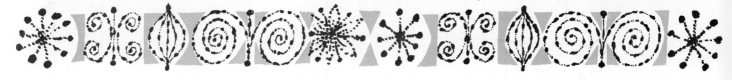

2 cups liquid nonfat dry milk
4 teaspoons liquid sweetener
   (cyclamate type)
⅛ teaspoon salt
2 tablespoons all-purpose flour
1 teaspoon butter
1 teaspoon vanilla, almond, or
   peppermint extract

Heat chocolate and 1½ cups of the milk in top part of double boiler over hot water. When chocolate is melted, beat with rotary beater. Add liquid sweetener and salt. Mix remaining ½ cup milk with flour to make a smooth paste. Stir into chocolate mixture and cook until thickened, stirring. Beat in butter and flavoring. Makes about 2 cups.

CHOCOLATE SYRUP

6 ounces (6 squares) unsweetened
   chocolate, melted, or 1 cup cocoa
1½ cups sugar
¼ teaspoon salt
1 cup boiling water
1 teaspoon vanilla extract

Mix melted chocolate with sugar and salt. Add boiling water and cook for 5 minutes, stirring constantly. Cool; add vanilla. Refrigerate. Makes 2 cups.

Quick Chocolate

For each serving, mix 1 to 2 tablespoons Chocolate Syrup with 1 serving cup hot milk.

CHOKECHERRY—This small, wild cherry (*Prunus virginiana* and *Prunus demissa*) grows on a large shrub, and is a native of North America. The flowers are white, and the fruit turns from red to black as it matures. Chokecherries have a puckery taste, and though they can be eaten raw, they are best used for jams and jellies.

Chokecherries are *not* to be confused with chokeberries, which belong to a different species, *Aronia,* and are the inedible fruits of a purely ornamental shrub.

CHOP—This can be either a noun or a verb. As a noun, a chop is a small tender cut of lamb, pork, or veal, with a part of the rib bone attached. Chops are usually cooked by dry heat, such as broiling or pan-broiling.

The verb "to chop" means to cut into small pieces, smaller than cubes or dices but larger than minces. For efficient chopping you need sharp knives and a wooden chopping board or bowl. Hold the knife blade by both ends and chop up and down rapidly, using the tip of the blade as the pivot. Keep pushing chopped food together under the knife.

CHOP SUEY, CHOW MEIN—These two dishes are the great favorites of American-Chinese cooking and they belong to a special category of their own, one which is neither Chinese or American. They are said to have been invented in San Francisco in the 19th century.

Both chop suey and chow mein are stews, consisting of combinations of shredded meat, celery, onions, Chinese cabbage, bamboo shoots, bean sprouts, water chestnuts, Chinese mushrooms, and other vegetables in chicken broth thickened with cornstarch. Both are served with rice and soy sauce, and the only difference between them is that chow mein is served with crisp fried noodles and chop suey without them.

Chow mein and chop suey are available in food stores, canned or frozen; crisp dry noodles in packages and cans.

CHOP SUEY

2 cups Chinese cabbage, shredded
2 cups sliced celery
2 medium onions, sliced
3 tablespoons cooking oil
2⅓ cups (one 1-pound, 3-ounce can)
   bean sprouts, undrained
½ cup water chestnuts, sliced
2 chicken bouillon cubes
3 tablespoons soy sauce
1 cup cooked chicken, cut into strips
3 tablespoons cornstarch
¼ cup water
2 cups cooked rice

In a large skillet, sauté cabbage, celery, and onions in oil for 8 to 10 minutes. Add next 5 ingredients and bring to a boil. Blend cornstarch with water and stir into chicken mixture; cook until clear and thickened. Serve on rice. Makes 4 servings.
Note: The same amount of cooked beef or cooked pork can be substituted for the chicken.

Chow Mein

Sprinkle finished chop suey dish with one 3-ounce can of crisp Chinese noodles.

CHORIZO—A Spanish or Mexican sausage made from coarsely cut meat, usually pork. It is seasoned with paprika, which gives it a piquant flavor and a colorful appearance. Chorizo can be bought in Spanish-American markets, either fresh, or dried and uncooked. It is also imported, canned in lard, from Spain.

CHOWDER—This is a thick hearty soup that probably originated in New England, but takes its name from a large French kettle, the *chaudière*. It usually contains fish or seafood, salt pork, vegetables, and milk. There are also all-vegetable chowders.

Chowder: a Great American Favorite

by Nika Hazelton

Ludwig van Beethoven, the great composer, once wrote to his friend Madame Streicher, in 1817 to be exact, that only the pure in heart can make good soup. I was imprudent enough to bring up this remark at a staid Boston supper party, in praise of a beautiful, creamy clam chowder sitting in front of me in its lovely Canton soup plate. The Bostonians beamed. But the guest of honor, a well known and spirited New York lawyer, and quite a cook himself, said that if purity of heart was gauged by a soup, the New York heart was a good deal purer than the New England heart because it was far more difficult to make a good, well-seasoned Manhattan clam chowder than a New England one. At once, passion was rampant on Mount Vernon Street and native reserve flew to the winds. The Bostonians, hot under the collar, ears flattened to the head like those of angry cats, hissed rather than spoke, praising their kind of chowder. The guest of honor, resembling an oil well tapped but not channeled, bellowed back. Oh such language, such strong sentiments! In my mind's eye, I could see poor purity of heart fleeing from the dinner table, wings folded over eyes like an angel weeping at the wickedness of man.

Whatever its name, a chowder is a thick, hearty soup that probably originated in New England. It usually contains fish or seafood, salt pork, vegetables, and milk. But it can also contain nothing but vegetables, or vegetables combined with meats, for soup is soup.

Ducking brickbats, I venture to say that the word chowder, used alone in a stark and naked manner, usually means a creamy clam or fish chowder, whereas the sub-versions are always qualified, such as Manhattan clam chowder, lobster chowder, and the most popular of vegetable chowders, corn.

Chowders, like soups all over the world, are based upon one of the verities of life, namely, that man eats what is accessible especially when it is for free. On the seashore, there is fish and seafood, his for the taking. Since soups are more nourishing, filling, and comforting than most dishes, what could be more natural than sticking the gifts of the sea into the soup pot? If company came along, it was always easy to throw another cup of milk or water into the chowder pot.

Whether it is New England or Manhattan clam chowder, to each his own, we say, feeling happy that along with baseball and pop art, there are still a few subjects on which we can disagree with passion, and no harm done.

NEW ENGLAND CLAM CHOWDER

2 dozen large chowder clams or 3 cans (10½ ounces each) minced clams
½ pound lean salt pork, diced
1 cup chopped onion
3 cups diced raw peeled potatoes
1 teaspoon salt
¼ teaspoon white pepper
2 cups light cream
2 cups milk
2 tablespoons butter
Paprika

Steam open chowder clams. Strain and reserve the liquid; coarsely grind or chop clams. If canned clams are used, strain and reserve liquid. Measure clam liquid, fresh or canned. Add water if amount is less than 4 cups. Fry pork in large kettle until golden. Remove pork and reserve. Drain off all but ¼ cup fat. Add onions and sauté for 5 minutes. Add potato, salt, pepper, and clam liquid. Simmer until potatoes are tender. Add clams, cream, milk, and butter. Reheat but do not boil. Top with crisp pork and sprinkle with paprika. Makes about 3 quarts.

MANHATTAN CLAM CHOWDER

¼ pound salt pork, sliced, or 4 slices of bacon, diced
1 large onion, sliced
½ cup green pepper, chopped
½ cup chopped celery
½ cup chopped carrots
½ cup chopped turnips
3 cups diced peeled potatoes
3 cups water
1 teaspoon salt
1 pint clams and liquid
⅛ teaspoon ground thyme
3 cups cooked or canned tomatoes
Salt and pepper
2 tablespoons chopped parsley

Sauté pork over low heat until soft and golden. Pour off all but 1 tablespoon of the fat. Add onion, pepper, and celery. Sauté until golden brown. Add carrots, turnips, potatoes, water, and salt. Shuck clams. Chop hard part of clams and add to soup with clam liquid; chop soft part of clams and reserve. Simmer, covered, over low heat for 30 minutes. Add chopped soft part of clams, thyme, and tomatoes. Simmer for 10 minutes. Season to taste with salt and pepper. Sprinkle with chopped parsley. Makes about 3 quarts.

New England Clam Chowder

Manhattan Clam Chowder

CORN CHOWDER

- 8 ounces salt pork, diced
- 2 onions, chopped
- ½ cup chopped celery and tops
- ½ bay leaf, crumbled
- 2 tablespoons all-purpose flour
- 4 cups water
- 3 cups diced potato
- 2 cups (one 1-pound, 1-ounce can) cream-style corn
- 2 cups evaporated milk
  Salt and pepper to taste
  Chopped parsley
  Paprika

In large kettle, cook salt pork until browned and crisp. Remove pork, and pour off all but 3 tablespoons fat. Add next 3 ingredients, and cook for 5 minutes. Blend in flour. Add water and potato; bring to boil, and simmer, covered, for 15 minutes. Add corn and milk; heat well. Season. Add pork. Serve with parsley and paprika. Makes about 2 quarts.

FISH CHOWDER

- 2½ pounds boned haddock
  Water
- 6 medium potatoes, cubed
- 1½-inch cube salt pork
- 3 medium onions, chopped
- 2½ quarts rich milk
  Salt and pepper
  Butter

Cook fish in 2 cups water for about 15 minutes. Cook potato in small amount of boiling salted water for about 15 minutes. Meanwhile, dice salt pork and fry until crisp but not brown. Add onion and cook for about 10 minutes more; do not brown. Add potato, pork, pork fat, onions, and milk to fish. (A little cream substituted for some of the milk improves the chowder.) Season to taste. Heat slowly almost to the simmering point. Do not boil. Put a little butter in each soup bowl, and serve with pilot or other crackers. Makes about 4 quarts, or 6 servings.

Note: Chowder can be cooled and reheated (do not boil) just before serving.

LOBSTER CHOWDER

- 2 tablespoons quick-cooking tapioca
- 1¼ teaspoons salt
- ⅛ teaspoon each of pepper and paprika
- 1 tablespoon minced onion
- 3 cups milk
- 1 cup light cream
- 1 can (6½ ounces) lobster or 1½ cups cooked lobster meat, cut in chunks
- 2 tablespoons butter
- 2 tablespoons sherry or brandy

In top part of double boiler mix tapioca, salt, pepper, paprika, onion, milk, and cream. Put over rapidly boiling water and cook for 15 minutes, stirring frequently. Add lobster and butter. Keep over hot water for 15 minutes to blend flavors. Add sherry. Serve at once, or cool, stir, then chill overnight. Makes 4 servings.

Crabmeat Chowder

Substitute 1 can (6½ ounces) crabmeat for the lobster.

at Christmas time

By CAMILLA R. BITTLE

At Christmas, when I was small,
    We placed the figures in the stall
(Mary, Blessed Babe, and all),
    Hung mistletoe high in the hall,
Made calendars for kitchen walls,
    And decked our tree with shiny balls.

On Christmas Eve beside the fire,
    We gathered round the wicker chair
To hear our mother's mother read
    Of sugarplums that danced in air,
Of moonlight on new fallen snow,
    And this we knew—as children know—
Was evidence of love below
    The great high arc of heaven's dome,
Of Christmases secured by home.

The cold—a stabbing, piercing knife.
    The stars—small, dazzling flecks of light.
Our breath rose up in columns white,
    And, oh, the still of Christmas night!

Each year we did the very same,
    Wrote cards, made lists, our cousins came.
On Christmas Eve out caroling,
    Our cheeks bared to the icy sting
Of snowy wind, grew tingling.
    We sang as loud as we could sing.

I ask myself—what did it mean,
    The stockings, tinsel, branches green,
The smell of oranges and pie,
    The wreaths, the bells, the winter sky
Where once a star shone for The Child,
    Whose birth we hailed with praises mild,
While overhead the Milky Way
    Was passage for Old Santa's sleigh.

We still hang up the mistletoe.
    My children's faces rosy grow,
Their boots squeak on the hard-packed snow.
    Their eyes with eagerness will glow,
And I'm the only one who'll know
    That it was different long ago.

The tree still flaunts its branches.
    The sky is jet, the stars wink light.
There is a hush to Christmas night,
    The songs are still sung out with might
And Santa's toys, a dazzling sight.

The only thing that's changed is me.
    It's not a fir with lights I see,
For only God can make a tree—
    This is what I see.
And children's eyes can only be
    Small windows on eternity.

And so with gifts, and cousins small,
    And so with garlands in the hall,
And firelight's shadows on the wall—
    God's handiwork, that's all.

Yet in this season of our joy
    There are still those who feel a toy
Is all that matters—not The Boy,
    Whose praises we should all employ,
Lest man all brotherhood destroy.

Come, take your stand—decry the whim
    That turkeys, gifts and greetings slim
Define the core—they are the rim
    And but the glossy surface skim
For in our hearts we kneel to Him.

Twelve Days Before Christmas
by Jean Hersey

I begin baking bread twelve days before Christmas. Now it is the day before, I've twenty-two loaves, I feel fresh as a daisy, couldn't be happier, and I'm no professional baker! Each morning right after breakfast, beginning twelve days before Christmas, I make two loaves of bread. I've a basic recipe and five variations, totaling six different kinds of bread. Each night I put the newly baked loaves in the freezer until there stands a neat stack of twenty-two (we ate the other two), each in its plastic bag held tight at the top by a clip clothespin. These are for our neighbors, for friends, and for people to whose houses we go for tea, for holiday festivities, and sometimes they are just for people. What a welcome and surprising present out of the clear sky is a loaf of homemade bread! Forgive me one small gloat and a boast. Each loaf is perfection, light as a feather but with substance. It is utterly heavenly to eat plain, with sweet butter, with or without honey. Toasted for breakfast, it is pure ambrosia. And what's more, while it is baking every-

one who comes to the door from the milkman to the electric-meter reader comments on the fragrance of our house. It always reminds them of something out of their past! Living here myself, it fills my days with a scent that is one of the best I know. If you never did eat bread it would be worth baking merely for the smell of it cooking. This fragrance carries you back many years, perhaps to your mother's kitchen, your grandmother's, your aunt's. It is the pure undiluted scent of nostalgia. Now I will tell you exactly, down to the last knead, how to bake this bread so you cannot fail even if you have never made a loaf before.

First of all you need two bread pans. The measurements should be 9" x 5" x 3".

Basic ingredients required for two loaves:

About 6 cups enriched white flour
2½ teaspoons salt
2 tablespoons soft butter
½ cup molasses (Black strap makes a dark bread, regular makes a lighter-colored bread. Honey can be substituted and is equally good.)
1 cup rolled oats
2 cups boiling water
2 packages active dry yeast
⅓ cup lukewarm water

This basic recipe can be made up as it is, or any of five variations can be made by adding one of the following:

(1) 1 cup seedless raisins

or

(2) herbs: ½ teaspoon dried parsley, 1 teaspoon dried basil, ½ teaspoon aniseed, 2 teaspoons dried summer savory, ¼ teaspoon powdered thyme

or

(3) herbs: 2 teaspoons leaf sage, crumbled; 1 teaspoon leaf marjoram, crumbled; ½ teaspoon caraway seed

or

(4) ¾ cup citron, dried fruits and peels

or

(5) ½ cup orange marmalade and only ¼ cup molasses

Each morning before breakfast I put the rolled oats in a large bread bowl, and pour the boiling water over it. It stands there while I get breakfast. About one-half hour later it will be still warm, and this is important. It will have softened up and all the little separate oats

will have blended together. And now you are ready to begin.

Step one is to soak the yeast. Pour it out of the packages on top of the lukewarm water. Let stand five minutes or so. Meanwhile you've other things to do. Add to the soaked oats the salt, molasses, butter, and special ingredients of the day, if any. (When my husband gets home at night he steps in the house, breathes deeply, and tries to guess the particular variation.)

By now the yeast has grown and is ready. Stir, and add it to the above mixture. Next add and stir in the first two cups of flour, then two more cups. The second two may be a little difficult to blend but they will gradually merge. The last two, you knead in.

One of the most fun things I know is kneading bread. You can feel the bounce of the dough; the yeast turns it elastic, and it purely lives in your hands and grows as you work it. Here is how you do this kneading, and it is not one bit difficult. Leave the dough in the large bowl. Roll up your sleeves. Scatter half a cup of flour on top of the dough. With the heel of your hand, press into the dough—one quick firm press. Then with your fingers get hold of and shift it around in the bowl, sometimes turning it over. As the flour you are working with gradually merges into the bread, add more, and continue kneading until the last two cups of flour are in. This might take ten minutes or five. If the dough is still very sticky, add a little more flour.

When the flour is all worked in, shape the dough into a mound in the center of the bowl, and cover with a clean dish towel and leave for several hours. The convenient part of this bread is that one hour more or less of rising doesn't matter, so you can go about your business. As it begins to rise a lovely smell spreads over the house, a scent more subtle than that of bread baking but equally nice. I'd suggest you let the dough rise about two hours in an average-warm room. No added heat from the stove is necessary. I can't say why but ours always rises faster on clear, sunny days.

When the dough has risen to about two times the size it was when you finished kneading and is gently lifting the covering cloth, you are ready for the next step.

Cut it down with a knife, which seems unfair after all its work of rising! But willy-nilly, cut back and forth a half dozen times through the dough while, like a punctured balloon, it subsides into never quite its original size but near it.

Now divide and place into the two well-greased bread pans, shaping the dough out to the ends, to cover entirely the bottom of the pans. Let the dough be fairly level and smooth on top. Cover and let it rise again. This time it comes up more quickly. In perhaps an hour or so it will rise into the lovely shape of the loaf you wish to have in the end, the top delicately rounded.

Put in the oven at 325°F. on a rack about four inches from the bottom. Bake for 50 minutes. If you have forgotten to turn the oven on, no matter; set in a cold oven, turning the gauge to 325°F., and bake 60 minutes. Either way is successful. This baking time is when the fragrance reaches its peak of delight. Ask a friend for tea just to sit there beside your glowing fire, with the bread baking.

There is something so solidly satisfying to me about making bread. Is it perhaps because, after all, yeast is a plant and it is always good to feel any plant grow in your hands? Or perhaps I like it because it takes me back to the basement kitchen of my youth and our old Irish cook, Delia. There, wrapped round by her brogue thick as a blanket, and her tales of Irish lore, I'd sit beside the old wood stove with the rich fragrance of pine and baking bread filling the room. Wherever bread is baking, long years ago or today, there is not only a fine smell but a comfortable feel of something basic. I don't quite know what it is, but I like it.

When you take the bread from the oven, turn it out of the pans immediately and set each loaf right side up on a wire cake rack so air circulates beneath. Butter the crust. When the loaves are cool, I pack each one in a plastic bag, seal the end with a clothespin, and put it in the freezer, except of course, the loaves we keep out to eat as we go along. We have to keep sampling.

Each of the twelve days before Christmas I've fresh loaves to store. The pile grows until December 24 when we begin to take them out, to go Merry Christmasing with them!

Hospitality Tables for the Christmas Season

Hospitality is as much a part of Christmas as the wreath on the door and the brightly bedecked tree in the living room. We welcome old friends and new to our home and good fellowship finds its most heartwarming expression in that festive tradition, the abundant table. For the friendliest gesture we can make is to share the good things from our kitchen with all who come to our house. In this spirit we have prepared menus and recipes for holiday entertaining, whatever the hour, whoever the guests.

AFTER-CAROLING PARTY

HERBED BOUILLON*   CRACKERS
OVEN-FRIED CHICKEN IN BREAD LOAF*
CRANBERRY FRUIT RING*
CREAM CHEESE-WATERCRESS BALLS*
BROWN BEAUTY CAKE*
COFFEE   MILK

HERBED BOUILLON

Combine 2 cans each condensed beef bouillon and tomato soup. Stir in 3 soup-cans water and dash of basil. Simmer for a few minutes. Top with slices of lemon. Makes 8 to 10 servings.

OVEN-FRIED CHICKEN IN BREAD LOAF

2 frying chickens, cut up
½ cup flour
2 teaspoons salt
½ teaspoon pepper
1½ tablespoons paprika
1¼ cups butter or margarine
1 large round loaf French or Italian bread
¼ cup each chopped parsley and green onion

Wash and dry chicken. Mix flour, salt, pepper, and paprika; roll chicken pieces in mixture. Melt ¾ cup butter in large shallow baking pan. Place chicken, skin side down, in melted butter. Bake in hot oven (400°F.) for 30 minutes. Turn chicken pieces and bake for 20 to 30 minutes longer, or until tender and brown. Remove from pan and cool. Cut bread in half crosswise and pull out a little of the inside of the bread. Melt remaining ½ cup butter in saucepan and add chopped parsley and green onion; spread on inside of bread. Fill bottom with fried chicken and cover with top. Wrap loosely in foil. Keep in cool place or refrigerate. One hour before serving, put in hot oven (400°F.); open foil last 5 minutes so that crust will be crisp. Cut top crust in wedges with knife or scissors, or break apart. Cut bottom after removing chicken. Serve with chicken. Makes 8 servings.

CRANBERRY FRUIT RING

1 pound (4 cups) fresh cranberries
1 orange
1½ cups sugar
2 cups hot water
2 packages spicy peach or lemon flavor gelatin
Cream Cheese-Watercress Balls

Force cranberries and orange through food chopper. Add sugar and mix well. Let stand while preparing gelatin. Add hot water to gelatin and stir until dissolved. When gelatin begins to set, stir in cranberry mixture. Pour into a 5-cup ring mold and chill until firm. Unmold on serving platter and fill with Cream Cheese-Watercress Balls. Makes 8 to 10 servings.

Cream Cheese-Watercress Balls

Cut 2 packages (8 ounces each) cream cheese into 10 pieces each. Roll each into ball, then roll in chopped watercress or parsley. Refrigerate until serving time.

BROWN BEAUTY CAKE

⅓ cup semisweet chocolate pieces
⅓ cup butterscotch pieces
¼ cup water
½ cup shortening
1¼ cups sugar
3 eggs
2¼ cups sifted all-purpose flour
1 teaspoon salt
½ teaspoon baking powder
1 teaspoon soda
1 cup buttermilk
Frosting

Combine chocolate and butterscotch pieces with water; heat until melted. Cool. Combine shortening and sugar and beat until creamy. Beat in eggs, one at a time. Blend in chocolate-butterscotch mixture. Sift flour with salt, baking powder, and soda; add alternately with buttermilk. Pour into 2 greased and floured 9-inch square or round layer-cake pans. Bake in preheated moderate oven (375°F.) for 25 to 30 minutes. Remove from pans. When cold, spread with Frosting.

Frosting

1 package (6 ounces) each semisweet chocolate and butterscotch pieces
½ cup strong coffee
3 cups sifted confectioners' sugar

Melt chocolate and butterscotch pieces over hot water. Remove from heat and stir in coffee and sugar, beating until smooth.

TRIM-THE-TREE SUPPER

SEAFOOD MEDLEY IN PATTY SHELLS*
SWEET-AND-SOUR MEATBALLS*
JELLIED VEGETABLE SALAD*
CURRY DRESSING*
AMBROSIA*
SMALL FROSTED CAKES*   TEA

SEAFOOD MEDLEY IN PATTY SHELLS

Combine 4 cans (10½ ounces each) frozen shrimp soup with 1½ cups milk; heat. Add 6 cups cooked fish and seafood such as flounder, cod, shrimps, crabmeat, lobster. Heat and add a little sherry, if desired. Makes 8 to 10 servings.

■ Patty Shells—Use ready-baked patty shells or buy frozen ones and bake according to package directions. Allow 1 per serving.

SWEET-AND-SOUR MEATBALLS

⅔ cup fine dry bread crumbs
2 teaspoons salt
¼ teaspoon pepper
1 tablespoon instant minced onion
Water
3 pounds beef chuck, ground
3 eggs, slightly beaten
Vegetable oil
2 cans (8¾ ounces each) beef gravy
⅓ cup vinegar
⅓ cup packed brown sugar
1 tablespoon soy sauce
1 pickled red pepper, cut up
10 tiny pickled onions (optional)
Parsley

Add bread crumbs, salt, pepper, and instant onion to 1 cup water; let stand a few minutes. Then add to beef with eggs and mix well. Shape into 30 balls and brown in small amount of oil in skillet. Add gravy, ¾ cup water, vinegar, and brown sugar. Cover and simmer about 35 minutes. Add soy sauce, red pepper, and pickled onions; heat. Sprinkle with parsley. Serves 10.

JELLIED VEGETABLE SALAD

Dissolve 3 packages mixed vegetable-flavor salad gelatin in 2¼ cups boiling water. Add 1½ tablespoons vinegar and 3 cups cold water. Put in 2½-quart mixing bowl. Chill; when almost set, divide in quarters. Section off one quarter at a time by holding 2 small plates in place; mix into each quarter one of the following: 1 cup shredded carrot; 1 cup thinly sliced celery and ¼ cup diced pickled red pepper; 1 cup thinly sliced green pepper; 1 cup well-drained canned diced beets. Chill until firm. Unmold; garnish with pimiento and parsley. Serve with Curry Dressing. Serves 10.

Trim-the-Tree Supper

◀ *Round-the-Clock Table*

▲ *Open-House Buffet*

Curry Dressing

Combine ¾ cup each mayonnaise and sour cream. Stir in 1 tablespoon each vinegar and curry powder.

AMBROSIA

Peel and section 6 to 8 large oranges. Combine with 2 cans (16 ounces each) pineapple chunks and 1 cup shredded or flaked coconut. Chill. Makes 8 to 10 servings.

SMALL FROSTED CAKES

Buy poundcake and cut into any desired shapes. Frost with packaged frosting mix prepared according to label directions. Decorate with ready frosting mix.

ROUND-THE-CLOCK TABLE

SPICY CRANBERRY PUNCH*
SHERRY   CHEESE
SAVORY HAM SPREAD*
ASSORTED CRACKERS   FRESH FRUIT
SOYED WALNUTS*   CANDY
CHRISTMAS TREE COOKIES*
HOLIDAY CHEESECAKE*

SPICY CRANBERRY PUNCH

    2 cups boiling water
    5 tea bags
    ¼ teaspoon cinnamon
    ¼ teaspoon nutmeg
    ¾ cup sugar
    2½ cups water
    2 pints cranberry juice cocktail
    ½ cup fresh orange juice
    ⅔ cup fresh lemon juice
      Orange slices
      Whole cloves

Pour boiling water over tea and spices. Cover; steep 5 minutes. Remove tea bags. Stir in sugar; cool. Add next 4 ingredients and chill. Garnish with orange slices stuck with cloves. Makes 2½ quarts.

SAVORY HAM SPREAD

    3 pounds canned ham, ground (7 cups)
    ¾ cup mayonnaise
    ⅓ cup sweet pickle relish
    ½ cup coarsely chopped parsley
    ½ cup cut sweet pepper

Combine ham with remaining ingredients. Pack into mold or mixing bowl and refrigerate. Unmold and garnish.
Note: Other cooked ham can be substituted for canned.

SOYED WALNUTS

    4 cups shelled walnuts (1 pound)
    ¼ cup butter or margarine
    ¼ cup soy sauce

Put walnuts in 13" x 9" x 2" pan. Roast in hot oven (400°F.) for about 15 minutes, stirring several times. Add butter and soy sauce; stir. Roast for 12 to 15 minutes longer, stirring often until nuts are coated and fairly dry. Makes 4 cups.

CHRISTMAS TREE COOKIES

    ¾ cup butter
    1¼ cups packed light-brown sugar
    1½ teaspoons vanilla extract
    1 teaspoon fresh lemon juice
    2 eggs
    3 cups sifted all-purpose flour
    2 teaspoons baking powder
    ½ teaspoon salt
      Frosting

Cream butter, add sugar, and beat until light and fluffy. Add vanilla and lemon juice. Add eggs one at a time, beating well after each addition. Sift flour, baking powder, and salt. Add to creamed mixture and mix well. Chill. Roll dough to about ⅛" thickness. Cut into medium and small Christmas trees, using cookie cutter or paper pattern. Bake in preheated hot oven (425°F.) for 5 minutes or until edges are lightly browned. Cool; cover with frosting; decorate. Makes 3 to 4 dozen.

Frosting

Heat and boil ½ cup butter in heavy saucepan until lightly browned; do not burn. Stir in 3 cups sifted confectioners' sugar and 1 teaspoon vanilla. Add a few drops of water until frosting is of spreading consistency. Frost cookies; then decorate with cake decorator, using colored frosting, and with colored sugar. To stand, set each in large ring of bought jellied candies.

HOLIDAY CHEESECAKE

      Cookie-Dough Crust
    5 packages (8 ounces each) cream cheese
    1¾ cups sugar
    3 tablespoons flour
    ¼ teaspoon salt
      Grated rind 1 lemon
      Grated rind ½ orange
    5 eggs
    2 egg yolks
    ¾ cup heavy cream
      Mandarin-orange sections

Make Cookie-Dough Crust. Let ingredients (except ½ cup cream) reach room temperature. Beat cheese until fluffy. Mix sugar, flour, and salt; gradually blend into cheese, keeping mixture smooth. Add grated rinds. Add eggs and egg yolks one at a time, beating well after each. Stir in ¼ cup cream. Turn into Crust. Bake in preheated very hot oven (475°F.) for 15 minutes. Reduce heat to 200°F., bake for 1 hour longer. Turn off heat; let stand for 15 minutes. Remove from oven. Cool on rack. When cold, remove sides from pan. Just before serving, garnish with ½ cup cream, whipped, and mandarin-orange sections.

Cookie-Dough Crust

    1 cup flour
    ¼ cup sugar

      Grated rind 1 lemon
    1 egg yolk
    ½ cup softened butter or margarine

Mix flour and sugar. Add remaining ingredients; mix well. Chill. Roll one third of dough to cover bottom of 9-inch springform cake pan. Bake in preheated hot oven (400°F.) for 8 minutes, or until lightly browned. Butter sides of pan; put bottom, with crust, inside it. Cool. Roll remaining dough into 2 strips, 2" wide and 14" long; press onto sides of pan.

OPEN-HOUSE BUFFET

HERRING ASSORTMENT
PICKLED SHRIMPS*
RELISH CHRISTMAS TREE*
HOT SAUSAGE SLICES*
ROAST FRESH HAM*
BAKED BARBECUED CORNED BEEF*
MUSTARD   ASSORTED BREADS
HERB SWEET BUTTER*   CHEESE BALL*
LIGHT FRUITCAKE*   COFFEE

PICKLED SHRIMPS

Cover 2 boxes (10 ounces each) frozen cleaned shelled shrimps with boiling water. Tie loosely in cheesecloth bag: ½ cup chopped celery tops and ¼ cup mixed pickling spices. Add to shrimps and cook 5 minutes, or until shrimps turn pink, breaking block apart with fork. Remove spice bag, drain shrimps and cool. Arrange shrimps and 2 cups sliced onion in alternate layers in bowl. Add 5 bay leaves and ½ cup pickled sweet red pepper. Mix 1¼ cups salad oil, ¾ cup white vinegar, 2 tablespoons capers and liquid, 1½ teaspoons each celery seed and salt, and dash of hot pepper sauce; pour over shrimps and onion. Cover and chill at least 24 hours. Drain.

RELISH CHRISTMAS TREE

Buy a piece of styrofoam shaped like a Christmas tree. Cover with a piece of heavy green wrapping paper. Stick with toothpicks and then with any assorted vegetables and pickles such as tiny tomatoes, pieces of cauliflower, radishes, pickled onions, and tiny cucumber pickles.

HOT SAUSAGE SLICES

Slice Polish or other type sausage and fry in small amount of butter or margarine until lightly browned and done.

ROAST FRESH HAM

Buy a whole fresh ham (pork) weighing 10 to 14 pounds. Rub with salt and pepper. Place fat side up on rack in open roasting pan. Insert a roast meat thermometer through the fat side into the center of the roast. Roast in preheated slow oven (325°F.) until thermometer registers 185°F. (well done), 6 to 7 hours. Score and garnish, if desired.

BAKED BARBECUED CORNED BEEF

5 to 6 pounds corned brisket of beef
1 tablespoon whole mixed pickling spice
  Whole cloves
2 tablespoons butter or margarine, melted
⅓ cup packed brown sugar
1 tablespoon prepared mustard
⅓ cup ketchup
2 tablespoons sweet-pickle juice or vinegar

Wash corned beef and put in large kettle. Cover with cold water. Add pickling spice. Bring to boil, cover, and simmer for 4 hours, or until tender. Cool beef in broth. Then put in shallow roasting pan and score fat layer. Insert whole cloves in fat. Mix butter, sugar, mustard, ketchup, and pickle juice. Pat on beef. Bake in preheated moderate oven (350°F.) for about 30 minutes. Serve warm, sliced thin for sandwiches. Makes 10 to 12 servings.

HERB SWEET BUTTER

Whip sweet butter and add a generous amount of fresh chopped or ground sage. Shape and chill until serving time.

CHEESE BALL

For a large cheese ball, shape 4 pounds soft-type Cheddar cheese into ball. (Keep cheese out of refrigerator until it is the right temperature to shape easily.) Chill. Cream 8 ounces cream cheese until of spreading consistency. Spread over ball. Cover ball with chopped parsley and press in lightly. Arrange strips of sweet red pepper down sides of ball and press in lightly. Top with a small tomato or a twisted strip of pepper.

LIGHT FRUITCAKE

1 pound almonds, blanched and slivered
½ pound candied red cherries, halved
¼ pound candied green cherries, halved
½ pound golden raisins
½ pound candied citron, chopped
¼ pound candied pineapple, chopped
4 cups unsifted all-purpose flour
1½ cups butter
2 cups sugar
6 eggs, separated
¾ cup milk
¼ cup brandy
1 teaspoon almond extract
1 teaspoon cream of tartar
  Candied strawberries
  Angelica

Grease a 10″ tube pan and line with brown paper and grease paper. Combine almonds, cherries, raisins, citron, and pineapple; sprinkle with ½ cup of the flour. Cream butter, gradually add sugar and beat until creamy. Beat egg yolks well and add to butter mixture; beat

thoroughly. Combine milk, brandy, and almond extract; add alternately with remaining flour to first mixture. Pour over fruit and nuts and mix well. Beat egg whites until foamy, add cream of tartar and beat until stiff. Fold into the first mixture. Pour into prepared pan. Bake in preheated slow oven (275°F.) for about 3 hours. Let stand for about 30 minutes. Remove cake from pan and carefully tear off paper. Cool to room temperature. Decorate with candied strawberries and strips of angelica. Wrap in moisture-proof paper and store in cool place.

CHRISTMAS BRUNCH

RAINBOW FRUIT*
DEVILED HAM STEAK*
CREAMY EGGS*
TOASTED ENGLISH MUFFINS
ORANGE-GINGER MARMALADE*
MUSTARD PICKLE
CHRISTMAS COFFEE RING*
COFFEE   MILK   COCOA

RAINBOW FRUIT

Arrange in individual serving dishes 2 kinds of chunky applesauce: one mixed with apricots and one with strawberries. Top each with a strawberry half and a sprig of mint, if desired.

DEVILED HAM STEAK

Buy 1 thick, center cut of ready-to-eat ham (about 2½ pounds). Put on rack in shallow baking pan. Combine 2 teaspoons dry mustard, ¼ cup packed brown sugar, and 2 tablespoons vinegar; sprinkle over ham. Broil under moderate heat until well browned. Turn and baste with pan drippings. Broil until lightly browned. Serves 6.

CREAMY EGGS

Hard-cook 1 dozen eggs; peel and cut in half. Put in shallow baking dish. Combine 2 packages of sour-cream sauce mix with 1½ cups milk. Beat to blend well. Heat and season with salt. Pour over eggs. Sprinkle with a few buttered bread crumbs. Put in preheated slow oven (300°F.) for 15 minutes, or until heated. Sprinkle with paprika. Serves 6.

ORANGE-GINGER MARMALADE

Add 2 tablespoons chopped preserved or crystallized ginger to 1 cup orange marmalade.

CHRISTMAS COFFEE RING

2 packages active dry yeast
½ cup warm water
1 cup lukewarm milk
5 cups unsifted all-purpose flour
  Sugar
½ cup butter or margarine

¼ teaspoon mace
¼ teaspoon cinnamon
¼ teaspoon nutmeg
¾ teaspoon salt
2 eggs
1 cup coarsely chopped nuts
1 cup seedless raisins
½ cup candied cherries, halved
¼ cup chopped citron
¾ cup mixed candied fruit

Dissolve yeast in water; let stand a few minutes. Add lukewarm milk, 2 cups flour, and 1 tablespoon sugar; beat until smooth. Let stand in warm place until bubbly and double in bulk. Cream butter and beat in ¾ cup sugar, spices, and salt. Beat in eggs. Stir down yeast mixture and add butter mixture. Beat in 2 cups flour. Then add nuts and fruit and enough flour to make a fairly stiff dough. Turn out on floured board and knead well. Put in greased bowl and let stand in warm place until double in bulk. Punch down in bowl and work dough well with hand for a few minutes. Pack into large well-buttered 3½-quart mold with hole in center. Let stand in warm place until double in bulk. Bake in preheated moderate oven (375°F.) about 35 minutes. Let stand a few minutes. Turn out and cool. If desired, frost with confectioners' sugar mixed with a little milk. Decorate with candied fruit.

The Merrie Christmas Cookie Cook Book

MORAVIAN COOKIES
*Thin, crisp rolled cookies with a good
ginger and molasses flavor.*

Sift together into bowl and reserve:
4½ cups sifted all-purpose flour
(Not instant type.)
¼ teaspoon baking soda
½ teaspoon salt
1 teaspoon ground cinnamon
½ teaspoon ground cloves
½ teaspoon ground ginger

Add
1 cup firmly packed light brown sugar
(Not granulated brown sugar.)

Mix well.

With pastry blender or 2 knives, cut in:
½ cup soft (not runny or whipped)
butter or margarine
½ cup soft lard

Gradually add:
1½ cups light molasses
½ teaspoon cider vinegar

Mix thoroughly.

Chill dough several hours, or until firm
enough to roll.

Using a small amount of dough at a
time, roll on floured board to ⅛-inch
thickness.

Cut with floured fancy cookie cutters.

Put on greased cookie sheets.

Bake in preheated moderate oven (350°
F.) for about 10 minutes, or until
browned.

Cool on wire racks.

Decorate with Confectioners' Sugar
Frosting (see page 410), tinted as desired, and with colored sugar. Makes
about 72.

To Store—Store cookies airtight. Can be
frozen. These cookies keep well but
may break in shipping.

ORANGE WALNUT-DATE BARS
*Cakelike cookies
with a creamy butter frosting.*

Sift together into bowl and reserve:
1 cup unsifted all-purpose flour
(Instant type can be used. Do not
sift, but mix with soda, spices, and
salt.)
½ teaspoon baking soda
½ teaspoon cinnamon
¼ teaspoon nutmeg
¼ teaspoon salt

Put
⅓ cup soft (not runny or whipped)
butter or margarine in large bowl of
electric mixer (or other bowl if mixer
is not available).

Add
¾ cup packed light brown sugar
(Not granulated brown sugar.)

Beat with mixer or wooden spoon until
mixture is light and fluffy.

Beat in:
1 egg
1 tablespoon grated orange rind
2 tablespoons fresh orange juice

Beat in flour mixture with mixer or
spoon, blending until smooth.

Stir in:
½ cup chopped pitted dates
¾ cup coarsely chopped walnuts

Spread evenly in greased and floured
baking pan (11 x 7 x 1 inches).

Bake in preheated moderate oven (350°
F.) for 25 to 30 minutes, or until
browned.

Spread with Orange Butter Frosting.

Sprinkle with ¼ cup coarsely chopped
walnuts.

Cut in 33 bars about 2 inches x 1 inch.

Orange Butter Frosting
Cream ¼ cup soft butter or margarine
until fluffy.

Add:
1 teaspoon grated orange rind
1 egg yolk
½ teaspoon vanilla extract

Beat until well blended. Gradually add 2
cups sifted confectioners' sugar, beating well.

Mix in:
2 teaspoons fresh orange juice, or
enough to make frosting of spreading
consistency

To Store—If cookies are not to be used

at once, do not frost. Cover whole pan
with moisture-proof wrap and store in
the refrigerator. Frost the day before
serving. Frosted cookies keep well in
the freezer. Will not ship well.

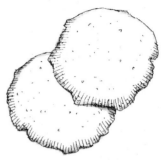

BROWN-EDGED BUTTER COOKIES
*Thin, crisp, buttery dropped cookies
with delicious flavor.*

Sift together into bowl and reserve:
¾ cup sifted all-purpose flour
(Instant type can be used. Do not
sift, but mix with salt. Cookies will
not be as thin.)
⅛ teaspoon salt

Put
½ cup soft (not runny or whipped)
butter or margarine in small bowl of
electric mixer (or other bowl if mixer
is not available).

Add:
⅓ cup sugar
½ teaspoon vanilla extract
1 egg

Beat with mixer or wooden spoon until
mixture is light and fluffy.

Add flour mixture.

Mix well.

Drop by half-measuring-teaspoonfuls onto
ungreased cookie sheets.

Bake in preheated moderate oven (350°
F.) for about 10 minutes, or until edges
are golden brown.

Remove to wire racks to cool. Makes
about 2 dozen.

To Store—Store cookies airtight. Can be
frozen. Good keepers but not good
shippers.

COCONUT SQUARES
*Chewy cookies in two layers
with coconut and nuts in the top layer.*

Put
½ cup soft (not runny or whipped)
butter or margarine in large bowl of

electric mixer (or other bowl if mixer is not available).

Add:
½ cup packed light brown sugar or ⅔ cup plus 2 tablespoons granulated brown sugar

Beat with mixer or wooden spoon until mixture is light and fluffy.

Add:
1 cup sifted all-purpose flour.
(Do not use instant type.)

Mix well.

Pat into greased pan (13 x 9 x 2 inches).

Bake in preheated moderate oven (375° F.) for 12 minutes.

Break 2 eggs into mixing bowl.

Beat slightly.

Add:
½ teaspoon salt
1 teaspoon vanilla extract
1 can flaked coconut
1 cup chopped nuts
¼ cup sifted all-purpose flour
1 cup firmly packed light brown sugar or 1⅓ cups granulated brown sugar

Mix well.

Spread evenly on mixture in pan.

Put back in oven; bake for 20 minutes.

Put pan on wire rack.

Cut in 24 squares. Cool in pan.

To Store—Store cookies airtight. They freeze and also ship well.

PECAN BUTTER BALLS
For a sweeter cookie, roll balls while warm in granulated sugar.

Sift together into medium bowl:
2 cups sifted all-purpose flour
(Do not use instant type.)
¼ cup granulated white sugar
½ teaspoon salt

Add:
1 cup soft (not runny or whipped) butter
2 teaspoons vanilla extract

Work with spoon or hands until well blended.

Add 2 cups minced pecans and mix well.

Shape in 1-inch balls.

Roll in 1 cup finely chopped pecans.

Put on ungreased cookie sheets.

Bake in preheated slow oven (325°F.) for about 25 minutes, or until pale brown.

Remove to wire racks. Makes about 4½ dozen.

To Store—Store cookies airtight. Can be frozen. These cookies are good keepers but do not ship well.

SUGAR COOKIES
Basic, rolled vanilla cookies that you frost and/or decorate.

Sift together into bowl and reserve:
2¾ cups sifted all-purpose flour (instant type can be used. Do not sift, but mix with baking powder and salt.)
1 teaspoon baking powder
½ teaspoon salt

Put
¾ cup soft (not runny or whipped) butter or margarine in large bowl of electric mixer (or other bowl if mixer is not available).

Add:
1 cup sugar
2 eggs
1 teaspoon vanilla extract or a combination of vanilla and almond extracts

Beat with mixer or wooden spoon until mixture is light and fluffy.

Beat in flour mixture with mixer or spoon, blending until smooth.

Chill 1 hour, or until firm.

Roll a small amount of dough at a time on floured board to ⅛-inch thickness.

Keep remaining dough in refrigerator until ready to use.

Cut in desired shapes with floured cookie cutters.

Put on greased cookie sheets.

Bake in preheated moderate oven (375° F.) for 8 to 10 minutes, or until pale brown.

Remove to wire racks to cool.

Decorate with Confectioners' Sugar Frosting (see page 410), tinted as desired, and with colored sugar. Makes about 4 dozen 3-inch cookies.

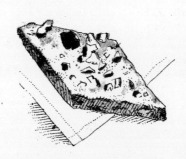

CINNAMON-NUT DIAMONDS
Thin, brown-sugar cookies with nuts in the dough and on top.

Sift together into bowl and reserve:

2 cups sifted all-purpose flour (Do not use instant type.)
½ teaspoon salt
1 teaspoon ground cinnamon

Put
1 cup soft (not runny or whipped) butter or margarine in large bowl of electric mixer (or other bowl if mixer is not available).

Add:
1 cup firmly packed light brown sugar or 1⅓ cups granulated brown sugar
1 teaspoon vanilla extract
1 egg yolk

Beat with mixer or wooden spoon until mixture is light and fluffy.

Add:
Flour mixture
½ cup ground walnuts or pecans

Mix well.

Spread in greased jelly-roll pan (15″ x 10″ x 1″).

Brush with 1 egg, slightly beaten.

Sprinkle with ½ cup ground nuts, pushing them into dough.

Bake in preheated moderate oven (350° F.) for 25 to 30 minutes.

Cut in 2-inch diamonds.

Remove to wire rack to cool. Makes about 2½ dozen.

To Store—Keep cookies in airtight container. Can be frozen. They keep and ship well.

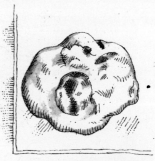

HOLIDAY FRUIT DROPS

Sift together into bowl and reserve:
3½ cups sifted all-purpose flour
(Instant type can be used. Do not sift, but mix with soda and salt.)
1 teaspoon baking soda
½ teaspoon salt

Put 1 cup soft (not runny or whipped) butter or margarine in large bowl of electric mixer (or other bowl if mixer is not available).

Add:
2 cups packed light-brown sugar or 2⅔ cups granulated brown sugar
2 eggs

Beat with mixer or wooden spoon until mixture is light and fluffy.

Add:
½ cup buttermilk
1 teaspoon vanilla extract
Flour mixture

Mix well.

Stir in:
   1½ cups chopped walnuts, pecans, or other nuts
   2 cups halved candied cherries
   2 cups cut-up pitted dates

Drop by teaspoonfuls on lightly greased cookie sheets.

Top each with a nut half, if desired.

Bake in preheated moderate oven (350° F.) for 12 to 15 minutes, or until lightly browned.

Remove to wire racks to cool. Makes about 8 dozen.

To Store—Store cookies airtight. Can be frozen. Good keepers and shippers.

LECKERLI

Sift together into bowl and reserve:
   2¼ cups sifted all-purpose flour
      (Do not use instant type.)
   1 tablespoon ground cinnamon
   1½ teaspoons each of ground cloves and nutmeg
   ⅛ teaspoon salt
   1 teaspoon baking soda

In large saucepan heat to boiling:
   ½ cup sugar
   ½ cup honey

To mixture in saucepan add:
   Grated rind ½ lemon
   ¼ cup each of chopped candied lemon and orange peels
   1 cup slivered blanched almonds
   2 tablespoons fresh orange juice
   Reserved flour mixture

Mix well.

Knead on lightly floured board until well blended.

Roll to ½-inch thickness, using as little flour as is necessary.

Put a sheet of wax paper on ungreased cookie sheet (15½ x 12 inches); grease paper. Carefully lift rolled dough onto greased paper.

Bake in preheated slow oven (325°F.) for about 25 minutes, or until golden brown.

Turn out on wire rack and at once peel off paper.

Turn right side up and spread top with Glaze.

Cool and store. Cut into small diamonds when ready to serve. Makes about 5 dozen.

Glaze

In saucepan mix:
   ½ cup sugar
   ¼ cup water

Cook until mixture spins a thread.

To Store—Keep cookies in airtight container at least 1 week before using. These cookies freeze well and are good keepers and shippers.

CHOCOLATE SQUARES

Sift together into bowl and reserve:
   ¼ cup sifted all-purpose flour
      (Instant type can be used.)
   ⅛ teaspoon salt

Over hot water melt:
   1 ounce (1 square) unsweetened chocolate (or substitute 1 envelope no-melt unsweetened chocolate)
   ¼ cup butter or margarine (not whipped)

Remove from heat and stir in:
   ½ cup sugar
   1 unbeaten egg
   ¼ teaspoon vanilla extract
   Flour mixture

Spread batter thinly in 2 greased pans (8 x 8 x 2 inches). (Pan size is important.) Sprinkle tops with ⅓ cup finely chopped filberts or walnuts.

Bake in preheated hot oven (400°F.) for 10 to 12 minutes. (Do not overbake.)

Cool slightly.

Cut each pan into 16 squares. When cold, remove to wire racks.

To Store—Store cookies airtight. Good keepers, not good shippers.

HONEY FRUIT BARS

Sift together into bowl and reserve:
   1⅓ cups sifted all-purpose flour
      (Instant type can be used. Do not sift, but mix with baking powder and salt.)
   1 teaspoon baking powder
   ¼ teaspoon salt

With rotary beater or mixer beat 3 eggs.

Add:
   1 cup honey
   1 teaspoon vanilla extract

Mix well.

Add:
   Flour mixture
   1¾ cups cut pitted dates
   1 cup chopped nuts
   ½ cup halved candied cherries

Mix well.

Spread in greased pan (13 x 9 x 2 inches).

Bake in preheated moderate oven (350° F.) for 45 minutes, or until browned.

Cool in pan on wire rack.

Cut in bars 3 inches x 1 inch.

Roll in fine granulated or confectioners' sugar. Makes 39.

To Store—Store cookies airtight. Can be frozen. Good keepers and shippers.

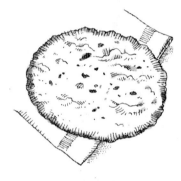

MELT-IN-THE-MOUTH COOKIES

Sift together into bowl and reserve:
   ¾ cup sifted all-purpose flour
      (Instant type can be used; batter will be stiffer. Do not sift, but mix with baking powder and salt.)
   1 teaspoon baking powder
   ½ teaspoon salt

Put
   ½ cup soft (not runny or whipped) butter or margarine in large bowl of electric mixer (or other bowl if mixer is not available).

Add:
   1 cup firmly packed light brown sugar
   1 egg
   1 teaspoon vanilla extract

Beat with mixer or wooden spoon until mixture is light and fluffy.

Beat in flour mixture with mixer or spoon, blending until smooth.

Stir in ½ cup finely chopped nuts.

Drop by scant measuring-teaspoonfuls onto ungreased cookie sheets.

Bake in preheated hot oven (400°F.) for about 5 minutes, or until browned.

Cool for ½ minute.

Remove carefully to wire racks. Makes about 6 to 7 dozen.

To Store—Keep cookies in airtight container. They freeze well but do not ship well as they break easily.

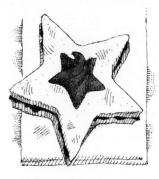

SANDWICH CREAM COOKIES

Sift together into bowl and reserve:
2¾ cups sifted all-purpose flour
(Instant type can be used. Do not sift but mix with salt.)
⅛ teaspoon salt

Add:
1 cup soft (not runny or whipped) butter or margarine
½ cup heavy cream

Stir with wooden spoon or mix with hands until blended.

Chill for several hours, overnight, or until firm.

Roll one fourth of dough to ⅛-inch thickness on board sprinkled lightly with sugar. Keep remaining dough in refrigerator until ready to roll.

Cut out cookies with floured 2¾-inch star cutter or round cutter.

Roll out remaining dough, one fourth at a time.

Cut all cookies with same cutter, but cut small stars out of centers of half of cookies with floured 1¼-inch star cutter. (If round cutter is used, cut half of cookies with same size doughnut cutter.)

Put cookies on ungreased cookie sheets.

Bake in preheated moderate oven (350° F.) for about 8 minutes. Do not brown. At once, carefully remove cookies to wire racks.

Cool. An hour or two before serving, put cookies together with cooled melted semisweet chocolate or with Confectioners' Sugar Frosting (see page 410), tinted as desired. Makes about 3½ dozen.

To Store—Store airtight and refrigerate or freeze. Not good keepers if filled more than a few hours before eating. Not good shippers.

CREAM-CHEESE-FOLDOVERS

Sift together into bowl and reserve:
2 cups sifted all-purpose flour
(Do not use instant type.)
¼ teaspoon salt

Put
1 cup soft (not runny or whipped) butter or margarine in large bowl of electric mixer (or other bowl if mixer is not available).

Add:
8 ounces soft cream cheese (not whipped)

Cream together until light and fluffy.

Blend in reserved flour mixture.

Chill for several hours, or until firm enough to roll.

Roll to ⅛-inch thickness on board sprinkled with confectioners' sugar. Cut in trapezoid shapes with knife, making shapes about 2 inches across widest side.

Spread with red jelly or jam.

Fold over once so that sides meet.

Put on ungreased cookie sheets.

Bake in preheated moderate oven (375° F.) for about 15 minutes. (Do not brown.) If desired, sprinkle with confectioners' sugar. Makes about 4 dozen.

To Store—Store cookies airtight and refrigerate. Will keep several days. Can be frozen. Not good shippers.

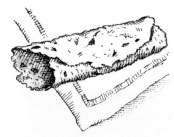

OATMEAL LACE COOKIES

Put
2¼ cups quick-cooking rolled oats in medium bowl.

Melt
1 cup butter or margarine (not whipped).

Stir in:
1½ cups firmly packed dark-brown sugar (do not use granulated sugar).

Pour over oats.

Mix well.

Let stand overnight at room temperature so that oats absorb butter.

Next day add:
½ teaspoon salt
1 tablespoon molasses
3 tablespoons all-purpose flour (Instant type can be used.)
1 egg, slightly beaten
1 teaspoon vanilla extract

Mix well.

Drop by half-measuring-teaspoonfuls 2 inches apart on well-greased cookie sheets.

Bake, one sheet at a time, in preheated moderate oven (375°F.) for 6 or 7 minutes, or until golden brown. Let stand half minute.

Remove quickly with spatula to wire racks to cool. (Or roll each quickly around handle of wooden spoon.) Makes about 7 dozen.

Variation—Substitute light brown sugar for dark; omit molasses.

Bake for 5 or 6 minutes.

To Store—Store cookies airtight. Can be frozen. Good keepers if kept in cool place. Not good shippers as they break easily.

CHOCOLATE PINWHEEL COOKIES

Sift together into bowl and reserve:
1½ cups sifted all-purpose flour
(Do not use instant type.)
¼ teaspoon baking powder
¼ teaspoon salt

Put
½ cup soft (not runny or whipped) butter or margarine in large bowl of electric mixer (or other bowl if mixer is not available).

Add:
¾ cup sugar
1 teaspoon vanilla extract
1 egg

Beat with mixer or wooden spoon until mixture is light and fluffy.

Add flour mixture. Mix until blended.

Over hot water or very low heat, melt 1 ounce (1 square) unsweetened chocolate. (Or use 1 envelope no-melt unsweetened chocolate.)

Cool.

Halve dough.

Add chocolate to one half.

Chill both halves several hours, or until firm enough to roll.

Roll white dough on floured, transparent plastic wrap to form a 16 inch x 6 inch rectangle.

Roll chocolate dough to same size on plastic wrap. Invert chocolate dough on white dough and peel off wrap.

Press gently with rolling pin.

Roll up like jelly roll, being sure center is tight.

Wrap in the plastic.

Chill overnight.

Slice ⅛-inch thick.

Bake on ungreased cookie sheets in preheated moderate oven (350°F.) for 10 to 12 minutes, or until lightly browned.

Remove at once to wire racks to cool. Makes about 3 dozen.

To Store—Store cookies airtight. Can be frozen. Good keepers but not good shippers as they break easily.

SPRITZ COOKIES

Sift together into bowl and reserve:
   2½ cups unsifted all-purpose flour
       (Do not use instant type.)
   ¼ teaspoon salt

Put
   1 cup soft (not runny or whipped) butter or margarine in large bowl of electric mixer (or other bowl if mixer is not available).

Sift into small bowl enough confectioners' sugar to make 1¼ cups.

Measure into bowl with butter.

Beat with mixer or wooden spoon until mixture is light and fluffy.

Beat in:
   2 egg yolks
   ½ teaspoon almond extract
   1 teaspoon vanilla extract

Add flour mixture.

Beat until blended.

Fill cookie press with dough.

Shape fancy cookies on ungreased cookie sheets.

Bake in preheated moderate oven (375°

F.) for 10 to 12 minutes. (Do not brown.)

Remove to wire racks to cool.

Decorate with Confectioners' Sugar Frosting (see page 410), tinted as desired, or decorate before baking with bits of candied cherries, colored sugar, or tiny candies. Makes about 5 dozen.

To Store—Store cookies airtight. Can be frozen. These are good keepers but not good shippers.

LIZZIES

Put
   3 cups seedless raisins in bowl. Add ½ cup bourbon. Mix well. Let stand for 1 hour.

Sift together into bowl and reserve:
   1½ cups sifted all-purpose flour
       (Instant type can be used. Do not sift; mix with soda, spices.)
   1½ teaspoons baking soda
   1½ teaspoons ground cinnamon
   ½ teaspoon each of ground nutmeg and cloves

Put
   ¼ cup soft (not runny or whipped) butter or margarine in large bowl of electric mixer (or other bowl if mixer is not available).

Add:
   ½ cup firmly packed light brown sugar or ⅔ cup plus 2 tablespoons granulated brown sugar
   2 eggs

Beat with mixer or wooden spoon until mixture is light and fluffy.

Beat in flour mixture with mixer or spoon, blending until smooth.

Stir in:
   Raisins
   1 pound (4 cups) pecan halves
   ½ pound citron, diced (1¼ cups)
   1 pound whole candied cherries

Drop from teaspoon onto greased cookie sheets.

Bake in preheated slow oven (325°F.) for about 15 minutes, or until firm.

Remove to wire racks to cool. Makes 7 to 8 dozen.

To Store—Store cookies airtight. Can be frozen. Good keepers and shippers.

LEBKUCHEN

Sift together into bowl and reserve:
   2¾ cups sifted all-purpose flour
       (Do not use instant type.)
   ½ teaspoon baking soda
   ½ teaspoon salt
   1 teaspoon each of ground nutmeg, cloves, cinnamon, and allspice

In saucepan heat to boiling, stirring until sugar is dissolved:
   ½ cup honey
   ½ cup molasses
   ¾ cup packed light brown sugar
       (Not granulated brown sugar.)

Cool and stir in:
   1 egg
   1 teaspoon grated lemon rind
   1 tablespoon fresh lemon juice

Beat in dry ingredients with mixer or spoon, blending until smooth.

Stir in:
   ½ cup chopped nuts
   ¾ cup diced candied citron

Wrap dough in moisture-proof paper and chill overnight.

Next day, roll dough a small amount at a time on lightly floured board to ¼-inch thickness.

Cut with round 2½-inch cutter.

Put on greased cookie sheets.

Arrange 3 blanched almonds on each and put half of a candied cherry in the center.

Bake in preheated hot oven (400°F.) for 10 to 12 minutes.

While hot, brush with Glaze. Makes about 2½ dozen.

Glaze

In saucepan, mix:
   1 cup sugar
   ½ cup water

Cook until a little of the mixture spins a thread when dropped from a spoon.

Remove from heat and stir in:
   Dash of salt
   ¼ cup sifted confectioners' sugar

To Store—Keep cookies in airtight container at least 1 week before using. These cookies freeze well and are good keepers and shippers.

Four Christmas Dinners to share with family and friends. Shown here, a yuletide feast featuring roast capons.

A Yuletide Feast
by
James A. Beard

In both remembrance and anticipation, I think of the Christmas holidays as a time of great rejoicing, wonderful food and drink, a colorful exclamation point marking the end of the year.

I believe I can recall almost totally the events of every Christmas in my life, but my most vivid memories go back to my childhood. Preparations in our home began weeks in advance, and as the days passed and the tempo of the activities increased, I became so excited that I could hardly bear to wait until the 24th of December.

We started by making the plum puddings and fruitcakes for the *next* year's holiday. When they were done and well bathed with cognac, they were stored away in a basement closet to mellow. Next came the baking for the Christmas coming up: poundcakes with a rich buttery, vanilla smell and hundreds of special cookies. There was always a cookie festival held at the home of one of my friends. Her mother, with the help of a few older children, did the baking. The rest of us sat around a table with bowls of icing and all sorts of decorative candies. Some of our creations would rival modern paintings!

During the week before Christmas our doorbell rang constantly, announcing the arrival of magnificent surprises. We lived in the Pacific Northwest, where game abounds, and many of our friends sent us ducks, pheasants, wild geese, and sometimes turkeys. Every year we received boxes of the famous Oregon apples: Spitzenbergs, Winter Bananas, a variety never seen any more, and giant Winesaps. The choicest came packed in individual boxes placed inside a wooden crate. As soon as they arrived the apples were stored in the cellar to be doled out for munching or for dessert during the rest of the winter. Sometimes we had pungent mandarin oranges shipped from China in exotic boxes.

Always our Chinese friends in the local Chinatown gave us strange Chinese sweetmeats and fine teas by the pound. My mother was a tea connoisseur and was noted for the blends she mixed with these teas.

A few days before Christmas, the decorating began and the woodsy smell of greens blended with the tantalizing odors from the kitchen. First, the huge tree was put up. We all joined in trimming it with many intricate baroque ornaments from Germany, bells of all colors, and colored tinsels. At the top we placed an elaborate crown with a glittering tassel-like cascade spilling down.

Our farmer delivered a load of mistletoe, pine branches, and plumes of dark cedar. The holly trees in our garden supplied bright green leaves and berries for wreaths and arrangements. What a hubbub! Everyone was busy making wreaths, hanging boughs, draping the mantel with greens, leaving no spot unadorned.

Our dining-table centerpiece for Christmas Day was an immense bowl of red roses. This was a family tradition, and one that I have maintained through the years. If I had to choose between red roses and a tree, I'd take the roses for memory's sake.

We had our tree on Christmas Eve, and after that an elaborate buffet. It was a large party: some of our special friends, anyone that Mother knew would be alone for the holiday, and many others who stopped by after church or after their own family parties.

The buffet featured a huge stuffed turkey and a big bowl of chicken salad plus other tasty dishes. These might be, variously, an oyster stew made with Olympia oysters, half cream and half milk and big pats of butter, and served with hot toasted homemade bread; a fine homemade pâté; delicate crabmeat patties; sometimes creamy eggs with homemade sausages, juicy and pungent with herbs.

Dinner on Christmas day was a quiet family affair. If we did have guests, there were never more than two or three old friends. We were leisurely and relaxed. The table, centered with red roses, was set with mother's choice old Haviland in the cornflower pattern, or with the gold-banded china, and with vintage-pattern silver.

A large ham usually occupied one end of the table, but the rest of the menu varied from year to year. A typical Christmas dinner might start with Mother's homemade cream of tomato soup, full of a true tomato-y flavor, rich with cream and butter and sparked with a hint of thyme. Balancing the ham, at the opposite end of the table, a lordly beef roast with browned potatoes, and onions smothered with cheese. Of course there were all sorts of tidbits: homemade pickled onions, pickled seckel pears, celery, salted almonds or filberts, and hot homemade rolls with sweet butter. Salad was often asparagus made with home-canned asparagus.

The desserts were always the same. The principal dish was the plum pudding made the previous year. It came to the table ablaze with cognac and with it went a choice of two sauces, cognac sauce or hard sauce. How could I choose? I took both. Then there was mince pie or mince flan made with apples and glazed with apricot and served with whipped cream. In those days no one thought of calories. We sat long at table, enjoying every morsel and stretching our appetites with judicious sips of wine. If we felt slightly groggy at the end, hot strong coffee and cognac could take care of that.

Though we eat less lavishly today, I still feel that Christmas is a time for elegant food. The holiday would not seem right to me if I did not carry on the tradition of serving friends with fine fare thoughtfully prepared. I don't hold large Christmas dinners, never have more than six or eight at table, because I like to preserve the feeling of an intimate gathering. For this reason, too, I dispense with help and handle everything myself.

I have a half-circle, 18th-century drinking table that can be rolled up to the dining table to serve as a buffet. On it I arrange the foods and there I preside as carver. I like a sit-down first course served with drinks. It could be a good pâté served with thin slices of French bread. At my last Christmas dinner, I served the two capons with the different stuffings suggested in the menu below. It was a great success for it offered a choice of seasonings. A ham, country-cured or Smithfield, seems important to me. Thin, thin slices of this smoky meat go well with the fowl or with salad. Root vegetables, such as the much-neglected turnips and parsnips, complement turkey, game, and capon. And Brussels sprouts cooked until just done but still bitey combine perfectly with mealy chestnuts, making an interesting contrast in texture and flavor.

Of course the proper end of the meal is plum pudding. I now lack the storage space at the right temperature to prepare it a year in advance as my mother did. I substitute a five-day pudding, and find it most satisfying. For a second dessert I have suggested a luxury that we could never enjoy in midwinter in my childhood: Bavarian cream with strawberries.

At the end of the meal, with the coffee, I like to offer the traditional Christmas sweets: good candies, cookies, fruitcake, and fresh winter pears. Then port and cognac, and as the hours go by, the candles burn down to the last drop of wax. All this to me means warm, satisfying Christmas cheer.

A YULETIDE FEAST
PÂTÉ LISE*
TWIN CAPONS WITH TWO STUFFINGS*
CAPON GRAVY*
APRICOT GLAZED HAM, MADEIRA SAUCE*
POTATO ROSETTES*
TURNIPS WITH MUSHROOMS*
BRUSSELS SPROUTS AND CHESTNUTS*
WATERCRESS AND CHERRY TOMATOES
PLUM PUDDING WITH RUM SAUCE*
PISTACHIO BAVARIAN WITH
STRAWBERRIES*

PÂTÉ LISE
1 pound pork liver
1 pound lean pork
1 tablespoon all-purpose flour
1 egg
1 onion, minced
2 tablespoons minced parsley
¼ teaspoon crumbled thyme
¼ teaspoon crumbled sage
1 teaspoon salt
 Pepper to taste
 Dash each of nutmeg, mace, and cloves
½ pound fat salt pork, sliced very thin
2 ounces brandy
1 bay leaf
 Flour-and-water paste

Grind liver and pork fine. Work flour into mixture well. Add egg, and mix well. Add onion, parsley, and spices. Line the bottom and sides of pâté mold or deep casserole with slices of salt pork. Pour in half of pâté mixture. Put over it a layer of salt-pork slices. Fill with remaining pâté. Add brandy. Cover top completely with salt-pork slices. Put bay leaf on top, and put on cover. Seal cover with thick flour-and-water paste to prevent steam from escaping. Place in pan of hot water in preheated slow oven (300°F.) for 3½ hours. Remove from oven, and let cool with pot still sealed. Then crack off seal, and chill. Unmold and garnish with sliced ripe olives and strips of pimiento, if desired. Makes 8 to 10 servings.

TWIN CAPONS WITH TWO STUFFINGS
You need 2 capons, 7 to 8 pounds each.

Stuffing Number 1
1 cup finely cut green onions or shallots
½ cup butter
1½ teaspoons salt
 Pepper to taste
1 teaspoon crumbled tarragon
½ cup chopped parsley
½ cup sherry or Madeira
5 to 6 cups fresh bread crumbs

Sauté the finely cut onions in butter until just soft. Add salt, pepper, tarragon, parsley, and sherry, and toss with fresh crumbs. Add additional melted butter, if desired. Stuff capon lightly. Secure vent, and truss.

Stuffing Number 2
 Gizzards, hearts, and livers of capons
½ cup butter
½ cup chopped onion
½ cup chopped parsley
⅓ cup finely chopped celery
1½ teaspoons crumbled thyme
3 cups fresh bread crumbs
1 cup pecans, coarsely chopped
 Salt and pepper
¼ cup bourbon

Chop or grind giblets very fine and sauté lightly in half the butter. Sauté onion in remaining butter with parsley and celery. Add to giblet mixture, along with thyme, crumbs, and pecans. Season to taste with salt and pepper; add bourbon. Toss lightly, and stuff the capon. Secure the vent, and truss.

■ **To roast capons**—Butter capons and place on their sides on a roasting rack. Roast in preheated slow oven (325°F.) for 25 minutes and turn capons to the opposite side. Roast for 25 to 30 minutes longer. Place capons on their backs, sprinkle with salt and pepper, baste with melted butter, and continue roasting until tender. Figure an additional 18 to 20 minutes per pound. Baste occasionally with pan drippings and additional melted butter to give a golden color to the skin. Serve on a large hot platter surrounded by Potato Rosettes. Makes 8 to 10 servings.

CAPON GRAVY
When the capons are removed to a hot platter, skim the fat from the roasting pan. Add about 2 or 3 tablespoons fat to the pan juices with 1½ cups cream. Season with salt and pepper, bring to a boil and stir for 2 or 3 minutes until the cream has blended well with the other ingredients. If you prefer a thicker sauce, small balls of butter and flour kneaded together may be added. A dash of sherry enhances it as well.

APRICOT GLAZED HAM
This may be any particular ham of your choice. The glaze is stewed, cooked-down apricot preserves and the decoration could be a poinsettia made of pimiento strips or candied or glazed fruits in a wreath with leaves of angelica.

MADEIRA SAUCE FOR HAM
Combine 2 tablespoons of ham fat from the baking ham, 1 can of beef gravy (10¾ ounces), and ⅓ cup Madeira. Bring to a boil and simmer for 3 minutes. Correct the seasoning.
Note: You may soak ⅓ cup golden raisins in the Madeira and add them to the sauce if you wish.

POTATO ROSETTES
6 Idaho potatoes
6 tablespoons butter
1½ teaspoons salt
½ teaspoon pepper
 Pinch of nutmeg
3 whole eggs
2 egg yolks

Peel and boil potatoes until tender. Mash with butter and seasonings and whip or put through a food mill to remove all lumps. Correct the seasoning, add eggs and yolks and blend well. To make rosettes, force potatoes through a large rosette tube of a pastry bag onto a buttered cookie sheet and put under the broiler or in a hot oven until delicately outlined with a dark brown crust. Arrange on a platter with the capons. Makes 8 to 10 servings.

TURNIPS WITH MUSHROOMS

- ¾ pound mushrooms, finely chopped
- Butter
- 1 large yellow turnip, peeled and sliced
- Salt and pepper

Sauté chopped mushrooms in 6 tablespoons butter very slowly until they have thrown off most of their moisture and have turned quite dark in color. You may leave these on extremely low heat for an hour or more, stirring occasionally. Salt to taste. Boil the turnip in salted water until just tender. Drain well and mash coarsely. Season with salt and pepper. When ready to serve, cut in mushroom mixture and add a dollop of butter to the dish as you serve it. Makes 10 to 12 servings.

BRUSSELS SPROUTS AND CHESTNUTS

Trim 4 cups (2 pints) Brussels sprouts and cook them until crisply tender in a small amount of boiling, salted water. Be careful not to overcook as they tenderize extremely fast. Heat 1½ cups peeled, whole, cooked chestnuts (they may be purchased cooked in brine or dried, shelled ones may be purchased) in 6 tablespoons butter and combine with cooked, crisp Brussels sprouts. Add more melted butter, if desired. Makes 8 to 10 servings.

PLUM PUDDING WITH RUM SAUCE

- ½ cup chopped dates
- ¾ cup dark seedless raisins
- ¾ cup golden raisins
- ¼ cup chopped candied citron
- ¼ cup chopped mixed candied fruits
- ¼ cup chopped candied orange peel
- 1½ cups beer
- 4 eggs
- 1½ cups firmly packed brown sugar
- ½ cup chopped nuts
- ½ cup fine dry bread crumbs
- 1 cup minced suet (¼ pound)
- 1 cup sifted all-purpose flour
- 1 teaspoon salt
- 1½ teaspoons baking powder
- ¾ teaspoon baking soda
- 1 teaspoon ground cinnamon
- ⅛ teaspoon each of ground cloves and allspice

Combine fruits and peel in bowl; add beer and let stand for at least 1 hour. Beat eggs with brown sugar and add fruit-beer mixture. Stir in nuts, crumbs, and suet. Sift dry ingredients and spices; stir into fruit mixture. Turn into 4 well-greased pint or two 1-quart pudding molds, filling three quarters full. Cover tightly with aluminum foil; tie securely. Put on rack in deep kettle; pour in boiling water to half the depth of the molds. Cover; steam for 2½ hours, adding more water if necessary. Remove from steamer; immediately remove foil covers. Cool completely. Re-cover and store in refrigerator. Before serving, steam for about 45 minutes to heat through.

Plum pudding may be served with a traditional Hard Sauce (see page 445) or the Rum Sauce below.

Note: When sending pudding as a gift, you may decorate the top with candied fruits. These can be removed during heating, replaced later.

Rum Sauce

Combine 1 cup heavy cream, 3 egg yolks, 2 tablespoons sugar, pinch of salt, and ⅓ cup rum in top part of double boiler and stir over hot water until it thickens slightly. Makes 10 to 12 servings.

PISTACHIO BAVARIAN WITH STRAWBERRIES

- 1½ cups milk
- ½ cup sugar
- 6 egg yolks
- 1 cup chopped pistachio nuts
- 1 teaspoon vanilla or pistachio extract
- 2 envelopes unflavored gelatin
- Touch of green coloring
- 1 pint heavy cream
- Fresh strawberries, sugared

Combine 1 cup of milk, sugar, and egg yolks and cook until thickened. Add the pistachio nuts and flavoring while mixture cooks. Soften gelatin in remaining milk. Add 1 cup of hot custard and stir until dissolved. Add remaining custard. Cool. When thickening starts, stir in green coloring and fold in heavy cream, whipped. Turn into a 3-quart ring mold and chill. Unmold on a serving dish and fill with sugared, fresh strawberries. Serve with additional whipped cream, if desired. Makes 8 to 10 servings.

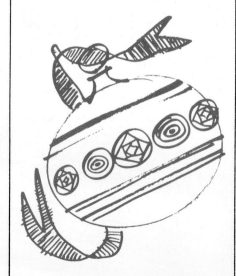

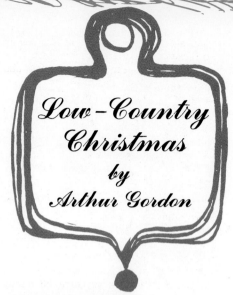

Low-Country Christmas

by Arthur Gordon

Down in the low country of the Georgia coast, when I was a boy, we never had a white Christmas, but this didn't bother us. We liked our Decembers the way they were, camellias glowing like rubies in their glossy foliage, sunlight like a golden rug on the amber pine needles, Spanish moss stirring faintly in the soft air. If we had stopped to think about it, we'd probably have considered all this snow-and-sleigh-bells stuff some kind of Yankee hoax. After all, there hadn't been any snow in Bethlehem, had there?

My brother and I went to boarding school so far in the frozen North that it took us almost two days on the train to get home. I don't remember these journeys, particularly, but I certainly remember the arrivals; the stampede up the steep steps of the old white-columned house, the wreaths in the windows, the smilax twined around the tall mirrors and the old portraits, the coal fires muttering in their grates under the black-marble mantels, and the indescribable blended smells of good food and old leather and coal smoke and furniture polish, the wonderful soaring knowledge that it was almost Christmas and we were home.

Usually it was early morning when we arrived and usually Elijah Green, our colored butler-teacher-adviser-companion-and-dearly-loved-friend, had prepared some kind of special breakfast. Sometimes the menu was quite exotic: shad roe and hominy, for instance (we never called it grits, and still don't); or hot biscuits and hash; or most likely Georgia cane syrup and waffles. The recipe for these waffles, "receipt" my mother called it, went back at least a hundred years, and had led to some belt-bursting eating contests in our house. President Taft came to stay with my grandfather and was said to hold the record with seven complete waffles, or twenty-eight quarters. But my brother and I were sure we would top this someday.

That first morning at home we usually spent looking for mistletoe and holly. We never had a Christmas Tree as such (now our children have about five); the old house itself became the symbol of Christmas. Climbing for mistletoe was hazardous but satisfying; once, I remember, my brother collected two baby squirrels as a sort of dividend. A few people had real English holly trees, but they would cut off your arm at the elbow if you tried to pick any of it, so mostly we were content with swamp or Florida holly, whose red berries were just as gay and perhaps more appropriate for a low-country Christmas.

As Christmas drew nearer, all sorts of edible gifts would begin to arrive from friends and relatives: bags of pecan nuts to be shelled and split and brushed with butter and salt and toasted in the oven; trays of Creole kisses, a sort of meringue with nuts that was my special favorite; and homemade fruitcakes. What I remember chiefly about these fruitcakes was their aroma: a rich, dark, mahogany-colored smell that lurked in the lower right-hand compartment of the big sideboard and rose up at you when you opened the door like a genie out of a bottle. There was none of this light-colored, namby-pamby, poundcake-with-raisin nonsense. These cakes were as black as the inside of a charred keg and as heavy as a cross section of cannonball. Furthermore they were so impregnated with brandy that I think if you had touched a match to them the whole house would have disappeared in a sheet of blue flame.

My mother used to cut these cakes up into small squares and serve them to friends who dropped in for eggnog on Christmas (or sometimes New Year's) morning. My father didn't drink, but he saw no reason why his friends shouldn't have a bit of Christmas cheer, and the eggnog, also an ancient southern formula, provided this. At larger parties, he might offer a deceptive and lethal concoction known as Chatham Artillery Punch, famous in our city since pre-Revolutionary days. Traditionally, it was set out when victorious generals or admirals came to the city to be feted. After

a few glasses, the conquering hero would usually try to make a speech. The orchestra leader was always given instructions to play the appropriate national anthem if the speaker became unintelligible for more than two minutes. The music was always played.

It was hard for us to keep a cook, even in those lavish days, because Elijah never got on with her. The kitchen was in the basement and the butler's pantry on the floor above, but even this geographical isolation was of no avail. Elijah would stick his head into the dumbwaiter and mumble such dreadful imprecations down the echoing shaft that his co-worker would lose her temper and walk out, sometimes in the middle of dinner. Usually, though, on Christmas Day the spirit of brotherly love would prevail, and the traditionally late (2 P.M. or 2:30 P.M.) midday dinner was always a masterpiece. The table would be set with white damask and silver candelabra or perhaps a pair of silver pheasants. The centerpiece might be a flat dish full of camellias, the golden-hearted Donklaari. The flat silver was the old Kirk pattern, long a favorite in the South; the china a royal-blue and white Spode, with gold edges. The wineglasses might either be ornate Venetian goblets or the plain and beautiful octagonal Irish glass brought to this country by my mother's ancestors in the eighteenth century. There would be celery and olives in long cut-glass dishes, nuts and chocolate mints in silver bonbon dishes. I even remember the salt-cellars, ovals of silver with ornamental rams' heads that seemed to stare solemnly at the assembled guests.

Dinner always began with a seafood soup, perhaps shrimp bisque, perhaps an oyster stew with the small, sweet Georgia oysters. I preferred the stew, because we always made a game of hunting for the little oyster crabs, bright red after being cooked, and no bigger than a child's thumbnail. They were supposed to be a great delicacy, but I always thought

they tasted like rather gritty Lima beans. Some of our guests took a dim view of the little crabs. One northern cousin, in fact, rashly yielded to our casual advice to "just crunch it," rolled off his chair in a dead faint, and landed on the carpet with a dull thud.

The entrée was usually a huge glazed turkey with aromatic stuffing; in my grandfather's day there were always two: a wild one and a tame one. But sometimes there was wild duck or a Smithfield ham from my mother's native Virginia, or both. Rice and gravy were inevitable at *every* midday meal, not just Christmas. This was a law as fixed and immutable as those of the Medes and Persians. The vegetables might vary: creamed cauliflower, perhaps; green beans with almonds grated over them; beets or eggplant. Candied yams were another must for Sundays or Christmas, so sweet and crusted with sugar and syrup that we put them on our butter plates to be eaten as a kind of semi-dessert.

Dessert itself might be a towering cylinder of vanilla ice cream, hand-churned, with strawberries clustered around the bottom. And spongecake. And fruitcake. And Creole kisses. And, oh, yes, I forgot, always pickled peaches somewhere along the line. I suppose I forgot them because I never liked them.

The wine was more ceremonial than customary. It might be champagne, with even the small children at the side table under the window being given a tiny sip. Or, more likely, the rich Madeira that was the wine most highly regarded in the days of the nineteenth-century merchant princes. Around the table it would go, carefully counterclockwise. And then the traditional toast, generations old and always the same: "To absent friends."

Then coffee in the living room (by now it was almost four o'clock) in tiny porcelain cups set in vermeil filigree holders, with my mother's Pekingese sitting up and waving his paws, begging for sugar, and what was left of the languorous afternoon stretching ahead, and the sense of repletion and gratitude and happiness.

Some things have changed. Christmas dinner in our house today is more likely to be a buffet than a lengthy sit-down affair. But the food and drink are still traditional and so, I hope, is the hospitality. Backgrounds may change, but the spirit of Christmas doesn't. It still means warmth and joy and fellowship and a toast to absent friends.

LOW-COUNTRY CHRISTMAS DINNER

SHRIMP BISQUE *
ROAST TURKEY *
BAKED SMITHFIELD HAM *
BUTTERED RICE   CANDIED YAMS *
BUTTERED BEETS *
CREAMED CAULIFLOWER *
GREEN BEANS WITH ALMONDS *
PICKLED PEACHES
CORN STICKS *   BUTTER
ICE CREAM   STRAWBERRIES
SPONGECAKE *   FRUITCAKE *
CREOLE KISSES *   COFFEE

SHRIMP BISQUE

1 pound shrimps
¼ cup butter
¼ cup all-purpose flour
4 cups milk
½ cup heavy cream
   Salt and pepper
   Worcestershire
   Sherry
   Thin lemon slices
   Paprika

Cook shrimps, remove shells, and clean. Force shrimps through food chopper, or whirl in blender. Melt butter and stir in flour. Add milk and cook, stirring, until thickened. Add shrimps, cream, and salt, pepper, Worcestershire, and sherry to taste. Put thin slices of lemon in warm soup cups or plates and add soup. Sprinkle lightly with paprika. Makes 6 to 8 servings.

ROAST TURKEY

Stuff turkey; put on rack in shallow pan, breast side up. Spoon about ¼ cup melted fat over turkey. Cover turkey loosely with foil. Roast in preheated slow oven (325°F.), basting several times with pan drippings. A 14- to 18-pound turkey will take about 5¾ to 6 hours.

BAKED SMITHFIELD HAM

Soak ham for 7 hours in plenty of cold water so as to completely cover the ham. Pour off the water and add same quantity of fresh water. Continue soaking for 7 to 8 hours longer. Cover with fresh water, bring to boil, and simmer for 4 to 5 hours, or until tender. From time to time, renew the water that boils away by adding more boiling water. Let the ham stand overnight in this pot liquor. Remove skin, dust ham thickly with brown sugar, stick with cloves, and bake in preheated moderate oven (375°F.) for about 1 hour. Serve hot or cold, sliced very thin.
Note: Ham can be purchased already cooked. Bake according to directions.

CANDIED YAMS

Boil 6 yams for 20 minutes, peel, slice lengthwise, and brown quickly in a little butter. Put in baking dish. Boil to thick syrup ⅔ cup sugar and 1 cup water. Pour over potatoes. Bake in preheated moderate oven (375°F.) for 25 minutes. Makes 6 to 8 servings.

BUTTERED BEETS

Heat 2 cans (1 pound each) whole beets in a little beet liquid. Drain, and pour over them a little melted butter. Makes 6 to 8 servings.

CREAMED CAULIFLOWER

Cook 1 medium head of cauliflower broken into flowerets, or 2 boxes frozen, in lightly salted water until tender. Pour a thin cream sauce over cauliflower. To make sauce, melt 3 tablespoons butter, stir in 2 tablespoons flour, and add 2 cups milk. Cook until thickened, stirring. Season. Makes 6 servings.

GREEN BEANS WITH ALMONDS

Cook 1 pound fresh or 2 packages frozen green beans until tender. Lightly brown ¼ cup slivered almonds in ¼ cup butter and pour over beans. Makes 6 servings.

CORN STICKS

    1 egg
    1 cup milk
    1 tablespoon shortening, melted
    2 cups water-ground white cornmeal
    2 teaspoons baking powder
    1 teaspoon salt

Beat egg; add milk and shortening. Add to dry ingredients and mix well. Spoon into well-greased corn-stick pans and bake in preheated very hot oven (450°F.) for about 15 minutes. Makes 12 to 14.

SPONGECAKE

    6 eggs, separated
    1½ cups granulated sugar
    1½ cups sifted cake flour
    1 teaspoon baking powder
    ½ teaspoon salt
    ⅓ cup cold water
    2 teaspoons vanilla extract
    1 teaspoon lemon extract
    1 teaspoon grated lemon rind
    ½ teaspoon cream of tartar
    Confectioners' sugar

Beat egg yolks until very thick and lemon-colored. Gradually add sugar, beating constantly. Add sifted flour, baking powder and salt alternately with water, flavorings and rind, blending lightly. Beat egg whites with cream of tartar until stiff, but not dry. Gradually and gently fold egg-yolk mixture into beaten whites. Pour into ungreased 10-inch tube pan. Bake in slow oven (325°F.) about 1 hour. Turn pan upside down with tube over neck of funnel or bottle. Cool and remove from pan. Put on serving plate and dust top with confectioners' sugar.

FRUITCAKE

    3 pounds pitted dates
    1 pound citron
    1½ pounds candied cherries
    1 pound candied pineapple
    3 pounds (12 cups) pecan meats
    5 pounds seedless raisins
    1 pint brandy
    1 cup light corn syrup
    2 cups butter
    3 cups sugar
    1 teaspoon lemon extract
    2 teaspoons vanilla extract
    12 eggs, separated
    6 cups all-purpose flour
    1 teaspoon baking soda
    2 teaspoons cream of tartar
    1½ teaspoons salt
    3 teaspoons cinnamon
    2 teaspoons nutmeg
    ½ teaspoon ground cloves

Cut fruit and nuts, except raisins, in fairly large pieces. Put with raisins in large bowl. Pour 1 cup brandy and the corn syrup over mixture. Let stand 24 hours, stirring several times. Cream butter and sugar together until fluffy; add flavorings. Beat in egg yolks. Beat egg whites until stiff, but not dry. Fold into first mixture. Stir in sifted dry ingredients. Add fruit mixture and blend thoroughly. Line bottoms and sides of 4 deep 9-inch tube pans with 2 layers of greased brown paper. Divide batter into pans. Bake in preheated slow oven (275°F.) for about 4 hours. When cakes begin to brown, cover with brown paper. When done, remove from pans and cool on racks. Pour remaining brandy over tops. Wrap in cloths and store in airtight containers. Moisten cloths with brandy occasionally to keep cakes moist. Store cakes 2 weeks to ripen before using.

CREOLE KISSES

    6 egg whites
    1 cup sugar
    ½ teaspoon cream of tartar
    1 teaspoon vanilla extract
    2 cups coarsely chopped pecans

Beat 1 egg white until stiff. Gradually beat in 2 tablespoons sugar. While beating constantly, add another egg white, then 2 tablespoons sugar. Continue this process until all egg whites are added. Mix remaining sugar with cream of tartar and gradually add to first mixture, beating constantly until very stiff. Add vanilla and nuts. Drop by teaspoonfuls onto cookie sheets lined with brown paper. Bake in preheated slow oven (300°F.) for 25 minutes, or until cracked on top, but not browned. Put paper on a damp surface and remove kisses with a sharp knife. Makes about 4½ dozen.

CHRISTMAS DINNER FOR 8

FRESH FRUIT AND SHERBET PARFAIT
RIB ROAST OF BEEF *
YORKSHIRE PUDDING *
OVEN-BROWNED POTATOES *
ONIONS AND CARROTS *
TOSSED SALAD
GREEN AND RED PEPPER RELISH
LIGHT PLUM PUDDING *   HARD SAUCE *
COFFEE

RIB ROAST OF BEEF

Wipe a 3-rib roast of beef with a damp cloth; place fat side up in open roasting pan. A rack is not necessary because the bones form a rack. Season with salt and pepper. Roast in preheated slow oven (325°F.) for 12 to 14 minutes per pound for very rare, 15 to 18 minutes per pound for medium rare, and 20 to 22 minutes per pound for well done, or until a meat thermometer inserted into the center of the rib-eye registers the desired degree of internal temperature. Allow roast to stand for 30 minutes after removing from oven (while Yorkshire Pudding is baking).

YORKSHIRE PUDDING

Beat 2 eggs well. Add 1 cup milk and continue beating. Add 1 cup sifted all-purpose flour with ½ teaspoon salt and beat until smooth. Put 3 tablespoons hot drippings from roast into 9-inch pie pan. Heat. When hot, pour in batter. Bake in preheated hot oven (425°F.) for 25 minutes.

OVEN-BROWNED POTATOES, ONIONS, AND CARROTS

About 45 minutes before roast is done, cook peeled potatoes, onions, and carrots in boiling salted water for about 10 minutes. Drain; arrange around roast in pan. When roast is done, transfer vegetables to another baking dish and continue cooking in oven while Yorkshire Pudding is being baked.

LIGHT PLUM PUDDING WITH HARD SAUCE

    ½ cup golden seedless raisins
    ½ pound dried apricots, cut into pieces
    ½ pound dates, cut into pieces
    Grated rind of ½ orange
    Grated rind of ½ lemon
    ½ cup chopped blanched almonds
    ¼ cup fruit juice or sherry
    ¼ cup butter or margarine
    1 cup firmly packed light brown sugar
    2 eggs
    ¾ cup grated raw carrots
    ¾ cup grated raw potatoes
    ¼ cup milk
    1 cup sifted all-purpose flour
    1½ teaspoons baking powder

1 teaspoon each of baking soda and salt
½ teaspoon each of ground nutmeg
  and mace
¼ teaspoon ground cloves
  Hard Sauce

Combine fruits, rinds, and nuts; add fruit juice. Cream butter and sugar. Add eggs, one at a time, beating until light after each addition. Add carrots, potatoes, and milk. Sift flour with remaining ingredients except Sauce and add to creamed mixture. Add fruit mixture. Put in well-greased 2-quart mold. Cover; put on rack in heavy kettle with about 1½ inches of hot water. Cover; steam for about 2 hours. Unmold. Serve with Hard Sauce. **Note:** Pudding can be made ahead, wrapped, and refrigerated. If frozen, thaw before resteaming. Allow about 1 hour for thorough heating.

Hard Sauce

Cream ¾ cup butter or margarine, 3 cups sifted confectioners' sugar, 1 tablespoon cream, dash of salt, and 2 teaspoons rum extract.

■ **To serve in lemon shells**—Cut around center of whole lemons with sharp knife and scoop out pulp. Pile sauce in shells and top with a few chopped candied cherries.

CHRISTMAS DINNER FOR 12

ROAST FRESH HAM *   GRAVY *
CRANBERRY APPLES *
OVEN-BROWNED WHITE AND
SWEET POTATOES *
CORN STUFFING BALLS *
BROCCOLI WITH PIMIENTO BUTTER *
WATERMELON AND
CANTALOUPE PICKLES
BLACK OLIVES
GREEN ONIONS, CELERY, CARROTS, AND
RADISHES
EGGNOG SNOW PUDDING *
ORANGE-AND-LEMON SAUCE *

ROAST FRESH HAM

Fresh ham is a leg of pork which has not been cured or smoked. Buy a whole leg, or a portion, allowing ½ pound per serving. Score top and season with salt and pepper. Put on rack in shallow roasting pan. Roast in preheated moderate oven (325°F.) for 40 to 45 minutes per pound, or until meat reaches 185°F. on meat thermometer. About 1¼ hours before meat is done, spread with a mixture of 1 cup light brown sugar, 1 teaspoon dry mustard, and 2 tablespoons vinegar.

GRAVY

Pour off clear melted fat from roasting pan. For each cup of gravy, blend 1 tablespoon fat with 1 tablespoon flour and add 1 cup water. Boil in roasting pan, stirring. Season.

CRANBERRY APPLES

Cook 1 cup sugar and 1 cup water for 5 minutes. Add 2 cups cranberries and cook until skins burst. Remove some of cranberries to stuff apples. Strain remaining cranberries and juice. Put enough juice and water to make 2 cups in large skillet. Add 12 cored and peeled medium cooking apples (or cook 6 at a time). Simmer, covered, for about 15 minutes, turning apples once or twice and basting often with syrup. Cool. Serve warm or cold. When ready to serve, stuff with reserved cranberries.

OVEN-BROWNED WHITE AND SWEET POTATOES

When adding brown-sugar mixture to ham, put 12 peeled medium white potatoes and 12 peeled small sweet potatoes around meat. Bake along with meat, turning potatoes occasionally.

CORN STUFFING BALLS

½ cup chopped onion
1 cup chopped celery
¼ cup butter or margarine
1¾ cups (one 12-ounce can) cream-style corn
1 cup water
1 teaspoon salt
¼ teaspoon pepper
1½ teaspoons poultry seasoning
  Pinch of ground thyme
1 package (8 ounces) prepared bread stuffing
3 egg yolks
½ cup melted butter

Cook onion and celery in butter. Add corn, water, salt, pepper, poultry seasoning, and thyme. Bring to boil. Pour over bread stuffing and mix lightly. Add egg yolks, and shape into 12 balls. Spread in shallow baking pan and pour melted butter over all. Bake in preheated moderate oven (375°F.) for about 15 minutes.

BROCCOLI WITH PIMIENTO BUTTER

Cook 4 packages (10 ounces each) frozen broccoli. Melt ½ cup butter, add 2 pimientos cut into strips, and pour over broccoli.

EGGNOG SNOW PUDDING

6 envelopes unflavored gelatin
1½ cups water
2 quarts prepared bottled eggnog
6 egg whites
½ cup sugar
½ teaspoon ground nutmeg
  Orange-and-Lemon Sauce

Sprinkle gelatin over water to soften. Stir over hot water or low heat until thoroughly dissolved. Gradually stir into eggnog. Chill until thickened. Then whip until light and fluffy. Beat egg whites until stiff. Gradually beat in sugar and nutmeg. Fold into gelatin mixture. Pour into serving dish and chill until set. Serve with Orange-and-Lemon Sauce.

Orange-and-Lemon Sauce

½ cup sugar
½ cup fresh orange juice
½ cup water
  Juice of 1 lemon
1 tablespoon cornstarch
2 tablespoons water
1 cup mixed candied fruits
½ cup chopped nuts

Combine sugar, orange juice, water, and lemon. Bring to a boil. Mix cornstarch and water to a smooth paste. Stir into hot fruit juice. Cook, stirring constantly, until clear and thickened. Add candied fruits and nuts. Chill before serving.

CHUTNEY

CHUTNEY—This word, of Hindustani origin, describes a well-seasoned relish that originated in India. Chutney is the standard accompaniment of curried dishes. It is made from a mixture of chopped fruits (mangoes are one of the characteristic ingredients) and spices. The two basic types are sweet and sour chutney, and there are a great many variations of each kind. Chutney can be served with other dishes as well as curries: stews, poultry, meat, and vegetables.

Commercially made chutney is available in food and gourmet stores, in jars of various sizes. Making it at home is a rewarding project.

MANGO CHUTNEY

    2 cups cider vinegar
 2¼ cups sugar
    2 large firm mangoes
  ¾ cup preserved gingerroot
    2 garlic cloves
    1 teaspoon mustard seeds
  ½ teaspoon salt
  ½ cup white raisins
  ½ cup seedless raisins

Combine vinegar and sugar in heavy saucepan; bring to boil. Peel and slice mangoes and add with remaining ingredients to syrup. Cook until mango slices are almost tender, 8 to 10 minutes; strain and reserve fruit. Bring syrup to boil and continue cooking until reduced to half the original volume and quite thick, about 15 minutes. Return fruit to syrup, bring to boil, and pour into hot sterilized jars. Seal. Makes about 6 cups.

PINEAPPLE CHUTNEY

    8 small dried hot red peppers
  ¼ cup cold water
    7 cups (two 1-pound, 14-ounce cans)
      pineapple chunks
    3 cups white vinegar
    2 cups firmly packed brown sugar
    2 teaspoons salt
    1 cup raisins
    2 tablespoons finely chopped
      candied gingerroot
    3 garlic cloves, crushed
    1 cup chopped blanched almonds

Soak peppers in cold water for 30 minutes, drain, and remove seeds. Chop peppers. Drain syrup from pineapple into kettle. Add peppers and next 6 ingredients. Bring to boil, reduce heat, and simmer for 10 minutes. Add pineapple and simmer for 45 minutes longer, or until thick. Add almonds; pour into hot sterilized jars; seal. Makes 6 cups.

TOMATO CHUTNEY

    2 pounds ripe tomatoes
 1½ cups sugar
    1 cup cider vinegar
    1 teaspoon instant minced garlic
    1 teaspoon salt
  ¼ teaspoon crushed red pepper
    1 teaspoon ground ginger

Wash and peel tomatoes and cut into eighths. Combine with sugar, vinegar, garlic, salt, and red pepper in saucepan; cook, uncovered, until syrup thickens and tomatoes are soft, about 45 minutes.

Add ginger and cook for 5 minutes. Makes about 1 pint.

CIDER—Cider is the juice of apples that have been ground to a pulp and pressed to extract their juice. Cider may be "sweet" or "hard," that is, nonfermented or fermented. There is a certain amount of confusion as to where apple juice ends and sweet cider begins, since the words are often used interchangeably. When made at home, apple juice and sweet cider are the same, but when made commercially, sweet cider has been processed to prevent spoilage. There is not too much difference in the taste of the two, the taste of sweet cider depending on the kind and quality of the apples used for pressing. Sweet cider may also be slightly fermented to produce a low alcoholic content of around 2 per cent.

Hard and fermented cider is the drink Europeans, great cider drinkers, usually refer to when they speak of cider. Its alcoholic content varies. Another form is applejack, a potent spirit distilled from hard cider.

Sweet cider is the native New England and American drink, whereas hard cider has always been much more popular in Europe. It is the traditional drink of England and Northern France, where it is called *cidre*. It is consumed in large quantities and with much relish in central Europe, in Germany, Austria, and Switzerland. Cider is made sparkling by a number of processes. Sparkling cider is a favorite of the British.

Caloric Value

☐ Sweet, bottled, 3½ ounces = 47 calories

CIDER SAUCE FOR PUDDING

    2 tablespoons butter or margarine
    1 cup firmly packed brown sugar
    2 tablespoons all-purpose flour
    1 cup cider
  ¼ cup raisins
      Ground nutmeg for sprinkling

Melt butter in saucepan. Combine brown sugar and flour and add gradually, stirring constantly. Add cider; bring to boil and let thicken just a little. Remove from heat. Add raisins. Pour into a small pitcher or serving bowl and sprinkle with nutmeg. Serve hot with bread, cottage or plain steamed pudding. Makes about 1 cup.

Note: If sauce becomes too thick, thin with a little cold cider.

CIDER GELATIN SALAD

    1 envelope unflavored gelatin
    2 tablespoons cold water
    2 tablespoons fresh lemon juice
 1¾ cups hot sweet cider
  ¼ cup sugar
 1½ cups diced apples
  ½ cup diced celery
      Lettuce, mayonnaise, chopped nuts

Sprinkle gelatin on combined cold water and lemon juice to soften. Add hot cider and sugar and stir until dissolved. Chill. When mixture begins to set, fold in apple and celery. Turn into 6 individual molds and chill until firm. Unmold; serve on lettuce and top with mayonnaise and chopped nuts. Makes 6 servings.

CIDER PIE

  ⅓ cup grated maple or brown sugar
  ⅓ cup sweet cider
    3 eggs, separated
  ½ teaspoon ground nutmeg
    1 teaspoon butter
  ½ cup seeded raisins
      8-inch pie shell, baked
  ⅓ cup granulated sugar

Combine sugar and cider; heat until dissolved. Beat egg yolks; stir into sugar mixture and cook until thickened. Add nutmeg, butter, and raisins. Pour into baked pie shell. Beat egg whites until foamy; add sugar gradually, continuing to beat until stiff. Spread over pie filling and bake in preheated slow oven (325° F.) for about 15 minutes, or until meringue is golden brown. Makes 6 servings.

HOT CIDER PUNCH

    2 cinnamon sticks
    1 tablespoon whole cloves
  ½ cup sugar
    8 cups sweet cider
  ¼ teaspoon salt
   12 pieces of lemon peel

Tie spices loosely in cheesecloth bag. Mix all ingredients except peel and bring to boil. Cool; then remove spice bag. Reheat and serve very hot, with a piece of lemon peel in each serving. Makes 12 servings.

CIDER VINEGAR—A mild, yellowbrown vinegar, made from hard (fermented) cider. Most vinegar used in the United States is cider vinegar.

CINNAMON—This reddish-brown spice comes from the dried bark of the shrub-like evergreen trees of the *Cinnamomum* family, which belongs to the laurel group. It is one of the very few spices not obtained from the seeds, flowers, or fruits of a plant.

The kinds of cinnamon most commonly used are cassia and Ceylon cinnamon. In its different subvarieties, cassia cinnamon is native to China, Indochina, and Indonesia. We import it from Indonesia and Vietnam. It has a reddish brown bark, and an aromatic odor accompanies its pungently sweet taste.

Ceylon cinnamon comes from Ceylon and it is used more in other parts of the world, especially Mexico, than in the United States. It is buff-colored and quite mild.

Cassia cinnamon has been in use much longer than Ceylon cinnamon. Chinese use of it dates back 2,500 years before the birth of Christ; the Egyptians, 1,700 years. Ancient Romans not only used cinnamon to make their food exotic; its essence grew to be in great demand as a love potion. The people of the Old Testament valued cinnamon highly as a spice and a perfume; they used it as one of the chief ingredients of the "holy oil" which Moses was commanded to use in the Tabernacle. There are repeated references both to cinnamon and to cassia in the Bible. And much incense used in churches around the world still contains cinnamon.

Perhaps the sweet smell of cinnamon is the embodiment of the scent of all spices. When we read in the Song of Solomon (4:16): "Awake, O north wind; and come, thou south; blow upon my garden, that the spices thereof may flow out" or in Milton's *Paradise Lost:* "Off at Sea North-East winds blow Sabean Odours from the spicie-shoare of Arabie the blest" we cannot help but think of cinnamon, a joy then, as today and tomorrow.

Cinnamon is sold both ground and whole, in sticks. Ground cinnamon is widely used in baking and in flavoring fruits and desserts. In Middle Eastern, Oriental, and South American cooking ground cinnamon is used in meat, seafood, and sauce cookery. A dash of cinnamon will give an indefinable, delicious haunting quality to many foods.

Whole cinnamon comes in sticks in order to minimize breakage. The young shoots of the cinnamon tree are cut back twice a year and stripped of their bark. The bark is then dried, cut, and rolled into the familiar sticks, or quills. A one-inch piece of stick cinnamon will work wonders for the stock from corned beef or smoked pork shoulder, and for the court bouillon for fish and shellfish, or for the water in which peas, dried or fresh beans, and other vegetables are cooked.

Oil of cinnamon is made both from the ripe fruit of the tree and residues of the bark.

CINNAMON TOAST DE LUXE

1 pound loaf fresh white bread
1 cup butter or margarine
1 cup fine granulated sugar
1 tablespoon ground cinnamon

Cut slices of bread diagonally. Sauté half the slices slowly, 2 or 3 at a time, adding butter gradually until each piece is golden brown on each side, but not dark. Remove slices from skillet and drop into a clean brown paper bag containing a mixture of sugar and cinnamon. Shake gently and serve warm. Makes 24 to 32 pieces. To pick up less sugar, put toast on a paper towel to dry for a minute after browning.

Note: For variety, combine sugar and cinnamon and add a little water to make a paste. Dip bread into paste and sauté in butter until browned. The sugar and butter caramelize and give the toast a delicious crisp crust.

CINNAMON STARS

2 cups blanched almonds or hazelnuts
4 egg whites
  Grated rind and juice of ½ lemon
5¼ cups sifted confectioners' sugar
  (about 1½ pounds)
2 tablespoons ground cinnamon

Grate almonds in rotary grater. Beat egg whites until stiff. Add rind, juice, and 2 cups sugar. Continue beating until very stiff, about 30 minutes. Measure 1 cup; reserve. To remaining mixture add almonds and cinnamon and chill for several hours. Put on board generously sprinkled with confectioners' sugar, and sprinkle top with sugar. Roll very thin with sugar-dusted rolling pin. Cut with star-shape cutter; put on brown paper on ungreased cookie sheets and let stand overnight. Spread with reserved egg-white mixture. Bake in preheated oven (250° F.) for about 30 minutes. Slip paper onto wet table or board. Let stand for 1 minute. Loosen stars. Makes about 5 dozen. Store airtight for 1 week before using.

LEOPOLD SCHNITTEN

½ cup soft butter
  Sugar (about ¾ cup)
1 cup unblanched almonds
1 cup sifted all-purpose flour
1½ teaspoons ground cinnamon
½ teaspoon ground cloves

Cream butter and ½ cup sugar until fluffy. Put almonds through finest blade of food chopper and add to butter. Sift together flour, ½ teaspoon cinnamon, and cloves. Add to butter mixture and pat into buttered pan (13 x 9 x 2 inches). Bake in preheated moderate oven (350° F.) for 20 to 25 minutes. While hot,

sprinkle with mixture of 3 tablespoons sugar and remaining cinnamon. Cut into 1½-inch squares. Store airtight. Makes about 4½ dozen.

CIOPPINO—This delectable fish stew is one of California's great contributions to gastronomy. No one knows when or by whom it was created but it is consumed with gusto in almost every fishing port in the state.

Cioppino is a complicated stew and the versions are many. Traditional seasonings vary from area to area and the fishes used vary with the day's catch. In addition, individual cooks often change the ingredients to suit their own tastes. Some prefer white wine to red; others use sherry. Many like to make it with the addition of exotic tidbits such as octopus, squid, or eel. Or the fish may be omitted and only shellfish used. Often dried mushrooms that have been soaked are included. Here is the basic recipe; master it and then try your own versions.

3 pounds sea bass, barracuda, halibut,
  or a variety of any firm fish
1 large live Dungeness (hard-shell) crab
  or 1 live lobster
1 pound jumbo shrimps (or more)
1 pint clams or mussels or oysters,
  or all three

Cut fish into good-size serving pieces. Crack the crab; remove top shell but keep it for making stock. If you use lobster, cut tail into pieces and reserve body to make stock; if you use eastern lobster, cut tail into sections and crack claws. Split shrimp shells down the back and remove the black vein. Steam the mollusks (clams, mussels, or oysters) in a small amount of water just until they open. Remove the top shells and save the juice.

Now to prepare the sauce:

1½ cups chopped onions
1 cup chopped green peppers
¼ cup olive oil
3 garlic cloves, thoroughly mashed with
  1 teaspoon salt
3½ cups (one 1-pound, 12-ounce can)
  tomatoes
  Juice from the mollusks
2 cups red table wine
2 cups tomato juice
2 cups fish stock made from crab shell
  or lobster body and fish trimmings
  Herb bouquet (bay leaf, parsley, basil)
½ cup minced parsley

Sauté onion and green pepper in olive oil until just soft. Add all the rest of the ingredients and cook for 10 minutes. Remove bouquet and taste for seasonings. Select a large casserole or kettle with a cover and in it arrange in layers all the fish except the mollusks. Pour sauce over fish and cover pan. Simmer over low heat or in the oven for 20 to 30 minutes, or until fish is just done. Three minutes before removing from heat, add the mollusks.

Cioppino

Serve in deep bowls, shells and all, and sprinkle liberally with minced parsley. Have plenty of big paper napkins on hand. This is finger food. With this hearty stew, serve hot crusty sourdough bread and a robust red wine. For dessert, a variety of fruits and cheeses. Makes 4 servings.

CITRON—This is the oldest of the citrus fruits; it grows on a small thorny tree whose flowers are purple and white. The citron resembles a lemon, and grows to a length of six to nine inches. It has a greenish-yellow, tough and warty, fragrant peel, and a scanty, acid pulp. The fruit is grown for its peel, which is used in baking, and it is a most important ingredient of fruitcakes. The peel is first treated with brine: to remove the bitter oil, to bring out the flavor, and to prevent spoilage. Then it is candied in sugar and glucose.

Citron probably came from northern India. It was the first of the citrus fruits to be used by Europeans, as long ago as the 4th century B.C. Today, it is grown chiefly in Corsica, Sicily, Greece, and the West Indies.

Citron is sold candied, by halves or diced, both in bulk and in jars of varying sizes.

Caloric Value

☐ 3½ ounces, candied = 314 calories

LITTLE WHITE FRUITCAKES

1 cup shortening
1 cup sugar
5 eggs
2 cups sifted all-purpose flour
1 teaspoon salt
1½ teaspoons baking powder
¼ cup pineapple juice
½ cup each of chopped candied
  cherries, finely cut citron,
  orange peel, and lemon peel
½ cup each of chopped pitted dates,
  chopped dried figs, and chopped
  dried apricots
1¼ cups chopped candied pineapple
1 cup golden raisins

2 cups flaked coconut
2 cups sliced blanched almonds

Cream shortening and sugar until light. Add eggs, one at a time, beating well after each addition. Sift 1½ cups flour, the salt, and baking powder. Add alternately with pineapple juice to first mixture. Dust fruits with remaining flour. Add fruits, coconut, and almonds to batter. Mix only until well blended. Pour into paper baking cups in muffin pans and bake in preheated very slow oven (275°F.) for 50 minutes. Store airtight. Makes thirty-two 2-inch cakes.

CITRON LOAF CAKE

⅔ cup shortening
1⅓ cups sugar
½ teaspoon vanilla extract
½ teaspoon lemon extract or rind
3 eggs
2⅔ cups sifted cake flour
2 teaspoons baking powder
¾ teaspoon salt
¼ teaspoon baking soda
1 cup dairy sour cream
⅔ cup thinly sliced or diced citron

Cream shortening; add sugar gradually. Add extracts. Add eggs, one at a time, beating until light and fluffy after each addition. Sift together cake flour, baking powder, salt, and soda. Add to batter alternately with sour cream, beginning and ending with dry ingredients. Beat until smooth. Fold in citron. Pour into greased and floured 9-inch tube pan and bake in preheated moderate oven (350° F.) for about 50 minutes. Cool for 5 minutes on rack. Turn out on cake rack to cool.

ARAB DATES

½ cup honey
½ cup chopped toasted almonds
¼ cup chopped candied citron
½ cup chopped walnuts
1 pound pitted dates
  Sugar

Mix first 4 ingredients. Stuff dates with this mixture. Roll in sugar, and store airtight.

CITRUS—A family of fruit trees, native to tropical Asia where they have been grown for thousands of years, but now grown in all parts of the world where the climate is favorable. The best-known species are oranges, grapefruit, tangerines, lemons, and limes, which are eaten for pleasure and health since they are outstanding sources of vitamins. They are grown in many varieties, both with and without seeds.

Not only the fruit, but the citrus trees as well, have captured the love of men. Their foliage is dense and evergreen; they grow in height to forty feet, and the flowers, which are small and mostly white, are abundant. They fill the air with an exotic fragrance which is irre-

sistible. Citrus trees, their flowers, and fruits have inspired poets and painters as symbols of the sunny south, balmy winds, and the sweet life. As trees, citrus have given shade and refreshment to weary travelers; in tubs, they have decorated the halls of palaces; as potted plants, they have brought beauty into the home. The sight of a golden orange nestling among dark-green leaves, or the fragrance of the white blossom, will lift the human heart above its cares.

From Asia, citrus trees spread to the Mediterranean countries, which grow citrus in abundance. (The one exception is grapefruit which is an American and not a European fruit.)

The first citrus fruits in the New World were brought to Haiti by Columbus; the first to grow in the United States were planted in St. Augustine, Florida, in 1565. Today, citrus is grown in Florida, California, Arizona, Texas, and Louisiana and on vast plantations in Brazil and other tropical Central and South American countries.

Americans consume from eighty to ninety pounds of citrus fruits per person, each year, in the form of fresh, canned, and frozen fruit; fresh, canned, and frozen juice; fresh and candied peel; and in flavoring extracts. The most popular of the citrus fruits is the orange. Grown in many varieties, oranges account for two thirds of the citrus consumption in this country.

MARKET VARIETIES OF CITRUS FRUITS

Citron—Yellow-green and oval-shape, it is 6 to 9 inches long, with rough skin and a small amount of acid pulp. It is grown for its peel, which is candied.

Grapefruit (Pomelo)—Ranges in color from pale yellow to russet to bronze; large, roundish fruit that grows in clusters. The pulp may be yellow or pink. The fruit is not native to or well known in the citrus-growing countries of Europe but is America's gift to the world. It is thought to be a mutation of the shaddock and probably originated in the West Indies.

Kumquat—Smallest of the citrus fruits, orange in color; oblong or round in shape, from 1¼ to 1½ inches in diameter, depending on the variety. Used for ornamentation as well as in cookery.

Lemon—Yellow and oval-shape, it is 3 to 5 inches long, and very sour.

Lime—Green and deep yellow in color with a smooth, thin skin, it is lemon-shape but smaller in size; very acid.

Orange, Sweet and Sour—The rind is orange while the flesh colors range from light orange to deep red. Because the rind tends to take on a greenish tinge late in the season, artificial coloring is

sometimes added. Some 200 varieties of oranges, the vast majority of them sweet, are grown in the United States.

King Oranges are probably a cross between a sweet orange and a Mandarin, with a sweet or slightly acid flesh.

Mandarin Oranges are a small, round fruit, native to China, with easily removable peel and loose segments. Extensively grown in Japan and in limited quantities in our Gulf States and California. Tangerines and satsumas are two well-known varieties.

Sour Oranges have a sour bitter pulp, and are used for making marmalade.

Temple Oranges are a hybrid between an orange and a tangerine.

Shaddock—Probable ancestor of the grapefruit. It grows to the size of a watermelon, weighs up to 20 pounds, has a coarse, thick rind and reddish, aromatic, but bitter flesh. Named after Captain Shaddock, who brought it from the East Indies to the West Indies.

Tangelo—The name is a combination of tangerine and pomelo (grapefruit), the two fruits which were crossed in 1897 to produce it. It has an orange rind and pale yellow flesh, is medium to large in size, with an accented fresh acid flavor. Two of the most successful varieties differ considerably in shape (pear or round) and in peel (smooth and thin, or rough and thick).

Tangerine—Variety of the Mandarin orange, tangerines are smaller than the orange, with flesh that is deep orange to red in color. They have a hollow pith and loose rind which permits easy separation of the segments.

Ugli Fruit—The rough, puffy appearance of this member of the citrus family belies its extremely pleasant flavor, which is a combination of that of oranges, grapefruit, and tangerines. Ugli fruits are larger than grapefruit, and not a citrus hybrid. They come from Jamaica and are imported in limited quantities.

CITRUS SALAD PLATE

On a bed of shredded salad greens, arrange orange, grapefruit, tangelo, and/or tangerine sections. Decorate with twisted slices of lemon and lime. Serve with Lime Dressing.

Lime Dressing

¼ cup salad oil
2 tablespoons fresh lime juice
Dash of cayenne
¼ teaspoon salt
⅛ teaspoon pepper
1 teaspoon sugar

Combine all ingredients and chill. Serve on fruit salads or tossed green salads. Makes ⅓ cup.

CLABBER—This is milk which has soured naturally and thickened. It contains definite curds, but they have not yet separated from the whey. Chilled clabbered milk is a pleasant, refreshing, wholesome dish that can be flavored in any desired way or eaten with fruit. For centuries it has been enjoyed wherever people have had their own cows and milk.

CLAM—The name is used to describe many bivalve mollusks found in various parts of the world. In the United States it most generally refers to *Venus mercenaria,* the round, hard-shell clam, and *Mya arenaria,* the long, soft-shell clam.

Soft-shell clams are found in Atlantic coastal waters from North Carolina to Greenland. They live in waters between tidemarks where they burrow into the mud or sand to a depth of several inches; they are dug up at low tide. Their meat is generally steamed or used for chowder.

Hard-shell clams range from Cape Cod to Texas and are also found off the coasts of Maine and New Brunswick. They are found beyond the low-water mark in waters from one to six fathoms deep. They are fished by raking, or dredged, like oysters. New Englanders often call them by their Indian name, "quahog." Young quahogs are called "littlenecks" and small ones, "cherry stones." The big ones are mainly made into chowder, and the small and medium-size ones eaten on the half shell, raw or cooked.

Off the West Coast there are a number of other varieties of clams, and the Atlantic varieties have also been successfully transplanted to Pacific waters.

Clams have always been an important item in the American diet. The Indians used them widely as food, and made parts of quahog shells into wampum. The colonists, enchanted with this food which was free for the taking, devised innumerable ways of preparing the gift from the sea.

As early as 1616 Captain John Smith was so thrilled by his adventures as an amateur clamdigger that he wrote this account to his fellow Englishmen: "You shall scarce find any bay or cove of sand where you may not take any clampes, or lobsters or both at your pleasure."

In fact, clams have become almost a ritual food which is associated with certain regions, such as New England. Unfortunately, mortality among young clams is high, and ruthless harvesting has also diminished the supply so that it no longer meets the demand.

Availability—Fresh clams are generally available at the shore where they are

CITRUS	TYPE AND AMOUNT	CALORIES	MILLIGRAMS OF VITAMIN C
WHOLE FRUIT			
Grapefruit	fresh, 1 raw, medium, 4¼-inch diameter:		
	white	50	50
	pink or white	55	48
	canned, water pack, 1 cup (solids and liquids)	70	?
	sugar pack, 1 cup (solids and liquids)	170	?
Lemon	fresh, 1 raw, medium, 2 1/5-inch diameter:	20	38
Lime	fresh, 1 raw, medium, 2-inch diameter	19	19
Orange	fresh, 1 raw, 2-4/5 to 3-inch diameter	60-70	75-76
Tangerine	fresh, 1 raw, medium, 2½-inch diameter	40	26
JUICES			
Grapefruit	fresh, 6 ounces	72	69
	canned, 6 ounces: unsweetened	75	63
	6 ounces: sweetened	96	58
	frozen, 6 ounces: unsweetened	75	72
	6 ounces: sweetened	87	63
Lemon	fresh, 6 ounces	45	85
	1 tablespoon	5	7
	canned, 6 ounces: unsweetened	45	77
Lemonade	water added, fresh or frozen diluted, 1 cup	110	17
Lime	fresh, 6 ounces	48	60
	canned, 6 ounces	48	39
Limeade	frozen diluted, 1 cup	105	6
Orange	fresh, 6 ounces, California	90	91
	Florida (average)	78	81
	canned, 6 ounces: unsweetened	90	75
	frozen, 6 ounces	82	84
Orange and	frozen, 6 ounces	82	75
Grapefruit	fresh, 6 ounces	87	50
Tangerine	canned, 6 ounces: unsweetened	78	42

dug: in local stores and from individuals.

Canned clams are available whole and minced. Bottled clam juice is available.

Purchasing Guide—Fresh clams are sold alive, in the shell, or shucked. If buying them in the shell, be sure the shells are tightly closed. Clams in the shell are graded according to size as:

HARD SHELL	SOFT SHELL
Chowder, Large	Large
Chowder, Medium	Steamers
Cherry stone	
Littleneck	

☐ 8 quarts, (1 peck) clams in-the-shell = 1 quart, shucked

☐ One 7½ ounce can, minced clams = about ½ cup clams and about ½ cup juice

☐ One 7½ ounce bottle clam juice = about 1 cup juice

Nutritive Food Values—High in protein, no fat, fair amounts of calcium and iron.

☐ Fresh, 3½ ounces, raw = 76 calories

☐ Canned, 3½ ounces, solids and liquid = 52 calories

Storage—Keep fresh clams in shells refrigerated. They should be eaten or cooked as soon as purchased.

☐ Fresh, refrigerator shelf, cooked: 1 to 2 days

☐ Canned, kitchen shelf: 1 year

☐ Canned, refrigerator shelf, opened and covered: 1 day

Basic Preparation—Discard clams with broken shells and shells that are slightly open.

All clams should be thoroughly scrubbed with a stiff brush before opening. Quick, gentle cooking will keep them from toughening.

Soak clams in a brine (⅓ cup salt to 1 gallon water). Sprinkle ¼ cup cornmeal over the clams, ¼ cup for every quart of clams. Let clams stand for at least 3 hours. This soaking whitens the shell, removes sand, and causes the clam to rid itself of its stomach contents. Using a strong thin knife or clam knife, insert the tip of the knife between the edges of the shell. Work over a bowl to catch the clam juice. Cut the muscle at the hinged back of the clam, exposing the meat.

If served raw, place six to eight clams on the half shell on a bed of crushed ice and serve with lemon wedges, tomato sauce, and horseradish. The smaller clams, littlenecks, and the medium clams, cherry stones, are best suited for eating raw. The larger clams with a stronger flavor are best suited for chowder. When preparing steamers, allow 1 quart unshucked steamers for each person.

STEAMED CLAMS

Allow 1 quart soft-shell clams for each

serving. Scrub shells thoroughly with brush, changing the water repeatedly until there is no trace of sand. Put clams in deep kettle; add 2 tablespoons water for each quart of clams. Cover and cook over low heat until shells open, about 15 minutes. Do not overcook. Remove skin from neck, or siphon, of clam. Remove to large soup plates and serve with individual dishes of melted butter. Strain the broth left in the kettle and serve with the clams. Lift each clam from the shell by the black neck. Dip into broth, then into butter, and eat all but the neck. Neck can be eaten if skin is removed. **Note:** Eat them piping hot as soon as the shells open.

CLAMS BROILED ON THE HALF SHELL

Crumple foil and place in baking dish. Place cherry-stone clams on the half shell on the foil, making sure the shells are steady. Top each clam with a dash of Worcestershire and a 1-inch piece of raw bacon. Broil until bacon is crisp. **Note:** Allow 6 to 8 clams for each serving.

DEVILED CLAMS

2 dozen cherry-stone clams
½ cup water
½ green pepper, minced
1 small onion, minced
3 tablespoons butter or margarine
½ cup dry bread crumbs
½ teaspoon each of ground thyme and marjoram
⅛ teaspoon hot pepper sauce
3 slices of bacon, minced
Parsley, lemon juice, paprika

Scrub clams with brush. Put on rack in kettle with water. Cover and heat gently until clams open. Remove clams from kettle; reserve liquid. Take clams from shells. Separate halves of shells and save. Put clams through food chopper, or mince with knife if preferred. Cook green pepper and onion in hot butter for 2 minutes. Add clams, crumbs, and seasonings. Put mixture in as many clam shells as it will fill, put on cookie sheet, and sprinkle each with a little bacon. Brown in broiler with medium heat for 10 to 12 minutes. Sprinkle with minced parsley. If desired, serve with small cups of any remaining clam broth, reheated with a dash of lemon juice and a little paprika. Makes 4 to 6 servings.

CLAM SOUP, ITALIAN STYLE

¼ cup olive oil
4 slices of Italian bread
1 garlic clove
2 parsley sprigs, chopped
¾ cup red wine
1 tablespoon ketchup
2 cans (7½ ounces each) minced clams with liquid
1 cup clam juice
¼ teaspoon pepper
½ teaspoon crumbled dried oregano

Heat 2 tablespoons oil in saucepan. Add bread and brown on both sides. Remove bread and add garlic to oil; cook for 2 or 3 minutes. Remove garlic. Add remaining ingredients to oil and simmer for a few minutes. Put a slice of bread in each bowl. Pour in soup. Makes 1 quart, or 4 servings.

CLAM FRITTERS WITH TOMATO SAUCE

2 cups all-purpose flour
2 teaspoons baking powder
1 teaspoon salt
¼ teaspoon pepper
1 can (10½ ounces) minced clams
Milk
2 eggs, well beaten
1 tablespoon melted butter or margarine
Fat for deep frying
1 can (8 ounces) tomato sauce
½ teaspoon Worcestershire
Juice of ½ lemon

Sift flour, baking powder, salt, and pepper together. Drain broth from clams into measuring cup and add enough milk to make ¾ cup. Add to eggs; stir into flour mixture and beat thoroughly. Add clams and butter. Drop by spoonfuls into hot deep fat (375°F. on frying thermometer) and fry until golden brown. Serve with tomato sauce heated with remaining ingredients. Makes 4 servings.

FRIED CLAM PUFFS

1 pint shucked clams and liquid
1 egg
1 teaspoon salt
¼ cup milk
1 cup all-purpose flour
1 teaspoon baking powder
Fat for deep frying

Remove black section from clams and put clams through food chopper. Beat egg and salt; add milk, clam liquid, and chopped clams. Sift flour and baking powder together; then add to clam mixture and stir well. Drop by tablespoonfuls into hot deep fat (375°F. on a frying thermometer) and fry until brown, about 5 minutes. Drain on unglazed paper. Makes 1 dozen.

WHITE CLAM SAUCE

2 dozen cherry-stone clams
1 cup water
¼ cup olive oil
2 garlic cloves, chopped
½ bay leaf, crumpled
¼ cup chopped parsley
Salt and pepper

Scrub and wash clams. Place in kettle and add water. Bring to a boil; lower heat. Simmer, covered, for 10 minutes, or until shells open. Remove clams from shells, strain broth, and reserve. Cut clams into small pieces. Heat olive oil. Sauté garlic, bay leaf, and parsley in it for 5 minutes. Add clam broth and bring slowly to a boil. Add clams; remove from heat. Season to taste with salt and pepper. Makes enough sauce to cover 1 pound of spaghetti.

Clambake
by James A. Beard

Surely the clambake is one of the most American forms of outdoor cookery and like many other primitive styles of preparing food it is "pit cookery." It originated on the shores of New England, where clams and lobsters abound. The method of cooking is this: One digs a large hole or pit and lines it with stones. These should not be wet stones or those gathered from under water, for they are apt to explode. A roaring fire is built in the pit and allowed to burn for two or three hours. The coals are shoveled out and a layer of wet seaweed is placed in the bottom of the pit. This is covered with some chicken wire and another layer of seaweed. Clams and lobsters are added—sometimes the latter are wrapped in muslin or cheesecloth—then another layer of seaweed; after that come potatoes and corn (husked or not, as you wish) and sometimes chicken halves. Often a top layer of clams is placed in the pit before the final covering of seaweed and a tarpaulin. Finally, the tarpaulin is weighted at the edges and some sand placed on top. The clambake is allowed to steam for anywhere from three quarters of an hour to two hours. One may lift the tarp and withdraw a lobster or chicken to test for doneness. It is usual to eat clams first, then lobsters, then chicken and corn. Copious quantities of butter and a good deal of beer help. Often clam chowder is served before, and watermelon is considered a traditional dessert.

Indoor clambakes with lobsters and clams are quite popular as well. These are done in large cauldrons with tight-fitting lids. The arrangement of seaweed and seafood, plus chicken, is essentially the same as the outdoor technique. There are a number of "farms" in Maine which send out complete clambakes in a large tin packed with sea water and seaweed and the necessary fish. The food may be "baked" in the same tin. These are shipped as far as the West Coast.

CLARET—Properly speaking, this is a red wine from the Bordeaux area in southwestern France. Claret is famous for its jewel-like color and its delicate flavor and bouquet. The principal grape variety used in red Bordeaux wines is Cabernet Sauvignon.

CLARIFY—In cooking, as in general usage, this word means to make pure and clear. It is generally applied to liquids and fats and it involves separating the solid parts from the liquid parts. The most commonly clarified foods are consommé and butter. Liquids are clarified by filtering; fats are clarified by slow heating; fruit juices and wines can be clarified by slight fermentation or by the addition of other substances, such as isinglass, a very pure animal gelatin. In the days when coffee was made by pouring boiling water over the grounds rather than by dripping or percolating it, it was often clarified with eggshell, to obtain a sparkling brew.

CLOVE—A clove is the dried, unopened flower bud of the stately evergreen clove tree, which belongs to the myrtle family and is grown mainly on the islands of Zanzibar and Madagascar, off the east coast of Africa. The name originated from the fact that the flower buds resembled small nails, and in French, nail is *clou,* in Latin, *clavus.* The Dutch call the clove *kruidnagel,* or "spice nail."

Very little is known about the early history of cloves, but their original home was in the Moluccas, the storied Spice Islands of the Far East, and we know they were used in China in 300 B.C., when courtiers held a clove in their mouths in the presence of the emperor. In the 4th century A.D. cloves were well known in the Mediterranean area, and by the 8th century they had made their way throughout Europe.

In the 17th century the Dutch, who ruled the Moluccas, enforced a policy limiting the production of cloves, creating a profitable monopoly. Toward the end of the 18th century, however, the French were able to get a few clove trees which they transplanted to various French colonies—in Cayenne, the West Indies, and some of their islands in the Indian Ocean. They are cultivated now in many tropical countries including Brazil, Java, and Sumatra.

The scent of cloves in bloom caused many a word to be written by poet and layman alike. Dr. Garcia da Orta, a Portuguese doctor who practiced in India in the early part of the 16th century, wrote the following in his *Simples and Drugs* in 1563: "The scent of the clove is said to be most fragrant in the world. I experienced this coming from Cochin to Goa (in India) with the wind from the shore, and at night it was calm when we were a league from the land. The scent was so strong and so delicious that I thought there must be a forest of flowers. On enquiring I found that we were near a ship coming from Maluco with cloves and then I understood the truth."

So pleasing is the scent of cloves that it is used to scent soaps, sachets, pomanders, and potpourris.

Cloves are sold whole or ground, and are one of the most useful spices. They are used in gingerbreads, spicecakes, and fruitcakes; chili sauce and pickles. They are good to flavor cooked beets and meat loaves. A clove-studded ham looks and tastes much better than a plain one. Cloves studding a whole onion give zest to creamed dishes and sauces, to stews and soups (remove onion and cloves before serving), an apple studded with cloves should be added to mulled wine and cider.

COAT—To coat food is to cover it with a thin layer of flour, fine crumbs, sugar, nuts, or frosting. Food is coated to preserve the inner moisture and to add flavor and texture contrasts between food and coating. In some cases, food is coated prior to cooking, as in sautéing, frying, or baking. In other cases cooked food is coated with gelatin or aspic, as a decoration: hams, chickens, cold meats, vegetables, and mousses, for example. Candy may be coated with chocolate, fondant, coconut, etc.

When coating, make sure dry coating materials are very finely crumbled. When coating with crumbs, it is necessary to dip the food first into a liquid, such as milk, cream, or beaten eggs, to make crumbs adhere to it. Once coated, chill the food before frying; in this way a crisper, firmer coating is formed. Some foods can be dipped into liquid, then into flour, then into eggs, and finally into crumbs for a firmer coating. This is usually done with veal cutlets.

When coating foods with gelatin or aspic, make sure that the food to be coated is absolutely cold. Add 1 envelope unflavored gelatin to every 1¾ cups stock or other liquid. When mixture has chilled and is of the consistency of unbeaten egg whites, spoon a thin layer of gelatin over food. Chill until firm. Repeat process until desired thickness is reached.

COBBLER—There are cobblers to eat and cobblers to drink. The first are desserts resembling a deep-dish fruit pie, where sugared fruit is covered with a single biscuit or pastry crust and baked. They are served with cream, custard, or with a hard sauce, and they are a fine, traditional American dessert, worth rejoicing in.

Cobblers to drink are also native, and consist of refreshing cold summer drinks spiked with wines or liquors, and garnished with fruits, such as oranges, lemons, and/or berries, and with mint.

The origin of the word is unknown. There has been speculation that it comes from "to cobble up," that is, to put together hurriedly.

OLD-FASHIONED PEACH COBBLER
1 egg
1 cup sugar
3 tablespoons butter, melted
⅓ cup milk
½ cup sifted all-purpose flour
2 teaspoons baking powder
½ teaspoon salt
4 cups sliced peeled peaches (7 or 8)
¼ teaspoon ground nutmeg
¼ teaspoon ground cinnamon

Beat together egg, ½ cup sugar, the butter, and milk. Sift together flour, baking powder, and salt. Beat into egg mixture. Combine peaches, remaining sugar, nutmeg, and cinnamon. Put in greased baking dish (12 x 8 x 2 inches). Top fruit with batter, spreading smoothly. Bake in preheated moderate oven (375°F.) for 30 minutes, or until crust is crisp and golden brown. Serve hot with cream, with custard, or with hard sauce. Makes 6 servings.

■ **Variation**—Instead of peaches, use 4 cups pitted cherries, plums, or berries.

SHERRY COBBLER
2 unpeeled oranges, thinly sliced
1 unpeeled lemon, thinly sliced
½ cup powdered sugar, or more to taste
Shaved ice
2 cups sherry
1 cup water
Mint or berries for garnish

Place alternate layers of orange and lemon slices into a deep bowl. Sprinkle fruit layers with sugar and shaved ice. Pour sherry and water over fruit. Stir thoroughly. Serve in goblets garnished with mint. Makes 4 to 6 servings.

COCKTAIL—The word is used to describe drinks, both alcoholic and nonalcoholic, and also a certain type of appetizer. The alcoholic beverage is a short, iced, and rather potent drink, made with liquors and flavoring ingredients. The nonalcoholic cocktail may be a chilled vegetable, fruit, or clam juice. The appetizer called a "cocktail" is chilled cut-up fruit or vegetables, or chilled seafood, served with a highly seasoned sauce.

The origin of the word cocktail is obscure. What is sure is that cocktails of all kinds are typically American inventions, which, in the case of alcoholic cocktails, have been enthusiastically taken over by Europeans.

TOMATO JUICE COCKTAIL

To one 6-ounce glass of tomato juice, add 1 teaspoon fresh lemon juice, dash of salt, ¼ teaspoon sugar, dash of Worcestershire, and dash of hot pepper sauce, if desired.

VEGETABLE COCKTAIL

Season canned vegetable juice with horseradish, Worcestershire, and fresh lemon juice; chill.

SIX FRUIT-COCKTAIL SUGGESTIONS

Always serve fruit cocktails in well-chilled sherbet glasses. If sweet fruits are chosen, sprinkle with some fresh lemon or lime juice to add that tangy flavor so necessary in appetizers.

Canned Fruit Cocktail—Drain chilled fruit cocktail and mix with diced unpeeled red apple, and orange and banana, if desired.

Citrus-Grape Cocktail—Combine diced orange and grapefruit sections with seedless grapes. Garnish with a fresh raspberry.

Melon-Lime Cocktail—Serve your favorite melon, cut into balls or cubes, with a wedge of lime.

Mixed-Fruit Cocktail—Combine a mixture of diced and whole small fruit (apples, pears, oranges, grapefruit, bananas, grapes, berries) and add some ginger ale or white wine. Experiment with flavors and colors: cranberry juice over grapefruit sections; grapes and red wine.

Pear-Orange Cocktail—Combine diced pear and orange sections. Top with mayonnaise mixed with orange juice.

Strawberry-Pineapple Cocktail—Arrange small chunks of pineapple and sliced strawberries in chilled glasses. Serve with a mixture of orange and lime juice.

SEAFOOD COCKTAIL

1 package (12 ounces) frozen shrimps, cooked, peeled, and deveined
2 lobster tails, cooked and cut up
1 package (6 ounces) frozen crabmeat
   Lettuce or watercress
¼ cup mayonnaise
¾ cup chili sauce
2 teaspoons Worcestershire
1 tablespoon chopped parsley
   Horseradish, hot pepper sauce to taste
   Salt and pepper to taste

Combine first 3 ingredients and chill. To serve, arrange seafood on lettuce. For sauce, combine remaining ingredients and chill. Spoon sauce over seafood before serving. Makes 8 servings.

AVOCADO-TOMATO COCKTAIL

1 avocado
2 tomatoes
   Small lettuce leaves
½ cup chili sauce
1 tablespoon horseradish
   Juice of ½ lemon
½ teaspoon salt
⅛ teaspoon pepper

Peel and dice chilled avocado and tomatoes. Put on lettuce in cocktail glasses. Mix remaining ingredients and serve as sauce. Makes 4 servings.

COCOA—The word comes from the Mexican Indian *cacahuatl* and describes a beverage and dessert flavoring made from the beans of the cacao tree which flourishes only in tropical climates. Today, the leading growers of cacao, or cocoa, beans are Brazil, the Dominican Republic, and Ecuador in the Western Hemisphere; and Ghana, Nigeria, Cameroon, and the Ivory Coast in Africa. The economies of these countries depend largely on the cocoa trade.

The cacao bean is also the source of chocolate. Cocoa differs from chocolate in fat and sugar content. After the beans are cleaned, dried, roasted, and ground, some of the fat, or cocoa butter, is removed. It is then ground again to form the powder known as cocoa. In Dutch-process cocoa, cocoa is treated with an alkali which gives it a darker color and a richer flavor. This process tends to prevent "settling out" of the cocoa when it is used as a beverage. Instant cocoa is a mixture of cocoa, sugar, flavoring, and an emulsifier, to be added to hot or cold water or milk for use as a beverage.

Storage—Cocoa should be stored, tightly covered, in a cool, dry place. When it is stored at too high a temperature or in too moist an atmosphere, it loses its brown color and becomes lumpy.

HOT COCOA

5 to 6 tablespoons unsweetened cocoa
4 to 6 tablespoons sugar
   Dash of salt
½ cup water
3½ cups milk

Mix cocoa, sugar, and salt in a saucepan or in top part of a double boiler. Stir in water. Place over low heat. Cook mixture in saucepan for about 2 minutes, in double boiler over boiling water for about 4 minutes, or until thick and smooth. Stir constantly. Stir in milk; heat to boiling, stirring occasionally, but do not boil. For a frothy drink, beat before

serving. Makes 6 cups.

Iced Cocoa

Follow recipe above for Hot Cocoa, using the larger measurement of cocoa. Pour warm beverage over ice in serving glasses; add a spoonful of whipped cream and a dash of ground nutmeg, if desired. Makes 4 large glasses.

HUNGARIAN CHRISTMAS BALLS

1 cup sugar
   Grated rind of 2 oranges
2 tablespoons fresh orange juice
1 teaspoon fresh lemon juice
1 cup finely ground walnuts
½ cup finely chopped candied fruits
½ cup Dutch-process cocoa

Over low heat melt sugar with grated orange rind, orange juice, and lemon juice. Cool. Add walnuts and fruits; with hands, work until well mixed. Pinch off pieces of dough and roll into ¾-inch balls. Roll in cocoa until covered. Makes 2½ dozen.

COCOA BUTTER—This is the fat removed from cacao beans during their conversion into chocolate and cocoa. It is used primarily in making candy and pharmaceutical products. Cocoa butter is whitish-yellow and smells refreshingly of cocoa.

COCONUT—The fruit of a palm, native to Malaya, which has been transplanted to all parts of the tropical and subtropical world. The coconut palm is a handsome, elegant tree that can grow to a height of one hundred feet, often leaning at a graceful angle. The trunk has few if any branches, and ends at the top in a crown of large, feathery, elongated leaves. The fruit is twelve to eighteen inches in length and six to eight inches in diameter. It takes about a year to mature. The outer covering is smooth, the husk fibrous, and a woody brown shell encases a layer of firm white meat with a milky fluid at its center. The palm goes on bearing fruit for some seventy years.

The coconut palm is one of the world's most indispensable plants. It yields not only coconuts and coconut milk, but also a vegetable, the cabbage palm, made from the tender young terminal buds, and a sap used to make palm-tree wine, liquors, and vinegar. The leaves of the coconut palm are used for thatching, mats, curtains, hats, and baskets, the wood for furniture, the shells for bowls, the roots for fuel, and the fiber around the fruit husk for fish nets, rope, and mattresses. The entire coconut forest is a source of shade from the tropical sun.

The coconut itself produces a white meat which can be grated or shredded and eaten as is or used for cooking, fresh or preserved. The water in the unripened fruit serves as a delicious drink which is always cool because the thick shell insulates it against the heat.

Most coconut meat, however, is dried to make copra, the only crop of many a tropical island. The coconut oil obtained from pressing copra is used for soap, toiletries, candles, and margarines and also for cooking. The oil also has many industrial uses. What remains of the meat after the oil has been pressed out goes into feed for stock and into fertilizer.

The coconut palm and its fruit, which are so important in the lives of so many people, have given rise to many beliefs and customs. In India, for instance, the plant is reputed to have been created by the sage Sisvamitra; when a boy is born in Malabar, his parents plant five coconut trees, enough to support him.

Fresh or otherwise, coconut is a delicious accompaniment to curry, and as an ingredient for baking and candy making.

Availability—Fresh coconuts are available all year. Peak season is October through December.

Coconut is also available in grated or flaked form, in cans or packages. It may be dry or moist, sweetened or unsweetened. Some toasted coconut and coconut with extra-long shreds is available in small quantities.

Purchasing Guide—Look for coconuts that are heavy for their size and sound full of liquid when shaken. Avoid coconuts with wet or moldy eyes (the three rings at one end).

☐ 1 medium coconut = 3 to 4 cups grated, about 1 cup coconut milk
☐ 1 cup grated coconut = 1⅓ cups flaked

Storage—Keep unopened coconut at room temperature. Keep grated coconut and unused pieces tightly covered in refrigerator or freezer. Renew softness by heating over hot water.

☐ Fresh, room temperature, unopened: 2 to 6 months, depending on age of nut and previous storage conditions
☐ Fresh, refrigerator shelf, cut and wrapped: 1 week
☐ Fresh, freezer, prepared for freezing: 9 months
☐ Fresh coconut milk, refrigerator shelf: 1 week
☐ Dried, shredded or flaked, kitchen shelf, unopened container: 6 months
☐ Dried, shredded or flaked, and canned, refrigerator shelf, opened and tightly covered: 1 month
☐ Dried, shredded or flaked, and canned, freezer, prepared for freezing: 1 year
☐ Canned, kitchen shelf, unopened: 1½ years

Caloric Values

☐ Fresh, 3½ ounces = 346 calories
☐ Dried, 3½ ounces, shredded = 548 calories

Basic Preparation—Pierce eyes with screwdriver or ice pick. Drain liquid; heat coconut in moderate oven (350° F.) for 15 to 30 minutes. Tap all over with hammer, then break open. Pry out meat and pare off dark skin. To grate white meat, use grater or whirl in blender. When measuring, pack lightly into cup.

☐ **To Toast**—Spread in shallow pan. Bake in moderate oven (350°F.) for about 15 minutes until light brown, stirring frequently.

☐ **To Tint**—Mix a few drops of food coloring with a few drops of water in bowl. Add coconut and toss lightly until evenly colored. Tinted coconut is used for decorating cakes, cookies, etc.

☐ **To Freeze**—Remove dark skin from coconut: Shred, grate, or coarsely grind meat. Pack into containers, allowing 1-inch headspace. Cover with coconut milk or with a mixture of half coconut milk and half white corn syrup.

☐ **To Make Coconut Milk or Cream, Fresh Coconut**—This is often used as a chilled beverage, or as an ingredient in cooking and baking. Crack open coconut. Drain the water. For a thin liquid use this in cooking. To obtain a thicker, creamier liquid, scrape out the white meat with a heavy metal spoon, stopping when the brown rind is reached. Place coconut on several thicknesses of cheesecloth and squeeze. Discard the coconut pulp. This thicker liquid can be used as is or combined with the drained liquid to get the desired consistency.

☐ **To Make Coconut Milk or Cream, Dried Coconut**—For 1 cup coconut milk, combine in a saucepan:

1⅓ cups (about) flaked coconut (or
   1 cup packaged grated coconut and
   1 cup milk)
1⅓ cups milk

Combine ingredients and simmer over low heat, stirring occasionally, until mixture foams, about 2 minutes. Strain. Use in curry sauce or other recipes that call for coconut milk. Or chill and serve as a beverage.

To use remaining coconut flakes, return coconut to saucepan. Add 3 tablespoons butter and 2 tablespoons confectioners' sugar. Stir over low heat until well blended. Spread coconut thinly on shallow baking pan. Place in moderate oven (350°F.) and toast for 25 minutes, or until delicately browned. Serve as accompaniment to a curry dish, or use as a garnish.

You can also use an electric blender to make coconut milk. To do so, place in blender:

1⅓ cups (about) flaked coconut
   (or 1 cup packaged grated coconut
   and 1 cup milk)
1⅓ cups milk

Blend until coconut is pulverized, about 15 seconds. Pour into saucepan and simmer over low heat, stirring occasionally, until mixture foams, about 2 minutes. Strain through double thicknesses of cheesecloth. Makes 1 cup coconut milk.

To use remaining coconut flakes, spread on a cloth to dry. Use as a garnish.

FRUIT SALAD WITH COCONUT DRESSING
2 bananas, sliced
1 cup strawberries, halved
2 cups diced fresh pineapple
2 tablespoons fresh lemon juice
1 cup heavy cream
2 tablespoons brown sugar
½ cup toasted, flaked coconut
   Dash of ground nutmeg
1 large cantaloupe cut into 4 wedges
4 lettuce cups

Combine cut fruits with lemon juice and chill. Make dressing: Whip cream and add next 3 ingredients; chill. Put a cantaloupe wedge in each lettuce cup on serving plates. Fill with fruits and serve with dressing. Makes 4 servings.

COCONUT PUDDIN'-PIE
2 tablespoons soft butter
1 cup sifted confectioners' sugar
3 eggs, separated
½ teaspoon vanilla extract
½ cup evaporated milk, undiluted
⅛ teaspoon salt
2 cups freshly grated coconut
   Ground nutmeg
   9-inch pie shell, baked

Cream butter and sugar. Add egg yolks, one at a time, and beat until mixture is very light and lemon-colored. Add vanilla and milk. Beat egg whites until foamy. Add salt and beat until stiff but not dry. Fold into creamed mixture. Fold in 1½ cups of the coconut. Pour into baked pie shell and sprinkle with nutmeg. Top with remaining grated coconut. Bake in preheated moderate oven (350°F.) for about 35 minutes, or until the filling is just set. Serve warm or cold. Makes 6 to 8 servings.

CHOCOLATE-COCONUT CRUST
Press a 12-inch square of aluminum foil on bottom, sides, and over rim of 9-inch pie pan so that it takes on shape of pan. In the foil put 6 ounces (1 package) semisweet chocolate pieces and 2 tablespoons shortening. Put in moderate oven (350°F.) for 2 or 3 minutes. Remove, and crimp foil edge over rim. With spoon, gently blend chocolate with shortening. Add ½ cup flaked coconut and mix lightly. Spread on bottom of foil. Chill for 7 or 8 minutes. Spread mixture up onto sides of pan (not over rim). Chill for at least 25 minutes. Remove crust with foil from pan, and start to

tear foil at rim. Holding crust in palm of hand, tear foil from half of rim. Using foil to cover fingers, invert crust; remove remaining foil. Return crust to pie pan. Use for chiffon or other gelatin-type pies.

CHOCOLATE COCONUT-CREAM PARFAIT

Alternate canned chocolate syrup and instant coconut cream pudding in parfait glasses. Chill. Top with whipped cream; sprinkle with candy shot.

COCONUT-CRUSTED APPLE DESSERT

    6 large tart apples, peeled, cored,
       and sliced
    1 cup brown sugar
 1½ teaspoons ground cinnamon
    ½ teaspoon ground mace
       All-purpose flour (about ½ cup)
    ¼ cup fresh orange juice
    ¼ cup butter or margarine
    ½ cup flaked coconut

Heap apples in greased 8-inch round baking dish 2 inches deep. Mix ½ cup brown sugar, spices, and 2 tablespoons flour; sprinkle over apples. Pour orange juice over all. For the topping, blend ½ cup brown sugar, the butter, and ⅓ cup flour with a fork until crumbly. Stir in coconut. Spread over apples. Cover with foil. Bake in preheated hot oven (425° F.) 20 minutes. Remove foil; bake about 15 minutes longer. Makes 6 to 8 servings.

FRESH-COCONUT CAKE

    1 cup shortening
    2 cups sugar
 3½ cups sifted cake flour
 3½ teaspoons baking powder
    ¾ teaspoon salt
    1 cup milk
    ⅔ cup freshly grated coconut
    6 egg whites, stiffly beaten
       Coconut Boiled Frosting
       Rich Chocolate Frosting

Cream shortening and gradually beat in sugar. Add sifted dry ingredients alternately with milk. Fold in coconut and egg whites. Pour into loaf pan (13 x 9 x 2 inches) lined with greased wax paper. Bake in preheated moderate oven (350° F.) for about 45 minutes. Turn out on cake rack to cool. Frost half with Coconut Boiled Frosting, half with Rich Chocolate Frosting.

Coconut Boiled Frosting

    ¾ cup sugar
    ¼ teaspoon cream of tartar
       Dash of salt
    ¼ cup hot water
       Few drops of almond extract
    2 egg whites, stiffly beaten
    1 cup freshly grated coconut

Combine sugar, cream of tartar, salt, and water. Heat, stirring to dissolve sugar; then boil without stirring to 240°F., or until a little dropped into cold water forms a soft ball that holds its shape. Gradually add syrup, with extract, to egg whites, beating constantly until stiff enough to spread. Frost top and sides of half the cake; sprinkle with coconut.

Rich Chocolate Frosting

 1½ cups sifted confectioners' sugar
    3 ounces (3 squares) unsweetened

Coconut Puddin'-Pie   **Chocolate Coconut-Cream Parfait**   **Coconut Cookies**

chocolate, melted
Dash of salt
2½ tablespoons hot water
3 egg yolks
½ teaspoon vanilla extract
¼ cup soft butter

Add half of sugar to chocolate. Mix well; add salt, water, and remaining sugar. Beat in egg yolks gradually. Add vanilla and butter and beat until well blended. Spread on top and sides of other half of cake.

COCONUT COOKIES
¾ cup butter (or use part margarine)
1 cup firmly packed dark brown sugar
1 egg
1 teaspoon vanilla extract
2 cups sifted all-purpose flour
½ teaspoon baking powder
¼ teaspoon salt
1 cup toasted grated coconut

Cream butter; gradually add sugar and beat until light and fluffy. Add egg and vanilla; beat well. Sift together dry ingredients; combine with coconut. Combine the two mixtures and knead until ingredients hold together. Shape into a ball and set in the refrigerator until firm, about 20 minutes. Roll small amounts of dough on a floured board to a thickness of ⅛ inch. Cut with cookie cutters or cut into 2-inch rounds and bake on ungreased cookie sheets in preheated moderate oven (350°F.) for 10 to 15 minutes, or until edges are brown and cookies are done inside. Loosen with spatula immediately; let cool on pans. Makes about 5 dozen.

COCONUT MACAROONS
2 egg whites
⅛ teaspoon salt
⅛ teaspoon cream of tartar
¾ cup sugar
½ teaspoon each of vanilla and almond extracts
1 can (3½ ounces) flaked coconut
Pink or green vegetable coloring (optional)
Candied cherries

Beat egg whites until foamy. Add salt and cream of tartar. Beat until soft peaks form. Gradually beat in sugar, 1 tablespoon at a time, beating until stiff and glossy. Fold in extracts and coconut. Tint pink or green if desired. Drop from teaspoon onto foil-covered cookie sheet. Put a cherry in the center of each. Bake in preheated slow oven (300°F.) for about 20 minutes. Makes about 30 macaroons.

COCONUT SNOWBALLS
Shape any flavor ice cream into balls; roll quickly in flaked coconut. Put in freezer until firm. Serve with chocolate or other sauce.

COCONUT ESKIMOS
Stick a plastic picnic knife into a thick slice of ice cream. Roll in toasted coconut; freeze.

COD—This soft-finned salt-water fish averages from three to four feet in length and seven to forty pounds in weight, although it can reach as much as one hundred pounds. The cod is brownish on the upper body and sides and creamy below, with small brown and yellow spots. It is extremely voracious and just as prolific; the roe sometimes constitutes a full half of the weight of the female fish. The flesh is firm, white, and delicious.

The cod is a cold-water fish. There are a number of varieties, such as Greenland and Pacific cod, which are found in the Alaskan waters and the Bering Sea and off Japan, but most cod comes from the North Atlantic and the Baltic. Scrod is a young cod weighing one and a half to two and a half pounds. Cod is eaten fresh or salted.

The history of Newfoundland, of New England, and many other North Atlantic coastal settlements is closely tied to this fish. Fishermen from the Basque region of France, in search of whale, discovered the abundance of fish along the Grand Bank of Newfoundland. New Englanders claim Boston as "the home of the bean and the cod." When fishing was the main source of income in our northern colonies, the codfish was a most profitable catch. So dependent was the economy of the Boston area upon this fish that on March 17, 1784, a painted wooden codfish, four feet, eleven inches long, was hung in the Boston State House, "as a memorial to the importance of the cod-fishery to the welfare of this Commonwealth." It remains to this day. A codfish was also on the seal of the Massachusetts Bay Colony. Early Bostonians referred to a strata of their society as the "codfish aristocracy." What is a

"Cape Cod turkey"? Why, a baked stuffed codfish, of course.

The economic importance of cod throughout history cannot be overestimated. To this day, cod largely regulates the economy of Norway and Iceland, where a large number of the people live by fishing for cod. The annual early spring cod fishing in Norway's Lofoten Islands, where tens of thousands of vessels congregate, must be seen to be believed. Equally unforgettable is the sight of drying codfish strung like curtains on tall, triangular racks along the coastal settlements of Norway, from where it is exported to southern Europe, to Latin America, and to the Orient, all parts of the world where dried cod is an integral part of the diet.

In the northern parts of Europe, fresh cod is a staple food and admirably prepared. Its vitamin-rich liver gave strength to the people long before it was made into cod-liver oil; to this day the livers are boiled and then sometimes sautéed. The tongues are another delicacy, eaten sautéed. Traditionally, in Norway they are given to the boys who help the cod fishermen: to sell on their own for pocket money.

Availability—Fresh cod is available all year; the best months are from September through December.

Cod steaks, fillets, and codfish cakes are available frozen.

Dried, salted codfish is available boneless, flaked, or shredded in small packages or jars.

Canned codfish cakes are available.

Purchasing Guide—Cod is marketed in the following forms: drawn, dressed, as steaks and fillets. Fresh fish should have firm, elastic flesh, bright skin, and a fresh characteristic odor.

Storage—Plan to use fresh fish within two days because it is very perishable. Cleaned and dressed fish should be wrapped in moisture-proof paper or placed in a covered dish in the coldest part of the refrigerator.

Keep frozen fish in its original package in the freezer compartment. Frozen fish will keep as long as it remains solidly frozen. If it thaws, it should be used immediately. Never refreeze fish that has thawed.

Keep dried, salted cod in a cool, dry place, unopened.

☐ Refrigerator shelf: 1 to 2 days
☐ Refrigerator frozen-food compartment, prepared for freezing: 2 to 3 weeks
☐ Freezer, prepared for freezing: 9 months

Nutritive Food Values—Cod is a lean fish, a good source of protein, some iron, calcium, and B vitamins.

☐ Fresh, 3½ ounces, raw = 78 calories

☐ Dried, salted, 3½ ounces = 130 calories

Basic Preparation—Wipe fillets or steaks with damp cloth or paper towel.

Fresh cod may be broiled, fried, sautéed, baked, steamed, or poached and served with a sauce. Baste codfish frequently with melted butter when broiling, to prevent dryness. Cook fish only until it flakes easily with a fork.

☐ **To Poach**—If convenient, poach cod fillets or steaks in a skillet in which you can serve them. This avoids the problem of breakage when removing fish from pan to platter. Put cod, cut in serving pieces if desired, in skillet and add just enough boiling water to cover. (Court Bouillon, page 486, can be used instead of water, if preferred.) Add 1 tablespoon white vinegar to each 2 cups water to keep fish extra firm. Add a few slices of onion, 6 peppercorns, a few sprigs of parsley, 3 or 4 whole cloves, and a little white wine, if desired. (If not using wine, add 1 or 2 teaspoons lemon juice.) Cover and simmer gently for 10 minutes, or until fish flakes easily with a fork. Drain and sprinkle lightly with salt. Serve hot with any desired sauce such as hollandaise, Newburg, mustard, horseradish, or barbecue sauce. Or cool fish, chill, and use for cocktails or salads. If you prefer to serve fish on a platter, tie uncooked fillets or steaks in cheesecloth before poaching.

☐ **To Freeze Fresh Fish**—Since cod is a large fish, it should be frozen in fillets or steaks. Dip pieces for 20 seconds into a brine solution (⅓ cup salt to every 4 cups water). Drain well and wrap tightly in a moisture-proof, vapor-proof wrapping. Be sure to exclude all air spaces as these cause deterioration of flavor.

☐ **To Cook Frozen Fillets**—Fish may be cooked before it thaws, but allow a longer cooking time at a slightly lower temperature. Use frozen fish interchangeably with fresh fish in recipes.

☐ **To Cook Dried, Salt Cod**—Soak to remove some of the salt before cooking. It is essential to break down its tough fibers; an old-fashioned but effective way is to slap the salt cod against a hard surface such as the legs of the kitchen table. Use in place of fresh fish in recipes. Salt cod is most frequently used in making fish cakes.

DEVILED COD STEAKS

  4 small cod steaks, about ¾ inch thick
  2 tablespoons each of prepared mustard and horseradish
  1 tablespoon each of chili sauce and ketchup
  1 teaspoon salt

Wipe cod steaks with damp cloth. Mix

remaining ingredients together and spread over fish. Arrange on greased ovenproof platter. Bake in preheated slow oven (325°F.) for about 35 minutes. Garnish with parsley, if desired. Makes 4 servings.

COD À LA CATALAN

  1 pound cod
  ¼ pound bacon, diced
  1 large onion, chopped
  1 red pepper, diced
  ½ cup chopped parsley
    Salt and pepper to taste
  1 pound potatoes, boiled and sliced
  2 tablespoons all-purpose flour
  3 tablespoons cooking oil

Simmer cod for 10 minutes in lightly salted water. Bone, and flake. In a covered pan place first the bacon, onion, red pepper, parsley, salt, and pepper. Cover with alternating layers of potatoes and cod flakes, dusting each layer of fish with a little flour. Then fill with water to the top layer, cover, and bring to boil. Add oil, cover, and simmer for another 10 minutes. Makes 4 servings.

COD FLORENTINE

  1 package (10 ounces) frozen chopped spinach, thawed
  1 pound cod fillets, fresh or frozen
  1 can cream-of-mushroom soup, undiluted
  1 tablespoon melted butter or margarine
  ½ cup soft bread crumbs
    Paprika

Divide spinach among 4 buttered small baking dishes. Cut fish into thin slices and put on spinach. Spoon undiluted mushroom soup over fish; top with buttered crumbs and sprinkle with paprika. Bake in preheated moderate oven (375° F.) for about 20 minutes. Makes 4 servings.

DROPPED CODFISH AND POTATO CAKES

  1 package shredded salted dried codfish
  2½ cups warm mashed potatoes
  1 egg, beaten
  1 teaspoon salt
  1 small onion, minced
  ¼ teaspoon pepper
  2 parsley sprigs, minced
    Fat or oil for frying

Freshen codfish according to directions on package. Mix fish and next 6 ingredients. Drop from tablespoon into a skillet of hot fat ½ inch deep. Brown quickly on both sides; drain on unglazed brown paper. Makes 4 servings, 16 codfish cakes.

Note: If desired, leftover mashed potatoes may be used in this recipe. Add a small amount of hot milk to potatoes and reheat.

CODFISH PROVENÇAL

  1 pound codfish, salted and dried
  3 medium onions
  3 garlic cloves
  ¼ cup olive oil
  ¼ cup butter
  3½ cups (one 1-pound, 12-ounce can)

    solid-pack tomatoes
  1 teaspoon crumbled dried rosemary
  1 bay leaf
  ¼ teaspoon fennel seed
  2 cups red wine
    6-ounce can tomato paste
  ½ cup pine nuts
  ¼ cup capers
  1 cup pitted black olives
    Salt and pepper
    All-purpose flour

First put salt cod to soak in cold water. It should soak for at least 4 hours. Meanwhile prepare the sauce. Peel and chop onions and garlic and sauté them in olive oil and butter. When they are just limp, add tomatoes, rosemary, bay leaf, fennel, red wine, and tomato paste and blend thoroughly. Cook gently until slightly thickened. Add pine nuts, capers, and olives; season to taste with salt and pepper and continue cooking gently for about 30 minutes. When the fish has soaked, drain it and cut into square serving pieces. Roll in flour and sauté in olive oil until nicely browned. Pour sauce over fish, and serve. Makes 4 servings.

Note: The sauce on this fish dish is a favorite in the south of France. It is called *rayte* and is often used as a dunk for crisp breadsticks or raw vegetables.

CODDLE—To coddle is to cook gently by letting the food stand in water that has been brought to the boiling point and then removed from the heat. The pan should be tightly covered.

What happens in coddling is that the food cooks gently in the cooling water and thus acquires a delicate, yet firm texture. Eggs are the most commonly coddled food. To coddle, place eggs in boiling water. Cover pan closely and let stand for 4 to 8 minutes, depending on desired consistency.

COFFEE—This is a beverage brewed from roasted and ground coffee beans. The beans themselves, whole or ground, are also known as coffee, as sold in food stores. The coffee plant, of the genus *Coffea,* is thought to have originated in Abyssinia or Ethiopia, but spread gradually to other countries bordering the Indian Ocean and the eastern Mediterranean. Around 1720 it was brought to the French West Indies, then on to Brazil, which is now the largest coffee producer. However Colombia, Guatemala, San Salvador, Costa Rica, Java, and Malaya also depend on coffee for much of their economy. It is a tropical plant and grown best in a hot moist climate at around 4,500 feet elevation. The trees themselves, as well as the picking and processing of the coffee, demand constant attention. The fruit of the tree, called the coffee cherry, must be picked by hand since blossoms, green cherries, and ripe cherries may all occur on the tree at the same time. The cherry consists of an outer skin, then pulp, a parchment-like skin, and then a thin silvery skin, all around two beans. To process, the outer skin and pulp are removed, then it is dried for about twenty days; it is hulled to remove the next two layers of skin; the beans are graded as to size and weight and then hand-inspected for color and imperfections. The beans are now ready for export. Later they will be roasted, ground, and in the case of instant coffee, still further processed by being brewed and then having the water removed. Decaffinated coffee is processed by having the caffeine removed. Coffee may be sold roasted whole, roasted ground, or as instant.

The United States consumes more coffee than any other country, but Scandinavians, Belgians, Italians, and South Americans consume and enjoy it in quantity.

Coffee has been the inspiration for more flights of fancy than any other non-alcoholic beverage. In Turkey coffeehouses abounded, where men sat crosslegged on cushions while the precious beans were roasted, pulverized, and brewed to their taste in front of them. Each tiny cup of thick coffee must have the proper amount of creamy foam on top. This was called the *kaimaik,* a symbol of hospitality without which the cup of coffee would be a disgrace. European coffeehouses were different in appearance but none the less enthusiastically received. London at the beginning of the 18th century had hundreds. For a penny you were admitted into the company of poets, philosophers, artists, and politicians, self-appointed or otherwise. Because of this, coffeehouses were sometimes called "penny universities."

So great a Universitie
I think there ne'er was any;
In which you may a Scholar be
For spending of a Penny.

In colonial America coffeehouses were common. Here coffee consumption was given additional impetus by the imposition of taxes on tea. Coffee in the early coffeehouses was served in shallow bowls and the habitué called for a "dish of coffee." Handles on the cups in which coffee was served were introduced in the middle of the 18th century. This did not deter the men from drinking their "dish of coffee," for under each cup there was a saucer which they continued to use for another century. Mustache cups were popular in the days of large mustaches.

More modern innovations are the coffee breaks in American offices and factories and the revival of the popularity of coffeehouses throughout the country. These offer coffee beverages of many varieties.

Throughout the centuries, poets and writers have sung of coffee with passion clad in flowery words. Its powers to stimulate moved the composer Bach to compose his beautiful *Coffee Cantata* in praise of it. Made in dozens of ways, drunk thick or thin, dark or light, strong or weak, pure or diluted with other substances such as chicory, coffee stands as a symbol of hospitality throughout the world.

Storage

- ☐ Whole beans, room temperature: 1 year
- ☐ Vacuum-packed, kitchen shelf, unopened: 1 year, with gradual loss of flavor
- ☐ Vacuum-packed, kitchen shelf, opened and covered: 2 weeks, with gradual loss of flavor
- ☐ Instant, kitchen shelf, tightly closed: 6 to 8 months, with gradual loss of flavor

HOW TO MAKE GOOD COFFEE

Making good coffee is not purely a matter of chemical formula. It depends on personal choices of the coffee, the roast, the grind, the brew, the water, the proportions of coffee to water, the method used, and the coffeemaker. However, there are certain rules which apply under all circumstances.

1. Once having arrived at a pleasing combination, don't change it.
2. Follow manufacturer's directions, at least the first time. If you want stronger or weaker coffee you can adjust the amounts later to your satisfaction.
3. Buy a brand you like in the grind appropriate to the coffeemaker you use. Buy regular or percolator grind for percolators, drip grind for drip or vacuum coffeemakers, and fine for certain vacuum-style coffeemakers.
4. Buy coffee in small amounts, unless it is used in large quantity. The sooner the coffee is used after it is ground, or after a vacuum-packed can of ground coffee is opened, the better the coffee. Grinding coffee beans at home just before use permits holding coffee on the shelf for longer periods of time without drastic loss of flavor, aroma, and strength. Be sure to set the grinder to the grind that is specified by the manufacturer of your coffeemaker.
5. Always use a clean coffeemaker. Most coffeemakers stress this in their directions. A few have surfaces to which the coffee oils cannot cling and so do not need to be and *should not be* scrubbed or scoured, but most need to be washed in hot water using a light-duty detergent to remove the oily residue, and then rinsed thoroughly. Spouts, percolator tubes, and other hard-to-reach areas should be cleaned with thin brushes available for the purpose.
6. Measure the coffee used and measure the water. Be consistent. The standard to start with is 2 level measuring tablespoons to ¾ cup (6 ounces) of water. Some coffeemakers have amounts marked on the sides of the coffeemaker for water and on the basket for the coffee so that these can be used as guides, and adjusted to individual taste.
7. Use freshly drawn cold water.
8. Use the right size coffeemaker for the amount to be used, that is, do not try to make 1 cup of coffee in an 8-cup coffeemaker.
9. Remove coffee grounds and serve coffee as soon as possible after brewing. If it must be kept hot, do so over low heat. Never boil coffee.

Percolator Method
(For Nonautomatic Percolators)
Measure fresh cold water into percolator (water level should always be below the

bottom of basket). Insert basket, and measure in required amount of regular-grind coffee. Cover and put over low heat. When water boils, percolate *slowly* 6 to 8 minutes. Remove from heat, and let stand a few minutes. Remove coffee basket, and serve.

Percolator Method
(For Automatic Percolators)
Follow manufacturer's directions. Remember to use the right grind of coffee and start with fresh cold water, just as you do for nonautomatic coffeemakers.

Drip Method
Preheat pot by rinsing with very hot water. Measure drip-grind coffee into filter section. Put upper container over filter section. Measure fresh boiling water into upper container, and cover. When dripping is completed, remove upper section and basket. Stir coffee, and serve.

■ **To Make Italian Espresso**—This coffee is made in a special pot similar to a drip coffeepot. Put ground espresso-roast coffee in basket; put over boiling water in bottom of pot. Put top part of pot in place and turn entire coffeepot upside down so water runs through coffee. Process may be repeated if very strong coffee is desired.

Vacuum Method
Measure fresh cold water into lower bowl. Put on heat. Put filter in upper bowl and add vacuum-grind or extra-fine ground coffee. When water boils, reduce heat, and insert upper bowl with slight twist. Let most of water rise into upper bowl. Stir water and coffee thoroughly. In 1 to 3 minutes, remove from heat. When brew returns to lower bowl, remove upper bowl and serve.

ICED COFFEE
Make coffee with half as much water as usual. When coffee is brewed, pour into glasses filled with ice cubes. Serve with fine granulated sugar and cream, or with sweetened whipped cream.
Note: To prevent dilution of the coffee by the melting ice cubes, pour coffee into freezer tray and freeze. Use coffee ice cubes in glass of iced coffee.

FROSTED COFFEE
Pour 3 cups hot extra-strong coffee over ice cubes in pitcher. Stir until thoroughly chilled. Pour half of coffee into a shaker and add 4 or 5 heaping tablespoons of ice cream. Shake until ice cream is dissolved. Repeat with remaining half of coffee. Pour into glasses and top each with ice cream. Makes 6 servings.

CAMPFIRE COFFEE
Measure coarsely ground coffee into thin cloth bag, using 1 heaping or 2 level tablespoons coffee for each coffee cup of water and adding 1 extra measure of

coffee. Tie bag with string. Put coffeepot or covered saucepan over red-hot coals until water boils. Add coffee bag and push pot to side of fire; allow coffee to simmer for 5 to 8 minutes. Do not boil. Remove bag, and serve.

COFFEE, CHURCH-SUPPER METHOD
Tie 3 cups percolator-grind coffee in two thicknesses of cheesecloth. Drop into 5½ quarts boiling water in large kettle. Turn off heat. Cover and let stand for 10 minutes. Remove bag. Makes 12 servings.

INSTANT COFFEE FOR A CROWD
Bring 5 quarts water to boil in large kettle. Turn off heat and stir in a 2-ounce jar of instant coffee. If necessary, keep hot over lowest possible heat. Makes 12 servings.

CAFÉ AU LAIT
With a pot of hot milk in one hand and hot coffee in the other, pour milk and coffee into cups simultaneously.

CAFÉ BRÛLOT
(*Also called* Café au Diable)
½ cinnamon stick
6 whole cloves
1 curl orange peel
6 lumps sugar
6 ounces brandy
   or 2 ounces rum and 4 ounces brandy
3 cups hot strong coffee

In a chafing dish or *brûlot* bowl mix all ingredients except coffee. Heat; ignite with lighted match. Stir with ladle and slowly add coffee. Serve in demitasse cups. Makes 6 servings.

MOCHA DE LUXE
1 ounce (1 square) unsweetened
   chocolate
1 cup rich milk or light cream
3 cups hot extra-strong coffee
⅛ teaspoon salt
3 to 4 tablespoons sugar, or to taste

In top part of double boiler over boiling water heat chocolate and milk. When chocolate is melted, beat with rotary beater until smooth and blended. Add coffee, salt, and sugar. Makes 4 servings.

Iced Mocha de Luxe
Prepare as above, omitting coffee. Chill. Add cold coffee just before serving in tall glasses.

IRISH COFFEE
Pour 1 jigger Irish whisky into a warmed goblet or coffee cup. Add 1 to 2 teaspoons sugar. Add hot strong coffee to within ½ inch of the top. Top with chilled sweetened whipped cream. Makes 1 serving.

TURKISH COFFEE
Put 2 cups water, 6 lumps of sugar, and 6 heaping teaspoons of espresso-roast ground coffee in small shallow saucepan. Bring just to a boil. Remove from heat and cool slightly. Repeat boiling process twice more. Drain the syrup from the grounds and serve syrup in demitasse

cups. Makes 6 servings.

COFFEE IMPERIAL
(*Sometimes called Oriental Coffee*)
4 cinnamon sticks
6 cups hot strong coffee
   Sugar
¾ cup heavy cream
   Chopped ice
   Few drops of vanilla extract

Add cinnamon sticks to hot coffee and let stand for 1 hour. Remove cinnamon. To coffee, add sugar to taste and ½ cup cream. Chill. Pour mixture into tall glasses and fill with ice. Whip remaining cream. Add a little sugar and vanilla. Use as topping for coffee. Makes 6 servings.

MOCHA
⅓ cup cocoa
⅓ cup sugar
   Pinch of salt
1 cup hot water
1 tall can (14½ ounces) evaporated milk
2 cups hot strong coffee

Mix cocoa, sugar, and salt in saucepan. Add water and stir until smooth. Cook slowly for 2 minutes or until thick, stirring constantly. Add milk and coffee; heat just to boiling. Beat, and serve. Makes 6 cups.

COFFEE SHAKE
2 cups extra-strong coffee
   Ice cubes
2 to 4 tablespoons fine granulated sugar
¼ to ⅓ cup heavy cream or undiluted
   evaporated milk
   Few drops of vanilla extract

Pour freshly made coffee over ice in shaker. Add remaining ingredients and more ice if necessary. Shake vigorously until foamy. Serve at once in tall glasses, topped with whipped cream if desired. Makes 2 servings.

COFFEE ICE-CREAM SODA
Several hours before making soda, mix 1 cup boiling water with ¼ cup instant coffee; add ½ cup sugar and dash of salt. Cool, and add ½ teaspoon vanilla extract. Chill. For each soda, put 2 to 3 tablespoons of mixture in large glass; add ¼ cup milk and large scoop of vanilla or coffee ice cream. Fill with chilled carbonated water; stir well.

COFFEECAKE—Coffeecakes are actually breads, usually with a sweetened filling or topping, which are served with coffee and especially with breakfast coffee. They may be made with or without yeast, in both large and individual sizes. Toppings and fillings include sugared crumbs, confectioners' sugar, frostings, fruit-juice glazes, fruits, nuts, and cheese. Coffeecakes should be eaten as freshly baked as possible, preferably straight from the oven. Aside from the smell of newly made coffee, few aromas are more pleasing and spirit-lifting than the fragrance of a freshly baked coffeecake. And few make for greater nostalgia for hearth and home, so that mothers, sweethearts, and wives cannot be sufficiently urged to learn how to bake at least one coffee-cake superbly.

YELLOW COFFEECAKE

2 cups sifted all-purpose flour
1 teaspoon baking powder
½ teaspoon baking soda
½ cup sugar
½ teaspoon ground ginger
⅓ cup shortening
1 egg
2 tablespoons molasses
1 cup sour milk or buttermilk
½ teaspoon salt

Sift flour, baking powder, soda, sugar, and ginger together. Cut in shortening. Remove ½ cup of mixture and save for topping. Beat egg lightly; add molasses, sour milk, and salt and pour into flour mixture. Beat with rotary beater just until smooth; pour into greased 9-inch square pan. Sprinkle dry mixture on top. Bake in preheated moderate oven (350°F.) for 30 minutes. Makes one 9-inch square.

APPLE COFFEECAKE

2 cups all-purpose flour
¼ cup sugar
2 teaspoons baking powder
½ teaspoon salt
¼ cup soft shortening
1 egg
⅔ cup milk
2 cups thinly sliced apples
½ cup firmly packed brown sugar
½ teaspoon ground cinnamon
¼ teaspoon ground nutmeg
⅓ cup butter, melted
½ cup slivered almonds

Sift dry ingredients; cut in shortening. Add egg and milk. Barely mix. Pour into greased 8-inch square pan. Lay apple slices evenly on top. Sprinkle with brown sugar and spices. Drizzle melted butter evenly over apples. Top with almonds. Bake in preheated hot oven (400°F.) for 25 minutes. Serve warm. Makes one 8-inch square.

PANETTONE (Italian Coffeecake)

2 packages dry yeast or 2 cakes compressed yeast
1 cup water*
4½ cups sifted all-purpose flour
½ cup sugar
½ cup butter or margarine
2 or 3 eggs
1 teaspoon salt
2 teaspoons grated lemon rind
2 tablespoons chopped citron
¼ cup yellow raisins
1 cup broken nuts
Melted butter

Use very warm water (105°F. to 115°F.) for dry yeast; use lukewarm water (80°F. to 90°F.) for compressed. Sprinkle or crumble yeast into water in a bowl. Let stand for a few minutes, then stir until dissolved. Beat in 1 cup flour.

Let stand covered until doubled in bulk. Cream sugar and butter until light and fluffy. Beat in eggs, one at a time. Add salt and lemon rind. Beat in yeast mixture. Gradually beat in 3½ cups flour. Beat for 5 minutes, until dough pulls cleanly from spoon when it is pulled out of the dough. Beat in fruits and nuts. Let stand covered until doubled in bulk. Stir dough and place in 2 greased 7-inch springform pans. Let rise in pans for 30 minutes. Brush tops of dough with melted butter. Bake in preheated moderate oven (350°F.) for 30 minutes, or until golden brown. Makes two 7-inch round loaves.

SCOTCH COFFEECAKE

1 cup packaged biscuit mix
3 tablespoons sugar
½ teaspoon salt
1 teaspoon baking powder
½ cup each of seedless raisins and chopped nuts
1 egg, well beaten
¼ cup melted shortening
¾ cup milk
¾ cup quick-cooking rolled oats
Topping

Combine biscuit mix, sugar, salt, baking powder, raisins, and nuts. Mix egg, melted shortening, milk, and rolled oats; add to biscuit mixture, mixing well. Pour into greased 9-inch square pan. Sprinkle with Topping. Bake in preheated hot oven (425°F.) for 25 minutes. Makes nine 3-inch squares.

Topping

¼ cup firmly packed light brown sugar
3 tablespoons all-purpose flour
½ teaspoon ground cinnamon
¼ teaspoon ground nutmeg
1 tablespoon butter or margarine

Combine dry ingredients; blend in butter with fork or fingertips.

COLA—The word covers a tree, a nut, and a complex syrup used for making America's favorite carbonated beverage. Native to tropical Africa, as well as extensively cultivated in the American tropics, the cola tree (also called kola) produces fruit containing numerous seeds. These brownish bitter seeds are the cola nuts from which the cola extract is obtained. Containing a small amount of caffeine, the cola nut is a mild stimulant. In this country the extract of the cola nut is widely used in the drug and beverage industries.

COLD CUTS—Daily life would be unthinkable without the assorted meats and poultry known as cold cuts and served cold, in slices. The meats may be roasted or boiled; fresh, cured, smoked, or corned; they may be canned; they may

be jellied; they may be sausages which require no cooking: bologna, salami, liverwurst. Thus a meal featuring cold cuts can range from a simple serve-your-self family dinner to an elaborate buffet supper for entertaining friends.

Availability—All year round, sold in bulk, or canned or packed sliced in moisture-proof plastic wrap.

Purchasing Guide—In addition to the meats and poultry, ham, roast beef, and turkey, for example, which are often served in cold-cut platters, the following meats and meat products are among those classified as cold cuts:

Corned Meat: Corned beef
Jellied Meat: Head cheese
Poultry: Pressed chicken loaf, turkey roll
Sausage: Bologna, bratwurst, braunschweiger, cervelat, ham bologna, Lebanon bologna, liverwurst, pepperoni, salami, thuringer (or blood) sausage, tongue-and-blood-sausage loaf, wienerwurst
Smoked Meat: Ham and cheese loaf, olive loaf, pickle loaf, prosciutto, spiced ham, tongue
Spiced Meats: Luncheon meats, meat loaf, pastrami, pimiento loaf, pork roll, pressed ham, scrapple, spiced beef

Storage—In general, refrigerate all meat and meat products. Refrigerate canned meats, too, if cans have been opened. Best temperature for them is as low as possible without freezing. Wrap well because they will absorb alien flavors.

Unopened canned meats may be stored in a cool, dry, ventilated place. However, some canned meats must be refrigerated even though cans have not been opened. Check label.

☐ Refrigerator shelf, covered: 1 week
☐ Refrigerator frozen-food compartment: 2 to 3 weeks
☐ Freezer: 6 months to 1 year
☐ Canned, kitchen shelf, unopened: 6 months

Nutritive Food Values—This varies for each meat, however, all are high in protein. Most processed meats are high in calories.

SUGGESTIONS FOR SERVING COLD CUTS

■ **Serve them sliced** arranged around a hearty potato salad. *Suggested cold cuts:* Tongue and corned beef. *Suggested salad:* Make it with packaged sliced potatoes and garnish with shredded carrot and chicory sprigs in green-pepper cups.

■ **Cut them into cubes,** pierce with toothpicks, and insert picks in an Edam cheese; add a pretty tiered fruit salad. Or put cubes in a hollowed-out cheese. *Suggested cold cuts:* Olive loaf, liverwurst, bologna, and salami. *Suggested salad:* Cut-up bananas, plums, pears, and strawberries piled on fresh pineapple slices and served with a smooth whipped-cream dressing.

■ **Make cornucopias** to serve with cheese molds and chilled mixed fruit. Use cottage cheese and blue cheese in the molds, garnishing them with thin pimiento strips. *Suggested cold cuts:* Cooked salami and pressed ham. *Suggested fruits:* Sliced peaches, grapefruit sections, and a sprinkling of blueberries.

■ **Arrange them in rolls,** with pears and dark grapes, around a gelatin salad. *Suggested cold cuts:* Spiced ham, pressed ham, ham and cheese loaf. *Suggested salad:* Lime gelatin, whole green grapes, and half cucumber slices, with a curry-mayonnaise dressing.

■ **Wrap them around broccoli spears** that have been chilled. *Suggested cold cut:* Boiled ham. *Suggested salad:* An egg salad, topped with mixed sweet pickles and tomato wedges.

■ **Cut them into slivers** to top a vegetable salad. *Suggested cold cuts:* Olive loaf and salami. *Suggested salad:* Frozen mixed vegetables with sliced green onions and tomato wedges.

COLESLAW—The Dutch words *kool* and *salade,* meaning "cabbage" and "salad," provide the most direct definition of coleslaw. Uncooked green or red cabbage is shredded and served with dressing. Other ingredients, such as chopped onion or celery, may be added. There are as many versions of coleslaw as there are cooks. To list a few of them: Crisp or wilted, flavored with French dressing, mayonnaise, sour cream, salad dressing, boiled dressing; hot or cold, seasoned with spices, chopped herbs, caraway seeds, celery seeds, pickles, crisp bacon, etc.

To prepare cabbage properly, cut cabbage into halves. Remove core. Remove leaves and trim tough ribs. Roll up leaves and shred very finely with a sharp knife or on a vegetable shredder. Cabbage can also be grated coarsely. Wash thoroughly and drain. Dry well. Place in refrigerator until ready to mix if a crisp coleslaw is desired. If a wilted slaw is desired, mix shredded or grated cabbage with salad dressing or other dressing immediately. Let stand in refrigerator until ready to serve. When a hot coleslaw is made, combine hot dressing with cabbage and serve immediately.

CUMBERLAND SLAW
4 slices of bacon, diced
½ onion, chopped
½ sweet pepper, chopped
2 teaspoons each of all-purpose flour and sugar
1 teaspoon salt
¼ teaspoon powdered mustard
⅔ cup vinegar

¼ cup water
2 tablespoons chopped pickle
¼ teaspoon celery seeds
3 cups shredded cabbage

Cook diced bacon until crisp; pour off half of fat. Add onion and pepper and cook for 2 minutes. Mix dry ingredients; add vinegar and water. Pour over bacon and onion mixture and cook until thickened. Add pickle and celery seeds and pour over cabbage; mix well, and serve. Makes 4 servings.

CELERY AND CABBAGE SLAW
2 tablespoons prepared mustard
½ cup salad dressing
2 tablespoons vinegar
½ teaspoon salt
⅛ teaspoon pepper
2 cups chopped red cabbage
¼ cup chopped celery

Mix mustard, salad dressing, vinegar, and seasonings. Add to the chopped cabbage and celery. Makes 4 servings. Chopped chives may be sprinkled over the salad if desired.

HOT SLAW
2 egg yolks
½ cup cold water
¼ cup vinegar
1 tablespoon butter or margarine
1 tablespoon sugar
¼ teaspoon powdered mustard
1¼ teaspoons salt
¼ teaspoon pepper
4 cups shredded cabbage

Beat egg yolks slightly in top part of large double boiler. Add water, vinegar, and butter. Mix sugar, mustard, salt, and pepper; add to liquid. Cook over boiling water until thickened, stirring constantly. Add cabbage and heat thoroughly. Makes 6 servings.

GERMAN CABBAGE SLAW
2 slices of bacon, diced
2 tablespoons vinegar
½ teaspoon salt
½ cup salad dressing
2 cups shredded cabbage
2 tablespoons chopped parsley
1 tablespoon chopped onion

Cook diced bacon until crisp. Add vinegar and salt. Stir well and add to salad dressing. Stir at once into cabbage, parsley, and onion. Makes 3 servings.

WISCONSIN DRESSING FOR SHREDDED CABBAGE
2 teaspoons garlic salt
1 tablespoon paprika
1 teaspoon celery salt
¼ cup sugar
1 cup salad oil
½ cup tarragon vinegar
2 tablespoons parsley
1 small onion, cut into fine pieces

Put all dry seasonings and sugar in mixing bowl. Add ½ cup oil and beat for 2 to 3 minutes. Then add 1 tablespoon vinegar and continue to beat. Repeat process, adding oil in a thin stream and alternating with vinegar, 1 tablespoon at

a time, until all has been used. Then add parsley and onions. Let stand for 1 hour before using. Shake well. Makes about 1½ cups.

COLLARDS—Collards are a member of the cabbage family and most closely related to kale. Their leaves are smooth, tall, and broad but they do not form a head as cabbage does. They withstand heat and drought better than other members of the cabbage family and are therefore grown mostly in the southern part of the United States, where they also are called "greens." The usual method of cooking them is to boil them with a piece of bacon or salt pork. The resulting juice is known as "pot likker" and is eaten with corn bread. Collards can also be cooked like spinach, chard, cabbage, or kale.

Availability—Available all year with peak season December to March.

Purchasing Guide—Look for crisp green, young, tender leaves; avoid wilted-looking yellow leaves. Avoid leaves with seedstems. Usually sold by the pound. Collards are also sold frozen.

Storage—Keep in refrigerator in moisture-proof container or bag. Remove discolored leaves and wash thoroughly before storing.

☐ Refrigerator shelf, raw: 3 to 8 days
☐ Refrigerator shelf, cooked and covered: 4 to 5 days
☐ Refrigerator frozen-food compartment, prepared for freezing: 2 to 3 months
☐ Freezer, prepared for freezing: 1 year

Nutritive Food Values—Excellent source of vitamin A, iron, calcium, and vitamin C; fair source of thiamine, riboflavin, and niacin.

☐ 3½ ounces, raw = 45 calories

Basic Preparation—Wash thoroughly in cold water to remove sand. Remove tough stems and midribs of leaves. Cut large leaves into pieces for cooking. Have about 1 inch of water boiling in saucepan. Add collards. Bring to rapid boil. Cover and lower heat to point where water will just continue to boil. Cook for 10 to 15 minutes. Cook the shortest time possible, to "just tender." Drain, season with salt and pepper to taste, add butter, and serve.

STEWED COLLARDS AND SALT PORK

2 pounds collards
½ pound salt pork or slab bacon, cut into 1-inch pieces
2 onions, sliced
Salt and pepper
½ cup water
Fresh lemon juice (optional)

Trim stems off collards unless very young and tender. Wash but do not drain. Cook salt pork in heavy saucepan until crisp. Remove meat and reserve. Pour off half of fat. Sauté onion in remaining fat until soft. Add collards, salt and pepper to taste, and the water. Cook, covered, over low heat for 15 minutes, or until collards are tender. If necessary to prevent sticking, add a little more water. Return meat to cooked greens. Heat through; add a little lemon juice if desired, and serve immediately. Makes 4 servings.

COLORING—In cookery, artificial tints, usually in the form of vegetable extracts, are added to foods to strengthen the natural color or, as in candies, to create a purely decorative effect. When using food colorings, it must be remembered that they are extremely concentrated, and that even two or three drops may be more than enough. Start with a drop at a time, and blend thoroughly into food before adding the next drop.

COMBINE—In cooking terms, the word means to put a number of different ingredients together in a bowl or saucepan. This is done prior to incorporating the ingredients by mixing, blending, stirring, etc.

COMPOTE—This is a dessert of fresh, canned, or dried fruits, cooked gently to preserve their shape, and served in their own juices hot or cold. Compotes may be flavored with spices, wines, liqueurs, and/or fruit juices. They may consist of single fruits or a combination of fruits. The word compote comes from Old French *composte* and conveys the thought of something that has been composed or put together. Compote is also the name given to the stemmed bowl from which the fruit is served.

Compotes are among the most delightful of desserts. With a little ingenuity in combining fruits and arranging and garnishing them, dishes can be produced whose elegance belies their thrift. The first requisite of a good compote is to combine fruits with an eye to their color, shape, and consistency. Apricots, plums, strawberries, and raspberries will add color to more subdued fruits. They will also add a texture contrast to harder fruits, such as apples or pineapple.

Each fruit in a compote should be cooked separately. Then the several syrups may be combined and cooked down to the desired consistency and poured over the fruit.

The cooking time of various fruits depends on their size and ripeness. If the fruit is very ripe, it is wise not to cook it at all. A hot sugar syrup may be poured over it. It is extremely important not to overcook fruit, or its texture and form will be lost.

The flavorings and seasonings of fruit compotes depend on individual tastes. The French use vanilla for apples, pears, peaches, and apricots; the Italians favor lemon rind. Mace, cloves, ginger, cinnamon, coriander, and nutmeg are also excellent and so are wines, both sweet and dry, and liqueurs. Fruit cordials, brandy, kirsch, and rum are also recommended. When spirits are used, they should be added to the cooked syrup. Or the fruits may be soaked in spirits and the hot syrup poured over them.

Compotes are sometimes thickened with flavored gelatin, or with cornstarch or potato starch.

Basic Preparation—For each pound or quart of each fruit, use 1 cup sugar, 1 cup water, plus the flavoring of your choice. Make a syrup by boiling sugar, water, and flavoring in covered saucepan for 5 to 10 minutes. Add washed fruit, a few pieces at a time, and poach over medium heat until done. Remove with slotted spoon. Repeat process until all fruit is used. If syrup is too thin, boil rapidly until the right consistency is achieved. Combine different fruits being used. Combine their syrups and pour over fruits; serve hot or chilled, with or without fresh cream.

FRUIT COMPOTE COMBINATIONS

■ Apples and blackberries
■ Apricots, peaches, and plums
■ Apricots and strawberries
■ Blueberries and peaches
■ Raspberries and pineapple
■ Strawberries and rhubarb

HOT APPLE-CRANBERRY COMPOTE

3 cups eating apples, peeled and sliced
2 cups fresh cranberries
2 cups orange sections
1 cup sugar

¼ cup water

Place fruit in alternate layers in 2-quart casserole. Combine sugar and water and bring to boiling point. Pour over fruit. Bake, covered, in preheated moderate oven (350°F.) for about 1 hour. Makes 6 servings.

CHILLED FRUIT COMPOTE

½ cup each of dried prunes and apricots
½ cup seedless raisins
1 cinnamon stick
2 cooking apples, peeled and sliced
2 fresh pears, peeled and sliced
2 cups undrained (one 1-pound can) unsweetened sour red cherries
1 box (3 ounces) cherry-flavored gelatin
1 cup boiling water
Lemon slices

In large kettle soak prunes, apricots, and raisins in 2 cups cold water for 1 hour. Add cinnamon, apples, and pears. Cover and simmer for 15 minutes, or until fruit is tender. Add undrained cherries and bring to boil. Dissolve gelatin in boiling water; stir gently into fruit. Chill. Serve with lemon. Makes 8 servings.

FRUIT COMPOTE AMANDINE

2½ cups (one 1-pound, 4-ounce can) pineapple chunks
6 to 10 pear halves (one 1-pound can)
6 maraschino cherries, halved
½ teaspoon grated orange rind
¼ cup fresh orange juice
⅓ cup toasted slivered almonds

Drain fruits, reserving 1 cup combined juice. Mix juice with remaining ingredients except almonds. Add canned fruits to juice mixture; simmer for 10 minutes. Chill until ready to serve. Garnish with almonds. Makes 6 servings.

CONCH—Pronounced "conk," this large shellfish, encased in a handsome spiral shell, inhabits southern waters. The muscle is edible, but it is unusually tough and must be tenderized. The most effective methods: pounding with the edge of a heavy plate, parboiling, or marinating.

Floridians and Italians prepare conch by cutting it in pieces, sautéing it, and serving it with scrambled eggs or as an omelet filling. The Italians call this *scungilli*.

Conch meat can also be ground, sliced thin, and fried, and made into stews and chowders.

Availability—Fresh conchs, live-in-the-shell, are available year round in Florida, the West Indies, and some fish markets in large northeastern cities. Summer is the peak season.

Frozen conch, cooked or uncooked, is also available. Canned conch is available in some Italian food stores.

Storage—As is true with any fresh fish, live conch should be cooked almost immediately. Cooked conch should be refrigerated.

☐ Fresh, refrigerator shelf, cooked: 1 to 2 days

☐ Canned, kitchen shelf: 1 year

CONCH CHOWDER

1 quart conch meat
1 carrot
1 green pepper
2 large onions
⅓ cup diced bacon
1 can (19 ounces) tomatoes, coarsely chopped
1 can (6 ounces) tomato paste
2 cups diced potato
4 cups water
Salt, pepper, and powdered thyme
¼ cup sherry

Force conch, carrot, green pepper, and onions through food chopper, using medium blade. Cook bacon until crisp. Add conch mixture, tomatoes, tomato paste, potato, and water. Season to taste with salt, pepper, and thyme. Bring to boil, cover and simmer 2 hours. Add sherry and more seasoning if necessary. Makes 3 quarts, or 6 to 8 servings.

STEWED CONCH

4 conchs
2 onions, chopped
3 cloves garlic, minced
⅓ cup olive oil
1 teaspoon dried basil
1 teaspoon salt
2 cups tomato puree
1 cup red wine

Tenderize the conchs. Cook onion and garlic in olive oil until golden. Add basil, salt, purée, and wine. Bring to boil and simmer for 30 minutes. Add conchs and cook just until heated through and tender. Add a little more wine if sauce becomes too thick. Season to taste, and serve on rice or spaghetti. Makes 6 servings.

CONCH IN MARINARA SAUCE

1½ pounds conch meat, thinly sliced
3 tablespoons olive oil
2 garlic cloves
1 small onion, thinly sliced
1 celery stalk, minced
2 cups (one 1-pound can) tomatoes
2 tablespoons tomato sauce
½ teaspoon salt
½ teaspoon each of ground oregano and basil
2 bay leaves
¼ teaspoon hot pepper seed (optional)

Cook conch in boiling water for about 15 minutes; drain. Put conch, oil, garlic, onion, and celery in skillet and brown well. Remove garlic and add next 3 ingredients. Cover and simmer until conch is tender. Add remaining ingredients and cook for 5 minutes longer. Hot pepper can be omitted, if preferred. Makes 4 servings.

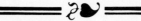

CONDIMENT—The word is applied to a seasoning, an acid, salty, or spicy addition to food to enhance its flavor. The origin of the word is the Latin *condire,* "to pickle" or "season." Condiments have come to mean prepared sauces or accompaniments, such as ketchup, mustards, pickles, or chutney, and steak sauce or other sauces.

CONFECTION—The word comes from the Latin word *confectus,* "prepared." Strictly speaking it can mean any prepared dish, but it especially applies to a sweet dish: a jam or fancy dessert, for example. Candies are often referred to as confections, and confectioners' shops are places where candy is sold.

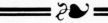

CONSERVE—A sweetmeat or preserve made of a mixture of fruits, generally with nuts added. Conserves are soft and spread easily.

GRAPE CONSERVE

4 pounds Concord grapes
½ cup water
Grated rind and juice of 1 orange
Grated rind and juice of 1 lemon
¼ teaspoon salt
1½ cups seeded raisins
4 cups sugar
1 cup chopped walnuts or pecans

Wash grapes, drain, and remove stems. Slip skins from pulp and reserve. Heat pulp to boiling and rub through coarse sieve to remove seeds. Add water, grated orange and lemon rinds, salt, and raisins. Cook for 15 minutes. Add orange and lemon juices and grape skins. Heat to boiling. Add sugar and cook until conserve is thick, stirring frequently to prevent scorching. Add nuts during last few minutes of cooking. Pour into hot sterilized jelly glasses and cover at once with ⅛ inch hot paraffin. Makes twelve 6-ounce glasses.

PEAR AND ORANGE CONSERVE

1 orange
2¼ pounds fully ripe Bartlett pears, about
⅓ cup finely chopped walnuts
5½ cups sugar
¾ cup water
1 box (1¾ ounces) powdered fruit pectin

Grate rind from orange and set aside. Section orange, removing membrane and seeds, and grind or chop the sections. Peel and core the pears and grind or chop very fine. Mix well with orange sections and rind. Measure 3 cups into large pan or bowl. Add chopped walnuts and sugar to fruit mixture, mix well, and let stand. Mix water and pectin in a small saucepan. Bring to a boil and boil for 1 minute, stirring constantly. Stir into fruit mixture. Continue stirring for about 3 minutes. There will be a few remaining sugar crystals. Ladle quickly into glasses. Cover at once with tight lids. When conserve is set, store in freezer. If conserve will be used within 2 or 3 weeks, it may be stored in refrigerator. Makes about ten 8-ounce glasses.

Note: Fruits may be prepared in a blender if desired. Place orange sections in blender, blend at low speed for a few seconds, and remove from blender. Place medium pieces of peeled and cored pears in blender so blades are just covered. Turn switch from low to off until fruit is finely chopped, not puréed. Remove. Repeat until all pears are finely chopped.

CONSOMMÉ—This is a clear soup made from the broth of slowly simmered meat or poultry which has been clarified to become sparkling clear. The word comes from the French *consommer* which means "to accomplish," or "to boil down." In beef consommé, beef is the principal ingredient from which the broth is made; in chicken consommé, it is chicken. Consommé is served hot or cold, plain or with the addition of vegetables, noodles, rice, and other ingredients. It is also used in cooked dishes as a flavorful substitute for water, and in gravies and sauces.

Consommé is an essential in French cooking and eating. Good, strong consommé is used as a curtain raiser to any meal. Served in cups with a salty cracker, consommé makes an excellent first course in any cuisine.

Availability—In addition to homemade consommé, consommé is available as a canned, condensed soup product, either plain or with rice or noodles added to it. Ready-to-serve consommé madrilène is also available.

Storage—Pour cooled consommé into jars; cover tightly and refrigerate.

☐ Canned, kitchen shelf: 1 year

☐ Homemade or leftover, refrigerator shelf, tightly covered: 3 to 4 days

☐ Homemade or leftover, refrigerator frozen-food compartment, tightly covered: 2 to 3 months

Caloric Value

☐ 1 cup = 10 calories

Basic Preparation—Cook ingredients in a tightly covered kettle or stock pot. Consommé should be simmered slowly to extract the best flavor.

To make jellied consommé, soak 1 envelope unflavored gelatin in ¼ cup cold water. Let stand for 5 minutes. Heat until gelatin is dissolved. Add to 2 cups cold consommé. Stir well and chill until firm.

CONSOMMÉ

    3 pounds boneless soup beef
    1 pound beef bones, cracked
    1 pound veal knuckle, cracked
    1 chicken carcass
    3 quarts cold water
    1 tablespoon salt
    1 or 2 small dried hot red peppers
    ½ teaspoon peppercorns
    2 or 3 bay leaves
    1 onion, sliced
    2 carrots, sliced
    2 celery stalks
      Parsley

■ **To Make Broth**—Cut meat into 1-inch cubes. Brown about ⅓ in heavy kettle. Add remaining meat and bones, the water, and salt. Let stand for 1 hour. Bring slowly to boil and boil hard for 3 minutes. Skim. Cover and simmer for 4 hours. Uncover, add remaining ingredients, and simmer, covered, for 1 hour. Strain through cheesecloth into bowl. Pour into quart jars and cool. When cold, cover and store in refrigerator. Do not remove layer of fat until ready to use broth. Makes about 2 quarts.

■ **To Clarify Broth to Make Consommé** —Before clarifying broth, all fat must be removed. Several methods are used. Chill the soup and then remove the hard layer of fat. If in a hurry, a paper towel will absorb most of the liquid fat, or it can be removed by skimming with a spoon or suctioning it off with a meat baster. After broth has been degreased, cool to room temperature. For every 5½ cups broth, beat 2 egg whites slightly and add them, with the broken-up eggshells, to the broth. Stir well. Cook over very low heat until broth just simmers. *Do not boil.* Simmer for 10 to 15 minutes over a very low heat. A white scum will rise to the top. Remove pan from heat and let stand for 30 minutes. Push scum carefully to one side. Spoon liquid from underneath and strain through several layers of cheesecloth.

Jellied Consommé Madrilene

Sprinkle 2 envelopes unflavored gelatin on ½ cup cold water to soften. Heat 1 cup clarified consommé, add to gelatin, and stir until gelatin is dissolved. Add 3 cups tomato juice, dash of cayenne, and salt, pepper, and grated onion to taste. Chill until firm. Break up with fork and put in chilled bouillon cups. Makes 4 to 6 servings.

CONSOMMÉ JULIENNE

    2 cans (10½ ounces each) condensed
      consommé
    2 cans water
      Few celery leaves
      Few slices of onion
    1 cup cooked vegetables such as celery,
      carrots, and green pepper, cut into
      julienne strips

Put first 4 ingredients in saucepan and simmer for 20 minutes. Strain, and add vegetables. Heat just to boiling, and serve. Makes 4 servings.

JELLIED WATERCRESS CONSOMMÉ

    1 can (10½ ounces) condensed
      consomme
    1 can water
    1 envelope unflavored gelatin
      Juice of 1 lemon
    ½ bunch watercress

Pour consommé into bowl; stir in water. Measure ¼ cup mixture into small saucepan. Sprinkle gelatin on mixture to soften. Stir over low heat until dissolved. Add to mixture in bowl with lemon juice. Force cress through food chopper, using finest blade. Add to mixture and chill until almost firm. Serve in chilled bouillon cups. Makes 4 servings.

COOKIE—At one time, what we now call a cookie was referred to as a small cake or sweet biscuit. We must thank the Dutch for providing us with a special name for it. It is derived from *Koekje* or *Koekie,* meaning a "small cake." The word cookie is an American usage; in England what we know as cookies are called biscuits.

There are more varieties of cookies than any other baked product because there are so many different shapes, sizes, textures, and flavorings possible. To the basic ingredients, often the same as those used in cakes, all kinds of flavorings may be added: extracts, spices, nuts, and fruits. Decorations of every sort are always in order. Cookies are usually classified according to the way in which the dough is shaped. The six classifications are: 1) bars and squares, 2) drop cookies, 3) rolled cookies, 4) pressed cookies, 5) molded or shaped cookies, and 6) refrigerator cookies. Bar and drop cookies are made with soft dough which has a comparatively high percentage of liquid. The other varieties call for stiff dough, usually less sweet and often higher in fat content than soft dough.

Storage

☐ Store unbaked cookie dough, tightly covered, in refrigerator: 2 weeks
☐ Most cookie dough and baked cookies may be frozen: storage life: 6 months to 1 year
☐ Store bar cookies in baking pan, tightly covered in a cool place
☐ Store soft cookies in tightly covered container in a cool place. If cookies tend to dry out, put a piece of bread or a wedge of apple in container with them to maintain moisture
☐ Store crisp cookies in a container with loose-fitting cover in a cool place. If cookies soften, place on cookie sheet in slow oven for about 5 minutes to recrisp
☐ Do not store soft and crisp cookies together

Basic Preparation

☐ **Cookie Sheets**—Usually cookie sheets are not greased unless the recipe specifies it. Be sure that sheets are at least 2 inches narrower and shorter than the oven rack so heat can circulate. Shiny sheets make browner cookies.

☐ **To Roll and Cut**—When rolling dough, be careful not to work in a lot of extra flour. For easier rolling, use a pastry cloth or canvas rolling-pin cover, or keep the dough chilled; take out the amount needed to roll and leave the rest in the refrigerator. Cut with a floured cutter, using a fairly plain one if dough is soft and short.

☐ **To Bake**—Because ovens vary, watch cookies closely. Since many ovens tend to overheat, second, third, and subsequent batches of cookies may take a shorter time to bake than originally specified in the recipe. Check for doneness just before the minimum baking time is up. If some cookies are thinner than others, you may have to remove them and bake the remainder a bit longer.

☐ **To Cool**—Unless otherwise specified in the recipe, remove baked cookies from the sheet to a cake rack as soon as you take them from oven. Wait until they are thoroughly cooled to stack them.

☐ **To Freeze**—Baked or unbaked cookies may be frozen. Shape stiff dough into rolls or bars and wrap carefully. Put soft dough in freezer containers and cover tightly. Cool baked cookies and pack carefully in freezer boxes or transparent film bags.

Thaw soft dough until easy to handle. Thaw stiff dough until it can be sliced. Thaw baked cookies at room temperature for about 15 to 20 minutes.

☐ **To Mail Cookies**—Select cookies that keep their fresh flavor for at least a week under average conditions and are thick and firm enough so they do not break easily.

Wrap separately in transparent plastic wrap or foil. Pack in crumpled tissue paper in a firm box so cookies cannot slide around. Gift wrap, then cover with corrugated cardboard. Put in a slightly larger box and mark it "FRAGILE."

1•*Layered Brazil-Nut Bars*

2•*Butterscotch Acorns*

3•*Lemon-Cheese Cookies*

4•*Brown-Sugar Nut Mounds*

5•*Almond-Butter Strips*

6•*Chocolate Fudge Meringues*

7•*Lace Cookies*

Making the Six Basic Types of Cookies

☐ **To Make Bars and Squares**—These are about the easiest and quickest to make. The ingredients are mixed, spread in a pan, and baked. The pan should always be the size recommended: if too large, the cookies will be thin and dry; if too small, they will be thick and may not bake through properly. When cool, use a sharp knife and a sawing motion to cut.

☐ **To Make Drop Cookies**—These are generally thick and round with a thin crisp crust and a soft center. Drop dough from a spoon onto a cookie sheet, pushing dough from spoon with another spoon or a spatula. Drop cookies spread more than other types during baking and need about 2 inches between each. Try to make cookies the same size so that they will be done at the same time.

☐ **To Make Rolled Cookies**—These cookies are crisp and tender. The dough is stiff and you chill it, often rolling it out on a lightly floured board or between 2 sheets of wax paper, in which case less flour will be needed and the cookies will be more tender. Scraps of dough should be collected and re-rolled at one time; these will be less tender. These cookies are usually cut with cookie cutters, or patterns may be cut out of cardboard and traced on the dough with a sharp knife. Dip the cutter or knife into flour before cutting the dough. Use a spatula to transfer cutouts to the baking sheet.

☐ **To Make Pressed Cookies**—Stiff dough is put into the hollow tube of a cookie press and, with the various tips supplied with the press, the dough is pushed through to form perfectly shaped cookies. For best results, follow directions supplied by the manufacturer of the press.

☐ **To Make Molded or Shaped Cookies** —The dough for these cookies is high in fat and is usually chilled to make handling easier. They may be shaped into balls or flattened, either with a fork in a crisscross pattern, or with bottom of a glass dipped into sugar. Or they can be molded in an infinite variety of shapes: fingers, crescents, rings, acorns, etc.

☐ **To Make Refrigerator Cookies**—These cookies, like rolled cookies, are thin, tender, and very crisp, but are often sweeter. The dough is usually shaped into long rolls, but may be molded into pinwheels, ribbons, and checkerboards. It is always tightly wrapped in wax paper or foil and kept for several hours in the refrigerator before baking. The dough is sliced with a sharp knife just before baking. If too firm to slice, let it stand at room temperature for a few minutes. The dough will keep for some time in the refrigerator, or it may be frozen.

COOKIE
COOK
BOOK

*A selection of deliciously varied
recipes for cookies
sweet or spicy, filled with nuts
or delicately plain*

● BARS AND SQUARES ●

COCONUT-ORANGE SQUARES
¼ cup soft butter or margarine
1 cup sugar
1 egg
1 tablespoon grated orange rind
1 tablespoon milk
1 cup flaked coconut
⅔ cup sifted all-purpose flour
½ teaspoon each of baking powder
    and salt

Cream butter and sugar until light. Beat in egg, orange rind, and milk. Add coconut, and flour sifted with baking powder and salt. Mix very quickly, and only enough to blend. Put in pan (8 x 8 x 2 inches) lined with wax paper, then greased. Bake in preheated moderate oven (350°F.) for about 25 minutes. Cut into 16 squares.

LAYERED BRAZIL-NUT BARS
¼ cup soft butter
1 cup plus 2 tablespoons sifted
    all-purpose flour
½ teaspoon salt
¾ cup firmly packed dark brown sugar
2 eggs, beaten
1½ cups minced Brazil nuts
½ cup flaked coconut
1 teaspoon vanilla extract
1 cup (one 6-ounce package) semisweet
    chocolate pieces
¼ cup light corn syrup
1 tablespoon water

Blend butter, 1 cup flour, and ¼ teaspoon salt. Press firmly into greased and floured 9-inch square pan. Bake in preheated moderate oven (375°F.) for 15 minutes. Beat sugar into eggs. Add remaining salt, 1 cup nuts, the coconut, and vanilla. Spread evenly over baked layer in pan. Return to oven and bake for 15 minutes longer. Cool in pan. Melt chocolate over hot water and stir in corn syrup and water. Spread on baked mixture and sprinkle with remaining nuts. Let stand until topping is firm, and cut into bars 1 x 3 inches. Makes 27.

RASPBERRY DELIGHTS
1¼ cups sifted all-purpose flour
½ teaspoon salt
    Sugar (about 1½ cups)
1 teaspoon baking powder
½ cup butter
1 egg yolk
2 tablespoons brandy or milk
¾ cup thick raspberry jam
2 eggs
2 teaspoons vanilla extract
6 tablespoons melted butter
2½ cups flaked coconut

Sift flour with salt, 1 teaspoon sugar, and baking powder; blend in butter; add egg yolk and brandy, and mix. Pat into buttered pan (11 x 7 x 2 inches). Spread with jam. Beat eggs until thick and lemon-colored; beat in 1½ cups sugar, vanilla, and melted butter. Add coconut. Spoon over jam. Bake in preheated moderate oven (350°F.) for 35 minutes. Cool. Cut into 1-inch squares. Makes 77.

FRUITED MOLASSES BARS
½ cup soft butter or margarine
½ cup sugar
½ cup molasses
1 egg
1 cup sifted all-purpose flour
½ teaspoon salt
¼ teaspoon ground cinnamon
⅛ teaspoon baking soda
1 cup chopped nuts
¼ cup seedless raisins
1 package (8 ounces) pitted dates,
    cut up
    Cinnamon Frosting

Cream butter, sugar, and molasses and add egg, beating until light. Add sifted dry ingredients, ¾ cup of the nuts, the raisins, and dates; mix well. Bake in greased and floured 9-inch square pan in preheated moderate oven (350°F.) for about 35 minutes. While warm, dribble with Cinnamon Frosting and sprinkle with remaining nuts. Cool in pan, and cut into 32 bars.

Cinnamon Frosting
Mix 2 cups sifted confectioners' sugar, 2 tablespoons hot milk, dash of salt, and ¼ teaspoon ground cinnamon.

PECAN BARS
2¼ cups sifted all-purpose flour
¼ teaspoon salt
1 cup granulated sugar
1 cup soft butter
2 egg yolks
1 tablespoon brandy
4 cups finely chopped pecans
½ cup firmly packed light brown sugar
1½ teaspoons ground cinnamon
4 egg whites, unbeaten
    Confectioners' sugar (optional)

Sift flour, salt, and ½ cup granulated sugar. Blend in butter; add egg yolks and brandy. Pat evenly into pan (15 x 10 x 1 inch). Bake in preheated moderate oven (350°F.) for 15 minutes. In heavy saucepan put remaining granulated sugar, the pecans, brown sugar, cinnamon, and egg whites. Cook, stirring, over low heat until sugars dissolve. Increase heat and cook until mixture no longer clings to sides of pan. Spread on baked mixture. Return to oven for 15 minutes. Cool slightly. Cut into bars 3 x 1 inch. Dust cookies with confectioners' sugar, if desired. Makes 50.

NUTMEG DATE BARS
1 package (8 ounces) pitted dates
1 cup pecans or walnuts
    Sifted confectioners' sugar
2 eggs, beaten
½ teaspoon salt
1 tablespoon cooking oil
1 tablespoon fresh lemon juice
¼ cup sifted all-purpose flour
¾ cup ground nutmeg

Force dates and nuts through food chopper, using medium blade. Add 1 cup confectioners' sugar, eggs, and salt; mix well. Add remaining ingredients and mix thoroughly. Spread in greased 9-inch square pan. Bake in preheated moderate

oven (350°F.) for about 30 minutes. Cool partially, cut into 18 bars and roll in confectioners' sugar.

FROSTED MINCEMEAT DIAMONDS
1 tablespoon soft butter
1½ cups firmly packed brown sugar
2 eggs
2 tablespoons molasses
2 cups sifted all-purpose flour
½ teaspoon each of salt and
    baking soda
1 teaspoon each of ground cinnamon
    and cloves
¼ teaspoon ground nutmeg
3 tablespoons hot water
⅔ cup chopped nuts, about
¼ cup seeded raisins, chopped
1 box (9 ounces) mincemeat, broken up
    with fork
    Frosting

Mix first 4 ingredients well. Add sifted dry ingredients and water; mix until smooth. Add ⅓ cup chopped nuts, raisins, and mincemeat. Spread thin in 2 greased pans (13 x 9 x 2 inches). Bake in preheated hot oven (400°F.) for 12 to 15 minutes. Spread with Frosting while warm and sprinkle with remaining chopped nuts. Cool, and cut into 2-inch diamonds. Makes 4 to 5 dozen.

Frosting
Mix well 3 cups confectioners' sugar, about ⅓ cup hot milk, 1 teaspoon vanilla, and dash of salt.

● DROP COOKIES ●

HERMITS
½ cup soft butter
1 cup firmly packed dark brown sugar
2 eggs
2 cups sifted cake flour
1 teaspoon baking powder
½ teaspoon salt
1 teaspoon ground cinnamon
¼ teaspoon each of ground cloves
    and nutmeg
2 cups seeded raisins, chopped
½ cup chopped nuts

Cream butter and sugar. Add eggs, one at a time, beating until light after each addition. Add sifted dry ingredients, raisins, and nuts; mix well. Drop by teaspoonfuls onto greased cookie sheets; bake in preheated moderate oven (350°F.) for about 10 minutes. Makes about 4 dozen.

OLD-FASHIONED ROCKS
⅓ cup boiling water
2 cups seeded raisins
½ cup soft butter or margarine
1½ cups firmly packed dark brown sugar
2 eggs
½ cup chopped walnuts
2½ cups sifted all-purpose flour
1 teaspoon baking powder
1 teaspoon salt
1 teaspoon ground cinnamon

Pour boiling water on raisins and let cool. Cream butter and sugar. Add eggs, one at a time, beating until light after each addition. Add nuts, sifted dry ingredients, and soaked raisins with water; mix well. Drop by teaspoonfuls onto greased cookie sheets and bake in preheated moderate oven (350°F.) for about 15 minutes. Makes 3 dozen.

LACE COOKIES

¼ cup butter
¼ cup shortening
½ cup light corn syrup
⅔ cup firmly packed light brown sugar
1 cup sifted all-purpose flour
1 cup finely chopped nuts (any kind)
1 cup semisweet chocolate pieces

Place butter, shortening, syrup, and sugar in top part of double boiler; bring to boil over direct heat and remove from heat immediately. Blend in flour mixed with nuts. Drop by rounded teaspoonfuls 3 inches apart onto greased cookie sheet covered with foil. Keep remaining batter warm over boiling water between batches. Bake in preheated slow oven (325°F.) for 8 to 10 minutes. Cool for 1 minute before removing from foil. Place chocolate over hot water and stir. When partially melted, remove from hot water; stir until melted. Then brush on each cooled cookie. (Too high a temperature of chocolate makes drying slow.) Makes about 6 dozen.

NUT-BUTTER WAFERS

½ cup soft butter or margarine
1 cup firmly packed light brown sugar
1 teaspoon vanilla extract
1 egg
¾ cup sifted all-purpose flour
1 teaspoon baking powder
½ teaspoon salt
½ cup finely chopped nuts

Cream butter and sugar. Add vanilla and egg and beat until light. Add sifted dry ingredients and nuts. Drop by scant teaspoonfuls onto ungreased cookie sheets. Bake in preheated hot oven (400°F.) for about 5 minutes. Cool for half minute. Remove to racks. Makes about 8 dozen.
Note: Use pecans, almonds, walnuts, filberts, or Brazil nuts.

BRANDY WAFERS

½ cup molasses
½ cup butter
1¼ cups sifted cake flour
¼ teaspoon salt
⅔ cup sugar
1 tablespoon ground ginger
3 tablespoons brandy

Heat molasses to boiling. Add butter. Add sifted dry ingredients gradually, stirring constantly. Stir in brandy. Drop by half teaspoonfuls 3 inches apart onto greased cookie sheets. Bake, 6 cookies at a time, in preheated slow oven (300°F.) for 8 to 10 minutes. Cool for 1 minute. Remove with spatula and roll at once around handle of wooden spoon. Makes about 5 dozen.

SUGAR CRISPS

1 cup soft butter
½ cup granulated sugar

⅓ cup firmly packed light brown sugar
2 eggs
Grated rind of 1 lemon
1½ cups sifted all-purpose flour
¼ cup seedless raisins
¼ cup slivered blanched almonds
¼ cup diced candied cherries
¼ cup each of finely diced candied orange peel and angelica or citron
3 tablespoons honey
½ teaspoon ground cinnamon

Cream butter and sugars. Add eggs, one at a time, beating until light after each addition. Add grated lemon rind and flour. Drop by teaspoonfuls onto greased cookie sheets. Spread thin with silver knife dipped into cold water. Mix remaining ingredients and top each cookie with a small mound of mixture. Bake in preheated moderate oven (375°F.) for 8 minutes, or until lightly browned. Makes 5 dozen.

ORANGE WAFERS

½ cup soft butter
¾ cup sugar
1 egg
1 teaspoon grated orange rind
1 tablespoon fresh orange juice
1½ cups sifted all-purpose flour
½ teaspoon baking powder
¼ teaspoon salt

Cream butter and sugar. Add egg and beat until light. Add remaining ingredients; mix well. Drop by level teaspoonfuls onto ungreased cookie sheets. Press flat with the bottom of a glass wrapped in cheesecloth which has been dipped in cold water and wrung out. Bake in preheated moderate oven (375°F.) for about 7 minutes. Makes about 8 dozen.

TOASTED FILBERT KISSES

3 egg whites
⅛ teaspoon salt
1 cup sugar
1 teaspoon grated lemon rind
½ teaspoon ground cinnamon
1 cup toasted and ground filberts

Beat egg whites until foamy. Add salt and beat until whites begin to hold their shape. Gradually add sugar and beat until stiff but not dry. Fold in lemon rind, cinnamon, and nuts. Drop by teaspoonfuls onto greased cookie sheets. Bake in preheated very slow oven (275°F.) for 20 to 25 minutes. Makes 6 dozen.
■ **To Toast Filberts**—Spread nuts in shallow baking pan containing 1 teaspoon melted butter. Brown in hot oven (400°F.), stirring every 5 minutes. Turn out on brown paper to cool.

CHOCOLATE FUDGE MERINGUES

4 egg whites
¼ teaspoon cream of tartar
½ teaspoon salt
1 cup sugar
½ teaspoon each of almond and vanilla extracts
Chocolate Fudge
Chopped Brazil nuts

Beat egg whites until foamy. Add cream

of tartar and salt and beat until whites begin to hold their shape. Gradually add sugar, beating until stiff but not dry. Add extracts. Drop by teaspoonfuls onto cookie sheet covered with heavy wax paper. With a teaspoon, make a depression in center of each and fill with Chocolate Fudge mixture. Sprinkle with nuts. Bake in preheated slow oven (300°F.) for about 25 minutes. Makes about 3½ dozen.

Chocolate Fudge

In top part of double boiler, melt 6 ounces (1 package) semisweet chocolate pieces with 3 tablespoons butter. Add 4 egg yolks slightly beaten with 2 tablespoons corn syrup. Cook, stirring, for 5 minutes. Remove from heat. Beat until of spreading consistency.

ROLLED COOKIES

CREAM-CHEESE BUTTER COOKIES

1 cup butter
8 ounces cream cheese
¼ cup sugar
2 cups sifted all-purpose flour
½ teaspoon baking powder

Cream butter and cream cheese; add sugar and mix until light. Sift flour and baking powder together; stir into first mixture. Mix well and roll into a ball. Wrap in wax paper or foil and put in refrigerator overnight. Roll out on floured board about ⅛ inch thick and cut into 1½-inch squares. Place on ungreased cookie sheets and sprinkle with sugar and ground cinnamon, or ground nuts and sugar, or spread with a favorite jam, or leave plain. Bake in preheated moderate oven (375°F.) until delicately brown. Makes about 8 dozen.

SPICY MOLASSES CUTOUTS

1 cup soft butter or margarine
1 cup sugar
1 cup light molasses
5 cups sifted all-purpose flour
2 teaspoons baking soda
1 to 3 teaspoons ground ginger
½ teaspoon salt
½ cup cold strong tea
1 teaspoon vanilla extract
Split almonds

Cream butter and sugar until light. Beat in molasses. Add sifted dry ingredients alternately with tea; mix well. Add vanilla. Chill for at least 24 hours. Roll out very thin and cut into fancy shapes. Arrange on well-greased cookie sheets and decorate with almonds. Bake in preheated moderate oven (375°F.) for 8 to 10 minutes. Makes 8 to 10 dozen.
Note: Make the dough a day ahead.

FILLED BUTTER RINGS

1 cup soft butter or margarine
½ cup sugar
3 cups sifted all-purpose flour

¼ teaspoon salt
Crab apple or other jelly

Cream butter and ¼ cup sugar; add flour and salt and mix well. Roll out to ⅛-inch thickness and cut with floured 2-inch cutter. Cut out centers of half of cookies with 1¼-inch cutter. Arrange on ungreased cookie sheets. Bake in preheated hot oven (400°F.) for about 10 minutes. Just before serving, spread whole cookies with jelly, piled higher at center. Top with cookie rings. Sprinkle confectioners' sugar around edges, if desired. Makes about 3 dozen.

ALMOND-BUTTER STRIPS
¾ cup soft butter or margarine
6 tablespoons sugar
½ teaspoon almond extract
2 cups sifted all-purpose flour
⅛ teaspoon salt
1 egg white, slightly beaten
⅛ teaspoon ground cinnamon
⅓ cup minced blanched almonds

Cream butter and ¼ cup sugar; add flavoring and beat until light. Add flour and salt and mix well. Chill until firm. Roll out to ⅛-inch thickness. With pastry wheel cut strips 1 x 2 inches. Put on ungreased cookie sheets and brush with egg white. Mix remaining sugar with cinnamon and almonds, and sprinkle on cookies. Bake in preheated moderate oven (350°F.) for about 8 minutes. Makes 6 dozen.

SAND TARTS
½ cup soft butter or margarine
1 cup plus 1 tablespoon sugar
2 eggs, separated
1 tablespoon milk
½ teaspoon vanilla extract
½ teaspoon salt
1 teaspoon baking powder
1½ cups sifted all-purpose flour
15 unblanched almonds, split
¼ teaspoon ground cinnamon

Cream butter and 1 cup sugar. Add egg yolks, milk, and flavoring and beat until light. Add sifted dry ingredients and mix well. Chill for at least 3 hours. Roll out dough very thin and cut with 3-inch star or other cookie cutter. Put on greased cookie sheets; put a split almond on each cookie. Brush with unbeaten egg whites; sprinkle with 1 tablespoon sugar and the cinnamon. Bake in preheated moderate oven (375°F.) for about 8 minutes. Makes about 2½ dozen.

SWEDISH CREAM COOKIES
2¾ cups sifted all-purpose flour
Dash of salt

½ cup heavy cream
1 cup soft butter or margarine
Sugar
1 cup (one 6-ounce package) semisweet chocolate pieces, melted over hot water

Mix first 4 ingredients thoroughly. Chill. Roll out on sugared board to ⅛-inch thickness. Cut with tiny fancy cutters. Bake on greased cookie sheets in preheated moderate oven (350°F.) for about 8 minutes. Put together with melted chocolate, putting a dot of the chocolate in the center of each. Makes about 10 dozen.

Jam Circles
Use recipe above. Cut half of cookies with 1¾-inch cutter. Cut remainder with 1¾-inch doughnut cutter. Bake as above. Fill with red jam or jelly. Makes about 6 dozen.

SPICED ORANGE FLOWERS
1 cup soft butter or margarine
1½ cups sugar
1 tablespoon grated orange rind
1 egg
3 tablespoons fresh orange juice
3 cups sifted all-purpose flour
1 teaspoon baking powder
½ teaspoon salt
½ teaspoon ground allspice
¾ teaspoon ground nutmeg
Candied cherries

Cream butter and sugar and add rind, egg, and juice, beating until light. Add sifted dry ingredients and mix until smooth. Chill if necessary to make stiff enough to roll. Then roll to ⅛-inch thickness and cut with 2-inch diamond-shape cutter. Put on ungreased cookie sheets and bring 2 longest points of each to center, overlapping slightly. Decorate with cherries. Bake in preheated hot oven (400°F.) for 8 to 10 minutes. Makes 8 dozen. (These are good keepers.)

ITALIAN WINE COOKIES
1 cup soft butter or margarine
2 cups sugar
2 egg yolks
5 cups sifted all-purpose flour
Dash of salt
⅔ cup sweet Marsala or sherry
1 egg white
Chopped nuts

Cream butter and sugar; add egg yolks and beat until light. Add sifted dry ingredients alternately with wine and mix well. Chill. Roll out thin on floured board and cut with 2-inch cookie cutter. Place on ungreased cookie sheets, brush with slightly beaten egg white, and sprinkle

with nuts. Bake in preheated slow oven (325°F.) for 8 to 10 minutes. Makes about 9 dozen.

SPITZBUBEN
Sugar
1 cup plus 3 tablespoons soft butter
2 cups ground blanched almonds
1 teaspoon vanilla extract
3¼ cups sifted all-purpose flour
½ teaspoon salt
Seedless raspberry jam

Mix 1 cup sugar and the butter; add almonds and vanilla. Add flour sifted with salt. Knead dough very well. On lightly floured cloth-covered board roll to ⅛- to ¼-inch thickness. Cut with simple cutters; place on ungreased cookie sheet. Bake in preheated slow oven (325°F.) until brown, about 15 minutes. Spread half of cookies with jam; top with matching cookies; dip into sugar and decorate. Makes about 5 dozen.

PRESSED COOKIES

BLACK-EYED SUSANS
½ cup soft butter or margarine
½ cup granulated sugar
½ cup firmly packed light brown sugar
1 egg
1 teaspoon vanilla extract
1 cup moist smooth peanut butter
1½ cups sifted all-purpose flour
½ teaspoon each of baking soda and salt
Semisweet chocolate pieces

Cream butter and sugars; add egg, vanilla, and peanut butter; beat until light. Add sifted dry ingredients and mix well. Force through spritz gun or cookie press onto ungreased cookie sheets, using a disc that will make a flower design. Put a chocolate piece in center of each. Bake in preheated moderate oven (350°F.) for about 15 minutes. Makes about 5 dozen.

LEMON-CHEESE COOKIES
1 cup soft butter or margarine
1 package (3 ounces) cream cheese, softened
1 cup sugar
1 egg yolk
½ teaspoon lemon extract
1 teaspoon grated lemon rind
2½ cups sifted all-purpose flour
½ teaspoon salt
Colored sugar, cinnamon sugar, or finely chopped nuts

Cream butter, cheese, and sugar; add egg yolk and flavorings and beat until light. Add sifted flour and salt; mix well. Force

through spritz gun or cookie press onto ungreased cookie sheets. Decorate as desired. Bake in preheated moderate oven (350°F.) for about 15 minutes. Makes about 6 dozen.

MOLDED OR SHAPED COOKIES

DREAM COOKIES

1 cup soft butter or margarine
1 cup sugar
1 teaspoon vanilla extract
2 cups sifted all-purpose flour
  Dash of salt
1 teaspoon baking powder
  Blanched almonds, split

Cream butter and sugar and beat until light. Add vanilla and stir in sifted dry ingredients; mix well. Form into small balls. Put on ungreased cookie sheets and press an almond half on top of each. Bake in preheated slow oven (300°F.) for about 20 minutes. Makes about 6 dozen.

HONEY-PEANUT BUTTER COOKIES

¼ cup butter or margarine
½ cup peanut butter
¼ cup sugar
⅓ cup honey
1 egg
¾ cup sifted all-purpose flour
¼ teaspoon baking powder

Cream butter and peanut butter with sugar until smooth. Beat in honey, then egg, and mix well. Add flour sifted with baking powder and mix well. Roll into walnut-size balls and put on ungreased cookie sheet. Press with fork to flatten, making lattice design, and bake in preheated moderate oven (375°F.) for 15 minutes. Makes about 3 dozen.
Note: Cream-style peanut butter gives a smooth cookie; chunk-style peanut butter a crunchier one.

BUTTERSCOTCH ACORNS

1 cup butter or margarine
¾ cup firmly packed light brown sugar
1 teaspoon vanilla extract
½ cup finely chopped pecans
2½ cups sifted all-purpose flour
½ teaspoon baking powder
1 cup caramel or butterscotch pieces
¾ cup pistachio nuts, chopped fine

Melt butter, remove from heat, and stir in sugar, vanilla, and pecans. Sift flour and baking powder; add to butter mixture. Form dough into 42 balls, using a rounded teaspoonful for each. Flatten one end by pressing on ungreased cookie sheet and pinching top to a point to resemble an acorn. Bake in preheated moderate oven (350°F.) for 15 minutes. Cool. Melt candy pieces over hot water; dip flat ends of cookies into butterscotch to depth of ¼ inch. Thoroughly coat melted candy with nuts. Makes 3½ dozen.

FINGERS

⅔ cup soft butter or margarine
6 tablespoons confectioners' sugar
1 teaspoon vanilla extract
½ teaspoon almond extract
2 cups sifted all-purpose flour
¼ teaspoon salt
1 cup chopped pecans or filberts
  Fine granulated sugar

Cream butter and confectioners' sugar until light. Add remaining ingredients except granulated sugar and mix well. With fingers, squeeze pieces of dough into 2-inch-long fingers. Arrange on ungreased cookie sheet and bake in preheated slow oven (325°F.) for about 30 minutes. While warm, roll in granulated sugar. Makes about 3½ dozen.

SUGARED BUTTER COOKIES

1 cup soft butter or margarine
  Confectioners' sugar
2¼ cups sifted all-purpose flour
1 teaspoon vanilla extract
¼ teaspoon salt
¾ cup chopped nuts

Cream butter and ½ cup sugar until light. Add remaining ingredients and mix well. Chill for several hours. Shape into 1-inch balls. Put on ungreased cookie sheets. Bake in preheated hot oven (400°F.) for 10 to 12 minutes. Roll at once in confectioners' sugar. Cool, and roll again in sugar. Makes about 4 dozen.

MOCHA NUT BUTTERBALLS

1 cup soft butter
½ cup granulated sugar
2 teaspoons vanilla extract
2 teaspoons instant coffee powder
¼ cup cocoa
1¾ cups sifted all-purpose flour
½ teaspoon salt
2 cups finely chopped pecans or California walnuts
  Confectioners' sugar

Cream butter, sugar, and vanilla until light. Add next 4 ingredients and mix well. Add nuts. Shape into 1-inch balls and put on ungreased cookie sheets. Bake in preheated slow oven (325°F.) for about 15 minutes. Cool, and roll in confectioners' sugar. Makes about 6 dozen.

FILBERT LEMON LOGS

1 cup butter or margarine
¾ cup firmly packed light brown sugar
1 teaspoon grated lemon rind
2½ cups sifted all-purpose flour
¼ teaspoon salt
1 tablespoon fresh lemon juice
1 cup chopped toasted filberts

Cream butter and sugar until light. Add lemon rind, sifted dry ingredients, and lemon juice. Mix well and chill several hours. Shape into fingers. Roll in nuts and put on ungreased cookie sheets. Bake in preheated hot oven (400°F.) for 10 to 12 minutes. Makes 3 to 4 dozen.

BROWN-SUGAR NUT MOUNDS

1 cup soft butter or margarine
1½ cups firmly packed light brown sugar
1 egg
4 cups sifted all-purpose flour

½ teaspoon each of salt and baking soda
2 teaspoons ground cinnamon
½ cup dairy sour cream
  Pecan halves

Cream butter and sugar and add egg, beating until light. Add sifted dry ingredients and sour cream; mix well. Shape into balls the size of a small walnut. Put on ungreased cookie sheets and press a pecan in center of each. Bake in preheated hot oven (400°F.) for 10 to 12 minutes. Makes about 7 dozen.

SWIRL COOKIES

1 cup soft butter
½ cup sifted confectioners' sugar
1 teaspoon vanilla extract
2¼ cups unsifted all-purpose flour
¼ teaspoon salt
  Red and yellow food coloring

Cream butter, sugar, and vanilla until light. Stir in flour and salt. Divide into halves. Color half with ¼ teaspoon red food coloring and about 7 drops yellow food coloring. Leave other half uncolored. Chill. Press together 1 level teaspoon of each color. Roll into pencil shape. Form each into a coil on ungreased cookie sheets. Bake in preheated moderate oven (375°F.) for about 8 minutes. Makes about 3½ dozen.

REFRIGERATOR COOKIES

LEMON-CARAWAY COOKIES

½ cup soft butter or margarine
1 cup sugar
1 egg
1¼ teaspoons caraway seeds
  Grated rind of ½ lemon
2 tablespoons fresh lemon juice
2½ cups sifted all-purpose flour
¼ teaspoon baking soda
½ teaspoon salt

Cream butter and sugar. Add egg and beat until light. Add caraway seeds, lemon rind and juice, and sifted dry ingredients and mix well. Shape into a roll 2 inches in diameter and chill. Cut into ⅛-inch slices and arrange on greased cookie sheets. Bake in preheated hot oven (400°F.) for about 10 minutes. Makes 6 dozen.

CHOCOLATE REFRIGERATOR COOKIES

1¼ cups soft butter or margarine
1½ cups sifted confectioners' sugar
1 egg
3 cups sifted cake flour
½ cup cocoa
¼ teaspoon salt
1½ cups chopped California walnuts
8 ounces (two 4-ounce bars) sweet cooking chocolate

Cream butter and sugar. Add egg and beat until light. Add flour, cocoa, and salt; mix well. Chill for several hours. Shape into 2 long rolls about 1½ inches in diameter. Roll in nuts until coated on all sides. Wrap in wax paper and chill overnight. Cut into ⅛-inch slices and arrange on ungreased cookie sheet. Bake in preheated hot oven (400°F.) for 8 to 10 minutes. Cool. Melt chocolate over hot water and spread in center of cookies. Makes about 8 dozen.

CARDAMOM COOKIES

1 cup soft butter or margarine
1 cup sugar
1 tablespoon ground cardamom
½ cup dairy sour cream
4 cups sifted all-purpose flour
¼ teaspoon each of salt and baking soda

Cream butter and sugar until light. Add remaining ingredients and mix well. Shape into 2 long rolls 2 inches in diameter. Roll up in wax paper and chill overnight. Cut into ⅛-inch slices and arrange on ungreased cookie sheet. Bake in preheated moderate oven (375°F.) for 8 to 10 minutes. Makes 10 dozen.

PRUNE REFRIGERATOR COOKIES

1 cup soft butter or margarine
1 cup firmly packed light brown sugar
½ cup granulated sugar
2 eggs
1 tablespoon vinegar
1 teaspoon vanilla extract
1 cup chopped cooked pitted prunes
4 cups sifted all-purpose flour
1 teaspoon each of baking soda and salt
1 cup chopped nuts

Cream butter and sugars. Add eggs, one at a time, and beat until light. Add vinegar, vanilla, prunes, and sifted dry ingredients; mix well and add nuts. Shape into 3 rolls about 2 inches in diameter. Wrap in wax paper and chill overnight. Cut into ⅛-inch slices and arrange on ungreased cookie sheets. Bake in preheated hot oven (400°F.) for about 12 minutes. Makes about 12 dozen.

■ **Variation**—Substitute ¾ cup finely cut dates for the prunes to make a delicious date cookie.

CHOCOLATE RINGS

1 cup butter or margarine
1 cup confectioners' sugar
2 teaspoons vanilla extract
1½ cups sifted all-purpose flour
½ teaspoon baking soda
1 cup uncooked rolled oats
Chocolate sprinkles

Cream butter, sugar, and vanilla until light. Sift flour and soda and add to butter mixture with rolled oats. Mix well. Refrigerate for 1 hour. Shape into 2 rolls 1½ inches in diameter and roll in chocolate sprinkles. Wrap in wax paper and refrigerate for several hours or overnight. Cut into ¼-inch slices and arrange on ungreased cookie sheet. Bake in preheated slow oven (325°F.) for 10 minutes. Makes 5 dozen.

Grandma Minnie's Cookie Crock

by
Minnie W. Muenscher

Keeping our cookie crock full is a never-ending joy to me. An even greater joy is to hear a clamor of voices requesting: "Grandma Minnie, may I have a cookie?" when the neighbor's children, cookie-crock raiders all, come around to hear a story, work a puzzle, or play a game with Grandpa. Their older brothers and sisters happily munch cookies as we visit, and even the college-age boys and girls take advantage of the standing invitation to help themselves. Afternoons, when friends drop in, there is always a cup of herb tea and a cookie waiting for them. To meet these varied demands, I try to keep on hand a supply of tempting but nourishing cookies, packed with vitamins, minerals, and whatever it takes to give growing youngsters pep and energy. Here are some of the cookies we like best, all good and good for you.

RAISIN-FILLED COOKIES

I have made no changes in this recipe. I think it might be better with part whole-wheat flour, and it could well have wheat germ added. The filling might be better with a tablespoon of lemon juice. But this is just as my sister Elsie and I used to make it fifty years ago.

Cookie Dough

½ cup sugar
½ cup shortening
1 egg
½ cup milk
2½ cups sifted all-purpose flour
¼ teaspoon salt
2 teaspoons baking powder
1 teaspoon vanilla extract

Add ingredients in order. Chill dough.

Filling

1 teaspoon flour
½ cup sugar
½ cup water
1 cup ground raisins

Mix flour and sugar; add water and

raisins, stirring carefully. Cook until thick. Let cool. Place between two thinly rolled cookies. Put on greased cookie sheets. Bake in preheated moderate oven (350°F.) for 15 minutes, or until browned. Makes 3 dozen.

STORMY-WEATHER JUMBLES

Of course these cookies can be enjoyed any time of the year; but they are especially good when the wind is howling, the rain is beating down, or the snow is swirling around the house. In this versatile recipe dark brown or white sugar can be used in place of the light brown. Sour milk or cream can be substituted for buttermilk; use less shortening if you use cream. The fruit can be seeded or seedless raisins, dates, dried figs, prunes or apricots, citron or other preserved fruits. I usually use seeded raisins. I use California walnuts; but almost any kind of nut could be used.

Blend together:

1 cup firmly packed light brown sugar
½ cup margarine

Add 2 eggs, one at a time, mixing after each addition. Then add:

2 tablespoons wheat germ
2 tablespoons brewers' yeast
½ cup white cornmeal (yellow can be used)
½ cup unsulphured molasses

Sift together:

1 cup sifted all-purpose flour
1 teaspoon each of salt, baking powder, and baking soda
1 teaspoon ground cinnamon
½ teaspoon each of ground cloves and ginger

Stir in:

1 cup whole-wheat flour

Add to mixture, alternating with ½ cup buttermilk.

Stir in:

1 cup chopped fruit
1 cup broken nut meats

Drop by teaspoonfuls onto ungreased baking sheets. Bake in preheated moderate oven (325°F.) for 15 to 18 minutes. Makes 6 dozen.

VIRGINIA'S OATMEAL CHOCOLATE COOKIES

This recipe comes from Elizabeth, our oldest daughter. (She was my helper with cookies and now she has twins to help her.) It is a variation of an old family favorite. The applesauce was added to the recipe several years ago for the benefit of Virginia's other grandmother who found the cookies a bit too crisp to be eaten comfortably. Virginia and her twin are responsible for the use of cooking oil and for the streamlined method of mixing, which make it safe to prepare with a baby on one arm. It will very likely be the first recipe Virginia uses when she begins to make cookies.

Sift together into large bowl:
½ cup sifted all-purpose flour
1 teaspoon baking powder
¼ teaspoon salt

Add and mix in:
½ cup whole-wheat flour
¼ cup wheat germ, soy flour, or whatever special flour is handy
¾ cup rolled oats
½ cup semisweet chocolate pieces

Mix in separate bowl:
1 egg, unbeaten
1 tablespoon applesauce
¾ cup firmly packed brown sugar
½ cup cooking oil
½ teaspoon vanilla extract

Add liquid ingredients to dry ingredients and mix well. Drop by teaspoonfuls onto greased baking sheets. Bake in preheated moderate oven (350°F.) until browned, about 18 minutes. Especially good while the chocolate is still soft. Makes 3 dozen.

HELEN'S MOLASSES CRINKLES

These cookies help to give Ralph and Peter, our older grandsons, the vigor they need for Alaskan winters. They are inexpensive and easy to make.

¾ cup margarine
1 cup firmly packed brown sugar
2 eggs
¼ cup unsulphured molasses
½ cup wheat germ
2 cups sifted all-purpose flour
½ teaspoon salt
1 teaspoon soda
½ teaspoon ground cloves
1 teaspoon each of ground cinnamon and ginger
1 cup whole-wheat flour
Granulated sugar
Blanched almonds

Stir together the margarine and brown sugar; add the eggs and stir well. Now mix in the molasses and wheat germ. Sift in all-purpose flour, salt, soda, and spices, stirring until well blended; add whole-wheat flour. Chill for at least 30 minutes. Form into balls the size of a walnut; dip into granulated sugar. Top each with an almond. Put on greased cookie sheets. Bake in preheated moderate oven (375° F.) for 12 to 15 minutes. Makes 5 dozen.

PEANUT-BUTTER DROP COOKIES

I decided to experiment with peanut butter in cookies and evolved this recipe.

Mix in order given:
½ cup peanut butter (smooth or crunchy)
½ cup softened margarine
1 cup firmly packed brown sugar
1 egg

2 tablespoons wheat germ
¼ cup milk
1 teaspoon vanilla extract

Sift together and add, stirring well:
1½ cups sifted all-purpose flour
¾ teaspoon baking powder
½ teaspoon each of baking soda and salt
½ teaspoon ground ginger

Stir in:
¾ cup raisins
½ cup Grape-Nuts

Drop by teaspoonfuls onto ungreased cookie sheets. Bake in preheated moderate oven (375°F.) for 10 to 12 minutes. This is a delightfully crunchy cookie. Makes about 4 dozen.

JOANNE'S SNICKERDOODLES

Joanne, our youngest daughter, makes mostly coffeecake and sweet rolls for her family instead of cookies. But she and her husband and small son like Snickerdoodles. I have added wheat germ to them and made a few other minor changes.

Mix together thoroughly:
1 cup soft shortening
1½ cups sugar
2 eggs

Sift together and stir in:
2½ cups sifted all-purpose flour
2 teaspoons baking powder
½ teaspoon salt

Add ½ cup wheat germ and 1 teaspoon vanilla extract and stir in. Chill dough. Roll into balls the size of small walnuts. Roll in mixture of 2 tablespoons sugar and 2 teaspoons cinnamon. Place 2 inches apart on ungreased baking sheet. Bake in preheated hot oven (400°F.) until lightly brown, 8 to 10 minutes. Makes 5 dozen.

MINT COOKIES

I have used caraway, poppy seeds, and aniseeds in cookies, especially Christmas cookies; but I wanted something different, so I tried dried peppermint, crumbling it almost to a powder. Spearmint or apple mint would do as well. If you cannot get the dried, you could probably get the same results with extract or essence of peppermint. This recipe could also be used with caraway seeds or nut meats.

Blend:
¼ cup margarine
½ cup sugar

Add, and stir well:
1 egg
1 tablespoon crumbled dried mint

Sift and stir in:
1 cup sifted all-purpose flour
1 teaspoon baking powder
¼ teaspoon salt

Drop by teaspoonfuls onto ungreased baking sheets and bake in preheated moderate oven (375°F.) for 10 minutes. Makes 2 dozen.

BLACK-WALNUT COOKIES

This is another very easy cookie to make, easy to eat, too. If you can't get black walnuts, use California walnuts.

2 eggs
⅔ cup cooking oil
1 tablespoon milk
½ cup wheat germ
¾ cup sugar
2 cups sifted all-purpose flour
2 teaspoons baking powder
½ teaspoon salt
1 teaspoon vanilla extract
½ cup broken black-walnut meats

Beat eggs with fork until well blended. Stir in oil, milk, and wheat germ. Blend in sugar until mixture thickens. Sift together flour, baking powder, and salt and stir into oil mixture. Add vanilla extract and black-walnut meats and stir. Drop by teaspoonfuls onto ungreased baking sheets. Space about 2 inches apart. Bake in preheated hot oven (400°F.) until nicely browned, 8 to 12 minutes. Makes about 5 dozen.

MAE'S DATE COOKIES

I added wheat germ and brewers' yeast and substituted whole-wheat flour for part of the flour in this recipe.

Mix well:
1 cup each of granulated sugar and firmly packed brown sugar
1 cup butter or margarine

Stir into this:
3 eggs, slightly beaten
3 tablespoons wheat germ
3 tablespoons brewers' yeast
1 teaspoon soda dissolved in 2 tablespoons cold water

Sift together and add gradually, stirring in well:
3 cups sifted all-purpose flour
1½ cups whole-wheat flour
1 teaspoon salt

Stir in:
1 cup each of cut pitted dates and chopped nuts

Drop by teaspoonfuls onto ungreased baking sheets. Bake in preheated moderate oven (375°F.) for about 12 minutes. Makes about 7½ dozen.

COQUILLE—In French, a *coquille* is a shell. In culinary language, it is a little dish in the shape of a shell, made from fireproof china, glass, or metal, or an actual shell, preferably the shell of a scallop. A *coquille* is also food placed into this kind of dish with or without a sauce, but covered with bread crumbs and/or grated cheese and browned in the oven or under a broiler. Any meats, fish, or vegetables, either singly or in combinations, can be served *en coquille*, provided they are at least partially cooked and cut into suitably small pieces. The best-known *coquille* dish is probably Coquilles St. Jacques, made with scallops, of which the most popular version is the one with a cream sauce.

Coquilles are elegant little affairs, and very well suited to a first course or a light luncheon entrée. They can be prepared in advance and browned at the last minute.

COQUILLES ST. JACQUES

1 pound mushrooms, sliced
Juice of 1 lemon
5 tablespoons butter
1 pound fresh or frozen sea scallops, thawed
1 cup dry white wine
¼ teaspoon ground thyme
1 bay leaf
½ teaspoon salt
⅛ teaspoon pepper
3 tablespoons all-purpose flour
1 cup light cream
¾ cup buttered soft bread crumbs

Sprinkle mushrooms with lemon juice. Cook mushrooms in 2 tablespoons of the butter until golden brown. Cut scallops into quarters. Place scallops, wine, and seasonings in saucepan. Simmer, covered, for 5 minutes. Drain, reserving 1 cup broth. Make a white sauce with remaining 3 tablespoons butter, the flour, broth, and cream. Add scallops and mushrooms. Spoon into 6 buttered scallop shells. Top with buttered crumbs. Bake in preheated hot oven (400°F.) for 10 minutes, or until browned. Makes 6 servings.

CORAL—The roe of a lobster is called coral. It is used in cooking to add color and flavor to sauces and to dishes featuring lobster meat.

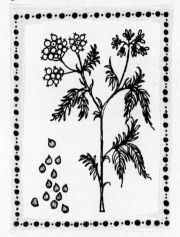

CORIANDER (Coriandrum sativum)—This spice seed is the dried fruit of a foot-tall herb which belongs to the parsley family. The foliage is leafy and the flowers are pinkish-white.

Coriander seeds are probably one of the first spices used in cookery. Native to the Mediterranean and the Orient, seeds have been found in Egyptian tombs of 960 to 800 B.C. In the Bible manna was likened to coriander seed. "And the house of Israel called the name thereof Manna; and it was like coriander seed, white; and the taste of it was like wafers made with honey" (Exodus 16:31). Persia in the 6th century B.C., the time of Cyrus the Great, was well aware of this flavorful seed. The Romans, lovers of exotic delicacies, cultivated coriander. Cato mentions it in the 3rd century before Christ. Seeds were found in the shops of Pompeii, and Pliny states that the best were imported from Egypt. The Romans introduced it into England and there it remained a favorite of the herb garden. Coriander was one of the herbs brought to this country from England. It was carried to Massachusetts before 1670.

Coriander has a pleasant flavor, not unlike that of a combination of aniseed, cuminseed, and orange. It has the delightful quality of becoming more fragrant the longer it is kept. Like so many spices, it can be used in a great variety of foods, depending on personal taste. Ground, it flavors cookies, candies, soups, Danish pastries, and gingerbreads. Cheeses, meats, and even salads benefit by the addition of this fragrant seed. Many blended spices, condiments, and curries contain coriander. Sugar-coated whole seeds make a sweet-tasting "comfit;" the jawbreakers of penny-candy times always held a coveted coriander seed in their centers. For a pleasant ending to a meal, crush a coriander seed in the bottom of the coffee cup.

CORIANDER RICE PUDDING

4 cups milk
¼ cup sugar
¼ cup uncooked rice
¼ teaspoon salt
1 teaspoon ground coriander seed

Put all ingredients in a 2-quart casserole and stir well. Bake for 1 hour in preheated moderate oven (350°F.); reduce to slow (300°F.) and bake, stirring every half hour, until milk is absorbed. This will be about 2 hours. If you wish, scald the milk first and bake in slow oven (300°F.) for 2 hours. Raisins may be added if desired. Makes 4 to 6 servings.

CORIANDER DROP COOKIES

1 cup vegetable shortening
1 cup sugar
1 teaspoon vanilla extract
2 eggs
3 cups sifted all-purpose flour
1 teaspoon baking powder
¾ teaspoon salt
2 teaspoons ground coriander

Cream shortening. Gradually add sugar and beat until light. Add vanilla, then eggs, one at a time, beating after each addition until blended. Add sifted dry ingredients and mix well. Drop by teaspoonfuls onto lightly greased cookie sheets. Bake in hot oven (400°F.) about 10 minutes. Makes about 5 dozen.

CORIANDER TOMATO MARMALADE

1 quart cherry and/or pear tomatoes
3 cups sugar
1 lemon
1 tablespoon whole coriander seeds

Scald and peel tomatoes. Add sugar and let stand overnight in a covered dish. (Do not use aluminum or other metal.) In the morning add lemon juice, finely sliced lemon peel, and coriander seeds. Stir well. Simmer, as slowly as possible, over lowest possible heat. Stir frequently until of the consistency of marmalade. This might take up to 3 hours. Put into hot sterilized glasses; seal with melted paraffin. Makes 3 to 4 half-pint glasses.
Note: If cherry or pear tomatoes are not available, use sliced large ones and add ½ cup more sugar.

CORN—To botanists, and to Americans, corn is very specifically the tall grass, *Zea mays,* which is also known as maize. It seems to have originated in Mexico—the word "maize" comes from the Indian word *mahiz*—and is America's great contribution to the cereal group. Its edible grain is cultivated for human food and for livestock feed; the entire plant is used for forage.

Originally the word corn was used to describe any small particle, as in "peppercorn," for instance, and then was used to describe the seed of whatever cereal plant was grown locally. In England, for example, "corn" stands for wheat. America's earliest settlers were introduced to maize and taught to grow it by the Indians, for whom it was a vital crop. The colonists, to distinguish the new grain from those they had known in the Old World, called it "Indian corn," and eventually, simply "corn."

Columbus and his men are considered the first Europeans to have seen corn. Magellan, De Soto, Cavendish, Champlain, great explorers in many different areas of the New World, all reported seeing this new grain. It was found growing in fields from Brazil to Canada, and from Chile to California. Many varieties were seen, indicating a very old culture. Its usefulness was not limited to food from the grain, for the Peruvians obtained sugar from its stalks, the Mexicans a honeylike substance, and a kind of beer or wine was made from it by all natives of the tropics. Corn was so important to the Incas, Mayans, Aztecs, American Indians of the southwest, Plains Indians, and the northern tribes that it entered into their mythology and religious practices. The plant appears as the Corn Mother. To the Iroquois of New York State, corn, beans, and squash represented three sisters. The corn dance is one of the most spectacular of ceremonial dances. It is performed by tribes dependent upon corn to insure a bountiful crop.

Corn came to be as universally accepted by the settlers as it had been by the Indian tribes throughout the country, and today corn is one of America's favorite vegetables, either fresh, frozen, or canned, and eaten by itself or in combination with other foods. It is also one of our great agricultural crops and the cornerstone of many industries.

Availability—Fresh corn is available May through December with peak diminishing after September.

Canned corn is available mainly as whole-kernel or cream-style corn and in combinations with other vegetables. Frozen corn-on-the-cob, cut sweet corn, and corn mixed with other vegetables are also available.

Purchasing Guide—When selecting fresh corn, look for bright green, snug husks with dark-brown silk at the husk end (a sign of well-filled kernels).

Cobs should have even rows well filled to the tip with tender, milky kernels large enough in growth to eliminate any space between and firm enough to resist slight pressure.

Buy for quick use. Texture, flavor, and half of sugar content is lost in first 24 hours after picking in summer temperature.

☐ 2 ears = about 1⅓ cups kernels

Succotash with Bacon
Double Corn Sticks

Storage

☐ Fresh, refrigerator shelf: as soon as possible
☐ Fresh, refrigerator frozen-food compartment, prepared for freezing: 1 month
☐ Fresh, freezer, prepared for freezing: 1 year
☐ Canned, kitchen shelf: 3 or more years
☐ Canned, refrigerator shelf, opened and covered: 1 to 4 days

Nutritive Food Values—Contains small amounts of a wide variety of vitamins and minerals.

☐ Fresh, 1 small ear = 85 calories
☐ Canned, 3½ ounces, whole-kernel = 66 calories
☐ Canned, 3½ ounces, cream-style = 82 calories
☐ Frozen, 3½ ounces, kernels on the cob, cooked and drained = 94 calories
☐ Frozen, 3½ ounces, kernels cut from cob, cooked and drained = 79 calories

Basic Preparation

☐ **To Prepare, Fresh Corn**—Remove husk and undeveloped tip from ear; pull out silk between kernel rows (a dry vegetable brush is handy to remove stubborn silk); rinse in cold water.

For whole kernels, cut kernels from cob, scraping well to remove all milk juice.

If you want grated or pulp corn to prepare cream-style, with sharp knife slit through center of each row and push out pulp and juice with dull side. Or cut tops off kernels and push out corn pulp and juice with dull edge of knife.

☐ **To Boil, Fresh Corn Ears**—Plunge husked corn into large kettle of rapidly boiling water (enough to cover ears). Do not salt during cooking; salt may harden the kernels. Cover and cook over high heat until tender, 8 to 10 minutes; less for very fresh corn. Drain at once and serve with butter or margarine, salt and pepper.

☐ **To Pan-cook or Steam, Fresh Corn Ears**—Soak husked corn in cold water for 10 minutes; put in Dutch oven or heavy skillet. Add ½ cup cold water; cover tightly; cook over medium heat for 5 minutes. Remove cover; let water evaporate. Add 1 teaspoon cooking oil and ⅛ teaspoon salt for each ear. Reduce heat and cook for 3 to 5 minutes, or until corn is done.

☐ **To Roast, Fresh Corn Ears**—Pull back husks from corn; remove silk. Replace husks and tie in place. Soak corn in salted water for 5 minutes; drain. Roast on grill over hot fire for 10 to 12 minutes, turning frequently. Remove husks and serve corn with butter or margarine and salt.

To roast in coals: Proceed as above, but after draining, bury corn in hot coals for 10 to 12 minutes. Remove husks; serve.

To roast ears in aluminum foil: Spread kernels of ear with softened butter or margarine; wrap in aluminum foil. Place over hot coals or in preheated moderate oven (350° F.) for 10 to 15 minutes on each side. To oven-roast corn-on-the-cob in its husk, use same temperature, roasting for 5 minutes longer.

☐ **To Steam, Fresh Corn Ears in Milk (for better flavor)**—Remove outer husks from corn; turn back inner husks and remove silk. Replace inner husks. Put corn in large heavy kettle. Cover with prepared nonfat dry milk and let stand for 15 to 20 minutes. Pour off most of milk, cover, and heat until cover gets very hot. Turn heat to low; steam for 15 to 20 minutes. Remove husks and serve immediately.

☐ **To Stew, Fresh Corn Kernels**—To kernels cut from cob add small amount of light cream, milk, or water. Cover and simmer for 5 to 6 minutes, or until corn is just tender. Season to taste with butter or margarine, salt and pepper.

☐ **To Freeze, Fresh Corn**—Process as quickly after harvesting as possible. For whole ears of corn, husk and remove silk. Scald small to medium ears in boiling water, covered, for 8 minutes, large ears for 10 minutes. Chill in running cold water. Wrap in moisture-proof wrapping.

Prepare kernel corn as above. Scald ears for 4½ minutes. Cut off kernels but do not cut too deeply or cob will be cut.

Cool, and package as above, allowing ½-inch headspace. Pack tightly to remove air spaces.

PARCHED CORN

Parched corn is corn dried slowly over fires. It is available in some western cities and towns. *Masa,* the basic ingredient for Mexican tortillas, is made from parched corn. *Masa* can also be bought ready-prepared in Mexican and Puerto Rican food stores.

☐ **To Make Masa**—Add 1 cup lime to every 5 to 7 pounds parched corn. Add water and cook for 30 minutes. Cool, and wash to remove all traces of lime and to remove all husks. Grind corn in a stone mortar. Wood ashes may be used instead of lime but this is not recommended. *Masa* after grinding is shaped between the palms of the hands into small thin pancakes. These are baked on a hot surface until white blisters appear on the underside of the tortilla. Turn and bake the other side in the same way. Serve by itself or filled with beans. After filling it may be fried until crisp.

POPCORN

This is a variety (*Zea everta*) of edible corn with small ears about six inches long. Kernels are very hard, small, pointed or round, depending on type, with a proportionately large amount of endosperm. Dry heat causes the moisture and air inside the kernel to explode into a starchy wrong-side-out white popped corn many times larger than its unpopped size. Popping quality depends on correct variety and proper uniform drying process. Popcorn, either whole or ground, is also consumed as a breakfast food.

Availability and Purchasing Guide—Available popped, plain or sweetened, and in specialty combinations. It is also available dry unpopped, in vacuum cans or packaged in a popping utensil.

☐ ⅓ cup unpopped = 5 cups popped

Storage—Opened containers of uncooked popcorn, as well as unopened packages, must be kept dry.

☐ Kitchen shelf, dry kernel, unopened: 1 year
☐ Kitchen shelf, popped, in plastic bags: 2 weeks
☐ Kitchen shelf, popped, opened: 2 days

Caloric Values

☐ Plain, 3½ ounces, popped = 386 calories

Basic Preparation—Use metal popper or wire mesh basket, skillet, electric popper, or package where packed as a popper container. For electric and package-popper, follow manufacturer's directions. For metal poppers and baskets use only a small amount of dry popcorn to allow space for the corn as it pops. An exploded kernel may be 5 or 6 times its original size. Shake over high heat until popping ceases. Add butter or margarine and salt, mixing well.

For skillet popping, 1 or 2 tablespoons of butter are melted in heated pan *before adding* popcorn; about ½ cup of popcorn is added. Sprinkle with salt.

SAUCES AND BUTTERS FOR CORN-ON-THE-COB

Bacon-Sour Cream Sauce—Crumble 2 strips of crisp bacon into small pieces. Blend with ½ cup dairy sour cream.
Sour Cream-Chive Sauce—Season dairy sour cream with chopped chives. (Good, too, with green onion.)
Corn Butters—Soften ½ cup butter and blend with any of the following:

- ½ to 1 teaspoon chili powder
- 1 teaspoon curry powder
- 1 teaspoon ground oregano
- ½ teaspoon ground dill seed.

CORN COOK BOOK

Sweet and tender corn, the great American vegetable, is as versatile as it is popular

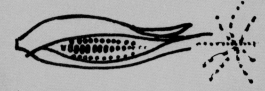

PENNSYLVANIA DUTCH CORN-CHICKEN SOUP

- 1½ cups cooked whole-kernel corn
- 1 can (10½ ounces) condensed chicken-rice soup
- 2 chicken bouillon cubes
  Water
  Salt and pepper
  Dumpling Batter

Combine corn, soup, and bouillon cubes in large saucepan. Add 3 soup cans water. Bring to boil; season to taste with salt and pepper. Dribble Dumpling Batter from spoon into gently boiling soup. Simmer for 5 minutes, or until dumplings are cooked. Makes 1½ quarts or 4 to 6 servings.

Dumpling Batter

Sift together ¾ cup all-purpose flour and ½ teaspoon salt. Cut in 1 tablespoon butter. Add 1 egg to ½ cup water and beat with fork just enough to blend. Add to flour mixture and beat with spoon until smooth.

CORN-HAM BAKE

- ½ small green pepper, chopped
- ¼ cup butter or margarine
- ¼ cup all-purpose flour
  Paprika (about ½ teaspoon)
- ¾ teaspoon salt
- ¼ teaspoon white pepper
- ⅛ teaspoon each of ground thyme and marjoram
- ½ teaspoon powdered mustard
- 2 cups milk
- 1 cup cooked cream-style corn
- 2 cups diced cooked potato
- 1 cup about (one 8-ounce can), onions, drained
- 2 cups diced cooked ham
- 1 cup shredded sharp Cheddar cheese

Sauté green pepper in butter for 5 minutes. Blend in flour, ¼ teaspoon paprika, and other seasonings. Gradually stir in milk and cook over low heat until thickened, stirring. Add corn and remaining ingredients except cheese. Mix lightly and put in shallow baking dish. Sprinkle with cheese, then with paprika. Bake in preheated hot oven (400°F.) for about 30 minutes. Makes 6 servings.

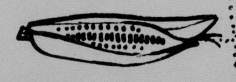

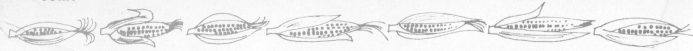

BARBECUED CORN AND MEATBALLS

Husk 4 ears of corn and remove silk. Wash and dry and break each ear in half. Season 1 pound ground beef and shape into 8 balls. On long, sharp skewers, alternately push corn and meatballs, putting 2 pieces of corn and 2 meatballs on each skewer. Put on broiler pan and broil for 10 minutes under medium heat, turning once. Then brush meat and corn with barbecue sauce and continue broiling for about 8 minutes longer, turning once and brushing with sauce. Makes 4 servings.

Note: Can be cooked on grill.

CORN AND MEAT ALL-IN-ONE

- 1 garlic clove
- 2 tablespoons cooking oil
- 1 pound beef, ground
- 1 bay leaf, crumbled
- 1 teaspoon ground sage
  Salt and pepper
- 4 cups thinly sliced raw potatoes
- 1 large onion, sliced
- 2⅓ cups (one 1-pound, 3-ounce can) tomatoes
- 2 cups cooked whole-kernel corn
  Paprika

Brown half of garlic clove in oil in large skillet. Discard garlic and brown meat slowly, breaking up with fork. Add bay leaf, sage, 1 teaspoon salt, and dash of pepper. Remove meat; brown remaining half of garlic clove in drippings; remove. Add potatoes and brown, stirring often; add onions and 1 teaspoon salt. Arrange layers of potato mixture, meat, tomatoes, and corn in 2½-quart casserole; top layer should be potato and tomato. Cover; bake in preheated moderate oven (375°F.) for about 1 hour. Sprinkle with paprika before serving. Makes 6 servings.

CORN AND SHRIMP CASSEROLE

- 2 cups (one 17-ounce can) cream-style corn
- 4 eggs, slightly beaten
- 3 tablespoons butter or margarine, melted
- 1 cup light cream
- 2 cups cooked shrimps, coarsely chopped
- ½ teaspoon hot pepper sauce
- 1½ teaspoons salt
- ⅛ teaspoon ground mace

Mix all ingredients thoroughly and turn into shallow 2-quart casserole. Bake in preheated slow oven (300°F.) for 40 minutes, or until set. Makes 6 servings.

CHILI CORN IN HUSKS

Trim ends off 8 large ears of unhusked corn. Remove about half of husks. Push remaining husks aside and remove silk. Put corn on a rack in a large covered kettle. Add about 2 cups water, cover, and steam for 20 minutes, or until corn is tender. Heat 2 to 3 teaspoons chili powder and ½ cup butter or margarine and brush on corn just before serving. Makes 4 servings.

CORN IN CREAM

- ⅔ cup light cream
- 2 tablespoons chopped parsley
- 1 teaspoon salt
- ¼ teaspoon white pepper
  Dash of garlic salt
- 4 cups whole-kernel corn

Combine all ingredients in top part of double boiler. Cover; cook over boiling water for 15 minutes, stirring occasionally. Makes 6 servings.

STEWED CORN MEDLEY

- 3 medium onions, thinly sliced
- 3 tablespoons butter or margarine
- 3 green peppers, sliced (optional)
- 3 tomatoes
- 2 cups cut fresh corn
  Seasoned salt and pepper to taste

Sauté onion in butter in saucepan for 2 to 3 minutes. Add peppers. Peel and chop tomatoes and add to mixture. Bring to boil, then simmer, covered, for 10 minutes. Add corn and simmer, covered, for 5 minutes, or until corn is tender. Season. Makes 6 servings.

Note: 2 cups (one 1-pound can) tomatoes can be substituted for the fresh. Drain tomatoes and chop.

CALIFORNIA SUCCOTASH

- 2 cups fresh Lima beans
- 4 ears of fresh corn
- 3 tablespoons butter or margarine
- ¼ cup slivered blanched almonds
- ¼ cup chopped black olives
  Salt and pepper

Cook Lima beans in small amount of boiling water for 10 minutes. Cut corn from cob and add to Limas. Cook for 10 minutes longer. Melt butter and brown almonds lightly. Drain succotash and add almonds and olives. Season with salt and pepper to taste. Makes 4 servings.

FRESH-CORN SOUFFLÉ

- 2 tablespoons butter or margarine
- 2 tablespoons all-purpose flour
- 1½ teaspoons salt
- ⅛ teaspoon pepper
- 1 cup milk
- 2 cups grated fresh corn
- 2 eggs, separated

Melt butter in heavy saucepan. Blend in flour, salt, and pepper. Gradually stir in milk. Cook over low heat, stirring constantly, until thick. Add corn and mix well. Beat egg whites until stiff and set aside. Beat egg yolks until thick and lemon-colored and stir into corn mixture. Fold in egg whites and pour into buttered 2-quart casserole. Bake in preheated moderate oven (350°F.) for about 30 minutes. Makes 4 to 6 servings.

CREAMY CORN BAKE

- 2 cups (one 1-pound can) cream-style corn
- 4 eggs, separated
- 1 teaspoon salt
- ¼ teaspoon white pepper
- 1 cup heavy cream
  Sautéed sliced fresh mushrooms (optional)

Put corn through sieve. Beat egg whites until stiff; set aside. Beat egg yolks until thick and add to corn with seasonings. Stir in cream. Then fold in egg whites. Pour into 1½-quart soufflé dish or casserole. Set in a pan of hot water and bake in preheated moderate oven (350°F.) for 30 minutes, or until firm. Serve at once with mushrooms. Makes 4 to 6 servings.

SAUTÉED CORN WITH GREEN ONION

Melt ¼ cup butter or margarine in skillet. Add 4 cups cut fresh corn and ½ cup sliced green onions with tops. Cook, covered, over medium heat for 5 minutes, or until corn is done, shaking skillet occasionally. Season with salt and pepper. Makes 4 to 6 servings.

SAUTÉED CORN AND MUSHROOMS

- 1 cup sliced fresh mushrooms or 1 can (4 ounces) sliced mushrooms, drained
- 1 tablespoon minced onion
- 2 tablespoons butter or margarine
- 3 cups cut fresh corn
- 1 teaspoon each of sugar and salt
- ¼ teaspoon pepper
  Few parsley sprigs, chopped
- 1 pimiento, cut up

Cook mushrooms and onion in butter in skillet for about 5 minutes. Add remaining ingredients except parsley and pimiento and sauté for about 5 minutes longer. Put in serving dish and sprinkle with parsley and pimiento. Makes 4 to 6 servings.

CORN QUICHE

- Pastry for 1-crust 9-inch pie, unbaked
- 1½ cups (one 12-ounce can) whole-kernel corn, drained
- ¼ cup grated Swiss or Parmesan cheese
- 5 eggs
- 1½ cups light cream
- 1 teaspoon instant minced onion
- 1 teaspoon seasoned salt
- ⅛ teaspoon pepper
- 4 slices of crisp bacon, crumbled

Line 9-inch pie pan with pastry. Mix corn and cheese and put in bottom of pastry-lined pan. Beat eggs with cream, onion, and seasonings. Pour over corn. Sprinkle with bacon. Bake in preheated hot oven (400°F.) for 25 minutes. Reduce heat to moderate (350°F.) and bake for about 20 minutes longer. Serve at once. Makes 6 servings.

Corn Fritters   **Sautéed Corn and Mushroom**

Baked Corn-Stuffed Tomatoes

Pennsylvania Dutch Corn Relish

Corn Relish

BAKED CORN-STUFFED TOMATOES

6 firm ripe medium tomatoes
5 or 6 ears corn, cooked
2 tablespoons each of minced onion and green pepper
1 tablespoon butter
2 tablespoons cream
  Salt and pepper
  Buttered crumbs or grated cheese

Cut off stem end of tomatoes and scoop out seeds and pulp, leaving shell intact. Turn upside down to drain. With sharp knife cut off kernels of corn and scrape out pulp with back of knife. There should be about 2 cups. Cook onion and green pepper in butter for 2 to 3 minutes and mix with corn and cream. Season to taste and fill tomatoes with the mixture. Put in shallow baking dish and sprinkle tops with crumbs. Bake in preheated hot oven (400°F.) for about 15 minutes. Makes 6 servings.

SUCCOTASH WITH BACON

Cut ¼ pound slab bacon into large cubes, and fry slowly until well browned and done. Remove bacon. Pour off all but 2 tablespoons fat from skillet. In remaining fat, sauté 1 small minced onion for 2 or 3 minutes. Cook ½ pound green beans, cut, and 2 cups Lima beans in small amount of boiling salted water for about 15 minutes. To beans, add corn cut from 4 to 5 ears and simmer for 5 minutes. Add onion and ½ cup cream; season with salt and pepper. Heat, and serve topped with bacon. Makes 6 servings.

CORN, TOMATO, AND CELERY SALAD

1 package (10 ounces) frozen cut corn
½ medium green pepper, diced
1 cup sliced celery
1 cup diced fresh tomatoes
  Salt to taste
  French dressing
  Chicory or other salad greens
  Onion rings

Cook corn as directed on the label; drain and cool. Add next 4 ingredients and French dressing to moisten. Chill, and serve on greens with a garnish of onion rings. Makes 6 servings.

BACON, EGG, AND CORN PANCAKES

4 slices of bacon
1 hard-cooked egg, chopped
1 cup cooked whole-kernel corn
1 raw egg
1¼ cups milk
2 tablespoons cooking oil
1 package (12 ounces) or 2 cups corn-muffin mix

Dice bacon and cook until crisp. Reserve bacon fat. Mix bacon with remaining ingredients. Spoon onto hot griddle greased with bacon fat and brown on both sides. Serve with butter and syrup. Makes about 2 dozen 3½-inch cakes.

CORN PIE

1¼ cups fine saltine-cracker crumbs
½ cup melted butter or margarine
1¼ cups milk
2 cups cut fresh or frozen corn
½ teaspoon salt
¼ teaspoon white pepper
2 tablespoons instant minced onion
2 tablespoons all-purpose flour
2 eggs, beaten
  Paprika

Combine crumbs and ½ cup melted butter. Set aside about ½ cup of mixture; with spoon press remainder into 9-inch pie pan to form a shell. Mix 1 cup milk, corn, salt, pepper, and onion in saucepan. Bring to boil, reduce heat, and simmer for 3 minutes. Blend flour and remaining ¼ cup milk; stir into hot mixture and cook, stirring, until thickened. Cool slightly. Gradually add eggs, stirring vigorously. Pour into lined pie pan and sprinkle with reserved crumbs and paprika. Bake in preheated hot oven (400°F.) for about 15 minutes. Cut into wedges and serve hot. Makes 6 servings.

FRESH-CORN CAKES

2 cups fresh cream-style corn
1 teaspoon baking powder
1 teaspoon sugar
¾ teaspoon salt
  Dash of pepper
1 tablespoon melted butter
1 tablespoon cream
2 eggs, separated

Combine all ingredients except eggs. Beat egg whites until stiff and set aside. Beat egg yolks until thick and lemon-colored. Stir yolks into first mixture, then fold in whites. For each cake drop 2 tablespoonfuls onto hot lightly greased griddle, and brown on both sides. Makes about 4 dozen 3-inch cakes.
Note: If cakes seem too tender to handle, stir a little flour into batter.

CORN FRITTERS

1 egg, beaten
½ cup milk
2 cups cut fresh corn
1½ cups sifted all-purpose flour
2 teaspoons baking powder
1 teaspoon salt
  Dash of pepper
1 tablespoon melted bacon fat or butter
  Fat for deep frying

Mix egg, milk, and corn. Sift dry ingredients and add to corn mixture. Add bacon fat and beat until well blended. Drop by tablespoonfuls into hot deep fat (375°F. on a frying thermometer) and cook until golden brown. Drain on ab-

sorbent paper, and serve hot. Makes 4 servings.

SKILLET CORN FRITTERS

1 package (10 ounces) frozen whole-kernel corn, thawed
  Milk
2 tablespoons butter, melted
½ cup unsifted all-purpose flour
¾ teaspoon baking powder
1 teaspoon salt
⅛ teaspoon pepper
2 eggs, beaten
  Fat for frying

Drain corn in strainer, pressing slightly against sides. Measure corn liquid and add milk to make ¼ cup. Mix all ingredients except fat until blended. Drop by tablespoonfuls into ½ inch of hot fat and fry until golden brown on both sides. Makes 4 to 6 servings.
Note: If using electric skillet, set temperature control for 375°F.

DOUBLE CORN STICKS

Prepare 1 package corn-muffin mix as directed on label. Add 1 cup cooked drained whole-kernel corn. Heat cornstick pans and brush generously with cooking oil. Half fill with batter and bake in preheated hot oven (400°F.) for about 20 minutes. To glaze, remove sticks from pan and brush tops with corn syrup. Makes 8 to 10.

PENNSYLVANIA DUTCH CORN RELISH

20 ears of yellow corn
6 green peppers, seeded and chopped
6 red peppers, seeded and chopped
4 large yellow onions, sliced
1 large head green cabbage, cored and chopped
4 cups sugar
2 tablespoons powdered mustard
2 tablespoons celery seed
2 tablespoons salt
1 tablespoon ground turmeric
5 cups cider vinegar
1 cup water

Cut corn off the cobs. Combine with all other ingredients. Cook for 20 minutes. Place in hot sterilized jars and seal at once. Makes 10 pints.

POPCORN WITH CHEESE

Pour a small amount of melted bacon fat over popped corn. Sprinkle with grated Parmesan cheese. Heat in preheated slow oven (325°F.) for 8 to 10 minutes, stirring often.

CORN, TO—This term covers a process by which protein foods, meats, poultry, game, and fish, are preserved in a liquid solution of salt, sugar, and saltpeter which is called brine. The salt actually preserves the food, the sugar keeps the salt from hardening the food, and the saltpeter intensifies and preserves the color. After corning, the food may be used as is, or processed further by smoking or drying.

Corning is a very old process of preserving meats. The term comes from the Old English word "corn," meaning "grain," or any small particle, and it is a reminder that originally corning was done with dry granular salt rather than in a brine.

Foods to be corned should be fresh. Foods that have been frozen do not corn well since their cellular structure, already softened by the freezing, would be softened further to a mushy, unpalatable texture by the corning process.

To Corn Meat

Remove bones and cut into uniform pieces. For each 25 pounds of meat allow 2 pounds of granulated plain, not iodized, salt. Use a wood or stone container. Starting and ending with salt, layer salt and meat. Let stand overnight. Make a brine of 1 pound sugar, 1 tablespoon baking soda, 2 tablespoons saltpeter, and 1 quart water. Pour brine over meat and weight top to keep meat under the brine. Keep in a cool place (under 45°F.). Cure for 4 to 6 weeks. Keep meat in brine until ready to use.

Note: The cuts of beef most generally used for corning are rump, brisket, and plate.

CORNED BEEF AND CABBAGE

Cover 4 pounds corned beef with boiling water in a kettle and bring to boil. Cover and simmer for 30 minutes. Drain, cover with fresh boiling water, and simmer until meat is tender. Do not boil. Cut 1 head cabbage into 8 wedges. About 15 minutes before beef is done, add cabbage. Cook, uncovered, for 10 to 15 minutes. Serve hot with boiled potatoes and mustard on the side. Makes 8 servings.

CORNED-BEEF HASH

2 cups chopped cooked corned beef
2 cups chopped boiled potato
1 tablespoon minced onion
⅓ cup cream, milk, or stock
    Salt and pepper to taste
2 tablespoons butter or margarine

Mix all ingredients except butter. Melt butter in heavy skillet, add hash, and pat down evenly. Cook very slowly until browned on the bottom. Fold like an omelet and turn out onto a hot platter. Makes 4 servings.

Note: If crisp brown bits are desired throughout hash, scrape up bottom occasionally.

■ **Variation**—For Baked Corned-Beef Hash spread hash mixture in shallow baking dish and bake in preheated moderate oven (375°F.) 15 to 20 minutes.

CORNMEAL—This is corn, coarsely ground. In "new-process" cornmeal the corn is ground after the hull and germ of the kernel are removed. In "old-process" cornmeal, the whole grain is ground into meal. Although old-process cornmeal is richer in vitamin-A content, new-process cornmeal keeps better because it has a lower fat content.

Cornmeal is used in many parts of the world in much the way we use bread or potatoes. Italy's famous *polenta* and Rumania's *mamaliga* are cornmeal cooked into a thick mush, served by itself, or with a sauce, milk, meat, or vegetables, or fried.

Availability—Both old-process and new-process cornmeal are available in either yellow or white meal. (The color depends on the variety of corn used.)

Storage—New-process cornmeal can be kept, tightly covered, in a cool, dry place. Old-process cornmeal should be refrigerated:

☐ New process, kitchen shelf: 6 months
☐ Old process, refrigerator shelf: 6 months

Caloric Value

☐ 3½ ounces, enriched, cooked = 46 to 50 calories

CORN BREAD

1 cup all-purpose flour
¾ cup cornmeal
2 teaspoons baking powder
¾ teaspoon salt
2 tablespoons sugar
1 egg, beaten
¾ cup milk
¼ cup butter or margarine, melted

Mix first 5 ingredients. Add egg, milk and butter. Stir until blended. (Do not overmix.) Spread into greased pan (8 x 8 x 2 inches) and bake in preheated hot oven (425°F.) for 20 to 25 minutes.

Corn Muffins

Prepare batter as in recipe for Corn Bread. Spoon into greased muffin pans, filling pans two thirds full. Bake in preheated hot oven (425°F.) for 25 minutes, or until lightly brown. Makes 8 large muffins.

DOUBLE-CORN SPOON BREAD

3½ cups milk
1 cup yellow cornmeal
2 teaspoons salt
2 cups (one 1-pound can) cream-style corn
2 tablespoons butter or margarine
5 eggs, well beaten

Heat 3 cups milk in top part of double boiler over hot water. Mix cornmeal with salt and remaining milk. Add to hot milk; cook, stirring, until thick; cover and cook for about 5 minutes. Add corn and cook for a few minutes longer. Add butter and stir until melted. Cool slightly. Fold in eggs. Put in greased 2-quart casserole. Bake in preheated moderate oven (375°F.) for 1 hour, or until firm but light. Serve at once with lots of butter. (Spoon bread will sink when removed from oven.) Makes 6 servings.

CORN OIL—A nonhydrogenated oil obtained from the kernel of corn. After refining it has no taste or odor. It is used extensively in the United States for salad dressings, for frying, and as a shortening in baking.

CORNSTARCH—This is a starch obtained from the endosperm portion of the kernel. It is used as a thickener in sauces, gravies, and puddings. It is also the basis of laundry starch. Cornstarch is used either alone or combined with white flour in much European baking, especially that of the Scandinavian countries. It gives cakes a finer, more compact, and drier texture. It makes them easier to slice and it insures their keeping quality.

COOKING WITH CORNSTARCH

■ When cornstarch is mixed with cold liquids, it will settle out on standing, so stir well just before using.

■ When cooking it, do not stir vigorously or mixture will not be smooth and even. A double boiler gives the best results and prevents scorching.

■ Cornstarch mixtures should not be overcooked because this causes "weeping" when mixture cools. Cook just to the boiling point and for 1 minute after. Then cool at room temperature without stirring. After cooling, mixture can be stored in the refrigerator. To keep a skin from forming on puddings, dust the top with sugar.

■ Acid affects the thickening quality. When making such things as citrus-fruit pies and puddings, cook cornstarch until thick before adding acids such as lemon juice and orange juice.

CORN SYRUP—This is a syrup obtained from cornstarch and is made in two kinds: light and dark. Light corn syrup has been clarified and decolorized. Dark syrup has a stronger flavor. Both are used in home cooking for ice cream, frozen desserts, frostings, candy making, canning, jams, and jellies. Corn syrup is also used as a pancake or waffle syrup.

In making frostings, candy, and frozen

deskserts, corn syrup is used to give a smooth, creamy texture. In canning foods, jams, and jellies, corn syrup gives a clear, sparkling product.

Caloric Value

☐ Table blends, 3½ ounces = 290 calories

COSTMARY (Chrysanthemum balsamita)—This hardy herb is a perennial which spreads from underground parts, forming clumps with erect stems reaching from three to four feet. The foliage is quite dense and the leaves have a sweet, minty, lemony fragrance. Costmary is native to western Asia and will grow in all temperate zones. It can be seen growing wild on the edges of old orchards or near old farms in the eastern and midwestern parts of the United States.

Costmary has a variety of popular names. "Bible leaf" comes from the use of its broad, long leaves by the early colonists as bookmarks in their Bibles. Known to the English as "alecost," it was used at one time to flavor beer and ale. In some localities, costmary is called "sweet Mary" or "sweet tongue." Like so many other herbs, it was introduced into Europe by Greek physicians who searched for plants they felt had great curative powers. In medieval times it was probably one of the sweet herbs strewn on floors and used for scenting the washing water at meals. The English planted costmary in their herb gardens and from England the colonists brought it here.

Costmary is a favorite in herb teas.

Fresh leaves may be used to flavor cakes, game, meats, and poultry. Caution in use must be exercised because the flavor is fairly strong.

COUPE—In French, this word means a "cup" or "goblet." It is also used to describe a dessert served in these dishes. This latter meaning is also the English one, and refers specifically to a dessert of ice cream topped with sauce, a syrup, a fruit, nuts, or whipped-cream garnish, served in a cupped glass dish.

Coupes are elaborate party desserts, but they can be prepared ahead of mealtime and refrigerated until serving time.

A coupe differs from a parfait only because a parfait is served in a tall, narrow glass. The ingredients are about the same.

COURSE—A course is a part of a meal consisting of one dish or of one dish plus the accompaniments served with it. There was a time when the formal dinner demanded no fewer than eight and often ten or twelve courses. The eight-course dinner was served in the following order: hors-d'oeuvre (small cold appetizers); soup (preferably clear); fish (often more than one kind); entrée (a variety of light dishes such as rissoles and croquettes plus fillets and cutlets); remove (the main course and usually a joint of meat served with vegetables, although poultry could be served instead or as an addition); roast (poultry or game); entremets (three minor courses comprising dressed vegetables, hot and cold sweets such as jellies and puddings, and savories such as cheese and sardines); dessert (fruit, ices, *petits fours*) and coffee.

With today's trend toward simpler dining, even the most formal dinner consists of only five or six courses, with little or no choice of dishes within a course. Soup or a fruit or seafood cocktail starts the meal followed by a fish or seafood course; a roast with vegetables; salad; dessert; and after-dinner coffee. The most commonly served courses in an informal or regular American dinner include an appetizer and/or soup; a main course featuring a meat, fish, poultry, cheese, or egg dish which may be accompanied by vegetables; a salad (sometimes served as the first course, or with the main course, or after it); and dessert and coffee.

COURT BOUILLON—"Short broth" is the literal translation of this French term, which stands for a liquid in which fish or seafood is poached. A court

bouillon can be as simple as salted water, or it can be a broth made with wine and seasonings.

A salt-water court bouillon is used for sea bass, red snapper, striped bass, and for fish that have a distinctive flavor in themselves so that they do not need artificial seasonings. The proportions used are one and a half teaspoons salt to one quart of water.

Salmon, halibut, cod, and seafood profit from a court bouillon pleasantly flavored with wine or lemon or vinegar, herbs, and spices, to which the bones and heads of fish may or may not be added for additional flavor. A flavored court bouillon may also be cooked down and used as an ingredient for fish sauces or as the base for aspics and glazes.

COURT BOUILLON, FLAVORED

2 pounds fish bones and heads
3 quarts water
4 cups dry wine, red or white
   Bouquet garni of thyme, parsley, and ½ medium onion
2 celery stalks with leaves
1 onion stuck with 2 cloves
2 carrots, cut into pieces
1 tablespoon salt

Simmer, covered, the fish bones and heads in 2 quarts of the water for 20 minutes. Strain. Add remaining water and other ingredients to broth. Simmer, covered, for 20 more minutes. Add fish and cook according to recipe. Makes about 3 quarts.

■ **Variation**—Omit fish bones and heads. Combine all other ingredients and simmer for 30 minutes.

Note: If the court bouillon is wanted for sauces or glaze, cook it down to about ⅓ of its volume.

FILLETS OF SOLE IN COURT BOUILLON

   Few parsley sprigs, chopped
2 green onions, chopped
1 teaspoon salt
⅛ teaspoon white pepper
1 cup white wine
½ cup water
2 pounds sole fillets
3 tablespoons butter or margarine
2 tablespoons all-purpose flour
1 cup heavy cream
1 egg yolk

To prepare court bouillon, put first 6 ingredients in skillet and bring to boil. Simmer for 5 minutes. Add fish and poach for about 10 minutes. Remove fish to a shallow broilerproof casserole; reduce liquid to 1 cup. In top part of double boiler melt 2 tablespoons butter and blend in flour. Add fish liquid and half of cream. Cook, stirring, until thickened. Mix remaining cream and egg yolk. Pour small amount of sauce over egg mixture, stirring. Pour back into double boiler and cook for a few minutes longer, stirring. Add remaining butter and pour over fish. Brown under broiler. Makes 6 servings.

CRAB—Crabs are crustaceans, animals with a shell, which have a short tail and ten legs. A crab's head has short feelers, two eyes on stalks, and feeding appendages around the mouth, and it is fused into one piece with the body. Walking or crawling sideways is their usual way of locomotion. There are many varieties of them, in waters all over the world.

Crabs live in salt or fresh water. Salt-water crabs are more numerous. They breed in rocks under water where they can seek refuge in the crevices from enemies.

Crabs are the second most popular shellfish in the United States (shrimp is first). The hard-shell, or blue, crab of the Atlantic, the Dungeness of the Pacific, and the Alaskan king crab are the most readily available in food stores.

The soft-shell crab is not a distinct species; it is simply the blue crab which has shed its shell. When a Chesapeake Bay fisherman spots crabs just about to molt, he sets these "peelers" off in special floats until they shed their shells. An extra hour in the water allows the new shell to harden enough to withstand shipping. Careful watch must be kept, for the whole process takes no more than eight hours.

Availability—Hard-shell (or blue) crabs are available live in-the-shell year-round in coastal areas. Soft-shell crabs are also available live, with peak season in July and August. Rock crab, a hard-shell variety, is available live in the New England area and Dungeness crab along the Pacific coast. Crabmeat can be purchased freshly cooked and iced.

Hard-shell crab is also available canned; Dungeness crab is available frozen; King (or Alaska) crab is available canned and frozen.

Purchasing Guide—Fresh crab in-the-shell should be alive when sold. Crabs have a fresh sea smell and are usually packed in seaweed.

You can get canned hard-shell crabs as lump meat, which is white in color and considered the choice meat; flake meat, also white in color; flake and lump meat combined; and claw meat, which is brownish in color on the outside.

The frozen Dungeness crab has body and claw meat packed together and is reddish in color.

Canned and frozen King crabmeat is reddish in color.

Storage—Cook fresh crabs immediately, refrigerate, and use as soon as possible.
- ☐ Fresh, refrigerator shelf, cooked and covered: 1 to 2 days
- ☐ Canned, kitchen shelf: 1 year
- ☐ Canned, refrigerator shelf, opened and covered: 1 to 2 days
- ☐ Frozen, refrigerator frozen-food compartment: 1 month
- ☐ Frozen, freezer: 6 months

Nutritive Food Values—Good source of protein, low in calories and fat; fair source of calcium and niacin.
- ☐ 3½ ounces, cooked or canned = 93 calories

Basic Preparation

☐ **To Cook Hard-Shell Crabs**—Live crabs should be plunged into boiling salted water or bouillon. Cover tightly. Simmer for 8 minutes per pound. Serve as is with melted butter and lemon; or cool, split body, remove back, and pull out meat. Split claws and remove meat carefully. Use as directed in cooked crabmeat recipes. If served whole, provide claw crackers and picks for removing meat.

☐ **To Prepare Soft-Shell Crabs for Cooking**—Stick a small sharp knife into body of crab between the eyes to kill it. Then lift up the pointed ends of the soft shell and remove the spongy white fibers (the gills). Turn crab over on its back and remove the aprons from the underneath part of body. All the rest is edible, including the small legs and fins. Wash crabs, drain, and cook at once. See recipes. Can be sautéed, broiled, fried.

☐ **To Prepare Canned Crabmeat**—Remove small shell pieces. Has a more crumbly texture than fresh or frozen crabmeat; should be handled carefully. It is generally used in recipes where crabmeat is flaked.

☐ **To Prepare Frozen Crabmeat**—Defrost, drain well. Cook as little as possible or it will toughen. Season and sauce delicately to enhance mild flavor of crabmeat. Use after thawing and draining as you would use cooked crabmeat.

Cook pieces frozen with shell in frozen state after washing off ice cover. Cook for 3 to 4 minutes under broiler, shell side up; turn and broil for 3 to 4 minutes, meat side up. Brush well with melted butter during cooking. Can also be sautéed.

CRAB, IN-THE-SHELL

MARYLAND STEAMED HARD-SHELL CRABS

Get as many crabs as you want, but allow at least 4 large crabs per person. Place on a rack that will fit into a large container with a tight-fitting lid. Pour vinegar, about ½ to ¾ inch deep, into container. Place container over heat and when vinegar begins to steam, place rack with crabs in container. Sprinkle crabs with 3 tablespoons salt, 1 tablespoon powdered mustard, and 1 tablespoon black or red pepper. Cover and allow to steam until crabs turn red and aprons can be readily lifted, about 25 to 30 minutes. Remove at once, drain on absorbent paper, and come and get it! Serve with buttered rye bread and beer. Have mallets and claw crackers handy.

FRIED SOFT-SHELL CRABS

Prepare as directed in Basic Preparation. Season with salt and pepper and fry in 1 inch of butter or margarine in a skillet for about 7 minutes on each side.

■ **Variation**—Dip the seasoned crabs into bread crumbs, then into egg, and again into crumbs, and fry in shallow fat until brown on both sides. Seasoned flour can also be used instead of bread crumbs, but real Marylanders prefer their soft crabs just seasoned and fried in butter or other fat. Serve on toast with tartare sauce and French-fries.

FRIED SOFT-SHELL CRABS AMANDINE

12 soft-shell crabs
    Paprika, salt, and pepper
¾ cup butter
3 tablespoons each of chopped shallots
    and parsley
¾ cup sherry
¾ cup almond slivers

Clean crabs (see Basic Preparation). Dust crabs liberally with salt, pepper, and paprika. Heat butter in skillet; add crabs, on backs, and sear. Lower heat, turn crabs, add rest of ingredients, and cook slowly for 20 minutes. Serve at once with crusty rolls and tossed salad.

BAKED STUFFED SOFT-SHELL CRABS

6 medium soft-shell crabs
    Salt and pepper to taste
12 wedges of cheese
1 egg, beaten
½ cup bread crumbs
1 small can (8 ounces) tomato sauce

Clean and dry crabs. Season with salt and pepper. Lift up back on each end of crab and place 2 wedges of cheese inside. Dip into beaten egg, then into bread crumbs. Place crabs in a greased baking dish, pour tomato sauce over them, and bake in preheated moderate oven (350° F.) for 40 minutes. Makes 6 servings.
Note: Serve with tartare sauce, French-fries, and tossed salad. Crusty rolls and a beverage complete a delicious meal.

CRABMEAT

CRAB NEWBURG

3 egg yolks
1 cup heavy cream
2 tablespoons butter
1 pound lump crabmeat
2 tablespoons sherry
    Frozen puff-pastry shells

In a saucepan beat egg yolks with cream. Add butter. Cook over low heat, stirring constantly until butter melts. Do not boil. Add crabmeat which has had fibers removed, and heat. Stir in wine. Heat, stirring, until piping hot. Serve over hot baked puff-pastry shells. Makes 4 servings.

CRAB CAKES

2 slices of bread with crusts removed
    Milk
1 pound fresh or canned crabmeat,
    flaked, with fibers removed
¼ teaspoon fish-herb blend
½ teaspoon salt
1 tablespoon each of mayonnaise,
    Worcestershire, chopped parsley, and
    baking powder
1 egg, beaten
    Fat for frying

Break bread into small pieces and moisten with milk. Press out excess milk. Mix with remaining ingredients except fat and shape into cakes. Fry until brown. Makes 4 servings.

DEVILED CRABS

1½ cups fresh or canned crabmeat
    Butter
¼ cup cracker crumbs
¾ cup milk or cream

2 eggs
¼ teaspoon salt
¾ teaspoon powdered mustard
1 teaspoon prepared horseradish
    Dash of cayenne
    Dash of hot pepper sauce

Flake crabmeat and remove fibers. Melt 1 tablespoon butter; add cracker crumbs and milk and bring to a boil. Remove from heat. Beat remaining ingredients and gradually stir in milk mixture. Add crabmeat and pack into crab shells or ramekins. Brush top with melted butter and bake in preheated moderate oven (375°F.) for about 20 minutes. Makes 4 servings.

IMPERIAL CRAB

1 pound fresh or canned crabmeat,
    fibers removed
    Crumbs from 2 slices of dry bread
    without crusts
½ cup mayonnaise
1 tablespoon each of prepared mustard,
    Worcestershire, fresh lemon juice, and
    drained capers
    Dash of hot pepper sauce
    Buttered crumbs

Flake crabmeat; mix with bread crumbs, mayonnaise, and seasonings. Fill buttered ramekins, cover with buttered crumbs, and bake in preheated moderate oven (350°F.) for 30 minutes. Makes 4 servings.

CRAB-MUSHROOM CASSEROLE

¼ cup butter or margarine
¼ cup all-purpose flour
2 tablespoons finely chopped onion
¼ cup finely chopped celery
¼ cup finely chopped green pepper
1 pound fresh mushrooms
2 cups chicken bouillon (can be made
    with bouillon cubes)
2 egg yolks, slightly beaten
¾ teaspoon salt
    Dash of ground ginger
1 pound fresh crabmeat
¼ cup grated cheese

Melt butter in saucepan, blend in flour and onion, celery and green pepper. Cook until golden. Clean mushrooms, slice, and add to mixture in saucepan; cook for 10 minutes. Gradually stir in bouillon. Cook over low heat, stirring, until mixture thickens. Remove from heat and stir into slightly beaten egg yolks, salt, and ginger. Stir in crabmeat with fibers removed. Pour into a 1½-quart baking dish, sprinkle with cheese, and bake in preheated moderate oven (350° F.) 45 minutes, or until top is browned. Serve hot in wedges with hot biscuits and a salad. Makes 6 to 8 servings.

CURRIED CRAB SALAD

3 pounds fresh lump crabmeat
1 cup mayonnaise
1 tablespoon heavy cream
½ teaspoon curry powder
1 tablespoon each of grated onion and
    minced parsley
¼ cup chili sauce
2 tablespoons each of sherry and lemon
    juice
¼ teaspoon pepper
    Lettuce cups
    Tomato slices

    Stuffed olives
    Parsley sprigs

Carefully remove fibers from crabmeat. Keep crabmeat chilled while combining rest of ingredients. Fold crabmeat lumps into the sauce carefully so as not to break lumps. Chill thoroughly. Serve in lettuce cups garnished with tomato slices, stuffed olives, and parsley sprigs. Serve with hot biscuits or rolls for a delicious meal. Makes 10 to 12 servings.
Note: This salad improves by standing for a few hours in coldest place in refrigerator. It is also excellent for picnics.

CRAB LOUIS

    Lettuce leaves
1 cup finely shredded lettuce
2 cups cooked flaked crabmeat
1 cup Sauce Louis
2 hard-cooked eggs, sliced
2 tablespoons finely chopped chives
    or green onion tops

Line a bowl with lettuce leaves. Place shredded lettuce on bottom of bowl. Pile crabmeat on shredded lettuce. Top with Sauce Louis. Surround with hard-cooked egg slices. Sprinkle with chives. Makes 4 servings.

Sauce Louis

½ cup mayonnaise
2 tablespoons heavy cream
2 tablespoons chili sauce
½ teaspoon Worcestershire
2 tablespoons minced green pepper
2 tablespoons finely minced onion or
    scallion
1 tablespoon fresh lemon juice
    Salt and pepper

Combine first 7 ingredients and blend well. Season with salt and pepper to taste. Makes about 1 cup.

CRAB APPLE—This is the fruit of a number of native American or Asiatic shrubs or small trees that belong to the rose family. Some of the trees are extremely ornamental. Crab apples are small and acid and are used for making jellies or for spicing. Spiced crab apples are served with meats.

Fresh crab apples are available in the fall. Spiced crab apples, packed in jars, are sold year round.

SPICED CRAB APPLES

6 pounds (about 4 quarts) red crab
    apples
    Whole cloves
4 cups cider vinegar
4 cups water
8 cups sugar
2 tablespoons broken cinnamon sticks
1 tablespoon whole allspice
    Red food coloring

Wash crab apples but do not remove stems. Stick 2 or 3 cloves into each. Combine vinegar, water, and sugar in large heavy kettle. Add cinnamon and allspice, tied loosely in cheesecloth bag. Boil for 10 minutes. Add a few drops of red food coloring and crab apples, a few at a time. Simmer each batch for about 10 minutes, or until tender. Fill hot sterilized jars with crab apples. When all are cooked and packed, strain syrup; bring to boil; fill jars to brim with boiling syrup, and seal. Makes about 4 pints.

CRACKER—This is a small to medium-size, thin, crisp, unsweetened, usually commercially baked product which Americans consume by the millions. In England, the word cracker is rarely used in this sense: "biscuit" is used instead, for both nonsweet and sweet products.

Availability and Purchasing Guide—Crackers come in dozens of types, shapes, sizes, thicknesses, textures, and flavors.

Cracker meal and cracker crumbs can be bought commercially packaged.

The crackers you choose depend upon use planned: Here are some of the common varieties with serving suggestions.

TYPE	APPROPRIATE USE
Animal, Arrowroot	For babies and young children
Bacon	As a snack; with vegetable juices or salads
Beef	As a base for canapes; for snacks; with cocktails or salads
Butter	With milk drinks; to crumble for toppings in cooking
Celery	As a snack; with cocktails or salads
Cheese	As a base for canapes; a snack; with cocktails, vegetable juices, or salads
Chicken	As a snack; with cocktails
Garlic	As a snack; with vegetable juices or salads
Graham	With fruit and milk drinks; baby food; to make dessert sandwiches with ice cream or frosting; to make pie crusts; crumbled as a topping
Onion	As a snack; a base for canapes; with vegetable juices or salads
Oyster, Pilot	With fish chowders, bisques, and stews
Pretzels	With vegetable juices, beer, other beverages; as a snack
Rye Wafers	With salads, soups, sharp cheese, vegetable juices, low-calorie meals
Saltines	With salads and cheeses
Soda Crackers	Crumbled as toppings; with seafood cocktails, salads, and soups
Triscuits, Water Biscuits, and Rusks	With cheese, peanut butter, etc., for snacks
Whole-Wheat Wafers	With cheeses and salads; as a base for canapes

Storage—All crackers should be stored in airtight containers in a cool, dry place.

Caloric Values

- ☐ Graham crackers, 4 small or 2 medium = 55 calories
- ☐ Oyster crackers, 10 crackers = 45 calories
- ☐ Saltines, 2 inches square, 2 crackers = 35 calories
- ☐ Soda crackers, plain, 2½ inches square, 2 crackers = 45 calories
- ☐ Cracker meal, 3½ ounces = 439 calories

CRACKLING—This is the crisp residue of the skin of fried or roasted pork, duck, or goose after the fat has been rendered during the cooking process. Crackling is also the crisp remains of rendered lard or salt pork. The flavor and texture of crackling are beloved by many, especially in the southern part of the United States, where crackling is baked into a popular corn bread.

CRACKLING CORN BREAD
1½ cups white cornmeal
¾ cup sifted all-purpose flour
2 teaspoons baking powder
½ teaspoon each of baking soda and salt
1 cup sour milk or buttermilk
1 cup diced cracklings

Mix dry ingredients. Add milk and stir until smooth. Fold in cracklings. Shape into small flat oblong cakes and put on greased cookie sheet. Bake in preheated hot oven (400°F.) for about 30 minutes. Makes 8 to 10.

CRANBERRY—A bright red berry of a plant, *Vaccinium*, of the heath family. In both the northern part of North America and in northern Europe different varieties of cranberries grow on low trailing woody plants in bogs and places with wet acid soil. In America, cran-

berries have been cultivated since 1840 and they form an important commercial crop. Massachusetts, in the Cape Cod region, grows about seventy per cent of the cranberry crop.

Wild cranberries were cooked with honey or maple sugar by the Indians and also dried for winter use long before the first settlers arrived on these shores. They were probably the first native American fruit eaten in Europe since, thanks to their excellent keeping qualities, they were packed in plain water and shipped by the ton to the Old World. Sailors ate them on long voyages as a scurvy-preventive.

Cranberries are highly prized in northern Europe, especially in the Scandinavian countries. Their local varieties, called lingonberries, are spicier than ours. Incidentally, cranberries are one of the rare cultivated berries that taste as good as the wild berries.

Availability—Fresh cranberries are available chiefly in fall and winter. Crop comes from Massachusetts, Wisconsin, Washington, and New Jersey.

Canned cranberries are available all year, jellied and whole in regular or dietetic sauce. Cranberry-juice cocktail is also available, as is a cranberry-orange relish. Frozen cranberries are available.

Purchasing Guide—Fresh berries should be firm and plump. A high luster indicates ripeness. Avoid soft, shriveled, dull-appearing cranberries. Color, which varies from bright to dark red depending on variety, also determines quality. Most common are medium-large bright-red fruit and smaller darker-colored kinds.

- ☐ Fresh, 1 pound bag or windowed box = 4 cups jellied or whole berry sauce
- ☐ Canned, 6 to 8 ounces, whole or jellied = ¾ to 1 cup
- ☐ Frozen fresh, 1 pound = 4 cups

Storage—Sort fresh cranberries, discarding any with soft, brown spots. Store them, unwashed but covered, in refrigerator until ready to use. Moisture hastens spoilage. Good-quality cranberries may be stored in the original package.

Store canned cranberries and cranberry juice in a dry cool place, away from direct light or heat.

- ☐ Fresh, refrigerator shelf: 1 to 4 weeks
- ☐ Fresh, refrigerator frozen-food compartment, prepared for freezing: 2 to 3 months
- ☐ Fresh or frozen, freezer, prepared for freezing: 1 year
- ☐ Canned, kitchen shelf: 1 year
- ☐ Canned, refrigerator shelf, opened and covered: 4 to 5 weeks

Nutritive Food Values—Cranberries are high in vitamin C.

- ☐ 3½ ounces, raw = 46 calories
- ☐ 3½ ounces, sauce = 146 calories
- ☐ 3½ ounces, juice = 65 calories

Basic Preparation—Sort fresh cranberries and wash before use.

Frozen berries may be cooked without thawing. They are ground more easily unthawed. Thaw frozen berries only when they are to be used without cooking.

□ **To Freeze**—Cranberries may be frozen after sorting and rinsing. Just pour cranberries into freezer package, allowing 1-inch headspace.

JELLIED CRANBERRY-TURKEY LOAF

Cranberry Layer
1 envelope unflavored gelatin
½ cup cold water
1¾ cups (1-pound can) whole-berry cranberry sauce
1 cup (one 9-ounce can) crushed pineapple
⅓ cup broken walnut meats
1 tablespoon fresh lemon juice

Turkey Layer
1 envelope unflavored gelatin
¾ cup cold water
¾ cup mayonnaise
2 tablespoons fresh lemon juice
Grated rind of ½ lemon
½ teaspoon salt
2 cups diced leftover cooked turkey
½ cup diced celery

■ **To Make Cranberry Layer**—Sprinkle gelatin on cold water to soften. Let stand for 5 minutes. Stir until dissolved over hot water or low heat. Blend in remaining ingredients thoroughly and turn into loaf pan (9 x 5 x 3 inches). Chill until almost firm.

■ **To Make Turkey Layer**—Dissolve gelatin as for cranberry layer. Stir in mayonnaise, lemon juice and rind, and salt. Chill until of the consistency of unbeaten egg whites. Fold in remaining ingredients. Spoon over cranberry layer. Chill until firm. Turn out on greens. Makes 6 to 8 servings.

BAKED CRANBERRY HAM CUBES
4 cups diced cooked ham
3 tablespoons butter or margarine
½ cup water
½ cup sugar
1¼ cups cranberries, washed
2 tablespoons grated orange rind
Salt and pepper to taste

Lightly brown ham in butter in skillet. Bring water and sugar to boil in saucepan, stirring until sugar is dissolved. Add ¾ cup cranberries and simmer, covered, for 15 minutes. Add orange rind and seasonings. Combine ham and cranberry mixture and pour into baking dish. Bake, uncovered, in preheated moderate oven (350°F.) for about 20 minutes. Add remaining ½ cup cranberries; bake 10 to 15 minutes longer. Makes 6 servings.

CRANBERRY-MINT SAUCE
Bring to boil 1¾ cups (1 pound can) whole-berry cranberry sauce. Stir in 3 drops of oil of peppermint and serve with lamb patties or roast lamb. Makes 6 to 8 servings.

CRANBERRY-RAISIN PIE
2 cups whole raw cranberries, washed
½ cup seeded raisins, halved
½ cup water
¾ cup sugar
1½ tablespoons all-purpose flour
Dash of salt
1 tablespoon butter
Pastry for 2-crust 8-inch pie, unbaked

Mix cranberries and raisins in saucepan. Add water and simmer for 5 minutes. Mix sugar, flour, and salt; gradually stir in cranberry mixture. Cook over low heat, stirring constantly, until thickened. Add butter. Line 8-inch pie pan with pastry and trim. Pour in filling. Roll out rest of pastry and cut into strips for lattice top. Arrange pastry strips crisscross fashion over all; seal edges. Bake in preheated hot oven (425°F.) for about 30 minutes. Serve warm or cold.

CRANBERRY ROLY-POLY
1 cup sifted all-purpose flour
1 teaspoon baking powder
¼ teaspoon salt
1 tablespoon sugar
3 tablespoons soft shortening
⅓ cup milk
2 cups whole-berry cranberry sauce, drained
Custard sauce or whipped cream

Sift together first four ingredients. Cut in shortening, add milk, and mix to form soft dough. Turn out on floured board and knead several times. Roll to form a rectangle ¼ inch thick. Spread with sauce to within ½ inch of edge. Roll up like jelly roll, dampen edge with water, and seal with tines of fork. Put on greased cookie sheet and bake in preheated hot oven (400°F.) for about 20 minutes. Cut into slices and serve with custard sauce. Makes 4 servings.

CANDIED CRANBERRIES
Wash 2 cups large firm cranberries; drain well and spread in bottom of buttered baking dish. Sprinkle with 1½ cups sugar and cover tightly. Bake in preheated moderate oven (350°F.) for 1 hour. Stir once to distribute sugar. Let berries cool in the syrup. Lift out onto wax paper. Sift a little sugar over berries and let stand until all are dry and firm. Makes about 2 cups.

CRANBERRY AND HORSERADISH RELISH
4 cups whole raw cranberries, washed
1 cup sugar
½ cup fresh grated horseradish or bottled horseradish, drained
Juice of 1 lemon

Grind cranberries with medium blade of food grinder. Combine with all other ingredients. Let stand in refrigerator for 2 days to allow flavors to blend. Makes about 4 cups.

CRANBERRY-ORANGE JELLY
4 cups (1 pound) cranberries
2 cups boiling water

Grated rind of 1 orange
1 cup sugar
¾ cup honey

Pick over, wash, and drain cranberries. Put in saucepan with boiling water and grated rind. Bring to boil and simmer, covered, for 20 minutes. Force through fine sieve. Bring to rapid boil. Stir in sugar and honey and boil for 3 minutes. Pour into hot sterilized glasses. Seal with paraffin. Makes about 1 quart, or three to four 8-ounce glasses.

CRANBERRY-CLARET JELLY
3½ cups sugar
1 cup bottled cranberry juice
1 cup claret
½ bottle fruit pectin

Put sugar in top part of double boiler. Add cranberry juice and wine; mix well. Put over rapidly boiling water and stir until sugar is dissolved, about 2 minutes. Remove from heat and stir in fruit pectin. Skim off foam and pour quickly into glasses. Seal at once with paraffin. Makes six 6-ounce glasses.

CRANBERRY PUNCH
2 cups cranberry-juice cocktail
1 cup fresh orange juice
¼ cup fresh lemon juice
½ cup each of pineapple juice, sugar, and water
Cracked ice

Mix all ingredients except ice. Put ice in punch bowl and cover with punch. Makes 8 servings, ½ cup each.

QUICK CRANBERRY DISHES
■ **Apple-Cranberry Dessert**—Heat whole-cranberry sauce, few seeded raisins, canned apple slices, and a little grated orange rind. Serve warm or cold, with cream, if desired.

■ **Banana-Cranberry Dessert**—Top sliced banana with cube of jellied cranberry. Garnish with whipped cream and chopped nuts.

■ **Crackers, Cheese, and Jelly**—Cut jellied cranberry with cookie cutter; top with cube of cream cheese. Surround with heated crisp crackers.

■ **Cranberries and Sour Cream**—Serve chilled sweetened whole stewed cranberries with dairy sour cream. Sprinkle with freshly grated ginger.

■ **Cranberry-Lemon Sherbet**—Serve canned or fresh whole-cranberry sauce with lemon sherbet. Garnish with pieces of green gumdrop.

■ **Pancakes with Cranberries**—Dust hot little pancakes with confectioners' sugar, and serve with cranberry-orange relish thinned with a little honey.

■ **Polka-Dot Fruit Salad**—Place a canned pear half and orange sections on salad greens. Fill pear with cottage cheese; top with drained whole cooked cranberries.

■ **Red-and-Yellow Dessert**—On a slice of orange chiffon cake or poundcake, place a canned peach half. Cover with a generous spoonful of cranberry-orange relish.

■ **Tapioca with Cranberries** — Prepare packaged orange-coconut tapioca according to directions. Serve chilled with canned or fresh whole-cranberry sauce.

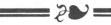

CRAPPIE

CRAPPIE—This is the name commonly applied to two small members of the fresh-water sunfish group. The average size is about one pound and the length one foot. Crappies are found mostly in the Great Lakes and in the Mississippi region. They are sporting fish, protected by the states. They make excellent pan fish.

PANNED CRAPPIES WITH CHIVES

2 pounds crappies
½ cup each of yellow cornmeal and all-purpose flour
2 teaspoons salt
¼ teaspoon white pepper
3 tablespoons butter or margarine
2 tablespoons chopped chives
1 lemon, cut into wedges

Clean fish, and remove heads if preferred. Wipe fish with damp cloth or paper towel. Mix cornmeal, flour, salt, and pepper. Roll fish in the mixture and fry for about 4 minutes on each side in hot butter, turning carefully to brown both sides. Sprinkle with chopped chives and serve with lemon wedges. Makes 4 servings.

CRAYFISH or CRAWFISH—A fresh-water shellfish, resembling the lobster in looks and in flavor, but only about six inches long. It is found in this country and in Europe. Here, it is available fresh principally in the Lake Michigan area, in the Pacific Northwest and California, and around New Orleans. Crayfish are available elsewhere canned.

Crayfish are among the most exquisite of shellfish and greatly prized by connoisseurs of fine food in France, Germany, and especially Scandinavia. In Sweden, in particular, Midsummer Day (June 24) is the time for a national crayfish festival, where these delicious crustaceans are consumed by the hundreds of tons and washed down with aquavit and beer, with much rejoicing from young and old.

The two names, cray and craw, are often inaccurately applied to the spiny lobster, rock lobster, or sea crawfish, a far-ranging coastal salt-water crustacean. The spiny lobster is much larger than the crayfish, but its first pair of legs is not enlarged into the claws which are found on the true crayfish or true lobster. The tail of the spiny lobster is the part chiefly used and it is commonly available frozen.

CRAYFISH IN COURT BOUILLON

40 crayfish
2 cups white wine
2 cups water
1 onion, chopped
1 carrot, sliced
1 bay leaf
2 small garlic cloves
  Salt and pepper to taste
  Few parsley sprigs

Wash crayfish in several waters. Mix next 7 ingredients and simmer, covered, for 30 minutes. Add crayfish and simmer for 12 minutes. Serve very hot, garnished with parsley. Makes 4 servings.

CREAM—This is the rich, fatty part of whole milk which rises to the top and which can be separated from the milk. The longer sweet cream stands, the thicker it will be. There are different kinds of cream, regulated by their butterfat content. Cream can be sweet or sour.

Cream, thick and sweet, rich and smooth, is an essential complement to fine cooking, and the word itself has come to stand for the best, the choicest, the quintessence of things, as expressed in such sayings as "the cream of the crop." Few other words in the language denote so much luxury and pleasure.

Purchasing Guide

Type	Butterfat Content	Calories per Tablespoon
Light or "coffee cream"	18 to 20%	35
Heavy or "whipping cream"	35 to 40%	55
Whipped cream	35 to 40%	28
Half-and-half (half milk and half light cream)	12 to 15%	20
Dried creams (milk solids plus light cream solids, stabilizer added)	Depends on brand; see label	Depends on brand

Storage—Cream is a highly perishable product. Keep in coldest part of refrigerator.

Whipped cream may be frozen and stored at 0°F. temperature; but liquid cream does not freeze successfully.

TO WHIP CREAM

Heavy cream when whipped should be light, smooth, and *doubled in volume*. (One cup heavy cream will yield about 2 cups, whipped.) To whip cream successfully, chill bowl and beaters as well as cream, preferably for a couple of hours. Use a rotary beater or a wire whisk.

If an electric beater is used, turn to medium speed until the chilled cream starts thickening. Then turn to low speed and beat only until the cream retains a soft shape and is still glossy. Do not overbeat, or cream will turn to butter.

Properly whipped cream will keep for 1 or 2 hours in the refrigerator.

If whipped cream is to be used for cake or other decorations, whip until it is about to turn into butter. If it turns into butter, whip in 1 or 2 tablespoons light cream or undiluted evaporated milk.

Fold sugar and flavorings into the cream after whipping it.

Small quantities of whipped cream can be frozen. Place a small amount, or a small decorative garnish, of whipped cream on aluminum foil. Freeze uncovered. Wrap when frozen and return to freezer.

SOUR CREAM

Also known as "dairy sour cream," sour cream is commercially produced and is made from homogenized pasteurized sweet cream to which a dairy culture is added for souring. Then, with proper timing and temperature control, the cream develops its characteristic flavor. Immediate chilling afterward stops the action of the dairy culture and fixes the tart flavor. Sour cream should be kept like all cream: covered and in the refrigerator.

Caloric Value

☐ 1 tablespoon, 18% butterfat content = 30 calories

CREAM, TO—A cooking term meaning to make foods soft and creamy by mashing or beating them with a spoon, a paddle, or any other tool. The word is most frequently applied to fats such as butter which must be creamed before flavorings or sugar are added, or the fat won't be receptive to them.

"To cream" is also used instead of "to blend," although the two processes are not quite identical. Creaming butter and sugar means that minute particles of each are thoroughly amalgamated, so that they don't show up separately. This takes some time to achieve. To blend the two means almost the same thing, but indicates that the mixing is done to a somewhat lesser extent.

Most creaming is done in baking, and an electric beater is an invaluable help. It should be set at low speed.

CREAMED—This is said of a food cooked or served in a creamed or creamy sauce: creamed chicken, creamed eggs, or creamed carrots, for example. Creaming a dish is a good way of stretching it.

CREAM OF TARTAR—A natural fruit acid in the form of fine white powder made from pressed grapes. It is an ingredient in commercial baking powders. Before their appearance, cream of tartar was combined with baking soda and used as a leavening agent. Some modern recipes also call for cream of tartar and baking soda as a leavener.

Cream of tartar is used in making frostings, candies, and in beating egg whites. In candies and frostings the addition of cream of tartar keeps the food white, gives it a creamier consistency and a less-sweet taste. In beating egg whites, when cream of tartar is added at the beginning of beating, it makes the egg whites firmer, and when they must be baked (as in meringues), they tolerate the oven heat better. When cream of tartar is added to egg whites, they may have to be beaten a little longer.

CREAM PUFF—This is an airy little cream-filled cake, brother to an éclair. Cream puffs are round, éclairs are oblong. They are of French origin and made by an entirely different method from other pastries. Cream-puff pastry is also called *chou* pastry, or literally translated from the French, "cabbage" pastry, because of the appearance of the finished product, which bears a vague resemblance to a miniature cabbage.

Chou or cream-puff pastry is made by adding flour to boiling water and butter and cooking the mixture until a thick paste is formed. Then the eggs are beaten in, one at a time. The eggs make the paste, which is nothing but a thick sauce, puff up during cooking. When finished, the puffs are cut open and filled with either a sweet or savory filling.

Cooks should rid themselves of the idea that cream puffs are hard to make. As a matter of fact, they are one of the easiest pastries. They are also extremely useful since they make all sorts of delightful desserts or, if the filling is not sweet, elegant appetizers and garnishes.

Furthermore, the paste can be put into a pastry tube and molded into all sorts of fancy shapes and sizes.

Perfect puffs should be firm, tender, and dry. There is only one secret to their perfection, and that is the baking. Hot puffs will seem just right when taken out of the oven, yet when cooled, they will be soggy because of an uncooked center portion. To prevent this, small puffs are punctured and large ones slit open, then replaced in the oven to dry out. If the center is soggy, it is often removed to keep outer shell dry.

CREAM PUFFS

1 cup water
½ cup butter or margarine
¼ teaspoon salt
1 cup sifted all-purpose flour
4 large eggs
   Vanilla Cream Filling
   Confectioners' sugar

In saucepan heat water, butter, and salt to full rolling boil. Reduce heat and quickly stir in flour, mixing vigorously with wooden spoon until mixture leaves the sides of the pan in a ball. Remove from heat and beat in eggs, one at a time, beating after each addition until mixture is very smooth. (An electric mixer at a low speed makes this procedure easier.) Drop dough from metal mixing spoon onto greased cookie sheets, or squeeze through pastry tube in any desired shape, forming mounds 3 inches apart. Bake in preheated hot oven (400° F.) for 10 minutes. Lower heat to moderate (350°F.) and bake for 25 minutes more. Puffs are ready when doubled in size, golden brown, and firm to the touch. Remove puffs from oven and cut the side of each with a sharp knife. Put them back into the turned-off oven. Keep oven door ajar and let stand for 10 minutes. Cool puffs on racks. Slit top; fill with Vanilla Cream Filling. Sprinkle with confectioners' sugar. Makes 12 large or 16 medium cream puffs.

Vanilla Cream Filling

3 cups milk
¾ cup sugar
6 tablespoons cornstarch
½ teaspoon salt
3 eggs, beaten
1 tablespoon butter
2 teaspoons vanilla extract

Scald milk in top part of double boiler over boiling water. Mix sugar, cornstarch, and salt. Stir into milk. Cook, stirring, until thick. Cover and cook for 10 minutes longer. Add small amount of mixture to eggs, return to double boiler, and cook for 5 minutes. Add butter. Put in bowl and sprinkle small amount of sugar over top to prevent skin from forming. Chill, and add vanilla.

Chocolate Cream Filling

Use recipe for Vanilla Cream Filling.

Melt 3 ounces (3 squares) unsweetened chocolate in milk and beat until smooth. Proceed as directed above.

SAVORY APPETIZER PUFFS

Use Cream-Puffs recipe. Measure exactly 1¼ teaspoons dough onto greased cookie sheet. Using this amount as a guide for size, drop remaining dough in same amounts onto cookie sheet. Bake in preheated hot oven (400°F.) for about 20 minutes. Replace in oven as in Cream Puffs. Fill (see below). Makes 8 dozen.

Fillings for Savory Appetizer Puffs

■ **Chutney-Cream Cheese**—Combine ¼ cup minced chutney, ¼ cup chopped almonds, 1½ teaspoons curry powder, 3 tablespoons syrup from preserved ginger, and 8 ounces cream cheese. Mix well.

■ **Crabmeat Filling**—Combine 2 cups flaked crabmeat (fibers removed), ½ cup chopped celery, 1 chopped hard-cooked egg, and mayonnaise to moisten. Mix well.

■ **Curried-Chicken Filling**—Combine 1 cup chopped cooked chicken, ½ cup finely chopped blanched almonds, 2 tablespoons minced scallions, 1 tablespoon curry powder, and mayonnaise to moisten. Mix well.

■ **Ham Filling**—Combine ½ pound chopped ham, ½ cup chopped black olives, ½ cup chopped hazelnuts, and mayonnaise to moisten. Mix well.

■ **Swiss-Cheese Filling**—Combine 2 cups grated Swiss cheese, 3 tablespoons chopped black olives, 2 tablespoons green pepper, and mayonnaise to moisten. Mix well.

CREAM SAUCE—A classic cream sauce is a white or Béchamel sauce which contains milk. It may also be made with cream rather than milk, or cream may be added to a reduced white or Béchamel sauce. Its thickness, like that of other white sauces, depends on the proportion of flour to liquid. Poultry, fish, eggs, and vegetables may be served in a cream sauce, or gratined in one.

CRÈME BRÛLÉE—The literal translation of these French words is *"burnt cream."* They stand for a glorious dessert of Creole origin made from a rich custard with a caramelized sugar topping. The interest of the dessert lies in the contrast between flavors and textures. The sweetness and smoothness of the custard are enhanced by the faintly bitter taste and the brittleness of the caramelized sugar. For a *Crème Brûlée* recipe, see page 494.

How to Cook Superbly: Crèmes and Custards

by Helen Evans Brown

Whether a custard is a simple baked one, flavored with nutmeg, or an elegant *crème brûlée,* with its soft rich cream covered with a brittle crust of burnt sugar, its base is milk or cream and eggs or egg yolks, and it requires gentle cooking to assure perfect smoothness, the secret of good custard-making. There are two basic kinds of custard, top stove and baked. Once these two, in their simplest forms, are mastered, many other variations can be made without effort: *crème renversée, pots de crème,* and *crème pâtissière* being the most useful for a budding *cordon bleu* cook to add to her repertoire. So let's get going.

EQUIPMENT

You'll probably already have everything needed for making simple custards. You need measuring cups and spoons, a whip, a rubber scraper, a strainer, a double boiler (when you get expert, a heavy-bottomed saucepan will do), and custard cups or larger casseroles or bowls. You'll also need a large pan about 2 inches deep for a "water jacket."

PLAIN BAKED CUSTARD

2 cups milk
2 eggs
2 egg yolks
3 tablespoons sugar
Pinch of salt
½ teaspoon vanilla extract or sprinkling of ground nutmeg

Set your oven at 325°F. (Custards can be baked at 300°F. or 350°F., in which cases they require more or less time, naturally.) Put the milk in a heavy saucepan and place over low heat. In a bowl mix together the eggs, yolks, sugar, salt, and vanilla, if you are using it. Mix well but don't beat. When tiny bubbles appear around the edge of the milk pan, pour about a third of it into the egg mixture and mix until well blended, then add this mixture to the remaining milk and again mix. Put 6 buttered custard cups (the 4- or 5-ounce size) in the larger pan and strain the custard mixture into them

If nutmeg is your choice, sprinkle a little on the top of each custard. Put pan in the oven, then pour hot water into the pan so that it comes halfway up on the custard cups. Be careful not to splash the water. Bake for 30 minutes, then check. If the custard wiggles like unset jelly, bake another 5 minutes, then insert a small knife near the center of one of the custards. If, when it's pulled out, the blade is shiny (not milky looking), the custards are done. If not, try 5 minutes more. (If baked in one large dish, allow a longer time for cooking; start checking after 40 minutes.) When done, remove from oven and lift cups from the hot water (tongs help here). Serve at room temperature or icy cold, whichever you think tastes best. Makes 6 servings.

Note: This custard can be made less rich if the egg yolks are omitted, richer by using half milk, half cream.

VARIATIONS OF BAKED CUSTARD
Caramel Custard (Crème Renversée)

All over Europe you will find baked caramel custard a favorite dessert. In Spain it's known as *Flan,* in France *Crème Renversée,* in Italy *Crema Caramella.* It is simply a baked custard that has been baked in caramel-lined mold and turned out on a dish so that it's glazed and sauced with amber caramel. Here is the way: have ready a large (2-quart baking dish) or 6 to 8 small custard cups. Prepare custard mixture. Double recipe for 2-quart dish. Put 1 cup of granulated sugar in a heavy skillet or saucepan and put over fairly high heat. Stir. It will start to melt and as you stir lumps will form. Don't let this bother you; the lumps will smooth out as the syrup forms. First you'll have a pale-amber syrup which will gradually turn darker. Watch it carefully. When it begins to smoke a very little, it's almost ready. Then it will start to bubble. Remove from heat at once and let the bubbles settle, then pour it into the baking dish and, using potholders or padded mitts, tip and turn the dish so that the bottom and sides are covered with a thin, even layer of clear brown glaze. If there is any surplus caramel, it will run down to the bottom when the dish is set down, and that's okay. If doing individual custards, you'll have to work quickly to get them all lined before the syrup hardens. However, many cooks simply pour about a tablespoon in the bottom of each cup. When the cups are lined, simply pour in the baked custard mixture and bake large dish about 1 hour. Bake cups for 30 to 35 minutes. Chill, and unmold by running a knife around the top edge, then putting a suitably sized dish on top and

quickly reversing the two. The custard should slip out easily. This dessert, made with some cream for extra richness, rates as an extra special one, suitable for sophisticated palates. Makes 6 to 8 servings (12, if made in 2-quart dish).

POTS DE CRÈME

Another very elegant dessert is a rich custard cooked and served in little covered pots, called *petits pots.* It's nice to have a set of these but if you haven't, custard cups or any similar containers can be used. Sometimes this custard is baked and sometimes cooked on top of the stove; this first one is baked.

POTS DE CRÈME À LA VANILLE
(Vanilla Cream Pots)

4 egg yolks
¼ cup sugar (less if desired)
Pinch of salt
1 teaspoon vanilla extract, or 1-inch vanilla bean
1⅓ cups cream

Mix yolks, sugar, salt, and vanilla extract, if used. Heat cream, adding split vanilla bean if that has been your choice. When bubbles form around edge of cream, proceed as in baked custard. (Remove vanilla bean but scrape the little seeds into the cream. They are a badge of honor.) Divide custard among 6 little pots and put in a pan of hot water. Press or prick any bubbles on top of the custard to break them. Cover, using rounds of aluminum foil if your pots lack tops. Bake in a preheated slow oven (325°F.) for 25 minutes, or until a knife inserted near the center comes out clean. Start checking at 15 minutes. The heavier the cream you use, the longer they take to set, but it's better to have them creamy in the middle than overcooked. Makes 6 servings.

TOP-STOVE CUSTARD

1 cup milk
3 egg yolks
1½ tablespoons sugar
A few grains of salt
½ teaspoon vanilla extract

Heat the milk in the top part of a double boiler. Mix egg yolks, sugar, and salt thoroughly, but don't beat. When bubbles appear around the edge of the milk, pour about a third of it into the egg mixture and blend well. Pour this into the remaining milk in the double-boiler top. Put over boiling water and cook, stirring constantly with a rubber scraper so that you can get into the corners and around the sides of the pan. When the mixture thickens and coats a spoon, it is done. Add vanilla, mix well, and cool. Makes about 1⅓ cups.

When you become expert, you can dispense with the double boiler and use a heavy saucepan over direct heat. Instead of regulating the heat by making it higher or lower, try this instant regulation: while stirring the custard with the right hand, hold the pan a few inches above the burner if it appears to be getting too hot, lowering it again as more heat is needed. Never, never let it boil. Remember that custard is thickened properly by the time it reaches 165°F. on a candy thermometer, and every degree higher than that brings it closer to curdling. And, dear cooks, if that dire thing should happen, don't throw it away. Simply remove it from the heat and beat vigorously with a wire whip or an egg beater. It will smooth, but it will become a little thinner and won't be quite as perfect as you'd like. Chill, and use custard as a dessert sauce, or double the recipe below for Floating Island.

VARIATIONS OF TOP-STOVE CUSTARD

Pots de Crème au Chocolat

Make a Top-Stove Custard as above, using 1 cup of milk or thin cream, 1 egg and 2 egg yolks, a pinch of salt, 2 tablespoons of sugar, and ½ teaspoon of vanilla. Allow to cool while you melt 2 ounces of semisweet chocolate over hot water. (When the chocolate begins to melt, remove from heat and stir until completely smooth.) Combine with the custard, mixing thoroughly. Pour into little pots, demitasse cups, or Chinese teacups and serve cold. Makes 4 servings.

Floating Island

Make a double recipe of Top-Stove Custard as above, and pour into a shallow serving dish; chill. Using 4 of the remaining egg whites, beat until fluffy, then gradually beat in a pinch of salt and 6 tablespoons of sugar. Continue beating until so stiff that the meringue (because that's what you've made) stands up in sharp peaks. Have ready a saucepan or skillet of simmering water and carefully drop tablespoonfuls of the meringue into it, one at a time. As soon as they set, in 2 or 3 minutes, lift out carefully with a slotted spoon and put on top of custard like little islands in a creamy sea. Chill before serving. Makes 4 to 6 servings.
Note: *Ile Flottant* is another thing entirely: a vanilla soufflé or spongecake surrounded by a moat of custard.

CRÈME BRÛLÉE

This is the most spectacular of all these custards and one that you can serve to your most epicurean guests. The technique is slightly different from regular top-stove custard, as you will see.

    7 egg yolks
    2 cups heavy cream
1⅓ cups firmly packed brown sugar
    Pinch of salt
    1 teaspoon vanilla extract,
      or 1 tablespoon Jamaica rum

Beat egg yolks until thick and light in color. Heat cream until bubbles form

A collection of crème and custard desserts: individual and large Caramel

around edges, and pour one third into the eggs; then add ⅓ cup of the brown sugar and the salt to the egg mixture, and add to the remaining cream. Cook, whisking constantly, until as thick as thin mayonnaise. (Do this over hot water or, if you are now sure of yourself, over direct heat as above.) Add extract and pour into a 10-inch fairly shallow baking dish. Chill for at least 4 hours. Two or 3 hours before serving, put the remaining brown sugar (1 cup) in a strainer and, pressing it with a rubber scraper, sift over the top of the cream, which will have set slightly. Make sure that the sugar is in an even, smooth layer, extending clear to the edge of the dish. None of the custard should show, and there should be no hills or valleys in the sugar. Put under a very

hot broiler, watching carefully, until the sugar melts completely; it may be necessary to turn the dish occasionally to insure even melting. Do this as quickly as possible. When the sugar has melted, return custard to the refrigerator. To serve, break through the hard crust with a spoon, and give each guest some crust as well as some cream. This is sometimes served with fruit, but it is sufficient unto itself. Makes 4 to 6 servings.

CRÈME PÂTISSIÈRE

This is the so-called pastry cream that French chefs use for filling cream puffs, lining tarts, and in many fancy desserts.

¼ cup all-purpose flour
⅓ cup sugar
  Pinch of salt

Custard with a rich, amber caramel glaze; Pot de Crème au Chocolat; Floating Island, and individual Baked Custards.

2 teaspoons butter
3 egg yolks
1 cup milk
½ teaspoon vanilla extract

Combine flour, sugar, salt, butter, and egg yolks, and mix. Heat milk and combine with mixture, and cook (over hot water or not) until very thick, stirring constantly. This, because of the flour, can take more heat and it should, or the flour will have a raw taste. When thick and smooth, add vanilla, and cover. Cool before using. Makes enough filling for 4 medium cream puffs or tarts.

CRENSHAW—This is a melon with a cream- and green-colored rind which is smooth, with no netting and very little ribbing. As the melon ripens the rind takes on a yellower cast. The flesh is salmon-colored, thick, juicy, and full of flavor. Crenshaw melons are at their best in the late summer and early fall.

Storage—When ripe, wrap in moisture-proof paper and refrigerate.
☐ Refrigerator shelf: 2 or 3 days

CRENSHAW FRUIT SALAD SUPREME
On a bed of salad greens arrange strips of melon, chunks of peeled banana, apricot halves or orange segments, and small bunches of seedless grapes. Serve with Fluffy Pineapple Dressing.

Fluffy Pineapple Dressing
1 cup pineapple juice

1 tablespoon butter
1 egg
3 tablespoons fresh lemon juice
⅓ cup sugar
2 tablespoons all-purpose flour
1 teaspoon each of celery salt and paprika
½ teaspoon powdered mustard
Seasoned salt
Whipped cream

Heat pineapple juice with butter in saucepan. Beat egg with lemon juice. Mix next 5 ingredients and beat into egg mixture. Stir in hot juice; return to saucepan and cook over very low heat, stirring constantly, until smooth and thickened. Add seasoned salt to taste. Cool; store in covered jar in refrigerator. Makes 1½ cups. To serve, mix with whipped cream in desired proportions.

 Menus

100 Menus
to help you plan
more varied meals
for your family with
the recipes in this volume

*Recipes for all starred dishes found in this volume.

BREAKFAST

Rainbow Fruit*
Hot Sausage Slices*
Skillet Corn Fritters*
Orange-Ginger Marmalade*

Honeyed Grapefruit
Creamy Eggs*
Toasted English Muffins
Coriander Tomato Marmalade*

Crenshaw Melon
Deviled Ham Steak*
Guatemalan Chocolate*

Orange and Grapefruit
Sections*
Canadian Style Bacon
Waffles
Whipped Cream Cheese
Molasses

Vegetable Cocktail*
Corned-Beef Hash*
Sliced Hard-Cooked Eggs
Cheese Fritters*
Pineapple Chutney*

Sliced Bananas with Orange
Juice
Bacon, Egg, and Corn
Pancakes*
Arab Dates   Pot Cheese

Tomato Juice
Baked Cranberry and
Ham Cubes
Creamy Corn Bake*
Panettone (Italian
Coffeecake)*

Whole Fresh Orange
Broiled Chicken Livers
and Bacon
Coddled Eggs*
Whole Wheat Toast

LUNCHEONS or SUPPERS

Prunes
Dropped Codfish and
Potato Cakes*
Stewed Tomatoes
Yellow Coffeecake*

Stewed Apricots and Raisins
Fried Ham Slice
Madeira Sauce for Ham*
Hominy Grits   Hot Biscuits
Crab Apple Jelly

Strawberries and Rhubarb
Compote*
Fried Catfish*   Lemon Wedges
Chantilly Potatoes*

Grape and Pineapple Juice
Welsh Rabbit* on Toast
Broiled Tomato Halves
Pennsylvania Dutch
Corn Relish*

Crab-Mushroom Casserole*
Shredded Green Cabbage
Wisconsin Dressing*
Cranberry Apples*
Spicy Molasses Cut-Outs*

Consommé*
Savory Ham Spread* on
Cheese Bread Toast
Sandwiches
Ambrosia*   Brown-Edged
Butter Cookies*

Pennsylvania Dutch Corn-
Chicken Soup*
Celery and Cabbage Slaw*
Coconut-Crusted Apple
Dessert*

Crab and Avocado Salad
Curry Mayonnaise
Hard Rolls
Herb Sweet Butter*
Holiday Cheesecake*

Chop Suey or Chow Mein*
Fried Noodles
Rice Soy Sauce
Preserved Kumquats
Hsing Jen Ping (Almond
Cookies)*   Tea

Corn Chowder*
Carrot Curls and Radishes
Toasted Rye Crisps
Butter
Midnight Lace Cake*

Pickled Shrimps*
Jellied Vegetable Salad
with Curry Dressing*
Surprise Chocolate Cupcakes*

Orange-Onion Salad
Chiffonade Dressing*
Homemade Herb-Cheese
Bread Loaf
Whipped Butter   Honey

Manhattan Clam Chowder*
Stuffed Olives
Oysterettes
Mandarin Oranges

Hot Baked Barbecued Corned
Beef* and Swiss Cheese
Sandwiches on Rye Bread
Dill Pickle Chips
Horseradish Mustard
Pineapple Sherbet

Crisp Bacon
Fruit Salad, Coconut
Dressing*
Corn Muffins*
Butter or Margarine
Caramel Custard

Tomato Soup
Popcorn with Cheese*
Jellied Cranberry-Turkey
Loaf*
Heated Assorted Crisp
Breads
Lizzies*

Shrimp Bisque*
Cheese Ball*   Rye Toast
Chocolate Fondant Cake*
with Fluffy White Frosting

Chicken Livers and Barley*
Sliced Tomato Salad
Italian Dressing
Provolone and Fresh Pears

Citrus Salad Plate*
Lime Dressing*
Toasted Sesame Seed
Crackers
Chocolate Ice Cream
Creole Kisses*

Crab Cakes*
Scrambled Eggs   Chili
Sauce
Celery and Radishes
Coriander Rice Pudding*

Roast Fresh Ham*
Cranberry-Claret Jelly*
Potato Rosettes*
Brussels Sprouts and
Chestnuts*
Asparagus Salad Vinaigrette
Eggnog Snow Pudding* with
Orange and Lemon
Sauce*

Cod Florentine*
Buttered Carrots
Head Lettuce and Russian
Dressing
Double Corn Sticks*
Queen Bona's Dessert*

Rib Roast of Beef*
Yorkshire Pudding*
Frenched Green Beans
Boston Lettuce and
Watercress Salad
Fruit Compote Amandine*
Sand Tarts*

Apricot Glazed Ham*
Oven-Browned White and
Sweet Potatoes
Broccoli with Pimiento
Butter*
Diva Cake with Brown-Sugar
Frosting*

Corned Beef and Cabbage*
Boiled Potatoes   Mustard
Crackling Corn Bread*
Waldorf Salad
Brown Beauty Cake*

Roast Capon*   Gravy*
Giblet Stuffing*
Creamed Cauliflower*
Buttered Beets*
Cider Gelatin Salad*
Fresh-Coconut Cake*
with Rich Chocolate
Frosting*

Avocado-Tomato Cocktail*
Corn-Ham Bake*
Spiced Crab Apples*
Chicory and Red Onion
Ring Salad   Lime
Dressing*
Chocolate Fudge Meringues*

Herbed Bouillon*   Corn
Chips
Deviled Crabs*
Cranberry Fruit Ring*
Seeded Hard Rolls   Whipped
Margarine
A Man's Chocolate Rum
Cake*

Jellied Watercress
Consommé*
Fillets of Sole in Court
Bouillon*
Buttered Peas
Double-Corn Spoon Bread*
Tomatoes and Cucumbers
Old-Fashioned Peach
Cobbler*

Cioppino*
Celery, Green and Ripe
Olives
Sourdough or Italian Bread
Butter
Pineapple-Cheese Pie*

Breaded Veal Cutlets
Noodles in Tomato Sauce
Mixed Green Salad with
Capers
Chilled Fruit Compote*
Cinnamon-Nut Diamonds*

Citrus-Grape Cocktail*
Panned Crappies with Chives*
French Fried Potatoes
Hot Slaw*
Parkerhouse Rolls
Floating Island*

Seafood Cocktail*
Cheddar Cheese Omelet
Cracked Wheat Toast
Lettuce, Green Lima Bean
and Sliced Radish Salad
with Garlic Vinegar and
Oil Dressing
Mocha Cake*

Lamb or Pork Chops
Preserved Kumquats*
Rice with Green Peas
Turnips with Mushrooms*
Dinner Rolls
Cherry Tarts*

Chopped Steak   Lima Beans
Corn on the Cob with
Chili Powder Butter*
Tomato Aspic on Sliced
Chinese Cabbage with
Russian Dressing
Chocolate Raspberry Cream*
Melt-in-the-Mouth Cookies*

Two Tone Cocktail*
Oven-Fried Chicken in
Bread Loaf*
Green Pepper Sticks
Cream Style Corn
Coffee Ice Cream
Orange Walnut-Date Bars*

Clams Broiled on the Half Shell*
Chicken Fricassee*
Brown Rice
Marinated Whole Green Bean
Salad on Greens
Sherry Cobbler*
Pecan Butter Balls*

Roast Leg of Lamb
Cranberry-Mint Sauce*
Oven Roasted Potatoes,
Onions, Carrots, and Parsnips
Romaine and Mandarin Orange
Salad—Wine Vinegar and
Oil Dressing
Black-Bottom Pie*

Baked Smithfield Ham*
Candied Yams*
Creamed Chopped Broccoli
Corn Sticks*
Pineapple-Spinach Salad with
Mustard French Dressing
Citron Loaf Cake*, Toasted
Orange-Ginger Marmalade*

Roast Loin of Pork
Corn Stuffing Balls*
Swiss Chard and Green
Onions*
Radish Roses
Secret Harbor Cheesecake*

Chi Tan Chuan
(Chinese Egg Rolls)*
Yang Jo Kao (Jellied Lamb)*
Chiang Lo Po (Sweet-and-Sour
Radishes)*
Ch'ao Fan (Fried Rice)*
Almond Cookies*
Green Tea

Chu Jou Pi Chi T'ang
(Pork and Watercress Soup)*
Corn and Shrimp Casserole*
Liang Pan Huang Kua
(Pickled Cucumbers)*
Panned Chicory*
Pears Hélène*

basil   dill   cloves   sage

salt   chives   rye   msg

Menus

Pork Chops with Cherries*
Cheese Spoon Bread*
Celeriac Salad*
Butter Pecan Ice Cream
Brandy Wafers*

Broiled Smoked Beef Tongue
Cheese Spinach Pie*
Crenshaw Fruit Salad Supreme*
with Fluffy
Pineapple Dressing

Smoked Boneless Butt
Cheese-Apple-Noodle
Pudding*
Jellied Vegetable Salad*
with Mustard Mayonnaise
Lemon Sherbet with
Grenadine
Spicy Chocolate Sticks*

Chicken Marengo*
Mixed Green Salad with
Anchovies
Crusty Italian Bread
Grapefruit and Orange
Sections
Almond-Butter Strips*

Chili Con Carne* on
Corn Bread* Squares
Shredded Lettuce, Sliced
Egg, Green Pepper, and
Pimiento Salad
Cream Cheese
Guava Jelly
Sesame Seed Crackers

Broiled Deviled Chicken*
Buttered Green Noodles
Baked Corn-Stuffed Tomatoes*
Tossed Green Salad with
Orange Segments
Italian Chestnut-Chocolate
Dessert*

Artichoke Hearts
Chiffonade Dressing*
Veal Chops Lucullus*
Fine Noodles with Butter
and Bread Crumbs
Apple-Cranberry Dessert*

Ham and Noodles*
Green Peas and Onions
Tomato Aspic
Shredded Cabbage
Mustard Mayonnaise
Pumpernickel Bread
Apple Sauce with Frozen
Raspberries

Veal Parmigiana*
Fresh-Corn Soufflé*
Pickled Beets and Cabbage
Salad
Crenshaw Melon with
Pineapple Sherbet

Clam Juice Cocktail
Fish Grill*
Green Beans with Almonds*
Spoon Bread
Cranberry-Lemon Sherbet*

Cheese-Baked Ham and
Vegetables (Casserole)*
Tomato and Lettuce Salad
Corn Muffins*
Cherry Dumplings*

Chicken Loaves* with Curry
Sauce
Buttered Asparagus
Mango Chutney*
Green Pepper and Carrot
Sticks
Toasted Sesame Crackers
Pistachio Bavarian with
Strawberries*
Cream-Cheese Butter Cookies*

Assorted Cold Cuts*
Creamy Macaroni and Cheese*
German Cabbage Slaw
Pumpernickel Bread
Sweet Butter
Charlotte des Pommes (Apple
Charlotte)*

Chi Tan T'ang
(Chinese Egg-Drop Soup)*
Wu Hsiang Ya (Spiced Duck)*
Rice*
Fried Celery*
Sugared Pineapple
Coconut Cookies*

Coq au Vin*
Whipped Potatoes
Mixed Green Salad with
Vinaigrette Dressing
Chestnut-Chocolate Vanilla
Tarts*

Sweet-and-Sour Meatballs*
Riced Potatoes
Brussels Sprouts   Rye Bread
Midnight Lace Cake* à la Mode

Jellied Watercress
Consommé*
T'ang Ts'u Chu Jo
(Sweet-and-Sour
Pork)*
Cauliflower in Cheese
Puff*
Pa Pao Fan (Eight
Treasures Pudding)*

Melon-Lime Cocktail*
Chicken in a Pot*
Green Beans
Cherry Tomatoes and
Watercress
Honey Chocolate Cake*

Celery and Radishes
Roast Chicken with Sausage-
Nut Stuffing*
Peas and Carrots   Creamed
Onions
Buttermilk Biscuits
Cranberry-Orange Jelly*
Grandma's Chocolate Cake*

New England Clam Chowder*
Chilled Boiled Ham
wrapped around
Broccoli Spears
Tomatoes Stuffed with
Egg Salad   Rye Crisp
Cherry Batter Pudding*

Supremes of Chicken
Jeanette*
Watercress
Marinated Green Limas,
Tomatoes, and Herbs
Hot Rolls
French Chocolate Mousse*

Barbecued Corn and
Meatballs*
Stewed Collards and Salt
Pork*
Mashed Sweet Potatoes
Sliced Tomatoes
Pineapple Cheesecake*

Crabmeat à la Dewey*
Spaghetti Parmigiana*
Zucchini and Escarole
Salad
Italian Bread
Grapefruit Sections with
Sweet Vermouth

Chicken Pilaf*
Bibb Lettuce and Sliced
Radish Salad
Onions Ménagère*
Seeded Hard Rolls
Cranberry-Raisin Pie*

Seafood Medley in Patty
Shells*
Chicken Salad*
Sliced Hard-Cooked Eggs,
Olives, Sliced Cucumbers,
and Tomato Wedges
Thin Onion Sandwiches
Strawberry Ice Cream
Sugared Butter Cookies*

———◆———

Vegetable Cocktail*
Deviled Cod Steaks*
Corn Quiche*
Spinach Slaw
Blueberries and Peaches*
Filled Butter Rings*

Fried Soft-Shell Crabs
Amandine*
Shoestring Potatoes
Swiss Chard
with Cheese Sauce*
Pancakes with Cranberries*

———◆———

Chicken Steamed in Lemon
Butter*
Stewed Corn Medley*
Romaine Hearts
Dessert Cheese Tray*
Fresh Fruit Bowl

Cottage-Stuffed Celery*
Crab Newburg* on Chive-
Scrambled Eggs*
Lettuce Hearts
Thousand Island Dressing
Whole Wheat Toast
Apricots with Grenadine
Mocha Nut Butterballs*

———◆———

Chicken Stew, Brunswick
Style*
Coleslaw with Celery Seed
and Sour Cream Dressing
Bread and Butter Pickles
Toasted Hard Rolls
Fresh Sour Cherry Pie*

Sardines in Mustard
Sauce Appetizer
Creamed Ham, Eggs
and Mushrooms*
Hashbrowned Potatoes
Marinated Peas and Onions
in Lettuce Cups
Chocolate Chiffon Pie*

———◆———

Crab Louis*
Chicken Gumbo*   Rice
Coconut Puddin'-Pie*
Café Brûlot*

Chicken à l'Orange*
Baked Yams
Cumberland Slaw*
Hot Biscuits
Unbaked Warsaw Chocolate
Torte*

———◆———

Country Captain*
Ripe Olives and Celery
Toasted Corn Bread Squares
Strawberry Pineapple
Refrigerator Cake*

Cheese Soufflé*
Broiled Bacon-Wrapped
Stuffed Olives
Stewed Tomatoes and Celery
Melon with Raspberry
Sherbet
Oatmeal Lace Cookies*

———◆———

Pea Soup with Rye Croutons
Frankfurters and Sauerkraut
New Potatoes with Caraway
Seed Butter
Horseradish Mustard
Grison's Steak House
Cheesecake*

Pot Roast of Beef   Gravy
Mashed Potatoes and Yellow
Turnips
Green Beans with Mushrooms
Pineapple Coleslaw
Cream Puffs*

———◆———

London Broil with Sautéed
Mushrooms
O'Brien Potatoes
Panned Mixed Greens
Sliced Melon and Grapes on
Lettuce   Lime Dressing*
Plain Baked Custard*

Lamb Stew with Potatoes,
Carrots, Onions, and
Peas
Minted Pineapple and
Watercress Salad
Double Corn Sticks*
Wisconsin Chocolate Cake*

———◆———

Lobster Chowder*
Pilot Crackers
Mexican Chick Pea Salad*
Sliced Tomatoes
Hot Seeded Rolls
Elena Zelayeta's
Postre de Mamon
(Mexican Cheesecake)*

Tuna Noodle Casserole
Marinated Mixed Vegetables
in Lettuce Cups
Dill Pickle Sticks
Honey Baked Apples
Moravian Cookies*

———◆———

Pork Sausage Patties
Corn on the Cob*
Sour Cream-Chive Sauce*
Stewed Tomatoes and Green
Peppers
Melon Cubes
Coconut Squares*

Chicken-Ham Mousse*
Cauliflower with Almond
Butter*
Orange and Avocado Salad
French Dressing
Sweet-Chocolate Cake*

———◆———

Spaghetti with White Clam
Sauce*
Grated Romano Cheese
Mixed Green and Red Cabbage
Salad with Capers
Italian Bread Sticks
Melon with Lemon Ice
Espresso

Jellied Consommé Madrilene*
Deep Fried Chicken*
California Succotash*
Escarole, Asparagus and
Pimiento Salad with
Blue-Cheese Dressing*
Strawberries with White
Wine   Dream Cookies*

———◆———

Chicken Hashed in Cream*
Fresh-Corn Cakes*
Cranberry and Horseradish
Relish*
Broccoli Spears and Lettuce
Fruit Cup   Toasted Filbert
Kisses*

Meat Loaf
Corn in Cream*
Dandelion Greens and Red
Onion Ring Salad
Garlic Bread
Stewed Plums
Black-Walnut Cookies*

———◆———

Danish Chicken*
Baked Tomatoes
Succotash with Bacon*
Cumberland Slaw*
Cottage Prune Soufflé*

Chicken Rosemary*
Wheat Pilaf Zucchini
Shredded Chinese Cabbage,
Raisins and Carrot
Salad with Mayonnaise
Chocolate Angel Food*
with Low-Calorie
Chocolate Sauce*

———◆———

Mixed Grill with Broiled
Peaches
Celeriac au Gratin*
Creamed Spinach
Romaine   Chiffonade Dressing*
Buttered Pecan Ice Cream
Swirl Cookies*

*Recipes for all starred dishes found in this volume.

GENERAL INFORMATION

The Ingredients and Measurements Used in Recipes

All recipes in this book have been tested in the Woman's Day Kitchens with standard American measuring cups (8 ounces = 16 tablespoons), measuring spoons (1 tablespoon = 3 teaspoons), and other standard kitchen equipment. All measurements are level. Liquids are measured in standard 8-ounce glass measuring cups, at eye level.

All sugar is granulated white sugar unless otherwise specified.

All flours, cake and all-purpose, are sifted before measuring unless otherwise specified. No self-rising flour is used.

All baking powder is double-acting baking powder.

All brown sugar is firmly packed when measured.

All confectioners' sugar is sifted before measuring.

All pepper is ground black pepper unless otherwise specified.

Fats and shortening are measured at room temperature, packed firmly into measuring cup and leveled with a straight knife. They are scraped out with a rubber spatula.

Salted butter or margarine, packed in ¼-pound sticks, is used unless otherwise specified. 1 stick = ½ cup = 8 tablespoons = ¼ pound.

1 tall can evaporated milk (14½ ounces) contains 1⅔ cups undiluted evaporated milk. Sweetened condensed milk is an entirely different product, and cannot be used interchangeably with evaporated milk.

⅓ to ½ teaspoon dried herbs can be substituted for each tablespoon fresh herbs. Crumble herbs before using to release flavor.

Before starting to cook or to bake, read the recipes carefully. Assemble all ingredients and equipment. Follow recipe exactly. Do not increase or decrease recipe unless you are a skilled enough cook to recognize what adjustments must be made as to ingredients, pan sizes, and/or cooking time.

Cooking Temperatures and Times

Cooking temperatures and times are approximate for meat. They depend not only on the weight and kind of meat, but also on its shape, temperature, and its bone and fat contents. A meat thermometer was used in testing.

Cooking times for meats are as recommended by the National Live Stock and Meat Board, 36 Wabash Avenue, Chicago, Illinois 60603.

Oven Temperatures

TEMPERATURES (Degree F.)	TERM
250 to 275	VERY SLOW
300 to 325	SLOW
350 to 375	MODERATE
400 to 425	HOT
450 to 475	VERY HOT
500 to 525	EXTREMELY HOT

Important—Preheat oven for 10 to 15 minutes before placing food in it. Many a cake has been spoiled by being placed in a barely heated oven. Baking times are based on the assumption that the oven is already at the stated temperature.

Check the oven temperature control frequently, especially if baking times vary from those given in recipes. (This can be done with a portable oven thermometer.) If a control is consistently off, call your public utility. They should be able to reset the oven temperature control.

Caloric Values

The caloric values, where mentioned, for each food are based on 100 grams, about 3½ ounces edible portion, as mentioned in Composition of Foods, Agriculture Handbook No. 8, Agricultural Service of the United States Department of Agriculture, Washington, D. C., revised December 1963.